Endorsed by

wjec cbac

WJEC GCSE
Religious Studies

Unit 1 Religion and Philosophical Themes

Steve Clarke, Joy White, Ed Pawson,
Amanda Ridley, Chris Owens

DYNAMIC LEARNING

HODDER EDUCATION
AN HACHETTE UK COMPANY

This material has been endorsed by WJEC and offers high quality support for the delivery of WJEC qualifications.
While this material has been through a quality assurance process, all responsibility for the content remains with the publisher.

Every effort has been made to trace all copyright holders, but if any have been inadvertently overlooked, the Publishers will be pleased to make the necessary arrangements at the first opportunity. Although every effort has been made to ensure that website addresses are correct at time of going to press, Hodder Education cannot be held responsible for the content of any website mentioned in this book. It is sometimes possible to find a relocated web page by typing in the address of the home page for a website in the URL window of your browser.

Hachette UK's policy is to use papers that are natural, renewable and recyclable products and made from wood grown in sustainable forests. The logging and manufacturing processes are expected to conform to the environmental regulations of the country of origin.

Orders: please contact Bookpoint Ltd, 130 Milton Park, Abingdon, Oxon OX14 4SE. Telephone: +44 (0)1235 827720. Fax: +44 (0)1235 400454. Email education@bookpoint.co.uk Lines are open from 9 a.m. to 5 p.m., Monday to Saturday, with a 24-hour message answering service. You can also order through our website: www.hoddereducation.co.uk

ISBN: 978 1 5104 1345 0

© Steve Clarke, Joy White, Ed Pawson, Amanda Ridley, Chris Owens 2017

First published in 2017 by
Hodder Education,
An Hachette UK Company
Carmelite House
50 Victoria Embankment
London EC4Y 0DZ

www.hoddereducation.co.uk

Impression number   10 9 8 7 6 5 4 3 2 1

Year   2020 2019 2018 2017

All rights reserved. Apart from any use permitted under UK copyright law, no part of this publication may be reproduced or transmitted in any form or by any means, electronic or mechanical, including photocopying and recording, or held within any information storage and retrieval system, without permission in writing from the publisher or under licence from the Copyright Licensing Agency Limited. Further details of such licences (for reprographic reproduction) may be obtained from the Copyright Licensing Agency Limited, Saffron House, 6–10 Kirby Street, London EC1N 8TS.

Cover photo © Serg_Velusceac/Getty Images/iStockphoto
Illustrations by Aptara Inc.
Typeset in India by Aptara Inc.
Printed in Italy
A catalogue record for this title is available from the British Library.

Contents

Introduction ... iv

Part A

Christianity ... **01**

1. Christianity: Beliefs and teachings ... 02
2. Christianity: Practices ... 28

Buddhism ... **50**

3. Buddhism: Beliefs and teachings ... 52
4. Buddhism: Practices ... 75

Islam ... **84**

5. Islam: Beliefs and teachings ... 89
6. Islam: Practices ... 104

Judaism ... **119**

7. Judaism: Beliefs and teachings ... 122
8. Judaism: Practices ... 138

Part B

Philosophical themes ... **156**

9. Issues of life and death ... 156
10. Issues of good and evil ... 200

Acknowledgements ... 250

Index ... 252

How to use this book

Introduction

This book covers the subject content of Unit 1: Religion and Philosophical Themes through the perspective of Christianity, Buddhism, Islam and Judaism, for the new WJEC GCSE Religious Studies qualification.

The book is set out in the order of the WJEC specification to help students and teachers work through any course of study in specification order.

The book includes information on all of the key concepts and detailed content for each part of the specification.

What is the assessment structure?

The assessment structure for the GCSE Religious Studies qualification requires students to complete two examination papers; one for Unit 1 Religion and Philosophical Themes and one for Unit 2 Religion and Ethical Themes.

The content below covers Unit 1 only. Unit 2 will be covered in a separate book to be published in March 2018.

Part A

Part A is the study of core beliefs and teachings of two religions.

For the first section of Part A students must study either Christianity OR Catholic Christianity. Only Christianity is covered in this title.

For the second section of Part A students must study a second world religion, we are only covering Buddhism, Islam and Judaism in this book.

The length of the examination paper for this unit is two hours.

Part B

Part B is the study of two philosophical themes:

- Life and death
- Good and evil

These must be studied through the perspective of Christianity (or Catholic Christianity though that is not covered in this title) and one other world religion, which should be the same as the second world religion you studied for Part A.

Assessment objectives

In each component there are different types of questions on the examination paper to assess the two different assessment objectives. The assessment objectives are referred to as AO1 and AO2 in the specification.

The two different assessment objectives test different dimensions of your religious knowledge and understanding.

In the GCSE examinations, each assessment objective is worth 50 per cent of the total mark.

Assessment objective 1

You need to demonstrate knowledge and understanding of religion and belief*, including:

- belief, practices and sources of authority
- the influence on individuals, communities and societies
- similarities and differences within and/or between religions and belief.

The form of questions for this assessment objective will vary but common rubric instructions for this assessment objective are:

- What is meant by …?
- Describe …
- Explain …

Assessment objective 2

You need to analyse and evaluate aspects of religion and belief*, including their significance and influence.

The form of question for this assessment objective will provide you with a statement followed by the rubric instruction:

Discuss this statement showing that you have considered more than one point of view. (You must refer to religion and belief in your answer.)

Answering the questions

It is important to know the structure of the exam paper and the type of questions that will be asked.

For all exam questions consider two questions:

- **How** many marks are awarded for the question? This will help you consider how much time should be spent on your answer and the depth of your answer.
- **What** is the question asking **you to do**? No question will ever ask you to write all that you know! What are the most important words in the question? Remember you can highlight them to help you focus on what the question is asking.

It is important to remember that there are **four types** of questions. The space in your exam booklet will give you an idea of how much to write though there is no requirement to fill all of the lines. It is also important to look at the marking grids so you can see what is required for each of the mark bands.

*The term 'belief' includes religious and non-religious belief as appropriate to the subject content requirements.

Question (a) – AO1

- 1 mark for each relevant point made (one point can be an example).
- 2 marks for either two separate points or one point which is developed/explained/elaborated.

These are always the first question in each unit. They ask you to state what the key concept means. Your responses can include an example.

Throughout the book you will find examples of the definitions of all the key concepts. There are 12 key concepts for the Part A and 8 key concepts for the Part B.

Remember there are only two marks available for these questions so it important you are able to give an accurate definition which is to the point.

Question (b) – AO1

In these questions you will be expected to describe a particular religious teaching, belief, idea, practice, place, event or view. There is a maximum of five marks for this type of question. To gain full marks you should be able to show your **knowledge** using appropriate **religious terms** and any **relevant sources of wisdom or sacred texts**.

Band	Band Descriptor	Mark total
3	An excellent, coherent description showing awareness and insight into the religious idea, belief, practice, teaching or concept.	4–5
	Uses a range of appropriate religious/specialist language and terms and, where relevant, sources of wisdom and authority, extensively, accurately and appropriately.	
2	A good, generally accurate answer showing knowledge and understanding of the religious idea, belief, practice, teaching or concept.	2–3
	Uses religious/specialist language and terms and/or sources of wisdom and authority generally accurately.	
1	A limited statement of information about the religious idea, belief, practice, teaching or concept.	1
	Uses religious/specialist language and terms and/or sources of wisdom and authority in a limited way.	
0	No relevant information provided.	0

Question (c) – AO1

These questions expect you to 'explain' a religious teaching, belief, idea, practice, event or view in the religions you have studied. There is a maximum of eight marks for this type of question. You need to use appropriate religious terms and relevant sources of wisdom or sacred texts.

In the Part B (Religion and Philosophical Themes), you will be required to consider **two religious** perspectives for the (c) questions. The two perspectives must come from Christianity and the other religion you are studying in Part A.

Band	Band Descriptor	Mark total
4	An excellent, highly detailed explanation showing awareness and insight into the religious idea, belief, practice, teaching or concept. Uses a range of religious/specialist language, terms and sources of wisdom and authority extensively, accurately and appropriately.	7–8
3	A very good, explanation showing awareness of the religious idea, belief, practice, teaching or concept. Uses a range of religious/specialist language, terms and sources of wisdom and authority accurately and appropriately.	5–6
2	A satisfactory explanation showing some awareness of the religious idea, belief, practice, teaching or concept. Uses religious/specialist language, terms and/or sources of wisdom and authority with some accuracy	3–4
1	A limited explanation showing little awareness of the religious idea, belief, practice, teaching or concept. Uses religious/specialist language, terms and/or sources of wisdom and authority in a limited way and with little accuracy.	1–2
0	No relevant information provided.	0

Question (d) – AO2

These are very important questions as they are worth 15 marks. The question requires you to read and understand a statement and then:

Discuss this statement showing that you have considered more than one point of view. (You must refer to religion and belief in your answer) (15)

Responses must analyse, evaluate, offer different and/or alternative views and reach well supported judgements.

Life and Death (d) question **must** include non-religious beliefs. Non-religious beliefs can be included (but don't have to be) in any appropriate (d) question that lends itself to a non-religious response.

Throughout the book there are tasks which will help you develop skills needed for the examination:

- Using religious and sacred text references.
- Using religious language and terms.
- Showing the diversity of beliefs and practices within a religious tradition.

Question 1(d), 2(d) and 4(d)

Band	Band Descriptor	Mark Total
4	An excellent, highly detailed analysis and evaluation of the issue based on comprehensive and accurate knowledge of religion, religious teaching and moral reasoning. Clear and well supported judgements are formulated and a comprehensive range of different and/or alternative viewpoints are considered Uses and interprets religious/specialist language, terms and sources of wisdom and authority extensively, accurately, appropriately and in detail.	12–15
3	A very good, detailed analysis and evaluation of the issue based on thorough and accurate knowledge of religion, religious teaching and moral reasoning. Judgements are formulated with support and a balanced range of different and/or alternative viewpoints are considered. Uses and interprets religious/specialist language, terms and sources of wisdom and authority accurately, appropriately and in detail.	8-11
2	A satisfactory analysis and evaluation of the issue based on some accurate knowledge of religion, religious teaching and moral reasoning. Some judgements are formulated and some different and/or alternative viewpoints are considered. Uses and interprets some religious/specialist language, terms and/or sources of wisdom and authority with some accuracy.	4-7
1	A weak analysis and evaluation of the issue based on limited and/or inaccurate knowledge of religion, religious teaching and/or moral reasoning. A limited and/or poor attempt or no attempt to formulate judgements or offer different and/or alternative viewpoints. Poor use or no use of religious/specialist language, terms and/or sources of wisdom and authority.	1-3
0	No relevant point of view stated.	0

Question 1(d) will also have 6 marks available for spelling, punctuation and the accurate use of grammar.

Question 3(d) – Life and death theme

Band	Band Descriptor	Mark Total
4	An excellent, highly detailed analysis and evaluation of the issue based on comprehensive and accurate knowledge of religion, religious teaching and moral reasoning. An excellent, highly detailed consideration of non-religious beliefs, such as those held by humanists and atheists. Clear and well supported judgements are formulated and a comprehensive range of different and/or alternative viewpoints are considered. Uses and interprets religious/specialist language, terms and sources of wisdom and authority extensively, accurately, appropriately and in detail.	12–15
4	A very good, detailed analysis and evaluation of the issue based on through and accurate knowledge of religion, religious teaching and moral reasoning. A very good, detailed consideration of non-religious beliefs, such as those held by humanists and atheists. Judgements are formulated with support and a balanced range of different and/or alternative viewpoints are considered. Uses and interprets religious/specialist language, terms and sources of wisdom and authority accurately, appropriately and in detail.	8-11
3	A satisfactory analysis and evaluation of the issue based on some accurate knowledge of religion, religious teaching and moral reasoning. A satisfactory, reasonably detailed consideration of non-religious beliefs, such as those held by humanists and atheists. Some judgements are formulated and some different and/or alternative viewpoints are considered. Uses and interprets some religious/specialist language, terms and/or sources of wisdom and authority with some accuracy.	4-7
2	A weak analysis and evaluation of the issue, based on limited and/or inaccurate knowledge of religion, religious teaching and/or moral reasoning. A very basic consideration or no consideration of non-religious beliefs, such as those held by humanists and atheists. A limited and/or poor attempt or no attempt to formulate judgements or offer different and/or alternative viewpoints. Poor use or no use, of religious/specialist language, terms and/or sources of wisdom and authority.	1-3
0	No relevant point of view stated.	0

Additional note

The complete WJEC specification is available on the WJEC website.

There are a variety of digital resources and other materials to support the teaching of this specification on the WJEC website.

Further information may be found in the specification content about alternative routes through the specification based on the study of other world faiths (Catholic Christianity, Hinduism, Sikhism) not included in this textbook.

Christianity

Key Concepts

Agape Selfless, sacrificial, unconditional love. Christianity holds agape to be the highest types of love, epitomised by Jesus' sacrifice on the cross for the salvation of humanity and in teachings such as 'Love your neighbour'.

Atonement The belief that Jesus' Death and Resurrection healed the rift between humans and God, thereby opening the way for God and people to be 'at one' again.

Divine command theory The belief that something is right because God commands it.

Holy Spirit One of the three persons of the Holy Trinity. Jesus promised the Apostles that he would send the Holy Spirit after his Crucifixion and Resurrection. Christians believe that the Holy Spirit is present as the power of God at work in the world.

Incarnation 'Made flesh' – the Christian belief that God became man in the person of Jesus, fully human and fully divine. God becoming human in the form of Jesus.

Inter-faith dialogue Different faith communities and groups coming together to better understand each other and to serve the wider community with a mutual respect that allows them to live peacefully alongside each other, in spite of differences in beliefs and ways of life.

Messiah The word means 'the Anointed One'. The Messiah is the one believed to be sent by God to be humanity's saviour. Christians believe this person to be Jesus.

Omnibenevolence The state of being all-loving and infinitely good – a characteristic often attributed to God.

Omnipotence The all-powerful, almighty and unlimited nature of God.

Omniscience The all-knowing nature of God.

Resurrection The belief that Jesus rose from the dead on the third day from when he was crucified, thereby conquering death. It is commemorated annually on Easter Sunday.

Trinity The three persons of God: God the Father, Son and Holy Spirit.

Core Questions

- What is God like?
- Did God create the universe?
- What does it mean to say God created human beings 'in his image'?
- What is Original Sin?
- How do we know what is right and wrong?
- What do Christians mean by 'love'?
- Why are there so many different branches of Christianity?
- What do Christians do to improve life for people in 21st century Britain?
- How do Christians work with other Christians and people of different faiths?

1 Christianity: Beliefs and teachings

■ God

▶ Attributes of God

God the creator

The first words of the Christian Bible are 'In the beginning, God created the heavens and the earth'. This gives two pieces of information.

1. The universe was designed and made; it did not come about by accident.
2. God was the designer and maker of the universe.

The Bible teaches that God created the universe and everything in it.

From these two pieces of information, Christians believe they are able to draw conclusions about what God is like. For example, if God created the universe, it follows that God existed before the universe. The universe has a beginning; before that, there was nothing but God. God created everything, and nothing exists that was not created by him. So God is somehow separate from his creation: he is **transcendent**. This means that he is the Supreme Being – there is none greater and he has no equal (see Beliefs and teachings on creation from the Genesis accounts, pages 7–12).

Transcendent Above and beyond anything in the physical universe.

God the sustainer

Christianity teaches that, having created the universe, God did not abandon it or leave it to its own devices, independent of him.

Christians recognise that the living world relies on God for its continued existence as well as its creation. God remains active in the universe, sustaining life as well as creating it.

The Bible teaches that everything in the universe depends on God. This dependence is absolute. If God ceased to exist, then the universe would cease to exist, too.

Christians often compare God's role as **sustainer** to that of a parent. A parent brings children into the world, but does not leave them to their fate. A good parent will provide the basic necessities required for children to grow: food, clothing, shelter and, importantly, love.

> **Sustainer** God's role in continuing to provide for and support the existence of the things he has created.

Christians think of God like a father.

As children develop, their needs become more complex, but parents still ensure they are met. They help their children to become independent, but, in reality, they are always there to provide support, guidance and assistance as long as they are able.

Christians refer to God as 'Father' to emphasise his role as sustainer. The Lord's Prayer, the Christian prayer first recited by Jesus, starts with the words 'Our Father'. It goes on to say, 'Give us this day our daily bread.' There are different ideas about what this means – it may refer literally to God's provision of food, or more generally the necessities of life – but it indicates the Christian belief that God sustains life.

Task

Look up the following Bible references. Use them to make a list of ways in which God is like a father to his creation.

- Matthew 6.26
- Matthew 18.12–14
- Luke 6.35–36
- John 16.27
- 1 John 3.1
- 1 Corinthians 8.6
- Psalm 68.5
- 2 Corinthians 1.3–4

The qualities of God start with the prefix *omni-*. This comes from a Latin word meaning *all*. So:

- omnipotent means *all powerful*.
- omnibenevolent means *all good*.
- omniscient means *all knowing*.
- omnipresent means *all present*.

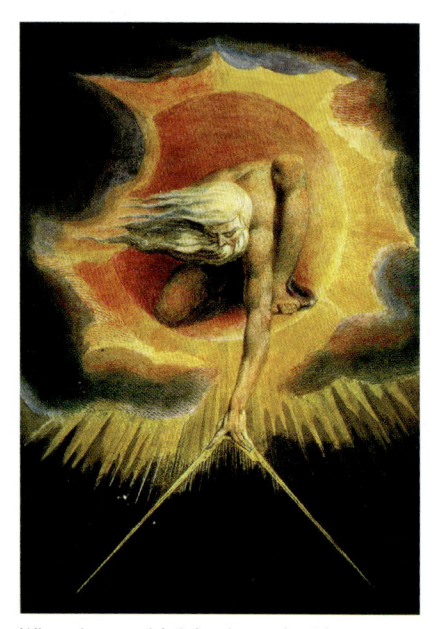

What do you think is shown in this picture? Look up Isaiah 40.12. What does this say about God's power?

Omnipotence

> **Key Concept**
>
> **Omnipotence** The all-powerful, almighty and unlimited nature of God.

Christians believe that God is **omnipotent**. He has power over everything he has created, and his power is without limit.

In the Book of Job in the Old Testament of the Bible, a man called Elihu talks about God's power. He says, for instance, that human beings rely on God for their existence, not the other way round:

> If you sin, that does no harm to God. If you do wrong many times, does that affect him? Do you help God by being so righteous? There is nothing God needs from you.

(Job 35.6–7)

Elihu goes on to say that God's power is so great that human beings cannot understand it:

> At God's command amazing things happen, wonderful things that we can't understand.

(Job 37.5)

Omnibenevolence

> **Key Concept**
>
> **Omnibenevolence** The state of being all-loving and infinitely good – a characteristic often attributed to God.

Christians believe that God is **omnibenevolent**. He is supremely good and loving.

According to the Bible, as God creates the universe, he declares his creation to be good at each stage. For example, after he has created the land and the sea, the sun and the stars, birds and fish, and land-dwelling animals, it says, 'God saw all that he had made, and it was very good' (Genesis 1.31).

Christians believe that, because his creation is good, God must be infinitely good. And because God created everyone to be equal, he is fair and just to everyone. Elihu says:

> Is he not the One … who shows no partiality to princes and does not favour the rich over the poor, for they are all the work of his hands?

(Job 34.19)

Christianity teaches that God's goodness shows itself in his love for human beings. Because of this, he is prepared to forgive people for their wrongdoings and sent his son, Jesus, to die as a sacrifice for human sin so that human beings could be saved.

1 Christianity: Beliefs and teachings

> **Task**
>
> Read the quote by Epicurus. Explain why the existence of suffering may cause a problem for Christians.

The problem of evil and suffering

Epicurus, an ancient Greek Philosopher, wrote the following about God and the idea of evil and suffering:

> Is God willing to prevent evil, but not able? Then he is not omnipotent.
>
> Is he able but not willing? Then he is malevolent.
>
> Is he both able and willing? Then whence comes evil?
>
> Is he neither able nor willing? Then why call him God?

This quote sums up one of the key reasons many people give for not believing in God – how can there be suffering in the world if God is both all loving and all powerful? (See page 238 in Issues of good and evil.)

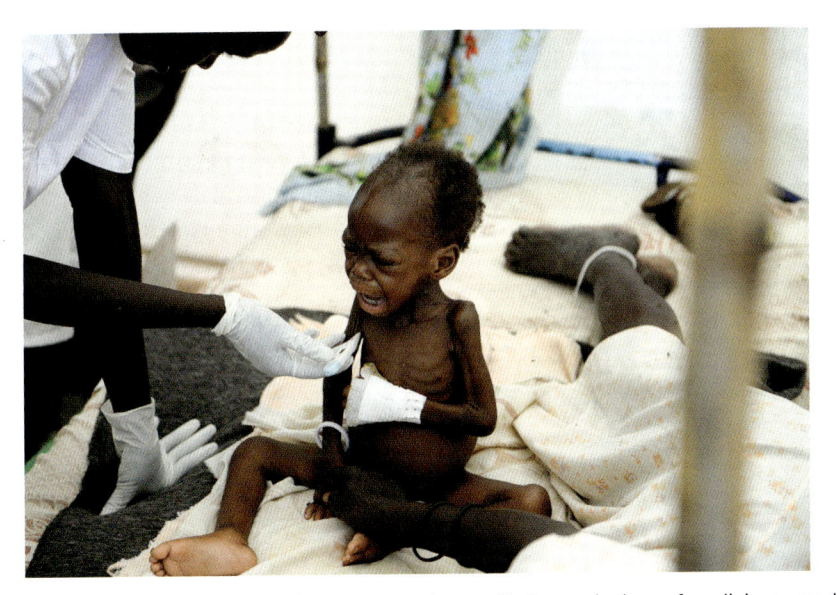

Why a loving God would allow innocent people to suffer is a major issue for religious people.

Omniscience

The Bible states:

> He determines the number of the stars and calls them each by name.
> Great is our Lord and mighty in power; his understanding has no limit.
>
> (Psalm 147.4–5)

This means that God knows everything there is to know because he created everything that exists.

For Christians, this knowledge includes knowledge of individual human beings. Psalm 139.1–4 says:

> You have searched me, LORD, and you know me. You know when I sit and when I rise; you perceive my thoughts from afar. You discern my going out and my lying down; you are familiar with all my ways. Before a word is on my tongue you, LORD, know it completely.

> **Key Concept**
>
> **Omniscience** The all-knowing nature of God.

Christians believe, therefore, that God has plans for each individual and a plan for the universe as a whole.

Some Christians believe that God's **omniscience** means that he knows the future. Certainly, the Bible gives examples of God having a direct influence over future events. For example, Luke's Gospel says that God sent an angel to Mary, the mother of Jesus, who tells her:

> 'You will conceive and give birth to a son, and you are to call him Jesus. He will be great and will be called the Son of the Most High. The Lord God will give him the throne of his father David, and he will reign over Jacob's descendants forever; his kingdom will never end.'
>
> (Luke 1.31–33)

Christianity teaches that God sent Jesus into the world knowing in advance that he would be killed.

For other Christians, the idea that God knows the future in perfect detail is at odds with the belief that human beings have free will to make their own decisions and actions about the future.

Omnipresence

The Christian belief in God's **omnipresence** is the belief that God is not restricted by space or time. It is related to the idea that if God knows and understands all things (is omniscient), then he must be in a position to observe and influence all things. This does not mean that God is spread throughout the universe, but that he is naturally present in everything at all times.

Omnipresence is not concerned with God's physical location. In any case, God does not have a physical form. Rather, omnipresence is a description of God's relationship with his creation. When a person says, 'I'll always be there for you', they are not talking about being present literally; they are saying that they are always available to provide support and guidance. Christians believe the same about God, except that his presence is infinite. In other words, he is omnipresent.

> **Omnipresence** The idea that God is everywhere throughout time.

> Where can I go from your Spirit?
>
> Where can I flee from your presence?
>
> If I go up to the heavens, you are there;
>
> if I make my bed in the depths, you are there.
>
> If I rise on the wings of the dawn,
>
> if I settle on the far side of the sea,
>
> even there your hand will guide me,
>
> your right hand will hold me fast.
>
> (Psalm 139.7–10)

Task

Copy and complete the table below, adding an explanation of the meaning of each of the qualities of God and a Bible quote to support each one.

Quality	Explanation	Biblical quotation
Omnipotent		
Omnibenevolent		
Omniscient		
Omnipresent		

1 Christianity: Beliefs and teachings

▶ Beliefs and teachings on creation

The story of the creation is set out in the first three chapters of the book of Genesis. Actually, these chapters contain two accounts that were originally separate.

The first account is contained in Chapter 1 and the first three-and-a-half verses of Chapter 2. This account describes:

- the creation of the universe
- the creation of the world
- the creation of the things that exist in the world, including human beings.

The second account is older than the first. It describes:

- the creation of the first human beings
- the temptation of the first human beings to disobey God
- their fall from God's favour.

Genesis 1.1–3

The Book of Genesis starts with these words:

> In the beginning, God created the heavens and the earth. Now the earth was formless and empty, darkness was over the surface of the deep, and the Spirit of God was hovering over the waters. And God said, 'Let there be light,' and there was light.

Genesis 1

The first (younger) account of creation provides an explanation of the creation of human beings and their importance relative to other created things. It describes how God puts the universe together over six days, resting from his work on the seventh day.

What does the story mean?

The story stresses that God is responsible for each stage of creation. The six stages unfold according to his plan. First, he creates environments: day and night, sea and sky, then dry land. Next, he creates those things that will inhabit those environments: sun, moon and stars, fish and birds, then animals and humans. The universe has order.

According to the Bible, God creates human beings 'to be like himself' (Genesis 1.27). It does not say in what ways humans are like God, but it suggests that they are important and share some of God's characteristics (see page 12).

The story establishes the position of human beings in the world. They are to be its rulers. God tells them:

> Have many children, so that your descendants will live all over the earth and bring it under their control. I am putting you in charge of the fish, the birds, and all the wild animals.

(Genesis 1.28)

So, humans are 'in charge' (**dominion**), but must ensure that the order God has created will be maintained (**stewardship**) (see page 166).

Dominion The role of humans as rulers and controllers of the world.

Stewardship The duty of human beings to care for the world and maintain balance in nature.

Day 1 – God creates night and day:
He calls the light day, and darkness, night.

Day 2 – God creates the sea and sky:
He makes the firmament (sky) and separates the waters that are under the firmament from the waters that are above it.

Day 3 – God creates land and plants:
He moves the waters under the firmament to make room for land to appear. He makes plants that carry seeds to ensure reproduction.

Day 4 – God creates the sun, moon and stars:
Having created day and night on Day 1, he now makes the sun shine in the daytime and the moon and stars to shine at night.

Day 5 – God creates fish and the birds:
He makes fish to swim in the waters and birds to fly in the sky.

Day 6 – God creates living creatures, including human beings:
He makes land animals first, then humans to have power over them.

Day 7 – God rests:
On the seventh day God has completed his work. (This is described at the beginning of Genesis 2.)

1 Christianity: Beliefs and teachings

Interpretations of Genesis 1

Literalists

A minority of Christians believe that the Bible contains the actual words of God and is to be taken literally. These believers, known as creationists, hold that God, as a matter of fact, created the universe in six periods of 24 hours in the order described in Genesis 1. Creationists believe that the universe was created exactly as it is today, and that life on earth was created exactly as it is today. Some creationists believe that the universe was created within the last 10,000 years. They are known as **young-earth creationists**.

Old-earth creationists

Some Christians maintain that the Genesis 1 account is essentially true, but that the six 'days' should not be seen as 24-hour periods. Instead, they are longer durations of time – thousands or millions of years. These Christians, known as **old-earth creationists**, believe that God created the universe as described in Genesis in six long stages, not six days. This interpretation is sometimes called **day-age creationism**.

Liberals

Most Christians see Genesis 1 as a pre-scientific attempt to explain the origins of the universe. They would say that the actual process of creation is not important. Instead, the importance of the creation account lies in the facts that God created the universe, that every aspect of it depends on him for its existence, and that humanity is the pinnacle of his creation. The world, in particular, was created for human beings, and everything in it is subject to their control.

As far as the origin and development of the universe are concerned, liberal Christians take a post-scientific view. They recognise that the biblical story was based on pre-biblical narratives, given the information they had at the time. They therefore have no problem in believing scientific accounts of the Big Bang theory (see page 158).

Creationism The belief that God created the universe exactly as described in the book of Genesis.

Young-earth creationism The belief that God created the universe in six 24-hour periods.

Old-earth creationism The belief that God created the universe over a long time.

Day-age creationism The belief that God created the universe over six long time-periods.

Task

Is it possible for a Christian to believe in the scientific explanation of the birth and development of the universe while believing that the Bible is inspired by God? Give reasons for your answer.

Are biblical creation stories consistent with the Big Bang theory?

Tasks

1. Reproduce the table below, explaining the different interpretations of creation in Genesis.

Attitude to the creation story	Interpretation
Young-earth creationists	They believe that...... 'Day' means ....
Old-earth creationists	They believe that...... 'Day' means ....
Liberals	

2. Why are there different interpretations of the Genesis account of creation?
3. Explain the four key beliefs about creation that most Christians agree on.
4. 'How the universe came about has no religious significance.'
   Discuss this statement showing that you have considered more than one point of view. (You must refer to Christianity in your answer.)

Genesis 2 and 3

The older account of creation in Genesis is less concerned with the origin of the physical universe, and more with the creation of humanity and the development of the relationship between humans and God.

It describes:
- the creation of the first human beings
- the temptation of the first human beings to disobey God
- their fall from God's favour.

Genesis 2

1. God creates the universe, including the earth. There are rivers and seas, but no rain, so no vegetation.
2. God creates the first man from the soil of the ground. He gives life to the man by breathing into him. The man is called Adam, which means 'ground' and came to mean 'human'.
3. God creates a garden of plants and gives the man the responsibility of looking after them.
4. In the middle of the garden are two trees: the Tree of the Knowledge of Good and Evil and the Tree of Life. God tells the man that he may not eat the fruit of the Tree of the Knowledge of Good and Evil.
5. God makes animals out of the soil as companions for the man.
6. God makes the first woman from a rib taken from the man while he is asleep. The woman is called Eve, which means 'life', since women bear new life.

At this point, the man and the woman are naked, but are not ashamed of their nakedness. This is because they have no idea of what is right and wrong.

Genesis 3

7. A snake tells the woman that they are not permitted to eat fruit from the Tree of the Knowledge of Good and Evil because, if they do, they will understand the difference between right and wrong. This knowledge would make them like God. The woman says that if they eat the fruit, they will die; the snake refutes this.
8. The woman eats fruit from the tree and gives some to the man to eat.
9. The man and the woman now understand right and wrong. They now realise it is wrong to be naked in front of each other and cover their bodies.
10. When they hear God coming into the garden, the man and the woman hide. God finds them. Seeing that they have covered their nakedness, God knows that they understand good and evil, so must have eaten the forbidden fruit.
11. God punishes the snake by making all snakes crawl on their bellies and making them enemies of women.
12. God punishes the woman by increasing the pain of childbirth, but not lessening her desire to bear children.
13. God punishes the man by making him work the hard land for life in order to get food.
14. God banishes the man and woman from the garden, fearful that, if they stay, they will eat fruit from the Tree of Life and live forever.

Can you identify the events of Genesis 2 and 3 in this painting?

What does the story mean?

There are clear differences between this creation story and that presented in Genesis 1. Most obvious, perhaps, is the emphasis of the two accounts. Genesis 1 is concerned with the development of the universe; Genesis 2 and 3 are concerned with the origin of human life.

Most significant in this account is the deterioration in the relationship between God and human beings. When the man and woman are created, their relationship with their creator is perfect. They have done no wrong. In fact, they can do no wrong, because they do not know what wrong and evil are.

The relationship becomes contaminated when the man and woman break the trust God has put in them. This contamination and breach of trust is what Christians call **sin**. Adam and Eve eat the fruit of the Tree of the Knowledge of Good and Evil despite being told not to. As a result, they become aware of right and wrong. They know they have done wrong and feel guilt and shame as a consequence. They have lost their innocence.

This event is called **the Fall**. The sin that lies at its core is called Original Sin. Although Genesis does not use the words 'Original Sin', Christianity teaches that human beings are responsible for bringing sin into the world by choice. Breaking the bond of trust with God was a deliberate act of disobedience and has tainted human beings' relationship with God ever since. Christianity teaches, then, that all humans are born with **Original Sin**; no one is morally innocent.

Another consequence of the Fall is that, by eating the fruit of the Tree of the Knowledge of Good and Evil, man and woman become mortal: human beings are destined to die.

> **Sin** Breaking God's laws.
> **The Fall** The transition of Adam and Eve from a state of innocence to one of disobedience.
> **Original Sin** The transference of Adam and Eve's breach of God's trust to all of humanity.

Task

> Therefore, just as sin entered the world through one man, and death through sin, and in this way death came to all people, because all sinned.
>
> (Romans 5.12)
>
> Explain this quotation from the Bible with reference to Genesis 3.

Interpretations of Genesis 2 and 3

Literalists

Those Christians who maintain that the Bible contains the actual words of God and is factually accurate tend to believe that Genesis 1–3 contains one continuous account of the creation of the universe, the world and human beings. They reject the idea that there are two separate stories. They would say that Genesis 1 gives a general account of the creation, while Chapters 2 and 3 give more detail about how human beings originated. They would emphasise the sinful nature of human beings since the Fall. Some would say that the story teaches not just that humans brought the possibility of sin into the world, but that it is now impossible for them not to sin.

Theistic evolution The view that God activated and guides evolution.

Task

Explain what theistic evolution means.

Liberals

Christian liberals believe that the story of Adam and Eve should not be taken literally. They accept the scientific explanation of the development of human beings through the process of natural selection according to the theory of evolution (see page 159). They would say that God was at the start of the evolutionary process; indeed, that he created the process as a way of sustaining life on earth. This is called **theistic evolution**.

Liberals may be less likely than literalists to emphasise what the story of the Fall teaches about human sinfulness. They would look more to the passage in Genesis 1 that says:

> God created mankind in his own image, in the image of God he created them; male and female he created them.

(Genesis 1.27)

They would say that this indicates the closeness between God and his human creations and the human capacity to love and do good.

Liberals would agree with literalists, however, that God is at the heart of creation, that he is the source of life, and that the created universe and everything in it depend on God for its continued existence.

Tasks

How might a Christian answer the following questions?
a) Why did God not want Adam and Eve to eat the fruit of the Knowledge of Good and Evil?
b) Why was Eve tempted to eat the fruit of the Tree of the Knowledge of Good and Evil?
c) What was Adam and Eve's sin?

▶ The nature of humanity

The accounts of the creation of the universe and of humanity in the Bible outline a view of human nature on which Christian teachings about the relationship between God and human beings are based.

The image of God

> Then God said, 'Let us make mankind in our image, in our likeness, so that they may rule over the fish in the sea and the birds in the sky, over the livestock and all the wild animals, and over all the creatures that move along the ground.' So God created mankind in his own image in the image of God he created them; male and female he created them.'

(Genesis 1.26–27)

Several passages in the Bible repeat the statement first made in the book of Genesis that God created human beings 'in his image' or likeness (some Christians use the Latin words *imago Dei* instead of 'in the image of God'). However, nowhere is it made clear exactly what this means. Very few Christians would suggest that it means that human beings look like God; rather that, in some way, they are like him.

What is clear is that human beings, out of all creation, are alone in being made in God's image. This means that human beings are different from all of God's other creations and have a higher place in the living universe than them. So understanding what being made in the image of God means entails looking at the qualities and characteristics that distinguish human beings from other living things.

- Some Christian thinkers claim that the meaning of being in God's likeness lies in the human ability to form complex relationships. Human relationships have a spiritual dimension. They are able to experience love, empathy and compassion. They can feel the emotions of others. In the same way, human beings are able to form a relationship with God on a spiritual level. The ability to form such relationships is unique to human beings – no other creature forms spiritual bonds – so some Christians believe this is the image of God in humans.
- Others see the image of God lying in the role and function of human beings in the world. The verse that follows the statement that God created mankind in his image says: 'God blessed them and said to them, "Be fruitful and increase in number; fill the earth and subdue it. Rule over the fish in the sea and the birds in the sky and over every living creature that moves on the ground"' (Genesis 1.28). Some Christians see verse 28 as an explanation of verse 27. In other words, bearing the likeness of God means carrying out one of God's functions: ruling over and caring for the earth and everything in it.
- Others maintain that being in the image of God means sharing some of his attributes and characteristics. Clearly, God has characteristics that no other being could have: **omnipotence**, **omnibenevolence**, omniscience and omnipresence, for example. However, there are features of human beings that do resemble some of God's and which are unique among other creatures. These include the possession of a spiritual element (soul), a sense of right and wrong (morality), the capacity to make choices and decisions (free will), intelligence and the ability to use reason and logic (rationality), and the ability to make order from chaos (creativity).

Soul The unseen, spiritual part of a person.

A 19th-century engraving showing the soul leaving the body at the moment of death.

Soul

Then the Lord God formed a man from the dust of the ground and breathed into his nostrils the breath of life, and the man became a living being.

(Genesis 2.7)

Christians today are divided in the beliefs about the **soul**. All accept that the soul is invisible and spiritual. Some believe that, after death, there is a 'bodily **resurrection**' and that the body and soul together rise to heaven. Others believe that when the body dies, the soul leaves it to be with God in a spiritual way.

> **Morality** Principles and standards that determine which actions are right or wrong.

Morality

Morality consists of the systems which individuals, societies and humankind as a whole use to ensure that people behave well towards each other and avoid bad or wrong behaviour that may hurt others.

Both Christians and non-Christians would agree that having a sense of right and wrong is unique to human beings; animals do not have moral understanding.

The creation story presented in Genesis 1 suggests that, as God created the universe, he built morality into it from the start. On the first day, he commands light to exist, and it does; he observes that 'it was good'. Both literalists and liberals would accept that the universe is a moral universe because God created it to be. They would also say that God created human beings to have a moral sense.

In the Book of Exodus, it is recorded that God sets out ten rules for human beings to follow. Four are religious and six are moral, to do with human behaviour. The ten rules are God's commands or Commandments. They are part of a contract or agreement between God and human beings. If humans obey his commands, then God will bless them and make them his people.

Free will

In the Genesis story of Adam and Eve, we have seen that, having been tempted by a snake, Eve chooses to eat fruit from the Tree of the Knowledge of Good and Evil, even though God has forbidden it. Adam follows suit. In making this decision, Adam and Eve exercise their **free will**, their ability to make choices using their own volition.

> **Free will** The ability to make choices voluntarily and independently.

Christianity teaches that human beings are born with free will. This is repeated throughout the Bible. St Paul reinforces the idea of free will in his letters to the Christians of Corinth:

> Each of you should give what you have decided in your heart to give, not reluctantly or under compulsion.

(2 Corinthians 9.7)

This is important because, if humans did not have free will, they could not be held accountable for their actions. If everything they did had been determined beforehand, it would be unfair to hold them responsible. On the other hand, if they do make choices and decisions about how to act, then they can be made to answer for their actions.

Christianity teaches that human beings are free to choose whether or not to believe in God. If human beings were 'programmed' to believe in God, then that belief could not be rewarded. Yet it is central to Christianity that belief is rewarded:

> For God so loved the world that he gave his one and only Son, that whoever believes in him shall not perish but have eternal life.

(John 3.16)

Tasks

1. Explain in no more than three sentences what problems are associated with free will.
2. Explain how the Fall relates to the idea that human beings are accountable for their actions.

Rationality

The Bible teaches that God created a planned and well-ordered universe in which logical rules are applied. When he created human beings, he created them to share his abilities to understand, think, plan and remember, in other words, to be rational beings that can use their reason and judgement to make informed decisions, including moral and religious decisions.

> For the Lord gives wisdom; from his mouth come knowledge and understanding.

(Proverbs 2.6)

Creativity

> **Creatio ex materia** The idea that God created the universe using matter already in existence.
>
> **Creatio ex nihilo** The idea that God created the universe out of nothing.

Christians today believe that, when God created the universe, he did so **ex nihilo** – from nothing. Clearly, human beings are not capable of this. Instead, Christians believe that God passed on to them the ability to create **ex materia**.

Some scholars believe that the writer of the Genesis account of Creation describes *creatio ex materia*: water and darkness already existed before God created the universe. If this is so, then it raises a problem: if God used pre-existing materials to make the universe, where did those materials come from?

When God created the first man, according to the Book of Genesis, he commanded him to tend the garden and make use of the plants in it. Human creativity in finding uses for plants in the world is almost limitless. Plants are used for food, for climate control, for clothing, for construction, for furniture, for medicines, and so on.

But Genesis makes it clear that the garden that Adam must look after contains plants that are 'pleasing to the eye' (Genesis 2.9). So Adam is instructed to make the garden a place of beauty; God makes him a craftsman and an artist.

Today, many Christian artists still use artistic skills to express their faith.

Fallen nature

> The Lord God took the man and put him in the Garden of Eden to work it and take care of it. And the Lord God commanded the man, 'You are free to eat from any tree in the garden; but you must not eat from the Tree of the Knowledge of Good and Evil, for when you eat from it you will certainly die.'

(Genesis 2.15–17)

We have seen that Eve then Adam disobeyed God. They ate fruit from the Tree of the Knowledge of Good and Evil when they were told not to. As a result, they came to understand right and wrong; but their perfect relationship with God had been broken. The event is known as the Fall.

Some Christians believe that a further consequence of the Fall is that all human beings since then carry with them Adam and Eve's Original Sin. This means that all humans, because of Adam and Eve, have a tendency to disobey God and sin. It is in their nature to do evil deeds. Their nature is said to be **fallen**.

The cross is an important symbol for Christians because it represents Jesus' death and Resurrection.

Grace God's undeserved mercy, love and forgiveness.
Fallen The state of inheriting Adam and Eve's Original Sin.
Redemption Being saved from sin.
Salvation Having one's sins forgiven and being granted eternal life.

Human beings cannot rid themselves of Original Sin, nor can they, on their own, mend their fractured relationship with God. It is only through God's grace – undeserved mercy, love and forgiveness – that they can be saved from the consequences of Original Sin. For example, Catholics believe that they receive God's **grace** through baptism and the belief that Jesus died on the cross so that their sins may be forgiven. Grace comes through the acceptance of God's love and forgiveness.

Humanity's fallen nature means that human beings are separated from God; their relationship with him is broken. Christianity teaches that Jesus' death on the cross was God's plan to mend the relationship. According to this teaching, the sin and guilt of human beings was borne by Jesus. God shows his love for human beings, a love they do not deserve, by allowing his son to be put to death. He shows his willingness to repair the damaged relationship with mankind in this act of **redemption**. Christians believe that Jesus' death offers the opportunity for **salvation** (being saved from Original Sin and its consequences).

Task

Explain what Christianity teaches about human nature. Think about the following: imago Dei, soul, morality, free will, reason, creativity, Original Sin.

▶ The Trinity

Key Concept

Trinity The three persons of God: God the Father, Son and Holy Spirit.

How great is God – beyond our understanding.

(Job.36.26)

The teaching of the **Trinity** is a way for Christians to understand what God is like. The word Trinity is not used in the Bible. However, the early Christians had started to develop their thinking about God as a Trinity within two hundred years of the death of Jesus.

The word 'Trinity' has two parts, a prefix *tri-* (three) and *unity* (one). So it literally means, three and one. It indicates that the one God is, at the same time, three different aspects. Each of the persons has all of the qualities of God – omnipotence, omnibenevolence, omniscience and omnipresence – yet they are distinct from each other.

The three persons of the Trinity are the Father, the Son and the **Holy Spirit**.

The three aspects are sometimes called 'persons', though this does not mean 'people' in the usual sense. Christianity teaches that God is not human and the three persons of God are not individuals. They are not three parts of God: each person is fully God. Christians do not worship three Gods, but one God.

Each of the three persons of the Trinity is fully God, yet distinct from the other two.

If this sounds complicated, it is! Christians believe that God is complex and beyond human understanding.

1 Christianity: Beliefs and teachings

16

God the Father

God the Father

Christians believe that God is the father of all because he is the creator of all. God created the universe and everything in it and God created humankind.

Christianity also teaches that God is father in relation to Jesus. Jesus claimed that his relationship with God the Father was unique and mysterious:

> No one knows the Son except the Father, and no one knows the Father except the Son and those to whom the Son chooses to reveal him.

(Matthew 11.27)

Christianity teaches that human beings can share in Jesus' relationship with his Father:

> To all who did receive him, to those who believed in his name, he gave the right to become children of God.

(John 1.12)

Yet the word 'father' does not just describe what God is like, it also describes the relationship God has with his creation – like a father to a child.

Christians believe that they can have a personal and loving relationship with God. God will show them his mercy and forgive them if they are willing to enter this relationship with him.

Tasks

1 Explain why Christians call God 'Father'.
2 Explain what the Parable of the Prodigal Son means to Christians and what it tells them about God.

The Parable of the Prodigal Son

Jesus tells the Parable of the Prodigal Son (Luke 15.1–32), about a young man who leaves his family to make his own way in the world. He is arrogant and ungrateful, yet his father gives him money to help him. However, he wastes the money and is reduced to poverty, sharing scraps of food with animals. Eventually he returns to his father, begging his forgiveness and asking to be allowed back. Without hesitation, his father greets him with love. The father's other son, who had remained faithful, cannot understand why his father has accepted his brother back so easily. But the father is clear that he does not prefer one child over the other.

> 'My son,' the father said, 'you are always with me, and everything I have is yours. But we had to celebrate and be glad, because this brother of yours was dead and is alive again; he was lost and is found.'

(Luke 15.31–32)

Christians see this as a metaphor for God's fatherly love for human beings. They also see it as an example of how humans should show love and forgiveness to each other.

Jesus Christ

God the Son

When Christians refer to God the Son, they mean Jesus. Jesus is called the Son of God because he was a human being. But Christians believe that, at the same time, Jesus was and is God, the second person of the Trinity, God the Son.

As the second person of the Trinity, God the Son existed before taking human form as Jesus. Christianity teaches that the Son was there at the creation of the universe. In the book of Genesis, God says, 'Let us make mankind in our image' (Genesis 1.26). Christians interpret the use of the plural 'us' as meaning that the three persons of the Trinity were present at the creation.

The writer of John's Gospel refers to God the Son at creation as the 'Word':

In the beginning was the Word, and the Word was with God, and the Word was God. He was with God in the beginning. Through him all things were made; without him nothing was made that has been made.

(John 1.1–3)

Later in the same chapter, John identifies the Word as Jesus:

The Word became flesh and made his dwelling among us. We have seen his glory, the glory of the one and only Son, who came from the Father, full of grace and truth.

(John 1.14)

God chose to reveal himself in the form of a human being.

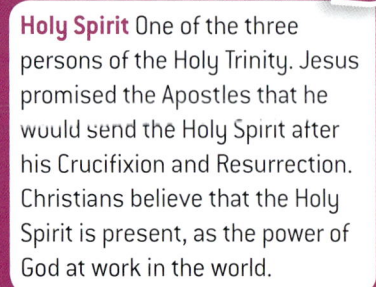

God the Holy Spirit

The word 'spirit' comes from the Latin word *spirare*, meaning 'to breathe'. When God created Adam, the book of Genesis states that God breathes into him and he comes alive. So the Holy Spirit is connected with life and the soul. Genesis also suggests that God the Holy Spirit was with the Father and Son at creation and before.

The Holy Spirit is closely associated with the life of Jesus. When the birth of Jesus is announced, Mary is told that she will become pregnant through the Holy Spirit. When Jesus is baptised by his cousin, John, in the River Jordan, Mathew's Gospel tells that the voice of God (the Father) declares that Jesus is his son, and the Holy Spirit descends upon him in the form of a dove.

> **Key Concept**
>
> **Holy Spirit** One of the three persons of the Holy Trinity. Jesus promised the Apostles that he would send the Holy Spirit after his Crucifixion and Resurrection. Christians believe that the Holy Spirit is present, as the power of God at work in the world.

The Holy Spirit represented as a dove in a stained glass window in St Peter's Basilica in Rome.

Jesus taught his disciples that the Holy Spirit would be with them to teach them and remind them of his teachings after his death:

> 'All this I have spoken while still with you. But the Advocate, the Holy Spirit, whom the Father will send in my name, will teach you all things and will remind you of everything I have said to you.'
>
> (John 14.25–26)

Christians believe that the Holy Spirit continues to act through people, producing in them characteristics that might be said to represent the ideal Christian. In his letter to Christians in Galatia, St Paul calls these characteristics 'the fruit of the Spirit' and lists nine of them:

> … the fruit of the Spirit is love, joy, peace, forbearance, kindness, goodness, faithfulness, gentleness and self-control.
>
> (Galatians 5.22–23)

Tasks

1 'The three persons of the Trinity are equally important.' Discuss this statement showing that you have considered more than one point of view. (You must refer to Christianity in your answer.)

2 Copy the diagram. Connect lines around each box with explanations of each of the persons of the Trinity and what they share as persons of God.

God the Father	God the Son
GOD	
God the Holy Spirit	

Jesus as God Incarnate

Incarnation

The word 'incarnate' comes from the Latin *carnem*, which means 'flesh'. So 'incarnate' means 'in flesh'. The idea of Jesus being God Incarnate, therefore, refers to the Christian teaching that Jesus, while being human, was, at the same time, God.

The Bible gives many examples of the Holy Spirit working in, through and around Jesus, providing evidence for Christians that Jesus was divine. For example:

- The angel told Mary that Jesus would be the Son of God because he was conceived by the Holy Spirit (Luke 1.35).
- The Holy Spirit was present at the baptism of Jesus in the form of a dove (Mark 1.10).
- Throughout his life, Jesus did good deeds, performed miracles and healed the sick through the power of the Holy Spirit (Acts 10.38).
- Jesus recognised the Holy Spirit working in him (Luke 4.38).
- The Holy Spirit spoke through Jesus (John 3.34).
- The Holy Spirit raised Jesus from the dead (Romans 8.11).

> **Key Concept**
>
> **Incarnation** 'Made flesh' – the Christian belief that God became man in the person of Jesus, fully human and fully divine. God becoming human in the form of Jesus.

> The expression 'God the Son' refers to the second person of the Trinity, God, eternal and transcendent, who became human. 'Son of God', on the other hand, refers to Jesus, the man who was God.

> **Tasks**
>
> 1. Explain why Christianity teaches that Jesus was divine.
> 2. Examine this photograph. Identify the three persons of the Trinity. Why are they depicted as they are? Would a Christian think this is an accurate portrayal of the Trinity? Why? Why not?

Jesus as Messiah

The word '**Messiah**' comes from the Hebrew word *moshiach*, which means 'one who is anointed'. Anointing is a process of sprinkling or pouring perfumed oil on someone. It formed an important part of the ancient Jewish ceremony for instating a high priest. Later, it became part of the ceremony enthroning a king. (It still is part of the coronation ceremony for monarchs in the United Kingdom today.)

The second king of the Jewish people was King David, regarded by Jews as their greatest king, who earned God's favour as 'a man after his own heart' (I Samuel 13.14).

Over time, Jewish prophets foretold the future coming of a new Messiah, a leader of the Jewish people who would combine the political functions of a king with the religious functions of a priest. It was (and is) said that the Messiah would be descended from King David.

> **Key Concept**
>
> **Messiah** The word means 'the Anointed One'. The Messiah is the one believed to be sent by God to be humanity's saviour. Christians believe this person to be Jesus.

1 Christianity: Beliefs and teachings

20

Jesus never claimed to be the Messiah. Nevertheless, the writers of the Gospels – accounts of his life in the Bible – give big clues that they thought he was. It was predicted in the Jewish Bible that:

- the Messiah would be a descendant of King David (Isaiah 11.1)
- he would be born in Bethlehem (Micah 5.2)
- he would be referred to as *Immanuel*, meaning 'God is with us' (Isaiah 11.1)
- he would be from the tribe of Judah (Genesis 49.10)
- he would be borne by a virgin (Isaiah 7.14)
- great kings would pay homage to him (Isaiah 60.6)
- he would ride into Jerusalem on a donkey (Zechariah 9.9)
- he would be rejected by his own people (Isaiah 53.3)
- he would be killed for the sins of humans (Isaiah 53.5).

The Gospel writers relate that all these things happened in the life of Jesus.

In his Gospel, Matthew says:

> When Jesus came to the region of Caesarea Philippi, he asked his disciples, 'Who do people say the Son of Man is?'
>
> They replied, 'Some say John the Baptist; others say Elijah; and still others, Jeremiah or one of the prophets.'
>
> 'But what about you?' he asked. 'Who do you say I am?'
>
> Simon Peter answered, 'You are the Messiah, the Son of the living God.'
>
> Jesus replied, 'Blessed are you, Simon son of Jonah, for this was not revealed to you by flesh and blood, but by my Father in heaven.'

(Matthew 16.13–17)

Jesus does not deny he is the Messiah. He suggests that (Simon) Peter identified him as the Messiah because it was revealed to him by God the Father.

> The Greek word for 'anointed one' (Messiah) is *Christos*. Christians refer to Jesus as the Christ to show their belief that he is the Messiah predicted by the Jewish prophets. It is possible that the Romans put Jesus to death fearing that, if he believed he was the Messiah, he might lead Jews against them.

Saviour

Christian teaching about the meaning and purpose of Jesus' life is set out at the beginning of Matthew's Gospel:

> She will give birth to a son, and you are to give him the name Jesus, because he will save his people from their sins.

(Matthew 1.21)

Notice that even the name Jesus – *Yeshua* in Hebrew – means 'the Lord saves'.

Atonement

We have seen that Christianity teaches that God planned Jesus' **incarnation** and death to repair the relationship with him that Adam and Eve damaged in the Fall. The crucifixion was an **atonement** for human sin.

In John's Gospel, Jesus' cousin describes Jesus as 'the Lamb of God, who takes away the sin of the world' (John 1.29). Christians believe that there are parallels between the Passover story, (see page 22), and the life and death of Jesus. They believe that Jesus' life was sacrificed, like the Passover lambs, and his blood shed, so that his followers would be saved from the slavery of sin and freed from death. Jesus' death and Resurrection open the door to eternal life for Christians:

Key Concept

Atonement The belief that Jesus' death and Resurrection healed the rift between humans and God, thereby opening the way for God and people to be 'at one' again.

> In the Old Testament of the Bible, in the story of the Passover, the ancient Israelites were held as slaves by the Egyptians. God sends plagues (disasters) to the Egyptians to persuade them to free the Israelites. But the Egyptian Pharaoh remains stubborn. Finally, God determines to kill the eldest child in every family. In order that the firstborn in the Israelite families will be saved, the Israelites are instructed to sacrifice a lamb and smear its blood around their doors. God will pass over these houses.
>
> In this story, the lives of the lambs are sacrificed to save the Israelites from death and free them from slavery.
>
> The Old Testament shows that there was a long tradition in the Hebrew religion of sacrificing animals to God in order to receive his forgiveness for sins. The book of Leviticus describes an ancient Israelite practice of sacrificing a goat and sending another out into the desert, symbolically carrying the sins of the people: the Scapegoat. This is known as atonement: it makes human beings 'at one' with God.

For God so loved the world that he gave his one and only Son, that whoever believes in him shall not perish but have eternal life.

(John 3.16)

Jesus himself tells his disciple, Thomas:

I am the way and the truth and the life. No one comes to the Father except through me.

(John 14.6)

Word

We have seen (page 18) that Jesus is referred to as the Word in John's Gospel. It is not clear exactly what is meant by this, and there are different Christian interpretations.

The statement in John 1.1 that the Word existed 'in the beginning' emphasises the eternal nature of the Trinity. The Word is identified with Jesus as God the Son, who is in turn identified with the other persons of the Trinity. Jesus himself explains to his disciples that he is part of the Trinity, indivisible from God. He says, for example, 'I am in the Father and the Father is in me.' (John 14.11). 'The Word' is a translation of the Greek word, '*Logos*'. *Logos* is the basis of the English word, 'logic', and implies systematic and strategic reasoning. So *Logos* refers to the organising principle of the universe. John is saying that Jesus, as *Logos*, 'was God' from the beginning, from before being 'made flesh'.

Another interpretation of the Word is that, just as words link human beings together as tools of communication, increasing understanding and co-operation, so Jesus is the link that connects human beings with God. Christians believe that Jesus reveals God's plans for and expectations of humanity through Jesus. At the same time, Christians believe that they can approach God through the worship of Jesus.

A painting depicting the birth of Christ. Christians believe that God became human in the form of Jesus.

▶ The birth, death, and Resurrection of Jesus

The events of the life and death of Jesus are recorded in four books in the New Testament of the Bible. They are named after their authors: Matthew, Mark, Luke and John. They are called 'Gospels'. The word gospel means 'good news'; the earliest of the Gospels (the Gospel according to Mark) starts, 'The beginning of the good news about Jesus the Messiah, the Son of God' (Mark 1.1).

The four accounts of Jesus' life record important events, but also offer interpretations of what they mean.

Jesus' birth

Only two of the four Gospels – Matthew and Luke – give accounts of the birth of Jesus. There are differences between the two versions, each designed to look at the Incarnation from a different angle.

Matthew 1.18–2.12

According to Matthew, Mary and Joseph were engaged to be married when Mary became pregnant. They married, but Joseph thought about divorcing her. However, an angel appeared to him and told him not to divorce Mary; Mary had become pregnant by the Holy Spirit. The baby was born and named Jesus.

Meanwhile, some mystics came from the east saying that they had seen a new star in the sky that indicated that a Jewish king had been born. They used Old Testament prophecies to work out where the birth had taken place. When the serving King Herod heard this, he thought his position as king may be threatened. He therefore asked the mystics to report back to him when they had found where the new king had been born.

The mystics found Jesus in a house in Bethlehem. They bowed down and worshipped him, presenting him with gifts of gold, frankincense and myrrh.

They were warned in a vision not to report back to King Herod, so went home by a different route.

In this account, Matthew is emphasising Jesus' divine nature as the Son of God. His birth is respectable and honourable: his parents are married, he is born in a house, he is visited by important people and given valuable gifts. However, the gifts themselves give clues about Jesus' life and its meaning. Gold and frankincense represent messiahship: gold for royalty, and frankincense, which is burnt in religious ceremonies, for priesthood. Myrrh was used to embalm dead bodies; Matthew seems to be giving a clue that Jesus' death would have deep significance.

Luke 1.1–20

Luke presents the birth of Jesus from a different point of view. According to him, Mary and Joseph were not married when Mary became pregnant and did not marry afterwards. However, Mary had been told in advance by an angel that she would become pregnant by the Holy Spirit.

Tasks

1. Read the Gospel accounts of the birth of Jesus in Matthew 1.18–2.12 and Luke 1.1–20.
2. Compare the two accounts. Draw a Venn diagram to show what is unique to Matthew's Gospel, what is unique to Luke's, and what they have in common. Underneath, write a paragraph to explain the symbols used in the two versions.
3. Explain why the Bible contains different accounts of the same events.

Blasphemy Insult or offence against God.

Meanwhile, the Romans were planning to conduct a census of the Jewish population. To facilitate this, Jews were required to return to the town of their birth to register. Joseph was born in Bethlehem – also the hometown of the great King David – so he and Mary travelled there from their home in Nazareth. When they arrived, there was no available accommodation. When Jesus was born, he had to be placed in an animals' feeding trough.

Some shepherds, tending sheep during the night, were visited by an angel and told that the Messiah had been born. They followed the directions they were given and found Jesus in the manger. They then spread the word of the Messiah's birth.

The Gospels of Matthew and Luke both present Jesus as the Messiah. But, whereas Matthew emphasises Jesus' divine identity, Luke shows his humanity. He is born in humble circumstances to unmarried people. He is not visited by important guests, but by ordinary working men, and he is given no gifts.

The Crucifixion

Jesus' teachings brought him into conflict with the Jewish authorities. They viewed him with suspicion and accused him of **blasphemy** because he claimed to be able to forgive sin. His followers believed he was the Messiah, and this was seen as a challenge to those in power. As a result, he was arrested in Jerusalem.

Jesus was first tried by a court of Jewish leaders. They found him guilty of blasphemy for claiming to be the Son of God. They did not have the authority to pass a death sentence, so they passed him on to the Roman Prefect, Pontius Pilate.

Pilate was not concerned about the charge of blasphemy since he was not Jewish. He discovered that Jesus came from Galilee, and, by chance, the Jewish ruler of Galilee, King Herod, was in town. He sent Jesus to Herod.

Herod was disappointed that his 'rival' as King of the Jews had no royal pretentions and gave no sign that he was divine. He sent him back to Pilate. Pilate was reluctant to have Jesus put to death and wanted to let him go. However, the crowd insisted that he should be killed. Fearing a riot, Pilate gave in to the crowd and ordered Jesus' execution.

A model of Jesus' crucifixion.

Tasks

1. Read the full Gospel account of Jesus' execution in Matthew 15.1–39.
2. Create a timeline of events for the Crucifixion of Jesus. Start with 'Jesus is arrested' and finish with 'Jesus dies on the cross'.
3. Explain why the Crucifixion of Jesus is important for Christians.

Key Concept

Resurrection The belief that Jesus rose from the dead on the third day from when he was crucified, thereby conquering death. It is commemorated annually on Easter Sunday.

The Roman form of execution was crucifixion. Its purpose was to ensure a criminal died in agony, and it was a powerful way to intimidate the civilian population. In the Gospel account, Jesus is one of a number of men crucified in Jerusalem at the same time. However, an unusual feature in the account of Jesus' Crucifixion is that the soldiers plait a crown of thorns and place it on Jesus' head.

Because Christians believe Jesus was both truly God and truly human, they believe that when he died on the cross he suffered like any other human being. Jesus participates in the suffering of humanity, and this is important to Christians because it means that God understands human suffering.

For Christians, the Crucifixion and death of Jesus open the way to salvation for those who believe in him.

The Resurrection

The **Resurrection** of Jesus is fundamental to the Christian faith. It refers to the belief that Jesus rose from the dead three days after his Crucifixion. This is the greatest miracle recorded in the New Testament and, for Christians, is evidence that Jesus was God.

In the passage below, Paul says that if Christians don't believe in the Resurrection of Jesus, then their faith is pointless and has no meaning:

> But if it is preached that Christ has been raised from the dead, how can some of you say that there is no Resurrection of the dead? If there is no Resurrection of the dead, then not even Christ has been raised. And if Christ has not been raised, our preaching is useless and so is your faith.

(1 Corinthians 15.12–14)

At the time of Jesus, many Jews claimed to be the Messiah. Many were travelling preachers, as Jesus was. For Christians, what makes Jesus different from the others and unique in history is that he rose from the dead. To be a Christian is not only to follow the teachings of Jesus, but to believe in the Resurrection as the only way to salvation.

The different Gospels disagree slightly on the exact events of the Resurrection, but they agree that on the Sunday following Jesus' Crucifixion, some of his followers went to his tomb. They found that the stone covering the mouth of the tomb had been rolled away and Jesus' body was not inside.

John's Gospel (20.1–21) records that Jesus first appeared to Mary Magdalene in a garden beside his tomb. Later he appears to his disciples, except for Thomas, in a locked room; then to all of his disciples, including Thomas, again in a locked room.

The Ascension

After Jesus rose from the dead there are few references in the Gospels to what Jesus did. He appeared to the disciples and groups of other people but the account is very short and vague. After a period of time, the Gospels record that Jesus ascended (rose up) to his father in heaven.

There are different understandings of what this actually means. Some Christians believe that Jesus physically ascended to heaven in a literal sense. Others believe that the description of Jesus physically rising up to heaven is just meant to be symbolic, showing that Jesus' time in human form on earth was over. Either way, for Christians, it is a very significant event. It marks an end to the presence of Jesus on earth in a physical way but includes an acceptance of Jesus' spirit at work in the world.

In the Book of Acts, Jesus tells his disciples that the Holy Spirit will enable them to tell others about his teachings, his death and Resurrection. The narrative continues:

> After he said this, he was taken up before their very eyes, and a cloud hid him from their sight.
>
> They were looking intently up into the sky as he was going, when suddenly two men dressed in white stood beside them.
>
> 'Men of Galilee,' they said, 'why do you stand here looking into the sky? This same Jesus, who has been taken from you into heaven, will come back in the same way you have seen him go into heaven.'

(Acts 1.9–11)

Task

Reproduce the table below, analysing the four key events in the life of Jesus. Complete it by giving a **definition** for each key term linked to the event, an **explanation** of what happened, an **outline** and a **quotation** linked to the event. (You will need plenty of space!)

Event	Definition	Explanation	Outline	Quote
Incarnation				
Crucifixion				
Salvation and atonement				
Resurrection				

▶ **End of Section Review**

Stickability

Key concepts:
- Agape
- Atonement
- Holy Spirit
- Incarnation
- Messiah
- Omnibenevolence
- Omnipotence
- Omniscience
- Resurrection
- Trinity

Key teachings:
- The nature of God
- The Creation
- The nature of humanity
- The Trinity
- The Son of God
- The Messiah
- Key events on the life of Jesus

Skills Link

1. What do Christians mean by 'Resurrection'?
2. Explain Christian beliefs about the Holy Spirit.

Knowledge Check

1. Write a short paragraph (roughly three sentences) to explain what Christians believe about the nature of God.
2. Write a long paragraph (roughly eight to ten sentences) to explain how Christians believe the incarnation and the resurrection are linked.
3. Explain at least three of the titles Christians use for Jesus.
4. Write a developed paragraph (approximately six to eight sentences) to explain different Christian interpretations of the Fall and Original Sin.

The Big Question

'Jesus is still relevant in the modern world.'

Your task

Respond to the statement above, showing that you have considered more than one point of view. Give reasoned judgements on the validity and strength of these views.

Task

You need to explain, in detail, religious teachings about **Creation**. Use the guidance below to help you to write a **developed explanation** for Christianity. Ensure that you use key terms fluently and frequently.

All/many/most Christians believe that _____ .

This comes from the teaching/Bible quote _____ .

This means that/Because of this they _____ .

Some/other Christians such as _____ believe that _____ .

This comes from the teaching/Bible quote _____ .

This means that/Because of this they _____ .

Finally, Christians such as _____ believe that _____ .

This means that/Because of this they _____ .

Their beliefs do/do not differ because _____ .

2 Christianity: Practices

■ Morality

▶ Approaches to ethical decision making

Most people would say that they know the difference between right and wrong, between good and bad behaviour. This does not mean, of course, that they always do the right thing (act ethically); but they know when they are doing wrong or behaving badly.

The question is, *how* do people know what is right and wrong?

> **Ethics** Principles of moral behaviour.

Moral absolutism

Some people would say that what is right and wrong is a matter of fact. Moral rules, such as 'It is wrong to kill' or 'It is right to keep promises' are universal truths – they are absolute. They apply to all people at all times in all situations. There are no circumstances in which it is morally acceptable to kill or to break a promise.

The question arises, how do we know what the moral rules are? Many religious people would say that what is morally right is whatever God has commanded, and what is wrong is whatever God has forbidden or condemned. This is known as **divine command theory**.

> **Key Concept**
>
> **Divine command theory** The belief that something is right because God commands it.

Moral relativism

Relativists would say that morality does not consist of hard and fast rules that apply in every situation. They would agree that there are certain moral principles, but they need to be adapted relative to specific circumstances. Some relativists would say that moral attitudes shift over time and between cultures. For example, at one time, keeping slaves was thought to be acceptable; today, it is not.

Most moral relativists would agree that this form of relativism is difficult to justify. They would, however, say that what is right and wrong depends on the specific circumstances of a particular situation. There are no universal or absolute rules. This is called situation **ethics**. For example, while accepting the general principle that it is wrong to kill, a situationist would argue that there are circumstances in which killing may be the best possible (or least bad) course of action.

> **Task**
>
> Explain the differences between absolute and relative morality. For each, give an example of a moral principle; explain why someone may hold it to be absolute, and why someone else may consider it relative.

The teachings of Jesus

When Jesus taught about morality, he linked it closely to his religious and spiritual teachings. His audiences and followers were Jewish and were familiar with Jewish moral teachings, especially those contained in the Jewish Bible. So Jesus' teachings were grounded in ideas that were already well known.

The Golden Rule

Matthew's Gospel records two occasions when Jesus teaches what has become known as the Golden Rule. He was not the first to do so; the Golden Rule appears in the Old Testament and in the moral teachings of many different religions and cultures. But Jesus claims that it summarises the whole of Jewish morality:

> So in everything, do to others what you would have them do to you, for this sums up the Law and the Prophets.
>
> (Matthew 7.12)

(In this quotation, 'the Law and the Prophets' refers to the Jewish Bible.)

Jesus is answering the question, 'How do we know what is right and good?' His answer is simple: your behaviour to others is right and good if it brings them the same benefits that you would like to receive. But Jesus goes further when he says in the previous verse that God will reward those who do what is right:

> If you, then ... know how to give good gifts to your children, how much more will your Father in heaven give good gifts to those who ask him!
>
> (Matthew 7.11)

The Kingdom of God

In another teaching (Matthew 25.31–46), Jesus explains that the reward for those who do good will be eternal life in God's Kingdom. On the other hand, those who fail to do good will receive eternal punishment. There are three further points to note.

1. Jesus himself will judge people's behaviour.
2. Punishment is not the consequence only of doing evil, but also of failing to do good.
3. The promise of eternal life should not be the motivation for doing good. In Jesus' teaching, those who receive eternal life are unaware of their good deeds; goodness comes naturally to them.

Elsewhere, Jesus explains that the way to heaven is not easy.

> Enter through the narrow gate. For wide is the gate and broad is the road that leads to destruction, and many enter through it. But small is the gate and narrow the road that leads to life, and only a few find it.
>
> (Matthew 7.13–14)

He is saying that entrance to heaven requires moral discipline, a challenge that is hard to meet.

Task

Was Jesus a moral absolutist or relativist? Give reasons and evidence to support your answer.

Agape (love)

> **Key Concept**
>
> **Agape** Selfless, sacrificial, unconditional love. Christianity holds agape to be the highest type of love, epitomised by Jesus' sacrifice on the cross for the salvation of humanity and in teachings such as 'Love your neighbour'.

Shortly before his death, Jesus gave his disciples an instruction:

> A new command I give you: Love one another. As I have loved you, so you must love one another. By this everyone will know that you are my disciples, if you love one another.
>
> (John 13.34–35)

In English, it is not very clear what this means. But the New Testament was written in Greek, and the Greek language is very specific. The word Jesus uses for 'love' is **agape**. Agape is not the kind of love that involves friendship or physical attraction. It means putting the welfare and interests of others before one's own.

In the Bible, Jesus sums up Christian ethics in these words: 'Love your neighbour as yourself' (Matthew 22.39). Again he uses the word agape. Luke's Gospel recounts a member of Jesus' audience, an expert in Jewish law, asking Jesus to clarify this statement. 'And who is my neighbour?' (Luke 10.29) he asks.

Jesus answers in the form of a parable, the story of the Good Samaritan (Luke 10.25–37).

> 'A man was going down from Jerusalem to Jericho, when he was attacked by robbers. They stripped him of his clothes, beat him and went away, leaving him half dead. A priest happened to be going down the same road, and when he saw the man, he passed by on the other side. So too, a Levite (priestly assistant), when he came to the place and saw him, passed by on the other side. But a Samaritan (inhabitant of the region of Samaria), as he travelled, came where the man was; and when he saw him, he took pity on him. He went to him and bandaged his wounds, pouring on oil and wine. Then he put the man on his own donkey, brought him to an inn and took care of him. The next day he took out two denarii and gave them to the innkeeper. 'Look after him,' he said, 'and when I return, I will reimburse you for any extra expense you may have.'

Jesus concludes by asking:

> 'Which of these three do you think was a neighbour to the man who fell into the hands of robbers?'
>
> The expert in the law replied, 'The one who had mercy on him.'

So, Jesus is asked, 'Which people deserve my love (agape)?' And his answer is, 'Anyone who needs it'.

> **Task**
>
> 'It is impossible to love everyone.'
>
> How might a Christian respond to this statement?

Forgiveness

The expression 'forgive and forget' is not one that Christians would agree with. There is a tendency to think that forgiving someone for a wrong they have committed means letting them get away with it and is a sign of weakness.

For Christians, forgiveness is a conscious decision to let go of feelings of anger and hatred that can be self-destructive. Forgiveness still requires that justice be done wherever necessary. A Christian who forgives would also want the offender to show remorse for what they have done, so that they can make their peace with God. They would pray for God to forgive them. But the person who forgives is free from painful and destructive feelings and is able to move on with life.

Letting go of destructive feelings means letting go of hatred and replacing it with love. Jesus says:

> You have heard that it was said, 'Love your neighbour and hate your enemy.' But I tell you, love your enemies and pray for those who persecute you.
>
> (Matthew 5.43–44)

As always, Jesus brings his teachings on forgiveness back to God. When he teaches how to pray, he includes the words, 'And forgive us our debts, as we also have forgiven our debtors' (Matthew 6.12). He then explains what this means:

> For if you forgive other people when they sin against you, your heavenly Father will also forgive you. But if you do not forgive others their sins, your Father will not forgive your sins.
>
> (Matthew 6.14–15)

It is a matter of simple justice.

Forgiveness does not require the offender to be sorry for what they did; it is unconditional. It is about setting the forgiver free, not the offender. Matthew's Gospel says:

> Then Peter came to Jesus and asked, 'Lord, how many times shall I forgive my brother or sister who sins against me? Up to seven times?'
>
> Jesus answered, 'I tell you, not seven times, but seventy-seven times.'
>
> (Matthew 18.21–22)

Jesus himself, as he hangs from the cross, forgives those who have put him to death:

> Jesus said, 'Father, forgive them, for they do not know what they are doing.'
>
> (Luke 23.34)

He asks God to forgive them; although they are unaware of the significance of the execution, they are still guilty and require God's forgiveness.

Jesus' words in Matthew 6.5–13 suggest that forgiveness is not so much about the relationship between the forgiver and the forgiven, but between each party and God.

Task

'Unforgiveness makes you a victim.'

This was said by Gee Walker, a Christian and mother of Anthony, who was murdered in a racially motivated attack. What do you think she meant by this?

▶ Treasures on earth and in heaven

We have seen that, for Jesus, moral goodness is motivated by love (agape). Good actions are selfless and result in benefits for others at least equal to those one would like for oneself.

But moral actions have a spiritual element. What is good is what is approved by God. As a result, God will reward moral righteousness after death.

In the Bible, Jesus compares performing good deeds to putting money in a bank or saving up treasure:

> Do not store up for yourselves treasures on earth, where moths and vermin destroy, and where thieves break in and steal. But store up for yourselves treasures in heaven, where moths and vermin do not destroy, and where thieves do not break in and steal. For where your treasure is, there your heart will be also.

(Matthew 6.19–21)

Worldly goods can perish or be stolen. But good deeds have a spiritual value that is revealed after death: 'treasures in heaven'.

On another occasion, Jesus relates a parable that explains not just that good deeds will be rewarded after death, but also that failure to do what is right will be punished. The parable of the Rich Man and Lazarus (Luke 16.19–31) concerns a man with considerable wealth who is aware that a poor beggar, Lazarus, sleeps rough outside his house, but he does nothing to help him. When they both die, the Rich Man goes to hell and Lazarus to heaven. Wealth and good fortune have no significance in the afterlife. How positively a person uses them while alive is what is important.

Jesus ends the parable by saying that this message is repeated throughout the Bible, yet people fail to take notice. The Rich Man in the story asks if Lazarus could go back to earth from heaven to warn his family of the consequences of failing to do good. Jesus says (possibly with reference to himself):

> If they do not listen to Moses and the Prophets, they will not be convinced even if someone rises from the dead.

(Luke 16.31)

Task

In two to three sentences, explain what Jesus means by 'treasures on earth' and 'treasures in heaven'.

Church

The diversity of Christianity

The history of Christianity has been one of expansion and division. The religion is practised by 2.4 billion people – a third of the world's population – in 197 of the 232 countries on earth.

The last census to be conducted in the United Kingdom in 2011 found that 59.3 per cent of the population of England and Wales declared themselves to be Christian. The figure was not significantly different in Wales at 57.6 per cent.

The first major division in the Church occurred in the eleventh century (the Great Schism), between the Churches that are today called the Eastern Orthodox Churches and the Catholic Church. Again, in the sixteenth century, disputes in the Catholic Church led to the foundation of Protestant Churches, which broke away from the Roman Catholic Church (the Reformation).

The Catholic Church in England and Wales was called the Church of England. At the time of the Protestant Reformation, King Henry VIII objected to the authority of the Pope and took over leadership of the Church of England himself.

As the British Empire spread to nations across the world, the Churches that were formed in those countries based themselves on the model of the Church of England. They linked themselves together as a community of Churches known as the Anglican Communion.

The Anglican Church in Wales is called the Church in Wales. Whereas the Church of England still has close ties with the British government as the established Church in England, the Church in Wales broke its ties in 1920 and became disestablished.

Protestant Churches that refused to conform or agree with all of the teachings and practices of the Anglican Church are known as Nonconformist. Dissatisfaction with the Church of England in Wales in the 18th and 19th centuries led to the growth of Nonconformist groups, including Methodists, Baptists and Independents.

The different groups and branches of the Christian Church are called **denominations**.

> **Denomination** A branch of the Christian Church.

The Roman Catholic Church

About half of all Christians in the world belong to the Catholic Church. The Catholic Church is led by the Pope. The Catholic Church teaches that the Pope has special authority that descends from Jesus himself. Catholic worship tends to be formal and ritualised. Local leaders are called priests; they are not allowed to marry, and women cannot become priests.

The Anglican Church

The Anglican Communion is an organisation of Churches from many nations that are in some way connected to the Church of England. The Anglican Church does not recognise the authority of the Pope and has the Archbishop of Canterbury as its figurehead. It allows a fair degree of freedom of belief, interpretation and practice, so there is a broad diversity of views and forms of worship. Most Anglican Churches allow women to become priests, but not all of them. Local leaders are usually called vicars. Priests, male or female, are allowed to marry.

The Church in Wales

The Church in Wales is the Anglican Church in Wales. As such, it has the same range of diversity as the other Anglican Churches. It is led by the Archbishop of Wales, who is also one of the Church's bishops, and it is estimated to have about 84,000 members.

Nonconformist Churches and Chapels

Nonconformist Churches are those Protestant Churches that split from the Catholic Church and also refused to conform to the teachings of the Anglican Church. There is a variety of them represented in Wales. Nonconformity started in the 18th century when Welsh Anglicans became unhappy that the Church of England in Wales had so few Welsh bishops and ministers. The three largest Nonconformist groups in Wales are the Union of Welsh Independents, the Baptist Church and the Calvinistic Methodist Church, or the Presbyterian Church of Wales. Men and women can be ministers in the Welsh Nonconformist Churches, and they can marry. Although they have differences, the Churches all consider the authority of the Bible to be their core principle. Many Nonconformist Church buildings are called chapels. Nonconformist denominations, especially those where worship is conducted in Welsh, are often called Chapel to distinguish them from the Anglican Church in Wales.

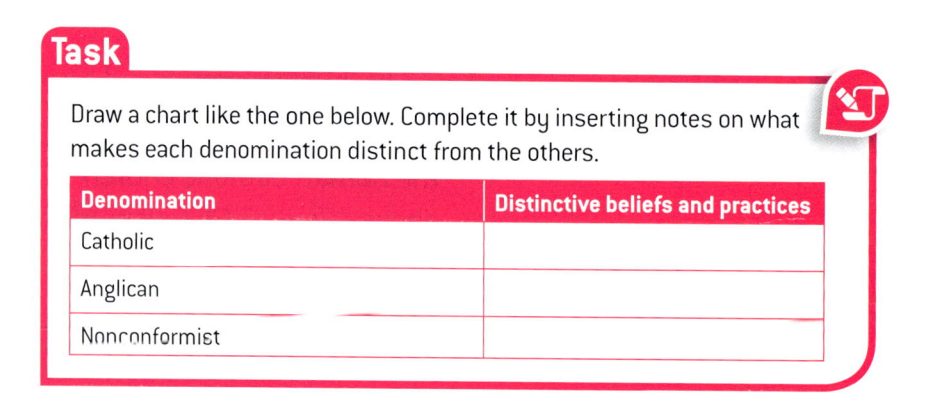

Task

Draw a chart like the one below. Complete it by inserting notes on what makes each denomination distinct from the others.

Denomination	Distinctive beliefs and practices
Catholic	
Anglican	
Nonconformist	

Tasks

1. Explain how the quotation from Matthew's Gospel relates to some of the activities carried out in churches and chapels.
2. Select five different activities run by the Church (for example, coffee mornings for the elderly). For each, outline how they serve the community.

The role of the local church

You are the light of the world. A town built on a hill cannot be hidden. Neither do people light a lamp and put it under a bowl. Instead they put it on its stand, and it gives light to everyone in the house. In the same way, let your light shine before others, that they may see your good deeds and glorify your Father in heaven.

(Matthew 5.14–16)

Primarily a church or chapel is a place of worship, but as part of living out the values Jesus demonstrated in the Gospels, they reach out into communities in a variety of ways. Some of the services the churches provide to the community might be religious in nature, for example, marking important rites of passage for individuals and families. Services such as baptisms, confirmations, marriages and funerals will be held in the church or chapel.

Many churches and chapels have a hall attached, and chapels also function as meeting houses. They may be used for a variety of activities, including:

- refreshments after Sunday services
- a weekly meal for the homeless provided by money donated by a congregation
- food banks
- coffee mornings for the elderly
- youth clubs
- Mothers' Union meetings
- crèche facilities for young mothers
- summer fêtes
- organisations like Cubs and Brownies
- fitness classes or slimming groups
- Christmas parties for old-age pensioners
- birthday parties
- family and community events
- concerts and shows
- charity sales
- Bible study and prayer groups
- adult education
- emergency shelters.

Notice board examples:
- The local Baptist church is opening a food bank every Friday
- Old Age Pensioners' Christmas Dinner to be held in Methodist church on Saturday
- Quakers to visit local prison to read with prisoners
- Catholic church opens SVP (Society of Vincent de Paul) shop in town centre to raise funds for those living in poverty
- Local Christian businessman funds street pastors in city centre: provided bottles of water and flip flops for distribution by the pastors working every weekend
- Crèche to open in local Anglican church three times each week
- Volunteers asked for in local churches to distribute Christian Aid collection envelopes

Churches are used for a variety of activities.

Diverse features of churches and chapels

The main function of churches and chapels is to conduct and participate in acts of worship. The architecture, layout and furniture of places of worship therefore reflect some of the beliefs and practices of the Christian religion in general and the denomination in particular.

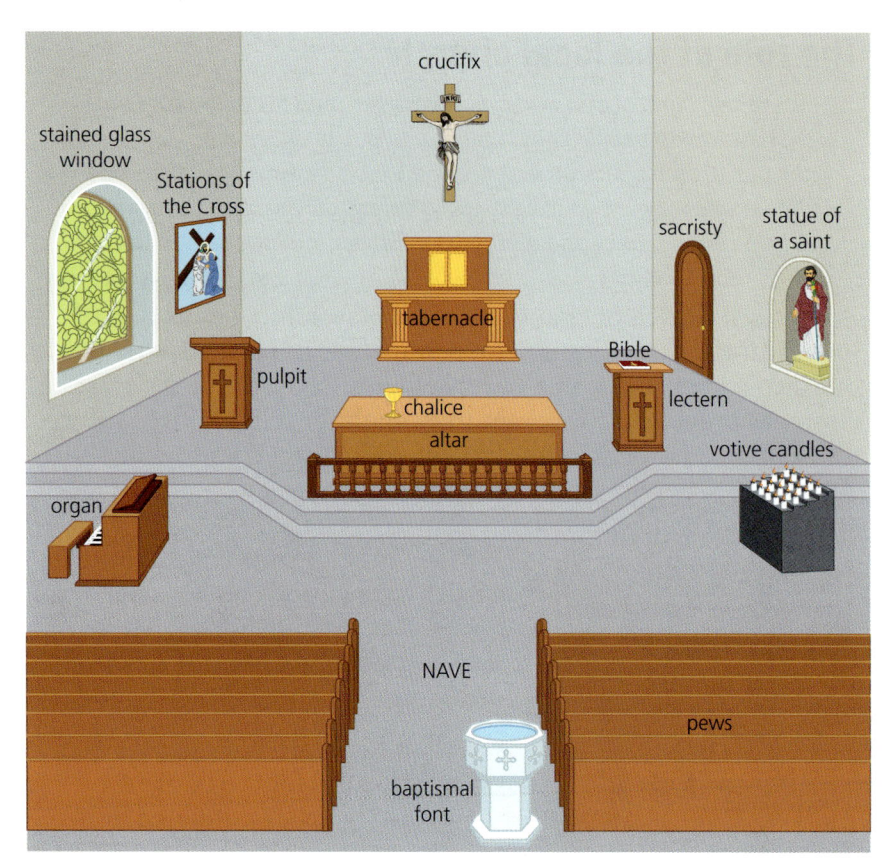

Inside a Roman Catholic church.

Catholic church

Catholic churches are traditionally, though not always, built in the shape of a cross. The top of the cross is at the east end of the building, facing Jerusalem, where Jesus died and is believed to have risen again.

The east end of the church is called the sanctuary. The central feature of the sanctuary is the altar, a table, often made from stone, on which bread and wine are blessed (offered to God) during the service of Eucharist. The bread and wine are kept in the tabernacle behind the altar.

Also in the sanctuary is a lectern, a reading stand from which passages of the Bible are read. On the other side is the pulpit from which the Gospel is read, and where the priest delivers talks or sermons.

A crucifix (a cross with the figure of Jesus on it) is displayed in a prominent position in the sanctuary, usually behind the altar.

There is a rail that separates the sanctuary from the main body of the church, the nave. The nave is where the congregation sits and takes part in the service that is led from the sanctuary. People typically sit in rows on benches called pews. On the walls are 14 pictures illustrating the events of Jesus' crucifixion; they are called Stations of the Cross.

Other features that are found in a Catholic church are:

▶ a font, a stone basin used to baptise babies using holy (consecrated) water
▶ a stoup, a smaller basin attached to the wall just inside the door also containing holy water. Catholics dip a hand in the water and cross themselves to renew their baptismal promises
▶ statues, paintings and stained-glass windows that tell important stories or illustrate religious teachings
▶ votive candles, lit by worshippers when praying before a statue
▶ an organ to accompany worshippers singing hymns
▶ confessional, a small cabinet in which the priest hears the confessions of individuals.

Anglican church

Because the Anglican Church was the Catholic Church in England until the Tudor era, many of their church buildings are very similar to Catholic churches. They are usually cross-shaped with a sanctuary at the east end containing an altar.

Task

Use the information on this page to write definitions of the following terms:

votive candle; stations of the cross; lectern; font; pew; crucifix; sanctuary; altar; nave; pulpit; confessional.

An Anglican church in Wales.

However, they are likely to be plainer, with fewer decorations. They do not have statues and votive candles to channel prayer, and the figure of Mary, the mother of Jesus, will not be prominent and may not be present at all.

In the sanctuary, the bread and wine used in Eucharist do not have a special container like the tabernacle in a Catholic church. It is more usual to have a simple cross rather than a crucifix. A font may be at the west end of the church, but there are no holy water stoups.

Nonconformist chapel

Chapels tend to be much simpler buildings than Catholic or more elaborate Anglican churches. Many churches have spires that reach up from the roof towards heaven, whereas most chapels have more regular pitched roofs. Churches are usually open inside to the roof, while chapels may have a gallery or balcony between the floor and ceiling; this allows more room for the congregation to sit. And while churches are normally oriented from east to west, chapels may not be.

The layout of a chapel reflects the primary purpose of it: to hear God's word and sing his praises. At one end, the focal point is a pulpit or lectern for the minister to read from the Bible and explain its teachings to the congregation. In front of the pulpit is a communion table for the celebration of Holy Communion. An organ is an important feature of the chapel to accompany the singing of hymns, and some may have space for a small band.

Baptist chapels have a door built into the floor in front of the pews where the congregation sits. The door can be opened to reveal the baptistry, a pool in which adults are baptised.

Task

Draw diagrams of different Christian places of worship and label them. Then write a sentence to explain each of the labels.

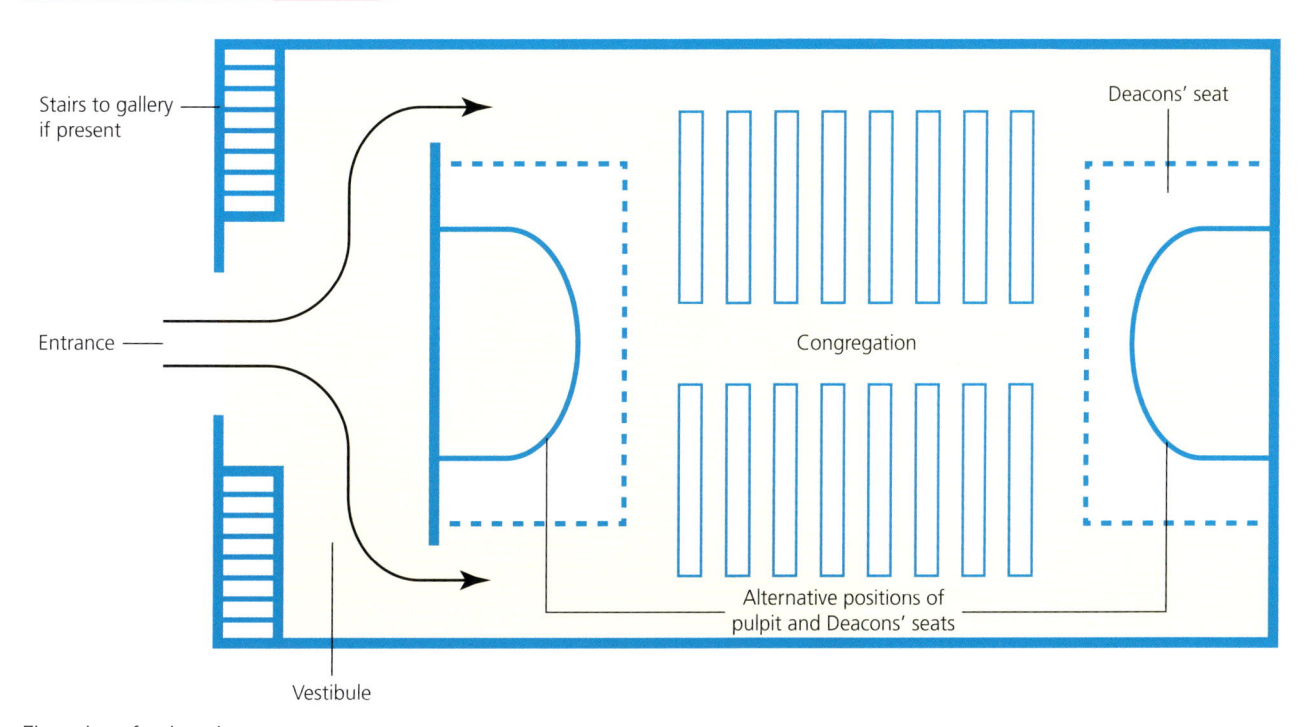

Floor plan of a chapel.

- Stairs to gallery if present
- Entrance
- Vestibule
- Deacons' seat
- Congregation
- Alternative positions of pulpit and Deacons' seats

Diversity of worship practices

Worship is an expression of adoration of and praise for God. Acts of worship and their importance are referred to frequently in the Bible. For example, in the Ten Commandments, the command 'to keep the Sabbath day holy' has been interpreted as a command to worship God.

There are many different forms of worship and different Christian traditions have different ways of worshipping God.

Individual worship takes place in addition to worshipping together in a church. Christians believe that it is important to form a personal relationship with God, and worshipping alone is often part of this. Some Christians do not feel the need to take part in public worship or belong to a formal or organised religious group, so worship individually.

Informal worship is public or 'corporate' worship that does not follow a set pattern or structure. The modern **charismatic** and **evangelical** approach to worship emphasises the importance of the Holy Spirit and spontaneous action and this shows itself in services, in worship and in prayer. In some churches this may involve worshippers falling into trances or even speaking in unknown languages ('speaking in tongues').

Liturgical worship is a form of worship that follows a set pattern and has established rituals as part of public church worship. Most Christian Churches have some form of liturgical worship. This might be a set pattern of prayers, or the use of a set service book, as in the Catholic Church and the Church in Wales.

In Wales, most liturgical worship is conducted in English, except for Chapel worship, which is usually conducted in Welsh.

Most denominations include the Lord's Prayer in their services (see page 42), which, because of its biblical origins, has real significance for all Protestant denominations. Worship in Nonconformist chapels has the Bible as the Word of God at its centre. Preaching God's word is the main feature of Chapel worship.

Charismatic A form of Christian worship that emphasises the work of the Holy Spirit, spiritual gifts and miracles.

Evangelical A lively form of worship that emphasises the worshipper's personal relationship with Jesus, often expressed through music.

Task

Explain why Christians worship God. In your answer, refer to the different ways in which different denominations worship.

A group of Christians coming together to worship is known as a congregation. Worship that takes place as a congregation is sometimes called 'corporate worship'.

For a full consideration of Sacraments and Eucharist see the Unit 2 textbook.

Sacrament An outward sign of an invisible and inward blessing by God, for example, baptism and Eucharist. The word comes from the Latin *sacramentum*, an oath of allegiance made by Roman soldiers in a ceremony. By the second century CE it had started to be used to describe Christian rites. By the fifth century it was defined by the early Christian thinker St Augustine in his writings as a 'visible sign of invisible grace'.

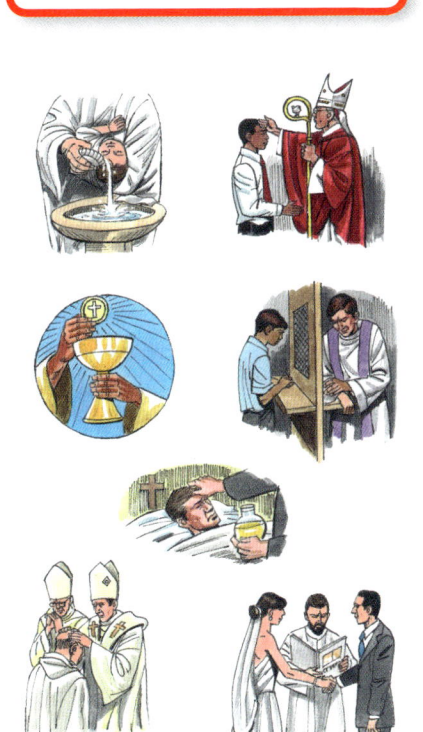

Diversity in worship: The sacraments

The sacraments are examples of liturgical worship. The word sacrament means a: 'visible sign of invisible grace'. This means that the actions, words and objects involved in each **sacrament** are a sign that Christians are receiving God's grace or blessing.

The Roman Catholic and Eastern Orthodox Churches recognise seven sacraments:

- Baptism initiates people into the Christian church.
- Confirmation takes place when a person reaches an age when they commit to the Church for themselves.
- Eucharist is the sharing of bread and wine in remembrance of Jesus' death.
- Penance is also known as the sacrament of reconciliation or confession. Catholics are required to confess their sins to a priest and repent them. The priest will then 'absolve' (or free) them from their sins on behalf of God.
- Anointing of the sick is performed when a Catholic is seriously ill or dying.
- Holy orders is the way people join the priesthood of the Church. Joining the priesthood is called being 'ordained'.
- Marriage shows the spiritual union of the couple and God.

Most Protestant and Anglican Churches only recognise two sacraments: baptism and Eucharist (or Holy Communion). This is because these were the only two sacraments documented in the Gospels as being practised by Jesus during his life. Some Protestants call them 'ordinances' rather than sacraments. They say they should carry them out because they have been instructed to, not in order to receive God's grace.

Some Protestant denominations, such as the Quakers (the Society of Friends) and the Salvation Army, do not even recognise these two sacraments. They believe that sacraments are an inward spiritual experience and that there is no need for external services or rituals.

The Eucharist service is an example of liturgical worship.

Different ways Christians understand the Eucharist

Eucharist is also known as Holy Communion or Mass. It remembers the death of Jesus and the significance it has for Christians. Jesus instructed his followers to maintain the tradition of the Eucharist during the last meal he ate before he died, the Last Supper. At this meal Jesus shared bread and wine with his disciples and told them that the wine represented his blood and the bread his body. He told them that they should share bread and wine when they gathered together after his death in his memory.

Christians today continue this tradition – taking bread and wine when they meet to worship in the sacrament of the Eucharist. They believe this brings them closer to God. The word 'Eucharist' is a Greek word, meaning thanksgiving: it is an act of thanksgiving for the life and death of Jesus and for the Christian faith.

The bread and wine shared during the Eucharist service are representative of Jesus' body and blood.

The Roman Catholic Church teaches that the bread and wine actually become the body and blood of Christ in a process called '**transubstantiation**'. Most Protestants reject this view.

Many Nonconformist denominations discourage the drinking of alcohol, so use alcohol-free wine or grape juice during Communion. They would then refer to it as 'the cup'. The Reformed and Presbyterian view of the Eucharist is that Christ is present spiritually rather than literally in the bread and wine. Other Protestants, such as Baptists, believe that Christ is not present in the bread and cup, but that the ritual is simply an act of remembrance. This is known as **memorialism**.

> **Transubstantiation** The Roman Catholic teaching that the bread and wine become the body and blood of Jesus in reality during the Eucharist.
>
> **Memorialism** The view that the taking of Communion is simply an act of remembrance.

Task

Why might some Christians think that the Eucharist is the most important of the sacraments?

The importance of prayer

Where two or three gather in my name, there am I with them.

(The words of Jesus, Matthew 18.20)

Prayer is about developing a special relationship with God. Prayer serves a number of purposes and is found in many different forms in different Christian denominations. Some of the most important types of prayer are:

- Adoration – deep love and respect for God
- Confession – statement of faith through prayer
- Contemplation – meditation
- Penitence – saying sorry
- Praise – expressing devotion, which might include singing hymns
- Thanksgiving – saying thank you
- Supplication – asking for something.

Prayer is how Christians believe they communicate with God. Through prayer, they believe that they are in contact with Jesus, and he with them.

For some there is a real sense of talking to God, whereas for others the means of communication is more mysterious. Jesus taught the early disciples to pray, encouraging them to pray to God as a father and this suggests that prayer is something to be learnt.

Private prayer

For Protestants, the importance of individual prayer cannot be underestimated. Praying alone gives Christians an opportunity to be alone with God and express their innermost feelings to him. They may create a prayerful atmosphere by lighting candles or kneeling before a cross. This may enable them to feel the presence of God. Catholics may use a rosary (prayer beads) to help them concentrate.

In the Catholic Church, one of the roles of a priest is to mediate between human beings and God, and Catholics ask saints to pray on their behalf. One of the great principles of the Reformation, which led to the creation of Protestantism, was a belief that each Christian is in their own way a priest. This means that Protestants believe that all Christians have direct access to God through Jesus; they don't have to go through another human being.

Prayer is a significant factor in making faith deeply personal. Many people pray alone but many people find tremendous spiritual support from praying together, believing that they are following the instructions of Jesus himself, who encouraged his followers to pray together.

For some Christians, prayer is a direct way of having a conversation with God.

Communal prayer

Often Christians feel that they need structure and discipline to their prayers. This means that they may wish to pray with other Christians. Communal prayers may take place at set times, perhaps in a place of worship, or informally whenever Christians meet together. They enable those who pray to connect with each other, as well as with God.

> *Our Father,*
>
> *who art in heaven,*
> *Hallowed be thy name.*
> *Thy kingdom come.*
> *Thy will be done.*
> *On earth as it is in heaven.*
> *Give us this day our daily bread.*
> *And forgive us our trespasses,*
> *as we forgive those who trespass against us.*
> *And lead us not into temptation,*
> *but deliver us from evil.*
> *For thine is the kingdom, and the power,*
> *And the glory, for ever and ever.*
>
> *Amen*

Source: From the Book of Common Prayer

In communal prayers, Christians will communicate the feelings of the community to God, perhaps expressing wishes for individual members or hopes for a group project.

Set prayers

Set prayers allow Christians to learn and repeat prayers that have a significant meaning for them. They allow prayer to become collective so when Christians recite the Lord's Prayer, for example, with others, their single voices become a communal voice.

The Lord's Prayer is recited in almost every Christian service. Jesus used the Lord's Prayer to teach his followers how to pray. Today, set prayers are part of the tradition and ritual of worship that goes back hundreds of years. Many ancient prayers are still recited in archaic language, like poetry.

The Lord's Prayer is the most important Christian prayer. Apart from the last sentence, it consists of the words Jesus gave directly to his followers (Matthew 6.9–13).

Tasks

1. Why is the Lord's Prayer so important for Christians?
2. Read the Lord's Prayer above. Explain, using quotes if necessary, three different things that it tells Christians about God.

Extemporaneous prayers

Extemporaneous prayers are non-formulaic, spontaneous prayers. Some Christians prefer these types of prayers because they believe that their spontaneity in some ways is more spiritually honest. Some Christians believe that when they pray in this way their choice and use of words are influenced by the presence of the Holy Spirit.

Some Christian denominations have gone so far as to reject set prayers other than the Lord's Prayer. They believe that by repeating set prayers, the real meaning is lost and people just end up repeating them without thinking carefully about the meaning. In Matthew 6.5–8, Jesus tells his followers that prayer is a private matter and should not be conducted to impress others.

Task

Draw a table of two columns. In one column, write a list of the advantages of private worship, and the advantages of communal worship in the other.

Informal prayers

Set prayers are written in formal Standard English. For example, God is referred to as 'Father' rather than 'Dad', as Jesus sometimes did. For some Christians, this very formal language means they feel they cannot really relate to the set prayers as they do not express their relationship with God; so they have adopted an informal voice in their prayers, speaking to God in more conversational or everyday language.

The social and community functions of churches

We have seen that, for Christians, spirituality and morality are closely linked. Jesus taught that his followers have a duty to God to do good to other human beings.

Although life in the twenty-first century is very comfortable for many people in the West, it is not comfortable for a significant number. Worldwide, more than three billion people live on less than $2.50 a day. Hunger is the greatest cause of death in the world.

The Churches consider it their duty to provide help for people who need it. This may take the form of food banks, advice on immigration or legal matters, help with accommodation or money management, or health information. Luke's Gospel tells of Jesus reading from the Jewish prophet, Isaiah, in a synagogue:

> The Spirit of the Lord is on me,
> because he has anointed me
> to proclaim good news to the poor.
> He has sent me to proclaim freedom for the prisoners
> and recovery of sight for the blind,
> to set the oppressed free,
> to proclaim the year of the Lord's favour.
>
> (Luke 4.18–19)

The Churches, too, consider this to be their mission in the world.

Task
Read the quotation from Luke's Gospel. How is this important for the Churches today? How might they apply this teaching?

Food banks

Food banks provide food packages for people who are at risk of not being able to afford to feed themselves and their families.

The Trussell Trust is a charity that co-ordinates a nationwide network of food banks. They work in partnership with local communities to alleviate the effects of poverty. Their aim is to eliminate poverty altogether.

The work of the Trust is based on Christian principles, in particular those expressed by Jesus in Matthew's Gospel:

> For I was hungry and you gave me something to eat, I was thirsty and you gave me something to drink, I was a stranger and you invited me in, I needed clothes and you clothed me, I was sick and you looked after me, I was in prison and you came to visit me.
>
> (Matthew 25.35–36)

Church Action on Poverty is also committed to tackling poverty in the UK. It works in partnership with churches of different denominations and with people in poverty themselves to find solutions to poverty, locally, nationally and globally. They believe they have a duty to help all people, as creations of God:

> At Church Action on Poverty, we believe that everyone is created in the image and likeness of God, and deserves equal treatment.
>
> (Church Action on Poverty website, October 2016)

Between 1998 and 2010, there were 16 food banks in Wales. This increased to 157 in 2016. The rest of the UK has seen a similar increase.

The Salvation Army

The Salvation Army is a Christian denomination. It uses military structures in the organisation of its personnel, declaring that it is at war against sin and social evils, such as poverty. It was founded in London in 1865 and today has over 1.5 million members in 127 countries in the world. Its mission is expressed in these words:

The Salvation Army… exists to save souls, grow saints and serve suffering humanity.

(Salvation Army website, October 2016)

Christians have set up charities to help the poor.

Task

Explain in your own words what the Salvation Army's mission statement means.

'Salvationists' work to bring salvation to the poor, by preaching the Word of God and offering material support. The ways in which they support people include:

- helping people who have lost the ability to provide for themselves
- helping in the rehabilitation of prisoners and providing probation care
- meeting the needs of the elderly, providing adult education, day care, regular meals and residential care
- fighting sexual exploitation and human trafficking
- reuniting families through tracing missing persons
- providing food for the poor
- providing food and accommodation for the homeless
- providing emergency disaster relief.

Homelessness

Housing Justice is a Christian charity that aims to ensure that everyone has access to a suitable home. The charity describes itself as 'the national voice of Christian action to prevent homelessness and bad housing' (Housing Justice website, October 2016). It is multi-denominational, being the result of a merger between the Catholic Housing Aid Society (CHAS) and the Churches' National Housing Coalition (CNHC).

Housing Justice Cymru was launched in September 2016 to work independently with and for homeless and badly housed people, and to support churches in meeting their needs. One of its projects aims to create affordable homes from the sale of disused churches, and it works with the Church in Wales to achieve this.

Another housing charity to be born from CHAS is Shelter, and Shelter Cymru works as an independent organisation. Its aim is that everyone in Wales should have a decent, affordable home. They provide advice and offer support services to those people who have no home or live in poor housing. They work with councils to ensure that they support people with housing needs and challenge bad landlords. They campaign to influence legislation in the Welsh Assembly to improve the housing situation in Wales.

Task

Explain how Christian organisations in Wales work to make society better.

2 Christianity: Practices

44

Christian groups working for social justice, reconciliation and inter-faith dialogue

Social justice

The Universal Declaration of Human Rights is international recognition that all people, throughout the world, no matter who they are, have freedoms and entitlements that nobody has the right to take away. The rights are basic needs that contribute to happiness and wellbeing.

Justice means fairness. When the rights and entitlements of humans are not met, it is said to be unjust. **Social injustice** occurs when certain rights and entitlements are denied or not met for groups of people. Examples of social injustice are unequal distribution of resources, unequal access to healthcare and unequal access to education. Social justice, on the other hand, is about equality of opportunity and treatment.

All Christian Churches actively support the promotion of social justice and fight against issues of social injustice. Many charities work in the field of social justice to ensure that people's rights and fair access to justice are met. Some of these charities have Christian foundations.

> **Social justice** Promoting a fair society by challenging injustice and valuing diversity. Ensuring that everyone has equal access to equal opportunities and rights.

Tearfund

Tearfund is a Christian charity whose aim is to put Christian beliefs and Jesus' command to 'love your neighbour' into action. Christians believe they are putting into practice the unconditional or unselfish love (agape) Jesus talks about in the Gospels.

The charity works through local church groups, giving help to the poor in many countries. Tearfund currently works in over 50 countries providing emergency aid when natural disasters occur and carrying out long-term projects to support local communities.

In the UK many people support Tearfund by raising money through coffee mornings and buying Tearfund Christmas cards. There is a lot of information about the work of Tearfund on its official website at tearfund.org.

Why is Tearfund important?

- Tearfund has a role in raising public awareness of social issues, such as poverty and discrimination in the world.
- Tearfund campaigns against the causes of poverty worldwide.
- Tearfund gives practical help in order to act out the teachings of Jesus to help others.
- Tearfund encourages self-help for both individuals and communities.

One example of how Tearfund puts Christian beliefs into action is their work with children and teenagers in Columbia. By working with partner agencies, churches and youth groups in the country, Tearfund has set up 30 sports clubs where children can attend football training. These clubs provide safe spaces for young people who are at risk of joining gangs to come and socialise. They also offer mentoring to equip them with life skills.

Reconciliation

Reconciliation is the idea that people should make up after an argument and move on. In the Christian Church some of the differences between the many denominations have led to conflict and tension in the past. Many Christians believe it is important for these denominations to resolve their conflicts and work together towards common goals. Today, living in a pluralist society, the need for the different Christian denominations to work together is greater than ever.

'**Ecumenical**' means relating to a number of different Christian Churches, and the ecumenical movement is an attempt to bring closer together the different Christian denominations and promote Christian unity throughout the world.

It began at the World Missionary Conference at Edinburgh in 1910. The movement aimed to unify the Protestant Churches of the world and ultimately all Christians.

As a result of the work of the ecumenical movement, there is increased co-operation between different Christian denominations, such as different Churches sharing a common building and holding ecumenical services. Although denominational differences still exist, today some Christians believe there should only be one Church. At a local level, many churches genuinely cooperate and work together.

> **Ecumenical** Relating to a number of different Christian Churches.

The World Council of Churches

The World Council of Churches is:

> A worldwide fellowship of churches seeking unity, a common witness and Christian service.

The aim of these Churches is to be 'a visible sign ... deepening communion ... sharing the Gospel together ... making connections'.

Each year, the World Council of Churches holds a special week of prayer for Christian unity. It brings together churches, denominations and church fellowships in more than 110 countries.

The Catholic Church is not a member of the World Council of Churches, but does take part in some national and local organisations.

Churches Together in Wales is a practical attempt to focus locally on the fellowship of those who share the Christian faith. Churches Together in Wales is named Cytûn, meaning 'of one accord', signifying togetherness. The aim is to offer practical ways of achieving greater unity. For example, Cytûn has coordinated the Churches of Wales to provide common responses to the arrival of asylum seekers to Wales. It has also brought the Welsh Churches together to mark national and international events and tragedies with acts of worship. The organisation offers advice, comment and assistance to support the activities of Welsh Churches as a means by which the Churches can be accessed and approached.

Key Concept

Inter-faith dialogue Different faith communities and groups coming together to better understand each other and to serve the wider community with a mutual respect that allows them to live peacefully alongside each other in spite of differences in beliefs and ways of life.

Inter-faith dialogue

The differences between the religions of the world can lead to tensions between them. These tensions can take the form of intolerance, prejudice and discrimination. They can develop into violence and war.

Those who promote **inter-faith dialogue** believe that tension between religious groups can be reduced through communication, and that communication can bring about peace.

Inter-faith dialogue is not an attempt to remove difference between religions, but rather to understand the differences and respect them, while remaining true to one's own faith.

Inter-faith Wales

Inter-faith Wales is an organisation made up of three separate bodies: the Faith Communities Forum (which is an agency of the Welsh government), the Interfaith Council for Wales and the Wales Inter-faith Network. It was set up after 9/11 to promote better understanding and respect between communities. Its membership comprises representatives of the major world faiths; the Welsh government is represented on the Interfaith Council by the First Minister.

The Council has the following aims:

- To advance public knowledge and mutual understanding of the teaching, traditions and practices of the different faith communities in Wales.
- To promote good relations between persons of different faiths and to be of service to the people of Wales.
- To promote awareness of the distinctive features of these faith communities and of their common ground.

An example of the work of Inter-faith Wales is its coordination of Inter-faith Week. This is a series of events that takes place annually to increase awareness and understanding of different faiths. So, for example, a 'Question Time' was held at Cardiff University at which representatives from a range of the University's faith and belief societies, as well as audience members, engaged in dialogue on a number of topics. The Inter-faith Council also organised 'Youth and the Rising Generation' at the Cardiff United Synagogue, with contributions from members of the Jewish, Christian, Hindu and Mormon communities.

The Christian Muslim Forum

The Christian Muslim Forum is the leading national forum for Christian–Muslim relations. It was launched in 2006, realising an initiative of the Archbishop of Canterbury. Its aim is 'to help Christians and Muslims to live and work together creatively and harmoniously in our plural society'.

Through the Forum, Christians and Muslims communicate with each other to respond to national and international events that may otherwise test their relationship. They are then able to present shared perspectives for the good of their communities and society as a whole.

The Council of Christians and Jews

The Council of Christians and Jews (CCJ) was founded during World War II, in 1942, when Jews across Europe were experiencing severe persecution from the Nazis. Today, Christians and Jews work together on the Council to fight against religious and ethnic intolerance.

The CCJ works to create constructive dialogue between Jews and Christians on a wide variety of topics, including the Israel-Palestine situation and the global economic crisis, providing a safe space for respectful dialogue, especially on difficult issues. It also encourages Jewish and Christian communities to work together on social action projects in the UK. For example, the CCJ has participated in high-level dialogues with the Parliamentary Committee against Anti-Semitism. It also organises an annual Christian/Jewish Leadership Study Tour of Israel/Palestine to equip participants with the knowledge that can help improve understanding between them.

▶ Persecution of Christians in the modern world

Christians believe they were given a divine commission from Jesus to spread the good news of the Gospel and that this may be in the face of personal danger. Christian **persecution** continues into the twenty-first century in a number of countries throughout the world.

In some parts of the world, Christians are treated unjustly in societies where the Christian faith is a minority religion. For example, terrorist organisations like Islamic State in the Middle East have targeted Christians, forcing them from their homes and subjecting them to violent attacks. Churches have been bombed, for example two Egyptian Coptic churches at Easter time in 2017; priests have been killed - even in Europe, a French priest was knifed to death for being a Christian. It is estimated that 100 million Christians in the world today face persecution for their faith.

Evangelical Christian organisations, such as Christian Freedom International and Open Doors, seek to help persecuted Christians. These organisations provide practical help to persecuted Christians, provide Bibles, and work actively for the human rights of Christians suffering persecution.

> **Persecution** Persistently cruel treatment, often due to religion or belief.

Task

> You will be hated by everyone because of me, but the one who stands firm to the end will be saved.
>
> (Matthew 10.22)

> Blessed are you when people insult you, persecute you and falsely say all kinds of evil against you because of me. Rejoice and be glad, because great is your reward in heaven.
>
> (Matthew 5.11–12)

Use these quotations to explain why so many Christians continue to practise their faith in spite of the possibility of persecution.

Open Doors

Open Doors was established in 1955 when Brother Andrew, a Dutch missionary, smuggled Bibles into the Soviet Union. Under the communist system in the Soviet Union, Christian Churches were persecuted.

Today Open Doors still supports persecuted Christians across the world in different ways:

- It distributes Bibles and other resources to those who might not have access to Bibles, or may have had them confiscated.
- It trains Christians and church leaders to deal with the trauma they may be suffering while maintaining their faith.
- It provides practical support for Christians who have been the victims of disasters.
- It speaks on behalf of persecuted Christians to raise awareness of their situation and gather support, for examples, by lobbying MPs in the UK government.

People in the UK support their work both practically and financially.

End of Section Review

Stickability

Key concepts:
- Divine command
- Inter-faith dialogue
- Agape (selfless love)

Key teachings:
- Ethical decision making
- Jesus' teaching about morality
- Forgiveness
- Treasures on earth and in heaven
- Practices of Christian denominations
- Prayer
- Social justice
- Reconciliation
- Inter-faith dialogue
- Persecution of Christians

Skills Link

1 Describe the role of the church in its local community.
2 "God must be sorry he ever created humans." Discuss this statement showing that you have considered more than one point of view. (You must refer to religion and belief in your answer.)

Knowledge Check

1 Write a short paragraph (roughly three sentences) to explain what Christians believe about prayer.
2 Write a long paragraph (roughly eight to ten sentences) to explain why some Christians believe the sacraments are important.
3 Explain, with specific reference to Roman Catholicism, Anglicanism and Nonconformity, why there are different Christian denominations.
4 Write a developed paragraph (approximately six to eight sentences) to explain why some people might argue that Churches are no longer necessary in twenty-first century Britain. Include three different reasons in your answer.

The Big Question

'You don't have to be a Christian to be a good person.'

Your Task

Respond to the statement above, showing that you have considered more than one point of view. Give reasoned judgements on the validity and strength of these views.

Task

Explain in detail religious teachings about the Eucharist. Use the guidance below to help you to write a developed explanation for Christianity. Ensure that you use key terms fluently and frequently.

All/many/most Christians believe that _____ .

This comes from the teaching/Bible quote _____ .

This means that/Because of this they _____ .

Some/other Christians such as _____ believe that _____ .

This comes from the teaching/Bible quote _____ .

This means that/Because of this they _____ .

Finally, Christians such as _____ believe that _____ .

This means that/Because of this they _____ .

Their beliefs do/do not differ because _____ .

Buddhism

Key Concepts

Buddha One who is fully enlightened; Siddhartha Gautama.

Dhamma (Dharma) Teachings of the Buddha.

Dukkha Suffering/unsatisfactoriness.

Four Noble Truths The Buddha's first teaching: suffering, the cause of suffering, the end of suffering and the means by which to end suffering.

Metta bhavana The development of the four types of loving kindness, usually through meditation.

Noble Eightfold Path The 'medicine' of the four Noble Truths. Eight steps towards overcoming suffering and desires and achieving Nibbana (nirvana). Commonly divided into three sections: Wisdom, Morality and Meditation.

Parinirvana (parinibbana) 1. Complete, final nirvana, afterdeath. The Buddha, after achieving nirvana in this life decided to remain in the world to share his teachings. Upon his bodily death he would be in the state of parinirvana/parinibbana. 2. Mahayana Buddhist festival commemorating the death of the Buddha, sometimes called Nirvana Day.

Samatha Calm, or breathing meditation.

Sangha The community of Buddhists. This can be lay or monastic.

Tanha Desire, wanting, craving of possessions, people, permanence.

Vipassana 'Insight' meditation enabling the individual to see the true nature of things.

Wesak A festival to commemorate the birth, enlightenment and death of the Buddha.

Core Questions

- What is a buddha?
- Who was the Buddha?
- What does it mean to be enlightened?
- Why do people suffer?
- Can people be permanently happy?
- What challenges face Buddhists in the twenty-first century?
- Why is meditation important for Buddhists?
- How do Buddhists remember important events in the life of the Buddha?

Monks from different Buddhist schools wear different coloured robes.

The Main Buddhist Schools

Buddhism began in Northern India, but expanded very quickly as missionaries and merchants spread the teachings far and wide. Different forms of Buddhism developed.

Theravada means the 'school of the elders'. The 'elders' refers to senior monks from the time of the **Buddha**. As such, it is very traditional in terms of teachings and monastic rules. Theravada Buddhists believe that human beings are able to eliminate desire and overcome suffering over many lifetimes. If they do they will then attain the state of nirvana (nibbana) (see page 66). It is the main form of Buddhism in Sri Lanka, Burma, Laos, Thailand and Cambodia. Theravada Buddhists tend to follow teachings that were recorded in the Pali language.

From about the first century BCE, a new movement grew up, which is now called the Mahayana, or "Great Way". There is no single Mahayana sect; rather it is an umbrella term that covers a great variety of sects. Most Buddhists are Mahayana. Mahayana Buddhists believe that everyone has the potential to become a buddha. The aim of Buddhism is to reveal the buddha nature, not attain it. It is found largely in China, Korea and Japan. Mahayana Buddhists tend to follow teachings that were recorded in the language of Sanskrit, and most spellings of Buddhist terms in this book reflect the Sanskrit.

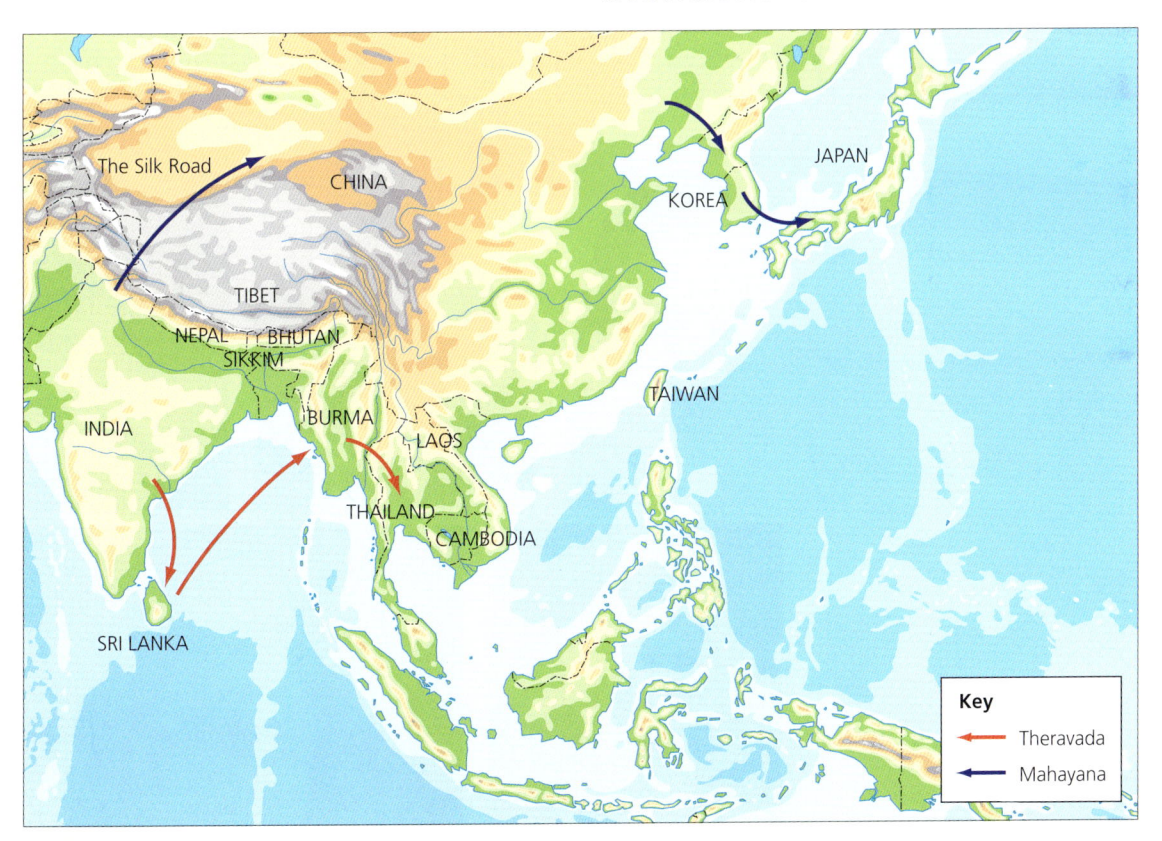

Buddhism spread from India, its place of origin.

3 Buddhism: Beliefs and teachings

■ Buddha

> **Key Concept**
>
> **Buddha** One who is fully enlightened; Siddhartha Gautama.

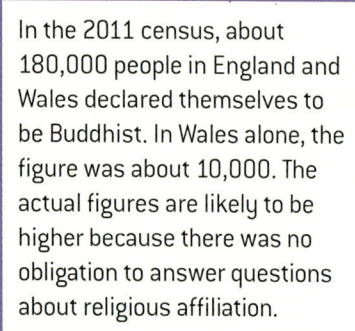

In the 2011 census, about 180,000 people in England and Wales declared themselves to be Buddhist. In Wales alone, the figure was about 10,000. The actual figures are likely to be higher because there was no obligation to answer questions about religious affiliation.

Like most religions, there are different schools of Buddhism, and over 20 are represented in Wales.

A buddha is an enlightened human being. This means someone who has come to understand the true nature of life.

Most people know very little about life. Some may know a lot about how it works, but few know why. Many people believe that their life has meaning or purpose, but few can explain easily what it is. A person who has reached a deep understanding of these things is said to be enlightened: a buddha.

Mahayana Buddhists would say that each of us has the capacity or potential to discover the truth about life and be a buddha. We all have the capacity to become angry or jealous or generous, and we show these qualities from time to time, given the right circumstances and stimuli. In the same way, these Buddhists believe that everyone has a buddha nature – the potential to be enlightened. The aim of the practice of Buddhism is to become enlightened.

A buddha is an ordinary human being who has gained enlightenment.

They would also say that, if anyone can become a buddha, presumably there have been buddhas in the past, there are buddhas today and there will be buddhas in the future.

Theravada Buddhists reserve the term Buddha for Siddharta Gautama (see below), to honour him having achieved enlightenment without anyone having to teach him. The aim of the practice of Theravada Buddhism is to learn, over many lifetimes, to become a perfect human being, an arahant. An arahant is not fully enlightened, but is able to find release from the cycle of birth, death and rebirth (see samsara, page 61). In theory, anyone can become an arahant, but in practice, monks are more likely to because they devote themselves completely to it.

The arahant (Theravada)

Those monks who are arahants have flaws destroyed, have lived the holy life, done what had to be done, laid down the burden, reached their own goal, destroyed the fetters of being, and are completely liberated through final knowledge. (Alagaddupama Sutta)

The buddha-nature (Mahayana)

At all times I think to myself:

How can I cause living beings

to gain entry into the unsurpassed way

and quickly acquire the body of a Buddha?

(Lotus Sutra)

Task

Explain what Buddhists mean by enlightenment.

▶ The Buddha

When Buddhists talk about the Buddha (with a capital B), they are generally referring to Siddhartha Gautama (Theravadins spell it Siddattha Gotama), the first buddha in history to have his life and teachings recorded.

It is important to understand that Buddhists do not worship the Buddha. They revere him, which means they regard him with the highest respect and would try to emulate him by following his example. But Siddhartha was a human being, not a god.

It is also important to understand that Buddhists do not believe in God. Some Buddhists may talk about gods, but when they do, they are referring to natural, unseen forces that operate in the universe.

▶ Early Life

Pre-birth

Siddhartha Gautama was born in a place called Lumbini in northern India (today, Nepal) around 563 BCE. His family was one of a number of leading families who governed the tribal groups of that part of India. Indeed, Siddhartha is sometimes known as Shakyamuni, which means 'wise man of the Shakya clan', to show his princely status.

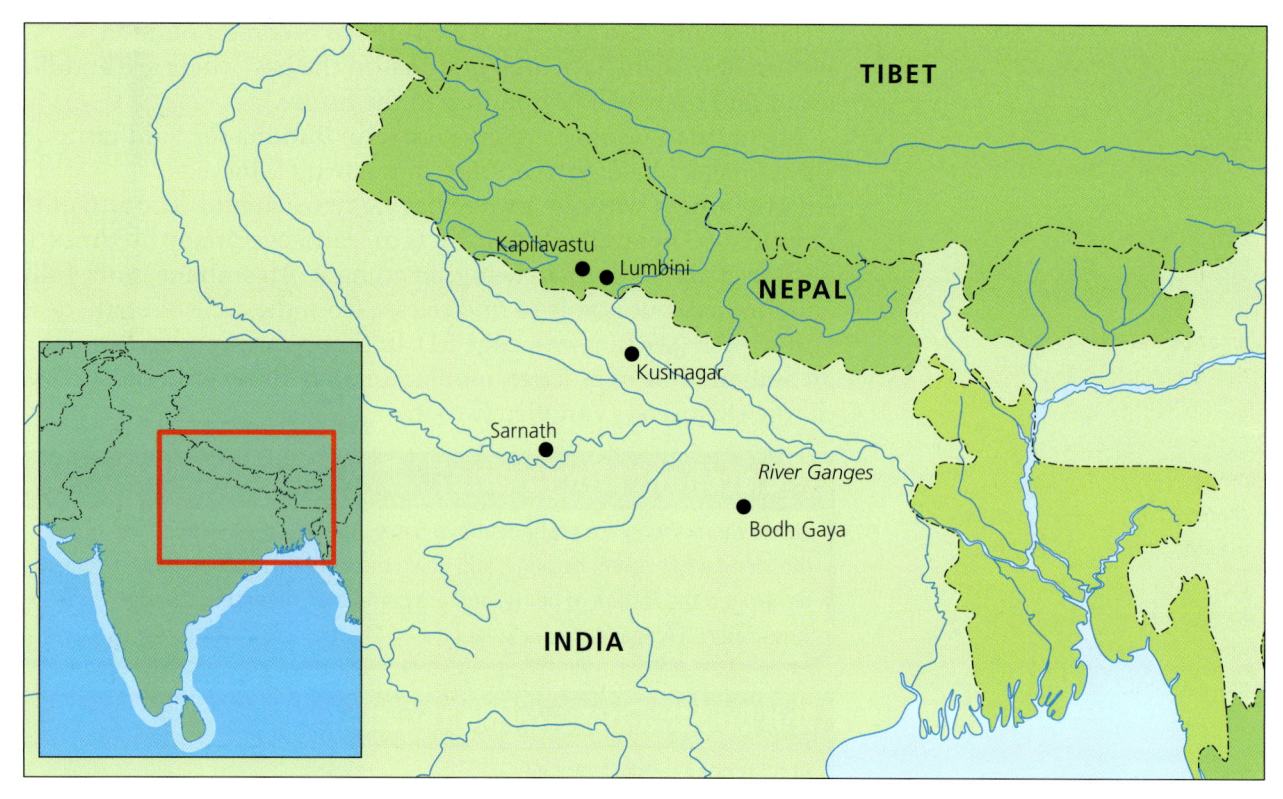

Northern India showing places associated with the life of Siddhartha.

His father was Raja Suddhodana of the Kingdom of Kapilavatsu; his mother was Queen Mayadevi. Legend has it that before Siddhartha was born, his mother dreamed that a pure white elephant with six tusks and a head covered in rubies came down from the highest heaven to enter her womb through her right side. Eight Brahmins (priests) told the King that this dream was a good omen, and that the child would be holy and achieve perfect wisdom.

Birth

Queen Mayadevi travelled to her parents' home to give birth, as was the custom. However, before she arrived, the birth process began. The Queen entered a garden at Lumbini, accompanied by her dancing women and her guards, and walked beneath a sala tree. The tree bent down and the Queen took hold of it and looked up to the heavens. At that point Siddhartha, the future Buddha, was born out of her side as she stood beneath the tree. He was fully formed as a human being and able to walk and talk. He immediately took seven steps towards each quarter of heaven, and at each of these steps there sprung up a lotus flower. He announced that he was the World-Honoured One, a title given to a buddha. He then declared that he would have to experience no more births, that this was his last body, and that he would pluck out by the roots the sorrow caused by birth and death.

The birth of Siddhartha.

The story of the Buddha's birth sounds like a fairy story. Yet Buddhists do not debate whether it actually happened or not; in fact, they are not particularly concerned whether or not it did. The story borrows images from several ancient myths and legends that show, for Buddhists, that Siddhartha was destined to be the Buddha for this universe in this age. For example, the seven steps the baby takes represent the seven directions of the universe in four dimensions (space and time): north, south, east, west, up, down, and here and now. The lotus flowers that spring up are common symbols of enlightenment.

A Buddhist monastery was built at Lumbini during the Buddha's lifetime. The exact spot where he is believed to have been born is marked by a stone. Today, only religious buildings are allowed to be constructed there.

Queen Mayadevi died seven days after Siddhartha's birth, and he was brought up by his aunt, Mahapajapati Gotami, who was also married to his father.

Prediction

Siddhartha would have been expected to follow his father and take his place as head of the family and as a local ruler. It was, and is, customary in Hindu families for an astrological chart to be drawn up to outline the course of a person's life. There is a tradition that, in drawing up Siddhartha's birth chart, a seer called Asita predicted that he would become either a great ruler or a religious teacher and a buddha. His father was anxious that he should rule. He was afraid that, if his son took an interest in spiritual matters and questions about the meaning of life, he would become too interested in religion and not enough in politics. So he tried to keep all knowledge of what life was like for people from the boy, and kept him in the lavish surroundings of the palace complex.

Life in the palace

By all accounts, Siddhartha was a very gifted young man, equally talented in the sports and the arts. He enjoyed a luxurious lifestyle, including a staff of young women to keep him amused. At the age of sixteen he was married to the princess of a nearby kingdom called Yasodhara and they had a son, Rahula.

Siddhartha's father continued to ensure that the young man had everything he could possibly want. In fact, he had three palaces: one for the summer, one for the winter and one for the rainy season. He had extensive grounds in which to go hunting, he trained in the martial arts, and played in a variety of sports.

By protecting Siddhartha from witnessing or experiencing anything but beauty and pleasure, King Suddhodana believed that he would remove the temptation for his son to want to see the real world. He was sure that, if Siddhartha knew what life was really like, he would want to follow a spiritual path and not become king.

Tasks

1 Explain what stories about the conception and birth of the Buddha say about the man he was to become.

2 In two to three sentences, explain why Buddhists are not concerned about the historical accuracy of stories about the Buddha.

The Four Sights – old age, sickness, death, and a holy man

Although Siddhartha's father tried to prevent his son from seeing how people suffer, the young man was deeply curious about the world around him, and he grew frustrated that he was not able to explore beyond the palace. He often begged his father to be allowed out of the palace to see the world beyond.

But the King was adamant that Siddhartha would see nothing of interest to him. Life could not be better than the one he enjoyed as a prince. What could be gained by seeing the world of ordinary people?

Siddhartha became more and more determined, however, to see the real world. Finally, he persuaded his father to make arrangements for him to tour Kapilavastu, the kingdom's capital city, with his charioteer, Channa. King Suddhodana organised the excursion in such a way that Siddhartha should see only happy, beautiful, youthful people; he should not be aware of any suggestion of imperfection.

Yet, in spite of his father's efforts to protect him from the realities of life, he saw four things that changed his life. They have become known as the Four Sights. The first three were:

- an old man,
- a sick person and
- a corpse.

Siddhartha understood for the first time what his father had tried to keep from him: the fact that all human beings suffer. No one can avoid it. Suffering is part of life. At this point Siddhartha is described as losing his taste for life. He was no longer able to enjoy all the luxuries of his life knowing that they could not protect him from old age, sickness and death.

Then Siddhartha saw:

- a holy man.

This was a **sadhu**, a man who devotes his life to the spiritual path. This fourth sight led Siddhartha to understand that there must be a cure for the world's suffering. Once he had seen the facts about life and the scope of human suffering, he felt compelled to do something about it. He was 29 years old.

> **Sadhu** Someone who devotes their life to the spiritual path.

> The Four Sights were a turning point in Siddhartha's life. He knew that suffering is a part of life from which no one can escape. He resolved at that moment to find out why. What is the cause of suffering? Can it be overcome? Is it possible for a human being to be perfectly happy, knowing that there is suffering in the world? What might that happiness be like? And how can it be achieved?

If Siddhartha could find the answer to the question of suffering, he would be enlightened; he would be a buddha.

Task

Explain what the Four Sights are and the realisations that Siddhartha had when he saw them.

Siddhartha's journey outside the palace gave him a new understanding of life.

Renunciation – leaving the palace and becoming an ascetic

When he returned to the palace, Siddhartha was very restless. He could not return to a life of luxury and pleasure having seen that his enjoyment of it could only ever be temporary. He knew now that he, like everyone else, would become sick and old. Neither his wealth nor his royalty could protect him from death.

He became obsessed with the idea that everyone suffers and that no one can avoid it. He became convinced that, if there was a way to overcome suffering and be permanently and deeply happy, then he would only discover it by becoming a sadhu – by leaving the palace and following a spiritual life.

Siddhartha told his father what he had been thinking and that he intended to leave his family to live the life of a sadhu. His father was devastated; Asita's prediction had been realised. He begged his son to stay. Siddhartha replied that he would stay if his father would make him a promise – that he would not get sick or old or die.

Naturally, the King was unable to make a promise that he had no chance of keeping. So Siddhartha made plans to leave the palace – leaving behind his father and aunt, his wife and son – unnoticed in the dead of night.

It is said that conditions conspired to help Siddhartha. Everyone was asleep, his horse made no sound, and the palace gates opened silently. Siddhartha rode into the night.

> It may seem selfish and irresponsible for Siddhartha to abandon his family in order to achieve a personal goal. However, leading the life of a sadhu has a long tradition in India. Siddhartha may have felt that staying with his family was holding him back from discovering something that would benefit them in the long term. It could be compared to the husband and father of a poor family leaving them temporarily to find work, later to return, able to support them better. As a Buddha, Siddhartha returned to his family and they became his followers. Some might see his leaving his family as a selfless act, making a sacrifice in order to achieve something greater.

Ascetic A person who follows a regime of strict self-discipline and denial of pleasure.

To start with, Siddhartha went to two different religious teachers and trained in meditation, but he failed to find the solution to suffering that he sought. He therefore went into the forest and joined a group of five **ascetics**. These were sadhus who tried to achieve spiritual benefit from living very simply and punishing the body through deliberate starvation. They attempted to overcome suffering by deliberately exposing themselves to it.

For six years Siddhartha followed this way of life. He assumed that the only way to become spiritually enlightened was to reduce his physical needs to an absolute minimum. It is said that, in doing this, he nearly starved himself to death, surviving on just one grain of rice a day.

One day Siddhartha went to bathe in the river, and, as he came out of the water, he saw a young cowgirl who offered him a bowl of milk-rice. Siddhartha realised that his ascetic

Siddhartha as an ascetic.

practices could never lead him to full insight. He had become too weak even to meditate. So he accepted the food. His fellow ascetics thought that he was going to return to his life of luxury. Disappointed at his apparent failure, they deserted him.

But Siddhartha had learnt an important lesson. He had discovered that his extravagant life-style could not protect him from suffering and so could not bring him deep and lasting happiness. Yet his ascetic existence brought him no closer to spiritual fulfilment. He realised that he would only become enlightened by living a Middle Way between the two extremes of luxury and hardship.

> **Task**
>
> Explain what the Middle Way is and why it is important in Buddhism.

▶ Enlightenment – seeing the world as it really is

Siddhartha Gautama was 35 years old. He had experienced both wealth and poverty and now lived the Middle Way. He sat in meditation beneath a pipal (fig) tree in the district of Gaya and determined that he would not move until he had achieved enlightenment. At first he had to struggle with temptations to abandon his quest, which came in the form of a 'devil' figure called Mara and his daughters. He fought against doubts that he could achieve his goal. Yet, after twelve hours of meditation, Siddhartha became enlightened.

Enlightenment A state of inner freedom and happiness which arises from within, which does not rely on sense pleasures or praise in activities like sports, exams and career, or anything external.

Mara

Mara is known as the Lord of Death in Buddhist mythology. He tries to prevent Siddhartha from continuing his quest for enlightenment by tempting him with worldly pleasures. However, Siddhartha is far enough advanced on his spiritual journey to know that he must overcome physical desire, and he defeats Mara.

Enlightenment is not about 'understanding' in the narrow sense of understanding facts. It is a whole new way of seeing and relating to life. It is impossible to convey exactly what Siddhartha understood as he became enlightened, because the understanding of it is **enlightenment**. You would have to be enlightened yourself to take it in fully. But we can see in general terms what he learned.

During his night of meditation, Siddhartha gained knowledge of his previous lives, and how his past related to the present. He came to realise the way in which all things come into existence and pass away again; that all things are constantly changing. He saw how negative feelings and cravings make people grasp at life, even though it brings them suffering. And, as the sun rose in the morning, he experienced the peace of nirvana, when all desires are overcome, and he became enlightened.

Mara is said to have demanded a witness to Siddhartha's enlightenment. In response Siddhartha touched the ground in front of him and Vasundhara, the earth goddess, appeared to support the Buddha's claim on enlightenment.

As we have seen, there is a problem with describing enlightenment: to understand it, you would need to be enlightened

The earth witnessed the Buddha's enlightenment.

3 Buddhism: Beliefs and teachings

58

yourself. But in the early writings of the Buddha's teachings there are descriptions of what it is like to overcome those things that prevent a person from moving towards enlightenment. They cannot describe what is experienced, but they suggest the sorts of feelings that arise when a person enters into deep meditation, and so give a glimpse of enlightenment.

Here are three of them:

> Suppose you are a slave. Life is difficult: you are trapped, unable to go where you want or do what you want. You are limited by what others tell you to do. Then suddenly you are released. You are no longer controlled by others. You are independent. You are free.

> Suppose you have been shut up in prison. You are not allowed beyond the four walls that confine you. Suddenly the doors are flung open and you are set free. You can return home; you feel safe and secure; you can start your life again.

> Suppose you have had to borrow a lot of money to start up a business. Debts pile up and you have to work hard to pay them. Then suddenly the business takes off. Money flows in. You can pay off your debts and have money to spare. Your worries are over.

The feelings these scenarios express are of overwhelming joy, liberation, security, and independence. We can assume that these are the feelings experienced by a buddha. They are accompanied by qualities of wisdom, compassion, courage, determination and sincerity.

> Gaya, the place where Siddhartha became enlightened, is today known as Bodhgaya (Gaya of the Buddha). A temple was built in his honour 250 years after his enlightenment. Behind the temple today is a pipal tree, a descendant of the one under which Siddhartha became a Buddha. It is called the Bodhi Tree.

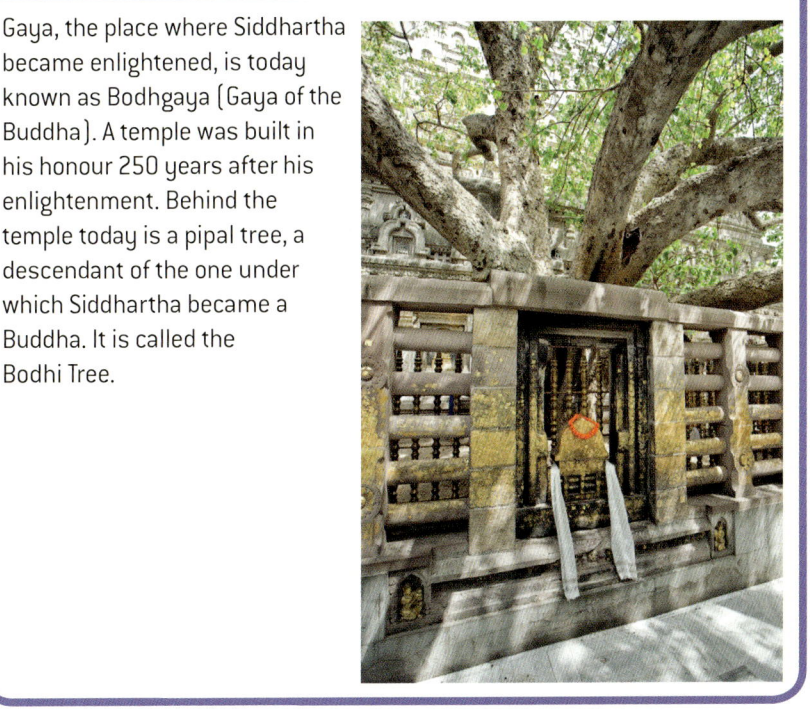

Task

Write a short paragraph to explain how believing in the possibility of achieving enlightenment might affect the life of a Buddhist.

(Notice that the question does not ask how enlightenment itself might affect a Buddhist's life, but refers to a belief in the possibility of achieving enlightenment. You will need to think about how our beliefs affect our lives and how we lead them.)

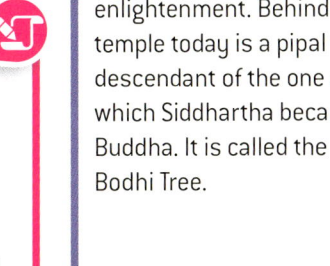

Teachings

After his enlightenment, Siddhartha can properly be called the Buddha. As a buddha, he now had to decide whether to keep his new knowledge to himself, or go out and teach it to others. At first he thought that others would not be able to understand it. But, as one story has it, he was approached by Brahma Sahampati, the King of the Hindu gods, who begged him to go out and preach.

The Buddha recognised that some people were ready to benefit from his new understanding of life, so he decided that he would teach them the means by which they, too, could overcome suffering and achieve peace.

The Deer Park Sermon (the First Turning of the Wheel of Dharma)

The first people to whom Siddhartha sought to explain his enlightenment were the Five Ascetics, who he joined when he began his religious quest. He met them in the Deer Park at Sarnath, near Benares. At first, they were dismissive of him, remembering that he had given up his ascetic practices. But Siddhartha explained that such severe hardship only confused the mind and made it impossible to see things clearly. Enlightenment is about being awake, alert, and having a sharp mind. He could only achieve enlightenment by following the Middle Way. So Siddhartha taught the Ascetics what he had learnt about suffering, its causes, and how to overcome it (the **Four Noble Truths**, see page 63). He taught them how to live the Middle Way (the **Noble Eightfold Path**, see page 67). As a result, they became enlightened themselves.

> The teachings of the Buddha are called the **Dhamma (Dharma)**. The word Dharma means 'to hold steady' or 'to keep firm'. It refers to something that is established, true and unchangeable. Dharma is therefore sometimes translated as 'law'. By extension, the teaching that Buddhists base their life on is also known as the Dharma: it is a foundation for knowing the truth.

Key Concept

Dhamma (Dharma) Teachings of the Buddha.

The Sermon (lecture) the Buddha gave to the Five Ascetics in the Deer Park at Sarnath is known as the First Turning of the Wheel of Dharma. Dharmachakra – or the Wheel of the Law – is an ancient symbol that indicates great change, for example, defeating enemies to bring about peace. In Buddhism, the First Turning of Dharmachakra refers to a spiritual change that came about in the Five Ascetics. It also suggests that, now the Buddha has started to teach his Dharma, it cannot be stopped.

This eight-spoked *dharmachakra* is often used as a symbol of Buddhism.

A stupa (a memorial monument) marks the place where the Buddha set in motion the Wheel of Dharma.

The Buddha visited the Deer Park at Sarnath many times after his enlightenment. A monastery was built to house his followers, a **stupa** – a memorial monument – was constructed at the place where Buddha first turned Dharmachakra, and another where the Five Ascetics meditated. The site was destroyed in the 12th century. Today, only one of the original stupas remains.

From then on the Buddha started to travel, teach and organise his followers. He had two types of followers. First, there were those who left their homes and families to wander, teaching others as they went. Second, there were householders who accepted the Buddha's teachings, but continued with their normal lives. This group is known as lay Buddhists.

For much of the year, the travelling followers went around the towns and villages of northern India, preaching and living off gifts of food from the lay people. During the rainy season, however, it was difficult to travel, so the full-time followers would meet together for study and meditation. Some wealthy lay believers donated pieces of land to them so that they could have places to meet on a regular basis. As they spent more and more time at these places, so they became monks and nuns.

The Buddha spent forty-five years travelling, teaching and giving others the benefit of his wisdom. By the end of his life, he had become the leader of a very large religious movement and had become well known throughout northern India.

Finally, old and weak, Siddhartha Gautama died of food poisoning at Kushinara, surrounded by his followers. His body was cremated, but his bones remained unburned. There was some dispute about who should have them, but eventually they were distributed among the various rulers of the northern Indian kingdoms, who built monuments – stupas – over them.

Samsara The eternal cycle of birth, death and rebirth.

Stupa A memorial, usually dome-shaped, placed over relics of important Buddhist figures.

A key Buddhist belief is that life does not end when the body dies. Unresolved issues of suffering and joy continue to exist to be resolved in another lifetime. The never-ending cycle of birth, death and rebirth is called **samsara**.

However, stories about the Buddha's birth relate that, as a new-born baby, he announced that he would have no more rebirths. When an enlightened being dies and escapes from the cycle of samsara, it is known as **parinirvana**. The death of the Buddha therefore coincided with his parinirvana.

Key Concept

Parinirvana (parinibbana) 1. Complete, final nirvana, after death. The Buddha, after achieving nirvana in this life decided to remain in the world to share his teachings. Upon his bodily death he would be in the state of paranirvana/parinibbana. 2. Mahayana Buddhist festival commemorating the death of the Buddha, sometimes called Nirvana Day.

A stupa was built at the place where it is believed the Buddha died. Several monasteries and temples were added over the centuries, some of which fell to ruins. The present **Parinirvana** Temple was built by the Indian government in 1956.

Kushinagar, the place where the Buddha died.

Tasks

1 Explain the importance of Siddhartha for Buddhists. Aim to make at least three points.

2 'Siddhartha is not a good role model for people today.'

Do you agree? Give reasons for your opinion, showing that you have considered other points of view.

Siddhartha's story provides an example of living the Middle Way. He rejected a life of luxury, yet saw that asceticism would not enable him to overcome suffering either. In working towards his enlightenment he showed determination and single-mindedness. He demonstrated the enlightened qualities of compassion, courage and wisdom in his dealings with others. In his religious life, he showed the practices that would lead his followers to become enlightened themselves.

The teachings of the Buddha Dhamma (Dharma)

The Dharma is how things are. The Buddha is the "One who Knows" this. The Buddha did not invent the Dharma, he re-discovered the Path to knowing it. Buddhists often prefer to call themselves 'followers of the Dharma', because they use the Dharma to guide their lives. So Buddhist teachings are not just a set of ideas: they offer a way of thinking and acting that helps individuals to become enlightened themselves.

The Dharma is a practical tool to be used for a purpose. The Buddha described his teachings as being like a raft that a person uses to cross a river. It is something to be used and then set aside.

When he saw the Four Sights, the Buddha understood that suffering is at the very core of life. Dharma, then, is about overcoming suffering and attaining happiness.

The Buddha taught the Dharma in two inter-related parts: The Four Noble Truths and the Noble Eightfold Path. These two teachings are perhaps the most well known and essential expressions of the Dharma.

▶ The Four Noble Truths

If you have an illness and want to cure it, you need, first of all, to find out what caused it. Then you can attack the cause of the disease and so recover from it. The Buddha said that the same technique can be used to overcome the sufferings of life. The method can be set out in four stages:

1. The problem
2. The cause of the problem
3. The way to overcome the problem
4. Strategies to overcome the problem

The four stages are called the Four Noble Truths.

> **Key Concept**
>
> **Four Noble Truths** The Buddha's first teaching: Suffering, the cause of suffering, the end of suffering and the means by which to end suffering.

> It is through not understanding, not realising four things that I, Disciples, as well as you, had to wander so long through this round of rebirths. And what are these four things? They are:
>
> The Noble Truth of Suffering
>
> The Noble Truth of the Origin of Suffering
>
> The Noble Truth of the Extinction of Suffering
>
> The Noble Truth of the Path that leads to the Extinction of Suffering
>
> As long as the absolutely true knowledge and insight regarding these Four Noble Truths was not quite clear in me, I was not sure that I had won that supreme enlightenment. But as soon as the absolute true knowledge and insight as regards these Four Noble Truths had become perfectly clear in me, there arose in me the assurance that I had won that supreme enlightenment.
>
> (Majjhima Nikaya 26)

First Noble Truth: life involves suffering (dukkha)

Dukkha is usually translated as 'suffering', but it is more than that. Buddhism teaches that there are three types of dukkha.

> **Key Concept**
>
> **Dukkha** Suffering/unsatisfactoriness.

- **Suffering of suffering** – *The dukkha of physical and emotional pain*
  This refers to the unavoidable sufferings of life, like tripping over, catching flu, being unable to sleep, or having a headache. But it also refers to the emotional suffering that goes with, for example, not having enough money, being insulted, getting embarrassed, or the general fact that things tend not to go the way we want them to.

- **Suffering of change** – *The dukkha of impermanence*
  This is suffering caused by the fact that life is constantly changing. We want pleasurable experiences, and we enjoy them for being pleasurable. But they do not last – everything changes, and nothing remains the same. People feel miserable when a holiday is over, sad when a precious possession breaks, bereft when a loved one dies. It is the loss of happiness that is painful.

▶ **Suffering of conditioning** – *The dukkha of life's nature*

There are undesirable happenings in life over which we have no control. There are forms of suffering that are unavoidable, like growing old or dying; they are bound to happen because that is the way life is. You can do nothing to stop them. We experience the effects of our actions according to the laws of **karma** (see box below). A great deal of the suffering of conditioning comes about as a result of one's own anger, pride, arrogance, selfishness or sheer stupidity.

Things just don't go the way we want them to.

Karma The law of cause and effect, Buddhism teaches that thoughts and actions have consequences.

Karma

Buddhism teaches that every deliberate thought or action has an effect on events. Good, positive and well-intentioned thoughts and deeds will have positive effects on one's own life in the future. Bad, negative or mean-spirited thoughts and deeds will have negative effects.

The effect is created at the time the cause is made, but it may take some time to come about. This means that each person has a store of karma, positive and negative, waiting to come into effect.

In most cases, it is not possible to work out which deed caused which effect. Indeed, it may not be possible to decide whether an effect is positive or negative. Situations that appear bleak can sometimes be turned into great opportunities, if handled skilfully.

Buddhists would say the practice of Buddhism is about how to live skilfully.

Task

Explain how a belief in karma might affect how a Buddhist lives.

Buddhism does not claim to be able to prevent you becoming ill, or getting old, or dying. These are things that will happen; they are not in themselves forms of suffering. Buddhism says that suffering is an experience of the mind, and following the Dharma can help prevent you from suffering from the pain and dissatisfaction that these events cause.

The Five Remembrances

The Buddha gave his disciples five things to remember each day, covering change, the types of suffering and the effects of karma:

1. I am of the nature to grow old. There is no way to escape growing old.
2. I am of the nature to have ill health. There is no way to escape having ill health.
3. I am of the nature to die. There is no way to escape death.
4. All that is dear to me and everyone I love are of the nature to change. There is no way to escape being separated from them.
5. My actions are my only true belongings. I cannot escape the consequences of my actions. My actions are the ground on which I stand.

(Anguttara Nikaya 5.57).

Task

Explain what Buddhists mean by dukkha.

Second Noble Truth: the cause of suffering (dukkha) is craving (tanha)

Tanha means craving, wanting or desire. It indicates that we form attachments to things, people and feelings, and we rely on them to make us happy. But these things are unreliable. Relying on things that are unreliable is bound to cause dissatisfaction.

Things are unreliable because they are impermanent – they change; they do not stay the same. We want things to stay the same, but they don't: they decay and die. When they do, we want more of the thing that gave us pleasure. We want the experience all over again, even though we know it will not last. Or we get bored with the things we are attached to; the pleasure does not last, and then we want something else.

What causes us to suffer is not the things that we rely on for our happiness, but the fact that we rely on them, knowing that, when the pleasure ends, it will be replaced by sadness.

Tanha refers to this relationship of reliance or attachment. We are drawn to things that give us pleasure and away from things that cause displeasure.

Buddhism identifies three types of tanha:

- *Kama tanha* (*craving for sensual pleasures*) is the simple desire to experience pleasure. It may be a desire for food, for designer clothes, for money or for gadgets. Buddhism encourages us to be aware of these cravings and not let them dominate us. By cultivating contentment and positive emotions our cravings lessens and we feel more naturally happy.
- *Bhava tanha* (*craving for being*) is the desire to be someone else. It may be a desire for a new job, to be famous, to be admired, or to be better at maths. There is nothing wrong with being ambitious, but if we can never appreciate and enjoy what we have now we are likely to suffer great dissatisfaction.
- *Vibhava tanha* (*craving for non-existence*) is the desire to get rid of unpleasant experiences and conditions of life. It may involve moving from one form of unhappiness to another, for example, by taking drugs or attempting to end one's life. It does not involve removing vibhava tanha itself.

Tanha causes us dukkha because our actions are motivated by Three Poisons: greed, anger and ignorance. These poisons are what cause us to grasp at things. We want things (greed), knowing that the pleasure they give will not last (ignorance). When the pleasure fades, we come become annoyed (anger), which causes us to want more or something different (greed), and the cycle continues.

Third Noble Truth: the way to overcome suffering (dukkha) is to overcome craving (tanha)

Quite clearly, if it is our desire for things that causes us to be frustrated with life, then we must overcome our desires. Then we can overcome our frustrations and dissatisfaction. The trouble is, wanting to overcome desire and craving is itself a form of craving. Wanting to get rid of desire is vibhava tanha; wanting to be enlightened is bhava tanha.

Key Concept

Tanha Desire, wanting, craving of possessions, people, permanence.

Task

Explain in your own words how craving causes suffering.

The practice of Dharma is understanding that we are not victims of desire. Desire only has power over us when we give in to it and try to grasp it. Dharma helps Buddhists let go of the need to grasp.

The ending of craving through the practice of Buddhism is called **nirodha**. The state of having achieved nirodha is **nirvana**. For Buddhists, the only way to stop craving is to discover inner satisfaction and an appreciation of life as it really is, to find happiness within instead of relying on other things, so there is no need to grasp.

> **Nirodha** The ending of craving and desire.
>
> **Nirvana** The state of peace and joy attained by extinguishing craving and desire.

Nirvana

The point at which all craving ceases (nirodha) is a point of peace called nirvana. The Buddha is said to have achieved this state at his enlightenment. A person who has achieved nirvana may still carry on living, eating, having relationships with other people (as the Buddha did for forty-five years after his enlightenment), but his or her actions would be done from a selfless motive, not driven by the Three Poisons, and so would not lead to further suffering.

Nirvana is not the same as extinction. Nor does it mean being so removed from life that you lose connection with it and feel nothing. Rather it describes a state of peace and happiness caused by the extinguishing of tanha.

Those who have achieved nirvana still experience things that others see as pain or pleasure, but they do not respond to them in the same way. The experiences will not be the cause of further craving and suffering.

> **Task**
>
> Draw a flow chart to show how the first three of the Four Noble Truths are connected. In the boxes of your flow chart, write an explanation of each of the Noble Truths.

Fourth Noble Truth: the way (magga) to overcome suffering is the Middle Way

A life of luxury is one of attachment, when we rely on things outside ourselves to bring us happiness. Yet we have seen that this will actually cause dissatisfaction in the long run. A life of hardship will cause us to crave and want those things that we do not have. It, too, is a life of suffering. The Buddha said that the way to overcome tanha is to live the Middle Way, a path that avoids the extremes of luxury and hardship. The word Buddhists use for the path is **magga**.

It is not called **the Middle Way** because it is a compromise between wanting luxury and comfort on the one hand, and the denial of pleasure and the cultivation of pain on the other. Rather, it rises above both extremes, avoiding the errors that each of them makes in the pursuit of happiness.

> **Magga** The path to end desire and suffering.
>
> **The Middle Way** A path that avoids the extremes of luxury and hardship.

The Middle Way ensures that the body is healthy enough to give strength to the mind. It is essentially a programme of mental training.

The Buddha's disciples needed further guidance. Living the Middle Way may enable you to overcome tanha, but how do you live the Middle Way? The Buddha gave various suggestions in response to this question. The best known is set out in the form of a path of eight steps: the Noble Eightfold Path.

> **Key Concept**
>
> **Noble Eightfold Path** The 'medicine' of the Four Noble Truths. Eight steps towards overcoming suffering and desires and achieving nirvana (nibbana). Commonly divided into three sections: Wisdom, Morality and Meditation.

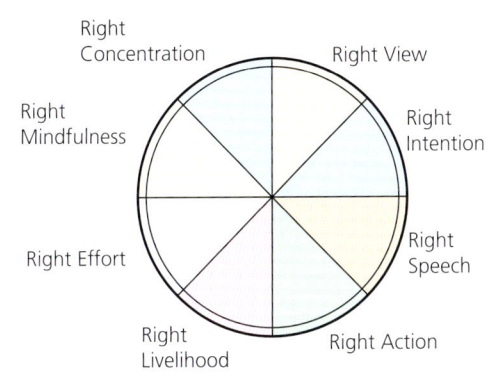

A wheel with eight spokes is often used as a symbol of Buddhism. It represents the Noble Eightfold Path.

The spokes are labelled: Right Concentration, Right View, Right Mindfulness, Right Intention, Right Effort, Right Speech, Right Livelihood, Right Action.

> **Prajna (Panna)** The Way of Wisdom: two stages of the Noble Eightfold Path: Right View, Right Intention.

The Noble Eightfold Path

The Noble Eightfold Path consists of eight things a Buddhist can do to overcome tanha and so achieve nirvana. Although the word 'path' implies a series of steps to be taken one after the other, the stages of the Noble Eightfold Path do not have to be done in any particular order, and can be done together.

The stages can be put together in three groups or disciplines:

1. the way of wisdom (prajna)
2. the way of morality (sila)
3. the way of mental training (samadhi).

Wisdom (prajna)

Wisdom involves true insight and a deep understanding of life. Wisdom is different from knowledge, which is just about learning facts. Wisdom is first about studying, listening and paying attention to the Dharma. Then it involves absorbing and internalising what has been heard, and reflecting on it in the light of experience. Finally, it means having the insight and perception to put the Dharma into action by following the Noble Eightfold Path.

There are two parts to the Way of Wisdom: Right View and Right Intention.

1 Right (or perfect) view (or understanding)

A Buddhist seeks to deepen his or her understanding of life by following the teachings of the Buddha. The right view of life is, therefore, the Dharma itself.

If you are about to go on a journey, you need to make sure you know the directions, you have the right documents, and you have packed what you need; you need to have planned your trip. In the same way, a person who is about to embark on the path to enlightenment needs to have a correct understanding of what it involves. Someone who has not thought about the origin of suffering or how to overcome it is unlikely to make progress towards enlightenment. The starting point, therefore, is a deep understanding of the nature of karma, the Four Noble Truths and the Noble Eightfold Path itself. The Buddha himself said:

> 'What now is right view? It is understanding of suffering (dukkha), understanding of the origin of suffering, understanding of the cessation of suffering, understanding of the way leading to the cessation to suffering.'
>
> (Digha Nikaya 22)

Right View does not just mean learning about the Dharma; it means accepting it as the basis of your life. Although Dharma can mean teaching, it is really about applying the teaching to living.

2 Right (or perfect) intention

It is one thing to hear or read about the Buddhist Dharma, quite another to decide to act on it, and to do so for the right reasons. Right Intention refers to what motivates Buddhists to follow the Buddhist path.

Buddhism teaches that being greedy, unkind and harmful are self-destructive and lead away from nirvana. If someone is motivated by these feelings, then their actions will cause suffering for themselves and others. If intentions are wrong, then actions are likely to be wrong.

On the other hand, if intentions are right, then actions will be right. The Buddha said that a person following the Path should be motivated by three intentions:

1 the intention to give up desires (tanha)
2 the intention to think and act with loving kindness (**metta bhavana**) (see page 76)
3 the intention to do no harm.

These three intentions come about by having Right View: a deep and thorough understanding of the Four Noble Truths.

Morality (sila)

The aim of following the Noble Eightfold Path is to overcome suffering and experience the joy and freedom of enlightenment. The law of karma says that well-intentioned actions cause positive effects to occur in one's own life. By the same token, mean-spirited actions have negative consequences and lead to suffering. It follows, then, that the path to enlightenment should involve guidelines on moral behaviour.

The third, fourth and fifth segments of the Noble Eightfold Path provide guidelines on moral behaviour. Morality is about what is right and wrong in terms of human behaviour. This is called **sila** (the Way of Morality).

Sila has three stages: Right Speech, Right Action and Right Livelihood.

> **Sila** The Way of Morality: three stages of the Noble Eightfold Path: Right Speech, Right Action, Right Livelihood.

3 Right (or perfect) speech

It is sometimes easy to underestimate the power of speech. It can be hurtful and break relationships, it can raise self-esteem, it can start wars and create peace. However, the effects of speaking are not always immediately obvious, so can be overlooked.

But verbal communication – speaking and writing – is one of the things that distinguish human beings from other animals. It gives dignity of expression to those who aim to extend loving-kindness to others.

In their dealings with others, Buddhists should avoid speaking to and about others in ways that would hurt them. They should avoid:

- telling lies
- spreading gossip
- speaking harshly
- wasting time with idle chatter.

Rather they should always try to talk positively to and about others by:

- being sincere, careful and accurate in what they say
- speaking in a way that promotes harmony between people
- being kind and gentle when speaking to others
- valuing silence when there is nothing useful to say.

4 Right (or perfect) action

Right Action differs from other stages in the Noble Eightfold Path in that it stresses the importance of behaviour and action rather than mental training. Yet, for Buddhists, our actions in life also require discipline and self-restraint.

In following Right Action, Buddhists observe five rules, known as the **Five Precepts**. They are:

- **Respect life**: do not harm or destroy life; protect all living things and the planet.
- **Develop generosity**: give freely of time and resources.
- **Avoid sexual misconduct**: this can cause pain to oneself and others.
- **Speak the truth**: no gossiping, speaking harshly or unfairly; be honest.
- **Be aware of what we consume**: eat healthy, avoid intoxicants, stay away from entertainments that are addictive.

These precepts apply to all who follow the Noble Eightfold Path. There are other precepts and rules for monks.

Five Precepts Buddhist guidelines on moral behaviour.

This Cardiff design company uses Buddhist principles in the running of their business. An article in Walesonline says, 'The staff aim to bring Buddhist practice to the workplace by following a code of ethics based on Buddha's five precepts, which include helping others, truthfulness and generosity.'

5 Right (or perfect) livelihood

If a person follows the Buddhist path, it is important that he or she should earn a living in a way that does not go against Buddhist principles. Work should be of benefit and should not harm others.

A Buddhist would not, therefore, have a job that involves violence or harm to another living being, human or animal. He or she would not earn a living by taking from others that which is not given willingly. Exploiting sex in order to make money would be unacceptable, as would be peddling lies or gossip about people, or trading in alcohol or drugs.

The Buddha himself lists five occupations that should be avoided: dealing in weapons, trading living beings (slaughtering animals as well as human trafficking), butchery, making and dealing in poisons, and dealing in intoxicants (Anguttara Nikaya 5.177).

A Buddhist is likely to seek a job that helps others, contributes to their well-being, respects their dignity, is honest and encourages thoughtfulness.

Meditation (samadhi)

Although this section of the Noble Eightfold Path is known as **samadhi** – the Way of Meditation – it is really about developing the spiritual and mental discipline to give up desire, overcome suffering and achieve nirvana. It includes the practice of meditation, but also includes the energy needed to maintain the practice, and the awareness to keep the mind focused and stable.

The Buddha was clear that all actions arise from thoughts, and all actions have consequences, negative or positive:

> All that we are is the result of what we have thought. It is founded on our thoughts; it is made up of our thoughts. If one speaks or acts with an evil thought, pain follows one, as the wheel follows the foot of the ox that draws the wagon.
>
> All that we are is the result of what we have thought. It is founded on our thoughts; it is made up of our thoughts. If one speaks or acts with a pure thought, happiness follows one, like a shadow that never leaves.

(Dhammapada 1.1–2)

The Way of Meditation aims to purify the mind, to abandon evil thoughts and cultivate good ones. It provides the conditions to develop two other sections of the Path: Wisdom (Prajna) and Morality (Sila).

Task

Make a list of jobs that a Buddhist is unlikely to have, and reasons why. Then make a list of jobs a Buddhist might have, and reasons why.

Samadhi The Way of Meditation: three stages of the Noble Eightfold Path: Right Effort, Right Mindfulness and Right Concentration.

6 Right (or perfect) effort

The first step in training the mind is to make a conscious effort to set aside negative thoughts and to replace them with positive ones. Another word for effort is 'energy'. Following the Noble Eightfold Path requires determination, discipline, single-mindedness and perseverance.

The Buddha stressed this when he said:

> 'I shall not give up my efforts until I have attained whatever is attainable by manly perseverance, energy, and endeavour.'
>
> (Majjhima Nikaya 70)

He goes on to specify where effort needs to be directed:

- to prevent the formation of unhealthy mental states
- to abandon unhealthy mental states that have already formed
- to form healthy mental states
- to maintain and perfect healthy mental states already formed.

Right effort recognises that a Buddhist should be aware of and be determined to shape the way he or she habitually thinks. In following this step, a Buddhist will always try to see the best in others.

7 Right (or perfect) mindfulness

Being mindful of something means having that thing right at the forefront of your mind; having your mind full of it. This stage of the Buddhist path aims to help people become more aware of themselves and everything around them.

People cannot be in control of their lives if they are unaware of these things. They need to have a mind that is clear and focused, not clouded and diverted. Mindfulness enables a person to be in control of their mind by observing the way it works. It enables them to anchor the mind, or fix it down, so it does not wander.

It can be applied in four different areas or 'foundations':

- Body – awareness of breathing, posture, and actions such as bending, stretching and turning the head.
- Feeling – pleasant, unpleasant or neutral.
- State of mind – greedy, angry, crowded, confused, and so on.
- External objects – mental hindrances to concentration, such as tiredness, doubt, worry or restlessness.

Mindfulness techniques have been found to be useful as tools for mental training for adults and children who are not Buddhists. They can improve focus and reduce distractions, enabling people to approach difficult situations calmly and make better decisions. Mindfulness has been found to be useful in overcoming mental health problems.

> **Task**
>
> Explain how the Noble Eightfold Path can lead a person to experience nirvana. Try to make at least one point for each of the stage of the Path.

8 Right (or perfect) concentration

This refers to training the mind through meditation practices. Its aim is to concentrate the mind onto a single point of focus. Buddhists believe that through meditation the mind is enabled to become calm, to develop loving-kindness, and also to gain insight into the truths of life – the Dharma.

- It leads to a state of joy, calm, well-being.
- It enables the mind to see things as they really are, leading to wisdom.

Concentration can be developed in two ways:

- the development of calmness (samatha-bhavana)
- the development of insight (vipassana-bhavana).

We will look at these forms of meditation in the next section (page 75).

> The Noble Eightfold Path is not a list of steps to nirvana that have to be taken one after the other. They can be undertaken in any order or in any combination. The Buddha suggested the following:
>
> > First establish yourself in the starting point of wholesome states, that is, in purified moral discipline and in right view. Then, when your moral discipline is purified and your view straight, you should practise the four foundations of mindfulness.
> >
> > (Samyutta Nikaya 47.3)

> **Task**
>
> What sequence of following the Noble Eightfold Path does the Buddha recommend?

▶ Challenges of living according to Buddhist teachings

While the number of people in the United Kingdom practising a religion or holding religious beliefs has fallen over the last two decades, the number of people who state that their religion is Buddhism has risen. In 2001, there were about 145,000 Buddhists in England and Wales; the figure rose to almost 180,000 in 2011. In 2001, there were 5,000 Buddhists in Wales, but, by 2011, this figure had almost doubled.

It may appear that the secularism – the process of a population becoming less religious – that affects other religions in the United Kingdom does not seem to influence the interest in Buddhism, especially in Wales.

Buddhism has aroused considerable interest since its introduction to the United Kingdom in the mid-twentieth century. In the 1960s, young Europeans and Americans travelled to the Far East, fascinated by the culture of 'the orient', especially that of Buddhism. At the same time, Buddhists from the East whose countries were torn apart by war and foreign invasion came to the West.

There were many superficial aspects of Buddhism that appealed to Westerners:

- It has close associations with the martial arts that were becoming popular.
- People began to experiment with 'exotic' beliefs and lifestyles, including Buddhism, as an object of curiosity.

Twenty-first century life presents many distractions.

More searching Westerners were attracted by religious ideas and practices that did not require belief in God, obedience to authority figures and motivation by guilt. They embraced a life-philosophy that was inclusive, promoted equality and the value of all life and promised results: enlightenment and peace.

However, what appears to be straightforward carries with it challenges and difficulties. Buddhism developed in countries whose cultures and lifestyles were very different from those in the West. In very general terms, life in the West is characterised by a decline in respect for religion and religious institutions, a rejection of ideas that cannot be verified by scientific enquiry, an emphasis on self-expression and personal development and a significant emphasis on materialism and consumerism which goes against Buddhist principles.

By contrast, Eastern cultures typically have deep respect for spirituality and religious traditions, an openness to accept abstract thoughts, and a greater concept of community and family. In the East, there is more of an ethos of duty and obligation, whereas in the West there is more of an emphasis on the rights of the individual.

These cultural differences present difficulties for those who practise the Dharma in West, especially if they have not absorbed Eastern culture.

- The pace of life in the West is such that it is difficult to set aside time for contemplative practices. There are distractions that challenge concentration and provide disincentives for practices such as meditation.
- As a result, there is a tendency for people to pick the parts of Buddhism that can be adapted to their secular lifestyle and abandon the rest. Buddhism then becomes watered down into a set of relaxation exercises or self-help therapies. This is compounded by the wealth of available information on different types of Buddhism that can lead to confusion and misunderstanding.
- The stress on individuality and individualism – valuing the self more highly than the group – in Western societies conflicts with Buddhist ideas of selflessness. Britain has been found to be the most individualist country in the world. Interestingly, individualism has shown to produce high levels of anxiety and depression.
- In addition, Western morality is often in conflict with Buddhist principles that are designed to purify the mind. For example, the easy availability of alcohol, drugs and sexual experiences make it hard to follow the Five Precepts.
- Secularism in the West suggests to many that religion has no relevance to modern life. It is possible to live happily and morally without a religious practice. The abundance of material goods and the comfort they afford seem to contradict the Buddhist idea that greed, desire and attachment cause suffering.
- In an age of war, international terrorism, global poverty and environmental destruction, Buddhism may appear to some to be naïve in its claims and goals. Ideas about inner peace and loving-kindness seem soft and unrealistic.
- Ideas about karma, samsara and rebirth have no scientific basis and cannot be upheld by science. If they cannot be proved, it is difficult for post-scientific societies to accept them.

Task

'It is not possible to practise Buddhism in twenty-first century Britain.'

Discuss this statement showing that you have considered more than one point of view. (You must refer to religion and belief in your answer.)

Stickability

Key concepts:
- Buddha
- Dhamma (Dharma)
- Dukkha
- Four Noble Truths
- Noble Eightfold Path
- Parinirvana
- Tanha

Key teachings:
- Early life of the Buddha
- Four Sights
- Renunciation
- Enlightenment
- First turning of the Wheel of Dharma
- Four Noble Truths
- Noble Eightfold Path
  - Wisdom: Right understanding, Right intention
  - Morality: Right speech, Right action, Right livelihood
  - Meditation: Right mindfulness, Right concentration
- Challenges of living the Dharma

End of Section Review

Skills Link

1 Explain what Buddhists do when following the Eightfold Path.
2 "The most important part of the Buddha's life was his experience as an ascetic."

Discuss this statement showing that you have considered more than one point of view. (You must refer to religion and belief in your answer).

Knowledge Check

1 Write a short paragraph (roughly three sentences) to explain why the Four Sights are important in Buddhism.
2 Write a long paragraph (roughly eight to ten sentences) to explain the causes of human suffering, according to Buddhist teachings.
3 Explain what Dharma means.
4 Write a developed paragraph (approximately eight to ten sentences) to explain why Buddhism teaches that the Noble Eightfold Path leads to the attainment of nirvana.

The Big Question

'Buddhism has no relevance in the modern world.'

Your Task

Respond to the statement above, showing that you have considered more than one point of view. Give reasoned judgements on the validity and strength of these views.

Task

You need to explain in detail religious teachings about enlightenment. Use the guidance below to help you to write a developed explanation for Buddhism. Ensure that you use key terms fluently and frequently.

All/many/most Buddhists believe that _____.

This comes from the teaching/quote _____.

This means that/Because of this they _____.

Some/other Buddhists such as _____ believe that _____.

This comes from the teaching/quote _____.

This means that/Because of this they _____.

Finally, Buddhists such as _____ believe that _____.

This means that/Because of this they _____.

Their beliefs do/do not differ because _____.

4 Buddhism: Practices

■ Meditation practices

▶ The significance and importance of meditation

Nirvana cannot be achieved without first mastering each stage of the Eightfold Path. Key to mastering each stage is the art of meditation. Meditation in Buddhism is usually called **bhavana**, which means 'cultivation of the mind' or 'self-development'. As well as underpinning the Eightfold Path, it also forms the eighth stage (Right Concentration, or training the mind through meditation practices).

The aim of meditation is to control the mind, not be controlled by it; to become free from habitual ways of thinking and to develop wisdom; to awaken the mind to the Dharma.

Broadly speaking, there are two aspects to meditation. The first is all those techniques which help us calm down, find inner stability and well-being (samatha).

Secondly, there are those techniques which encourage us to understand the nature of reality (vipassana). The Buddha was clear that both are important.

> **Bhavana** Cultivation of the mind, or self-development.

▶ Types of meditation

Samatha, including breathing meditation

If you want to find something in a full and untidy cupboard, it is sometimes helpful to empty the cupboard first: to clear it out completely, get rid of the unwanted stuff, and then you will be able to see what you are looking for. When you do this with your mind it is called samatha. The word samatha has a range of meanings, but our word 'tranquillity' covers all of them. You do not have to be a Buddhist to practise samatha, but Buddhists use it to clear the mind of clutter. So samatha is not, in itself, a form of meditation, but is often used as a preparation for meditation. It is a state of having the mind empty but still fully awake. Some Buddhists call it 'bare awareness'.

The idea of samatha is to choose something on which to focus the mind, something simple to start with. The mind may wander off it, but you should gently try to bring it back to the subject again; and as the mind wanders again, you should keep trying to refocus.

This kind of concentration is a skill, like riding a bicycle or playing a musical instrument. The more you do it, the better you become at it. And the better you become, the more easily you are able to tackle more complicated exercises. Someone who is well practised in samatha will choose complex ideas to focus on. An angry person may focus on the idea of peace; a greedy person may choose generosity.

> **Key Concept**
>
> **Samatha** Calm, or breathing meditation.

Breathing meditation is a form of samatha.

Anapanasati Breathing meditation.

A commonly used method of concentration, particularly for beginners, is known as **anapanasati**, breathing meditation. Here breathing itself is the object of concentration. Anapanasati is a type of samatha.

Anapanasati (breathing meditation) in action

The first stage is to sit in a comfortable position. Buddhists usually sit in the lotus position: cross-legged with each foot resting, sole up, on the opposite thigh. This may be rather difficult to start with, so simply sitting cross-legged on the floor, or in an upright chair is fine. The back should be straight, and the body in such a position that it will not get restless. The idea is to fix the mind on the point at which breath leaves the nostrils. Breathing should not be forced, but natural. To start with, you could count the breaths, both in and out, to keep the mind focused, but after a while this should not be necessary. Note the breath as it enters and leaves the body, and observe the movement of the body as it happens. In time, breathing will become more delicate, and it may even appear to stop altogether. There is no thought involved, simply observation. It is the observation that should fill the mind: remember that the object of the exercise is mindfulness.

You could try breathing meditation for yourself, following the instructions on this page. Remember, you do not have to be a Buddhist, or even religious, to practise samatha.

Samatha, then, means paying attention to the movements of the body and the changing states of the mind in order to discover their real nature. The important thing is not to associate them with yourself, because your feelings, perceptions, ideas and consciousness are yours; you are attached to them, and you are trying to rid yourself of attachments. Observe your movement and mind objectively, as things in themselves.

Kasina An object of focus in meditation.

An object that is used as a focus in samatha is called **kasina**. It could be almost anything: a coloured disc, a stone, a tree, a candle flame. Concentration on it should become so focused that you can see the kasina as clearly with the eyes shut as with them open. This is what mindfulness is: complete concentration. At this point, sense activity ceases: all there is mindfulness.

▶ ## Brahma vihara bhavana, including metta bhavana (meditation on loving-kindness)

Key Concept

Metta bhavana The development of loving-kindness (i.e. the development of loving-kindness through meditation.)

In Buddhism, the **brahma viharas** are considered to be the ideal qualities for a person to develop, the highest emotions, the things that promote harmony between people. The words brahma vihara mean 'excellent place'. The brahma viharas are used by some Buddhists as objects of concentration for tranquillity (samatha), but can be used for deeper meditation. They are love, compassion, joy for others and peace.

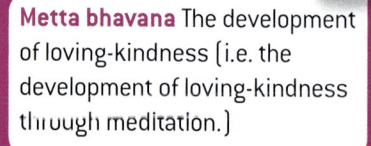

Brahma viharas The highest emotions

The brahma viharas are just emotions, ways of feeling. It may seem strange to try to develop emotions, because it seems that they just happen without our having any control. We just 'feel happy' or 'get angry'. We might be able to control what we do about it: if you get angry, you can restrain yourself, for example, by preventing yourself from hitting someone. But it is far more difficult to control the anger. Can you choose not to be angry?

Buddhism says you can. And you can choose to be serene, compassionate, joyous and full of loving-kindness. Meditation in itself cannot produce these emotions, but it does create the conditions in which they can develop. When meditating on the brahma viharas, the idea is to develop the qualities in oneself and, at the same time, spread them to all beings.

A person who has cultivated the brahma viharas is unable to hate or experience feelings of prejudice or anger. For Buddhists, then, it is important not just to try to be guided by the brahma viharas, but to meditate on them in order to draw on and develop the qualities inside oneself. This form of meditation is known as brahma vihara bhavana and meditation on the brahma vihara of metta is called metta bhavana.

Although metta means 'love', it is usually translated as 'loving-kindness' because it is difficult to say what love is. Metta is not the Christian idea of agape, which involves the notion of self-sacrifice. It is not being affectionate or 'nice'. It is about respect for the lives of others, simply because they are alive. It is about showing that respect in being considerate, kind and polite. It is rejoicing in others' joy and success, being happy for them. It is sometimes called 'universal friendliness'. The Buddha described it in these words:

> As a mother even with her own life protects her only child, so should one cultivate immeasurable loving-kindness towards all living beings.
>
> (Metta Sutta)

Moreover, developing loving-kindness (**metta bhavana**) leads to the eradication of desire (tanha):

> For one who mindfully develops
>
> Boundless loving-kindness
>
> Seeing the destruction of clinging,
>
> The fetters are worn away.
>
> (Itivuttaka 1.27)

In metta bhavana one starts with wishes for one's own happiness:
May I be free from ill will and danger.
May I be free from mental suffering.
May I be free from physical suffering.
May I take care of myself, happily.

This is used as a base from which to spread the same wish to others. First, you may think of loved ones, friends or family, and make the same wish to them:
May they be free from enmity and danger.
May they be free from mental suffering.
May they be free from physical suffering.
May they take care of themselves, happily.

Then the wish can be extended to acquaintances (people you know a little), then to enemies (which is more difficult), and finally to all beings (more difficult still). Then the barriers between these groups can be broken down so that metta is communicated to enemies as sincerely as it is to loved ones.

The aim of metta bhavana is to embed metta firmly in the mind so that it drives away all other thoughts, words and deeds spontaneously.

Vipassana (insight meditation)

Vipassana means 'insight'. Insight is the ability to see things clearly, to get to the heart of things. It means to recognise the truth of something, often suddenly, in a flash.

It is rather like getting the punchline of a joke. With some jokes, some people get it and some do not. Some do not at first and then out of the blue it dawns on them. It is like suddenly understanding something, maybe a mathematical principle that baffled you before.

Vipassana means having insight into the nature of life. The nature of life, as we have seen, is described as the Dharma. It is one thing to read about it and understand the logic of it. It is another thing to actually feel the truth of it.

Vipassana meditation is the means to gain this insight. It is a technique that cannot be learned from a book: it must be taught by a master. Only one who is skilled in it can pass it on to pupils. Samatha is sometimes used as a preparation for vipassana. Samatha is not, strictly speaking, a meditative practice: it is a system of concentrating the mind. But it paves the way for deep meditation: vipassana.

> Samatha is about concentration, but vipassana is about mindfulness. Concentration means focusing your mind on a single thing, blocking out everything else; it could be breathing or loving-kindness or even homework. But mindfulness involves observing it, thinking about it, taking in all its meanings. Someone may practise samatha to overcome attachments and then practise vipassana to develop the wisdom that comes from overcoming attachments.

The aim of vipassana is to reveal the wisdom of a buddha. There are four stages in this process:

1 Seeing connections between the mind and the body.
2 Seeing the unity of mind and body effortlessly.
3 Experiencing only concentration and happiness.
4 Insight, wisdom and freedom from suffering.

Key Concept

Vipassana 'Insight' meditation enabling the individual to see the true nature of things.

Task

In two or three sentences, explain how vipassana can help a person achieve nirvana. You should refer to the Noble Eightfold Path in your answer.

Task

Why is meditation an important practice for Buddhists? Use the quotation from the Dhammapada and other information from this section in your answer.

Practising vipassana

Vipassana is usually practised in a sitting position, with legs crossed and the feet resting, soles upward, on the thighs. The back should be perfectly straight, at 90 degrees to the legs. This is known as the lotus position. However, someone who is well practised in vipassana can do it while sitting, walking, standing or lying down.

A Buddhist practising vipassana.

> Wisdom springs from meditation; without meditation wisdom wanes. Having known these two paths of progress and decline, let a man so conduct himself that his wisdom may increase.
>
> (Dhammapada 282)

Festivals and retreats
Wesak

> **Key Concept**
>
> **Wesak** A festival to commemorate the birth, enlightenment and death of the Buddha.

Vesakha is the name of the ancient Indian month that roughly corresponds with the month of May in the modern calendar. **Wesak** is the festival that takes place on the day of the full moon of that month. It commemorates the birth, enlightenment and death of the Buddha. It is probably the most important and widely celebrated festival in Buddhism.

The coming of an enlightened being to this world is seen as a rare and important event. The Buddha and his teachings can be compared to a light that illuminates the darkness of samsara. Therefore, light is used as a symbol of all three aspects of the festival: the Buddha's birth, enlightenment and passing away. Festival goers light lanterns, carry them through the streets and hang them outside houses. In Sri Lanka there are great processions in towns and cities with brightly lit floats. In the UK, where Buddhism is a minority faith, Wesak is an opportunity for Buddhist centres to open their doors to local people so that they can share their understanding of life. Some British Buddhist communities organise children's activities, such as puppet shows of Buddhist stories and face-painting depicting characters from Buddhist mythology. They also give talks on Buddhist beliefs and teachings.

At Wesak, lay believers, that is Buddhists who are not monks (sometimes called householder Buddhists), make a special effort to make donations to the monks. In addition to the Five Precepts that they usually undertake as part of the Noble Eightfold Path (Right Action), some take on five extra Precepts usually reserved for monks. So, just for the duration of Wesak, they will also undertake:

- to refrain from eating after midday. Human beings need to eat in order to live, but a Buddhist whose mind is occupied with thoughts of supper is craving, and so is making very slow progress towards buddhahood.
- to refrain from dancing, singing and watching unsuitable entertainments. Enjoyment of such things increases worldly attachment. Buddhists are not against entertainment and would not wish to stop anyone else from enjoying such things. But during Wesak, when Buddhists are making extra effort to progress towards nirvana, they choose to avoid them.
- to refrain from using scents or garlands. The Dharma is life itself. You cannot improve life by making it smell better!

Wesak is a festival of light.

> **Task**
>
> Explain why light is used as a symbol.
>
> Think about the properties of light: its abilities to give illumination and heat, life and death. Think, too, about the ways in which human life is affected by light or its absence. Finally, consider how and why Buddhists use light as a symbol at Wesak and compare it with the ways in which light is used symbolically in other religious traditions.

> **Key Concept**
>
> **Sangha** The community of Buddhists. This can be lay or monastic.

> **The Sangha in Wales**
>
> There are over 30 different Buddhist groups in Wales representing a variety of Buddhist traditions. Many are members of the Buddhist Council of Wales, which aims to ensure that Buddhist views are expressed nationally.

Wesak is sometimes called Buddha Day.

Task

What reasons might lay Buddhists have for undertaking the five monastic Precepts during Wesak?

- to refrain from sleeping on a high or broad (in other words, luxurious) bed. During Wesak, Buddhists think of sleep as a necessity, not as an enjoyable pastime. One can become enlightened only when awake and alert. So Buddhists sleep on a thin mat that they roll up during the day.
- to refrain from handling gold and silver (including money). This is an obvious way of breaking an attachment to worldly things.

Monks and lay believers will spend the day together in the temple attending lectures on the scriptures, learning about aspects of the Buddha's life, chanting from religious texts and meditating. Stupas are lit up, and so are the paths around them as families walk around them. Stalls are set up to give away food and drink to passers-by.

▶ Rain retreats

The Buddha's first teaching, the First Turning of the Wheel of the Law, is believed to have been given in the ancient Indian month of Asalha, which is, roughly, July. It is commemorated on the day of that month's full moon, known as Dharma Day, when monks chant the Buddha's first sermon, the Dhamma Cakka Sutta, in the Pali language.

The rainy season lasts in South-East Asia for about three months.

Asalha marks the beginning of the Vassa, the three-month rainy season. Monasteries were established during the Buddha's lifetime for monks to stay in during the monsoons. It was seen as an opportunity to reflect, to study and to meditate. The tradition of rain retreats has continued, and today monks use the Vassa as a time to recharge their batteries and re-energise their commitment to the Dharma. Lay people, too, use the Vassa to advance their spiritual progress. They commit to giving up old habits, like smoking or eating certain foods, that form the attachments that slow down their progress. In the Theravada tradition, some lay believers become ordained as monks for the rainy season, returning to their regular lives at the end of it.

Kathina

During the Vassa, the monks and lay people have had little to do with each other. Now it is over, the monks will start to move on. Before they do, the lay (householder) and monastic communities get together in a festival of unity called **Kathina**.

Many of the rituals associated with the Vassa began in the time of the Buddha. He forbade his monks to travel during the rainy season for fear that they might trample crops and injure animal life. So as soon as the rains started, they had to stay where they were.

It is said that one year a group of monks were travelling to see the Buddha to spend the Vassa with him. But the rains started unexpectedly and the monks were not able to get to him. For three months they strengthened their practice together and when the season was over, they continued their journey to see the Buddha.

The roads were still wet and muddy from the rainy season and the monks' robes got dirty and torn. When they arrived at the place where the Buddha was staying, they were ashamed of the poor state of their clothes. But monastic rules say that monks may not have spare robes. They cannot make robes from new cloth and cloth must be donated by a lay Buddhist: they have no money with which to buy any.

The Buddha saw the sorry state of the monks and saw, too, how ashamed they were. He had been given cloth for new robes by a follower and he gave it to the monks, telling them to make new robes from it and to give them to whichever of them they chose.

Still today, lay believers contribute robes and other essential equipment to monasteries. One or two monks receive the gifts and pass them on to whichever monks they feel need them most. The word 'Kathina' refers to a sewing frame on which the robes used to be made.

Some families, whose sons have been monks for the rainy season, welcome them home again, and all congratulate the monks on their retreat, for it is believed that they have created merit (blessings and good fortune) for the whole community.

Kathina can take place at any time during the month following the Vassa (usually October or November). The lay community provides a meal for the monks in the morning and the robes are presented at a ceremony in the afternoon. It is seen as a way of creating positive karma for those who are generous enough to contribute.

> **Kathina** Festival that marks the end of Vassa (the traditional retreat for monks during the rainy season).

> **Task**
> Explain why Kathina is important for monks, on the one hand, and lay (householder) Buddhists, on the other. Aim to write a short paragraph (2–3 sentences) for each.

▶ Parinirvana Day

Buddhists believe that, when he attained enlightenment, the Buddha also achieved nirvana.

In attaining enlightenment, he saw life as it really is; he gained perfect wisdom, seeing that all things and all events are interrelated and nothing has independent existence. He saw that everything changes because everything depends on everything else, that nothing has a permanent identity. He awoke to the Four Noble Truths, that because everything changes, nothing can bring lasting happiness; on the contrary, desiring and forming attachments only brings suffering, but that suffering can be overcome.

As a result of his enlightenment, the Buddha was able to extinguish desires and craving, thereby becoming free from suffering and entering the peace and joy of nirvana.

However, this nirvana was only, in a sense, temporary, because the Buddha still lived in the world of material things and beings. When he died, his nirvana became complete: being free from desire and suffering, he was free from the karmic cycle of samsara, to be reborn no more.

The completion of his nirvana is called parinirvana. Mahayana Buddhists celebrate it on **Parinirvana Day** (or Nirvana Day) which takes place on 15 February each year. (Theravada Buddhists mark the Buddha's parinirvana (parinibbana) at Wesak [see page 79].) Parinirvana Day is a day of celebration, because it marks the time when the Buddha became free of suffering. As he lay dying, he told his disciples:

> 'Do not grieve! Have I not taught from the very beginning that with all that is dear and beloved there must be change and separation? All that is born comes into being, is compounded, and is subject to decay. How can one say: "May it not come to an end?" This cannot be.'

(Mahaparinibbana Sutta 58)

After the Buddha died, Anuruddha, one of his followers said:

> 'The Blessed One has not passed away. He has entered the state of the cessation of perception and feeling.'

Parinirvana Day is also a day of reflection. Buddhists read the teachings the Buddha gave as he lay dying and meditate on the impermanent nature of life and death. Some Buddhists make a pilgrimage to Kushinagar, where the Buddha died (see page 62).

The Buddha attained parinirvana when he died.

Parinirvana Day Day to commemorate the Buddha's release from samsara.

Tasks

1. What is the difference between nirvana and parinirvana?
2. Why did the Buddha tell his followers not to grieve for him after his death?
3. Find out what the Buddha's last words were and what he meant by them.

▶ **End of Section Review**

Stickability

Key concepts:
- Metta bhavana
- Samatha
- Sangha
- Vipassana
- Wesak

Key teachings:
- Importance of meditation
- Samatha (including breathing meditation)
- Loving-kindness meditation (metta bhavana);
- Insight meditation (vipassana)
- Wesak
- Kathina
- Parinirvana Day

Skills Link

1. What is meant by 'samatha'?
2. Describe the ways in which Buddhists celebrate Kathina.

Knowledge Check

1. Write a short paragraph (roughly three sentences) to explain why Buddhists meditate.
2. Write a long paragraph (roughly eight to ten sentences) to explain the different types of Buddhist meditation.
3. Explain what metta means.
4. Write a developed paragraph (approximately eight to ten sentences) to explain why Buddhism teaches that the Noble Eightfold Path leads to the attainment of nirvana.

The Big Question

'Festivals are just a good excuse for a party.'

Your Task

Respond to the statement above, showing that you have considered more than one point of view. Give reasoned judgements on the validity and strength of these views. Refer to Buddhism in your answer.

Task

You need to explain in detail religious teachings about festivals. Use the guidance below to help you to write a developed explanation for Buddhism. Ensure that you use key terms fluently and frequently.

All/many/most Buddhists believe that _____.

This comes from the teaching/ quote _____.

This means that/Because of this they _____.

Some/other Buddhists such as _____ believe that _____.

This comes from the teaching/ quote _____.

This means that/Because of this they _____.

Finally, Buddhists such as _____ believe that _____.

This means that/Because of this they _____.

Their beliefs do/do not differ because _____.

Islam

Key Concepts

Adhan Call to prayer, usually performed by a muezzin.

Du'ah Varying forms of personal prayer.

Hadith Saying; report; account. The sayings of the Prophet Muhammad, as recounted by his household, descendants and companions. These are a major source of Islamic law.

Halal Any action or thing which is permitted or lawful, often used in reference to foods that are permitted.

Qur'an That which is read or recited. The divine book revealed to the Prophet Muhammad. Allah's final revelation to humankind.

Saddaqah Voluntary payment or good action for charitable purposes.

Salat Prescribed communication with and worship of Allah, performed under specific conditions, in the manner taught by the Prophet Muhammad, and recited in Arabic. Muslims believe that the five times of Salat are fixed by Allah.

Sawm Fasting from just before dawn until sunset. Abstinence is required from all food and drink as well as smoking and sexual relations.

Shahadah Declaration of faith, which consists of the statement, 'There is no god except Allah, Prophet Muhammad is the Messenger of Allah'.

Shirk Association; regarding anything as being equal or partner to Allah.

Tawhid 'Oneness' in reference to God and is the basic Muslim belief in the oneness of Allah.

Zakat Purification of wealth by payment of annual almsgiving. An obligatory act of worship.

Core Questions

- The word Islam means 'submission'. Why do Muslims believe they need to live their lives in submission to God?
- What are Muslim beliefs about the afterlife and God's plan for our lives?
- Why is Prophet Muhammad known as the 'Seal of the Prophets'?
- What is the Qur'an and why is it important in Islam?
- Why do Muslims fast?
- What is meant by the Greater and Lesser Jihad?
- What are the Five Pillars of Islam?
- How do Muslims make decisions about right and wrong?

▶ Introduction

Allah The Arabic word for God. Muslims believe that they worship the same God that spoke through Musa (Moses) and Isa (Jesus).

Islam The name given to the Muslim religion. Literally translates as submission or peace.

Muslims believe in one God (**Allah**), whom they worship as the divine creator. Islam teaches that, through the centuries, God revealed his truth to many special people (known as prophets). However, most importantly, God spoke to the last and greatest Prophet, Muhammad, in special messages that were collected together in the form of the Qur'an. According to **Islam**, submission and obedience to the will of God (Allah) is the only way in which a person can fully experience true harmony in heart and mind. In fact, the word Islam means 'submission' in Arabic. Another meaning of the word Islam is 'peace', and this is why Muslims are committed to establishing a fair and respectful society. They believe that God has given a clear set of laws (called the Shari'ah) to guide human beings, allowing them to live together in peaceful communities, as he has intended.

> The spelling of words used in Islam can cause problems. Arabic uses a different script from European languages, so there can be disagreement about how words should be translated from the original. This book uses generally accepted spellings. Throughout the book the word 'God' has been preferred to the word 'Allah' to emphasise to the non-Muslim reader that Muslims worship God, not some other being. It was Prophet Muhammad's belief that he was worshipping the same God as the Jews. The WJEC specification uses the word Allah and either term will be accepted in the exam.

Islam worldwide

There are an estimated 1.6 billion Muslims in the world today (23 per cent of the world's population), making Islam the world's second largest religion after Christianity. It is also the fastest growing religion in the world. Islam originates from the Middle East: Prophet Muhammad lived in Arabia (modern-day Saudi Arabia), and the most important Islamic holy sites are in this part of the world. The Middle East and North Africa have the highest concentration of Muslim population today: 93 per cent of people in this region are Muslims. However, nearly two-thirds of the world's Muslims live in the Asia-Pacific region (in countries including Pakistan, India, Bangladesh and Indonesia).

Tasks

1. Create your own word diagram/mind-map on Islam. Use headings, words and topics from these pages and try to organise a word picture that links some of the main ideas in Islam. This will help you to organise your thoughts on the topic as you begin to study this religion.
2. In your own words, explain why Muslims believe they should submit to God.

Muslims believe that Islam did not begin with Prophet Muhammad; it goes right back to the earliest humans (Adam). Islam is the natural religion of all people and, while Prophet Muhammad is understood to be the final prophet, he is not the founder of Islam.

Task
Explain why Muslims challenge the idea that Prophet Muhammad was the founder of Islam.

Task
What's it like for young Muslims in Wales today? Read this article online. Make notes on what it says about: a) being Muslim, and b) being Welsh.
www.walesonline.co.uk/news/wales-news/what-life-like-young-muslims-10392557

Islam in Britain

In Britain today, there are nearly three million Muslims, making up approximately 4.5 per cent of the population. Up until the mid-twentieth century there were very few Muslims in the UK, but, from the 1950s onwards, significant numbers of people came from the former colonies, taking up the offer of work in post-Second World War Britain. Some of the first were East African Asians, while many others came directly from South Asia.

The 2011 census shows that Britain is now home to one of the most diverse Muslim communities (ummah) in the world. The largest groups originate from India, Pakistan and Bangladesh, but many come from Arab and African communities, as well as Muslims from South-East Asia, the Balkans and Turkey. There are also many Muslims who have converted from other faiths.

Some Muslims in Britain describe themselves as Sufis. Sufis try to find the heart of the religion, and they practise a more mystical version of Islam. There is also a significant Ahmadiyya community in the UK. They believe the long-awaited Messiah (Mahdi) has come, in the person of Mirza Ghulam Ahmad, to renew the faith and remind people today of Prophet Muhammad's teachings. However, many British Muslims (including the Muslim Council of Britain) regard the Ahmadiyyas as non-Muslims.

The majority of British Muslims are Sunnis (95 per cent), with the remaining five per cent coming from the Shi'a tradition. Within the Sunni community there are groups such as the Deobandi, Barelvis and Salafi. Types of Shi'a groups include the Twelvers, Zaydis and Ismailis.

Islam in Wales

According to the 2011 census, there are about 50,000 Muslims currently living in Wales, making Islam the largest non-Christian faith in Wales. The biggest population of Muslims in Wales is in Cardiff. It was in Cardiff that the first mosque in the UK was opened in 1860, and Cardiff is also the site of the first purpose-built mosque in Wales, built in 1947. For many hundreds of years, the busy seaport of Cardiff has been a convenient place for sailors from all around the world to settle. Records show that Muslim sailors from Yemen and Somalia were living in the city more than a century ago. Today, many Welsh Muslims trace their ancestry back to South Asia, such as India, Pakistan and Bangladesh.

Peel Street Mosque, Cardiff (taken in 1964): the first purpose-built mosque in Wales. (Due to redevelopment work it was demolished in 1997.)

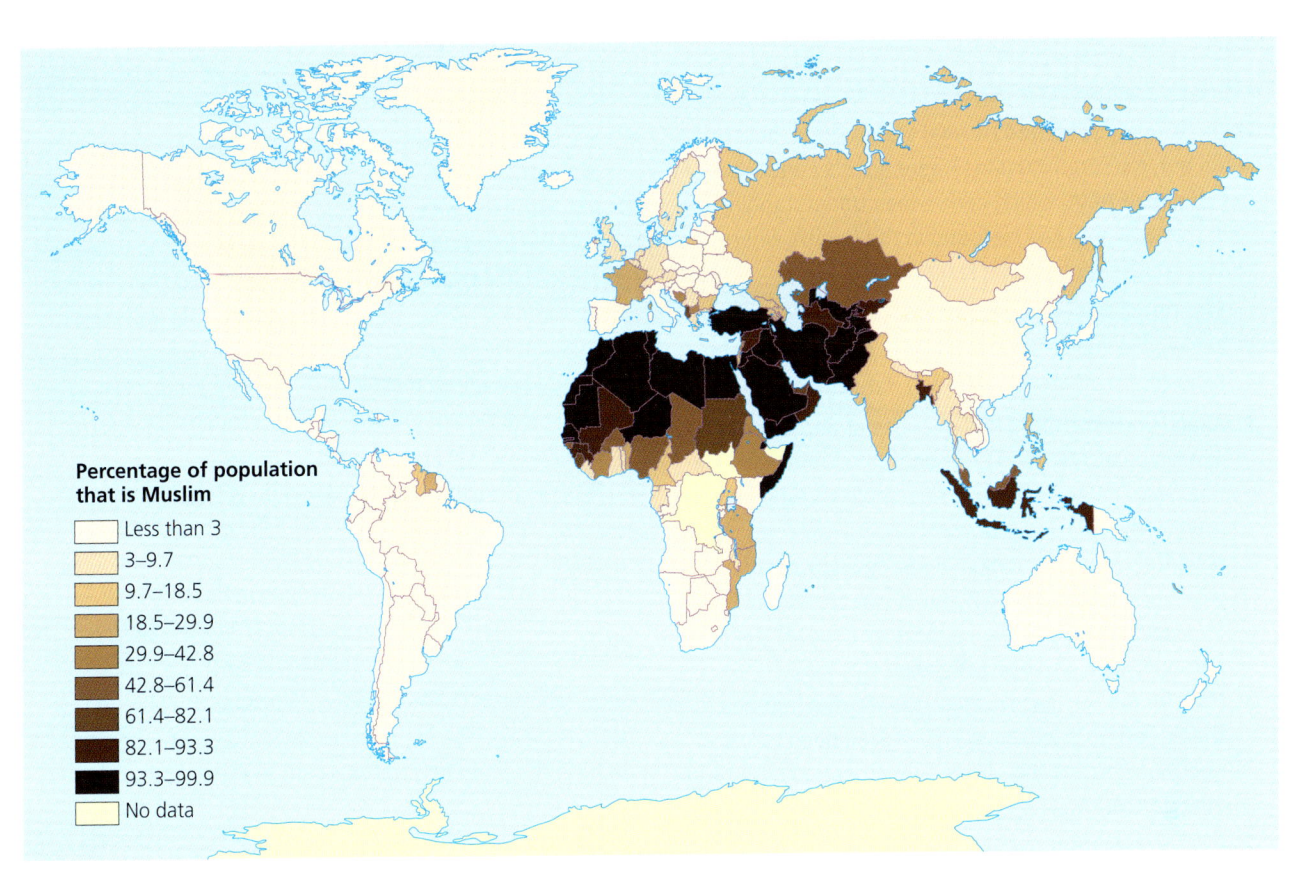

World map showing the distribution of Muslims.

Percentage of population that is Muslim
- Less than 3
- 3–9.7
- 9.7–18.5
- 18.5–29.9
- 29.9–42.8
- 42.8–61.4
- 61.4–82.1
- 82.1–93.3
- 93.3–99.9
- No data

A useful infographic showing diagrams and statistics relating to different Islamic sects, schools and groups can be found at: www.informationisbeautiful.net/visualizations/islamic-sects-schools-branches-movements.

Sunni One of the two main branches of Islam. Literally means 'one who follows the Sunnah' (the Sunnah is the book that describes the way the Prophet Muhammad lived). For Sunnis, there is no overall leader of the Islamic community. Leaders are chosen locally and called *imams*.

Shi'a One of the two main branches of Islam. Literally means 'from the House of Ali' (Ali was a close relative to Prophet Muhammad). Shi'as believe that Ali, Muhammad's cousin and closest living relative, should have become the first leader of the Muslims after Muhammad's death, and all subsequent leaders should be descended from Muhammad.

Sources of authority

It is important for Muslims that they can trust the information they have about how to live in the world. Their sources of information must have authority.

For Muslims, the ultimate source of authority is their holy book, the Qur'an. This is because they believe that the Qur'an contains the actual words of God that were passed to Prophet Muhammad who remembered them with perfect accuracy.

Other sources of authority include the **Hadith** and the Sunnah. These are accounts of what the Prophet Muhammad said and did. The moral and religious rules that are prescribed in the Qur'an, the Hadith and the Sunnah are known as Shari'ah.

In addition, over the centuries, imams and Islamic scholars have made judgments and rulings based on their expert reading of the texts and these too are sources of authority.

The Islamic community

One of the major divisions in Islam is the split between **Sunni** and **Shi'a**. Sunnis form the majority of Muslims in the world today (87–90 per cent), most of them living in North Africa, the Middle East, South Asia and Indonesia. Only about five per cent of British Muslims are Shi'as. Although they share most central beliefs, they do have significant differences in the way they understand religious truth, laws and practices.

The six articles of faith in Islam

There is no official **creed** (formal statement of beliefs) in Islam but, for Sunni Muslims, there are six central beliefs, or **articles of faith**, which define their understanding of God. This teaching can be found in the Hadith, where Muhammad is recorded as saying:

> You must believe in Allah, his angels, his holy books, his messengers, in the Last Day and in fate (both in its good and in its evil aspects).

1. **Allah** (God) The unity and oneness of God is called **Tawhid**. Like Jews and Christians, Muslims believe in one God. The Arabic word for God is Allah, which simply means 'the (al) God (ilah)'.
2. **Malaikah** (angels) God created angels to interact with human lives, bringing his divine message. Each Muslim has two guardian angels who record that person's good and bad actions.
3. **Holy books** God has revealed his word to humans in the Qur'an. This tells Muslims all they need to know about how to live their lives. Other inspired scriptures include the Tawrat of Musa (Torah), the Zabur of Dawud (Psalms) and the Injil of Isa (Gospels).
4. **Risalah** (prophethood) God has spoken through numerous prophets throughout time, including Adam, Nuh (Noah), Ibrahim (Abraham), Musa (Moses) and Isa (Jesus). However, Muhammad is the greatest prophet.
5. **Akhirah** (the afterlife) Belief in the final judgement and life after death. This life is a preparation for the eternal life that follows. On the last day there will be a time of judgement, when all people will have to account for their lives. Muslims whose good deeds outweigh their bad deeds will go to Paradise. Those who have led wicked lives will be cast into hell.
6. **Al-Qadr** (God's divine plan) God is responsible for everything and has set out a divine destiny for all things. God has written down all that has happened and all that will happen in the universe (predestination). However, Islam teaches that this does not take away our human free will.

Although these six beliefs are central to the Islamic faith, they are not the only important beliefs. Others include the jihad and submission to the will of God (see page 92).

> **Creed** A set statement of faith that all religious believers follow.
>
> **Six articles of faith** The six central beliefs of Islam.

Task

Create a mind map around these six articles of faith. Write out the six key beliefs on a large sheet of paper and add in the following ideas, linking them in where you think they belong:

- Prophet Muhammad
- Angel Jibril
- The Qur'an
- Free will or predestination?
- The afterlife
- One God (Tawhid)
- Ibrahim, Musa and Isa
- Two guardian angels
- Revelation from God

Can you think of six more ideas to add to the diagram?

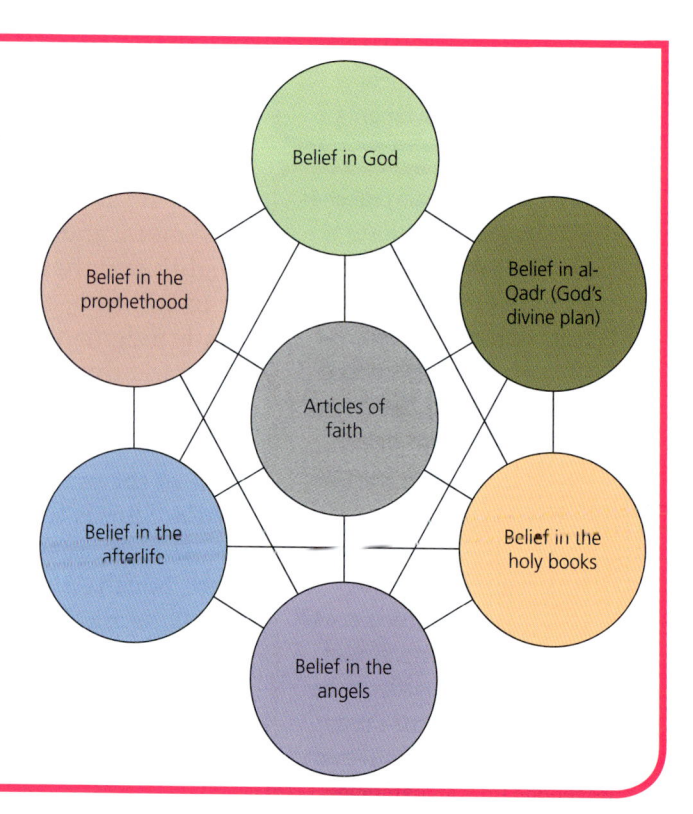

5 Islam: Beliefs and teachings

The nature of God
Allah as one God: Tawhid

Beget To bring a child into existence, or to create offspring.
Surah A chapter in the Qur'an.

Key Concept

Tawhid 'Oneness' in reference to God and is the basic Muslim belief in the oneness of Allah.

Islam is a monotheistic faith: it teaches that there is only one God. There are no other divine beings and it is a sin to compare God to other 'false' gods. Muslims reject the Christian belief that Jesus is the Son of God. The passage 'He neither **begets** nor is born' (Qur'an 112.3) makes it clear that God has no children and he is not the child of anyone.

The oneness and unity of God is the single most important belief in Islam. It is called tawhid. There is one God (Allah) who is the universal God of all humanity. The Qur'an teaches that 'there is no deity except Him, the Exalted in Might, the Wise' (Qur'an 3.18).

Tasks

This mind map shows **Surah** 112. 1–4 from the Qur'an with notes around it to explain some of its meaning. This passage sums up the nature of God and is one that many Muslims will learn by heart.

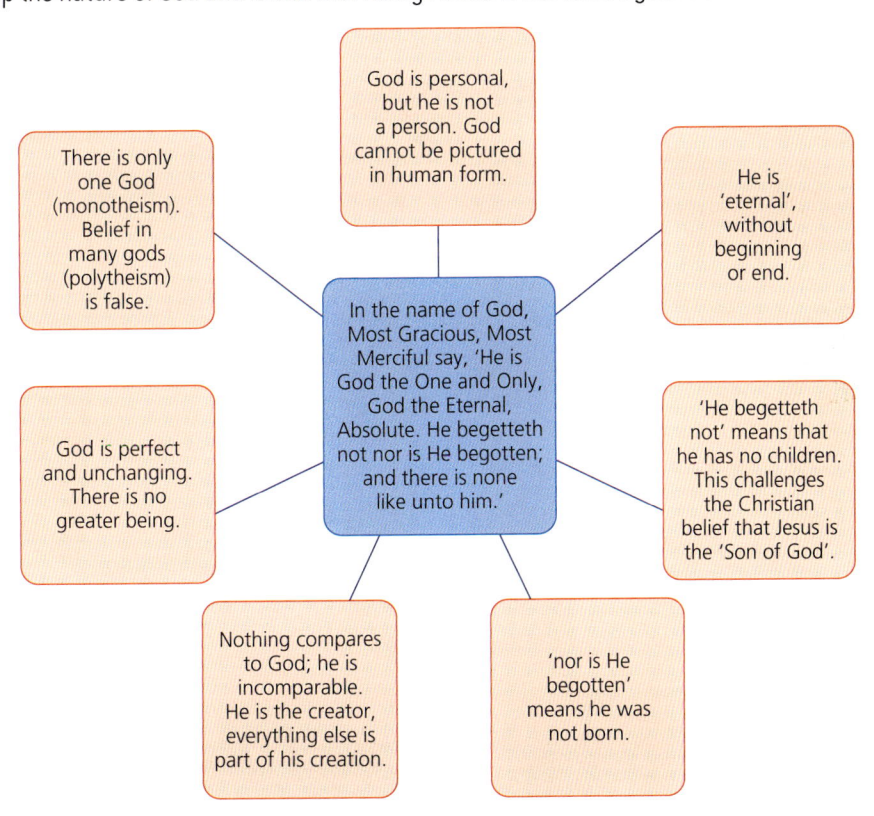

- In the name of God, Most Gracious, Most Merciful say, 'He is God the One and Only, God the Eternal, Absolute. He begetteth not nor is He begotten; and there is none like unto him.'

- There is only one God (monotheism). Belief in many gods (polytheism) is false.
- God is personal, but he is not a person. God cannot be pictured in human form.
- He is 'eternal', without beginning or end.
- 'He begetteth not' means that he has no children. This challenges the Christian belief that Jesus is the 'Son of God'.
- 'nor is He begotten' means he was not born.
- Nothing compares to God; he is incomparable. He is the creator, everything else is part of his creation.
- God is perfect and unchanging. There is no greater being.

1. Make a list of the qualities and attributes of God mentioned in Surah 112.
2. Using the information above, write a paragraph to explain what Muslims believe about God. Include two short quotations from Surah 112.

The qualities of God

Muslims believe that God is:

- **Immanent** God is always close by. The Qur'an says that God is closer to each one of us than the veins in our necks (50.16).
- **Transcendent** God is beyond all things, not limited by the rules of nature.
- **Omniscient** God has all knowledge; nothing can be hidden from him.
- **Omnipotent** God has unlimited power. The Qur'an teaches that it was God 'Who created the heavens and the earth' and that 'He is over all things competent.' (Qur'an 46.33).
- **Beneficent** God is always kind; he loves us.
- **Merciful** God is always fair; he forgives us if we are sorry.
- **Judge** On the last day, God will be our judge.
- **Creator** God is the beginning; he is the cause of all that exists.

Many of these qualities are expressed by Muslims in the Al-Fatihah. Al-Fatihah is the first surah (chapter) in the Qur'an. It means 'the opening' and many Muslims learn to recite it from memory in their daily prayers.

> In the name of Allah, the Entirely Merciful, the Especially Merciful. [All] praise is [due] to Allah, Lord of the worlds – The Entirely Merciful, the Especially Merciful, Sovereign of the Day of Recompense. It is You we worship and You we ask for help. Guide us to the straight path – the path of those upon whom You have bestowed favour, not of those who have evoked [Your] anger or of those who are astray.
>
> (Qur'an 1.1–7)

We tend to think of the word Allah as the term that applies to the God that Muslims worship. However, in countries in the Middle East, where Arabic is the spoken language, Christians refer to God as 'Allah'. Allah is not a name, it simply means 'the (one) God'. Muslims believe there is only one God, the same God that is worshipped by Christians and Jews.

Al-Fatihah in Arabic calligraphy.

Tasks

1. Copy out the al-Fatihah in your book.
2. Why do you think Muslims might try to learn this passage by heart?
3. Choose three things it says and write down what they teach Muslims about God.

> Whenever I am in a difficulty, I remember God with his words and through his names. There are 99 names for God, and we remember them for different purposes.
>
> (Musarat S)

The 99 beautiful names of God

In Islam, God is not to be confused with any living creature. He is beyond all things (transcendent) and cannot be pictured as a physical being. God is outside our human understanding, but for Muslims he lies at the very centre of everything they think and do. So, how do Muslims 'see' God?

The Qur'an and the Hadith have many different 'names' for God – not as a person, but using words that describe his qualities and attributes. They use names like King, Protector, Wise, Eternal and Light. These are known as the 99 beautiful names of God (or sometimes, the 'beautiful names' of God).

In fact, there are different lists of these names, recorded through different traditions of Muslims, and reciting these names has been a powerful form of prayer for Muslims through the centuries. Most of these names are dotted throughout the Qur'an, for example:

> Vision perceives Him not, but He perceives [all] vision; and He is the Subtle, the Acquainted.
>
> (Qur'an 6.103)

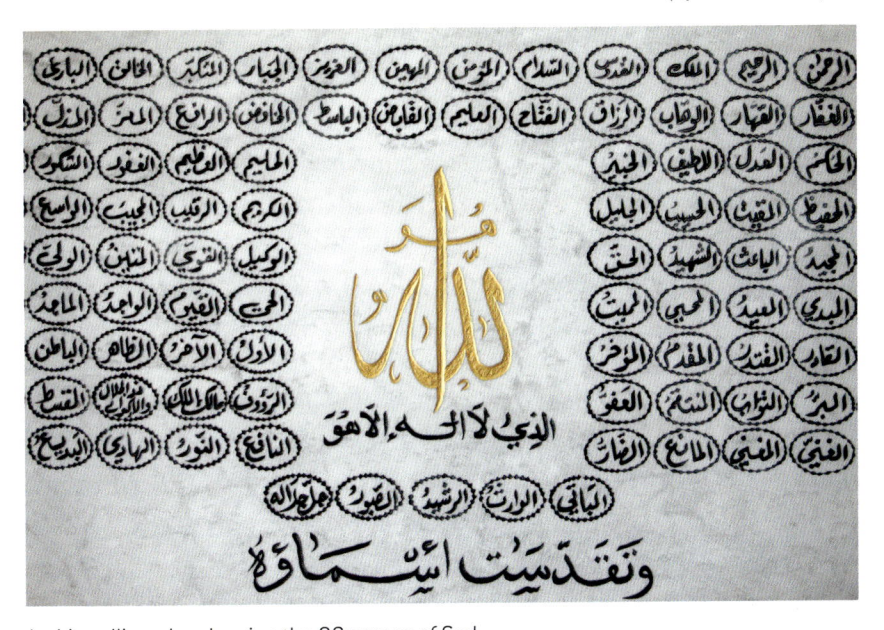

Arabic calligraphy showing the 99 names of God.

Task

Here are some of the 99 names of God: compassionate, patient, almighty, sublimely exalted, nourisher, generous, giver of life, utterly just, all-hearing, magnificent, irresistible, kind, pardoner, all-encompassing, infinite, forgiving.

Copy out the table below. Put each of the names of God from the list above into the column you think it most relates to.

Then compare your table with your neighbour's. Did you have different ideas? Why?

Immanent	Transcendent	Omnipotent	Beneficent	Merciful

> 'There's nobody and there's nothing like Allah. I love him. I can't see him, but I know he's beneficent, merciful, master of the Day of Judgement.'
>
> K Farzana (From *Committed to Islam* by Sylvia and Bary Sutcliffe)

▶ Submission to the will of God

The word Islam means 'submission' in the Arabic language. Muslims believe in one God (Allah) and they worship him because he is the divine creator. They believe that all of God's creation is in submission to him, following the natural laws he has put in place. The sun follows its natural course in the sky. Plants grow according to natural laws. Uniquely, as his greatest creation, human have been offered choice. Islam teaches that God has sent prophets and messengers to earth to guide people so they can learn how to live in submission to him. Accepting the will of God means following the Five Pillars (religious practices) (see page 104) and the rules of Shari'ah law (see page 203). These are the signs of being a true Muslim.

Jihad: the struggle to follow the way set out by God

The Greater and Lesser Jihad

The struggle to follow the path set out for human beings by God is called Jihad. It means striving to do what is right for God. The Greater Jihad is the struggle that each person has, as an individual, to follow God's will in their life. The Lesser Jihad is the fight to defend Islam (holy war).

Following the Greater Jihad

The Greater Jihad is the spiritual struggle with oneself. It is the desire and commitment to live the perfect Muslim life:

- to perform the Five Pillars with devotion
- to practise the path set out by Prophet Muhammad (as set out in the Sunnah)
- to seek justice and fairness for all
- to rise above one's own greed and selfishness.

Examples of how Muslims might apply the Greater Jihad include:

- **The need to control desires** Islam teaches that Muslims need to control their desires and behaviour, to follow the Five Pillars and live a life that is pleasing to God. This will ensure that when the last day comes and they are brought to judgement by God, they will be worthy to receive God's favour and thus to enter paradise.
- **The battle against laziness** There is a prayer of Prophet Muhammad that says: 'God, I seek thy protection against helplessness and laziness, and against cowardice... and miserliness.' This describes the Greater Jihad. It is the commitment to make the effort to be a better person and live as God has instructed. The Greater Jihad is the spiritual fight against the tendency to be lazy: to get up for prayers before dawn, to only eat food that is **halal** (permitted), to show kindness and generosity towards other people.
- **Encourage what is right** This process is partly about removing evil from oneself, but also about making the world a better place.

The Prophet Muhammad says:

Whoever amongst you sees an evil, he must change it with his hand. If he is not able to do so, then with his tongue. And if he is not able to do so, then with his heart, and that is the weakest form of faith.

(Hadith)

▶ **Respect for the beliefs of others** The Qur'an encourages Muslims to be tolerant and respectful towards the beliefs of others: 'For you is your religion, and for me is my religion' (Qur'an 109.6). Muslims should live in peace and harmony in society, celebrating differences and obeying the law. The Qur'an makes it clear that every single life is precious:

Whoever kills a soul … it is as if he had slain mankind entirely. And whoever saves one – it is as if he had saved mankind entirely.

(Qur'an 5.32)

▶ Shahadah, the declaration of faith

The first of the Five Pillars of Islam is the **Shahadah**. It declares that 'there is no god but Allah (God), and Muhammad is the prophet of God'. This statement forms the central support for the 'House of Islam': the other four pillars are all outward expressions of this deeply held belief.

Arabic calligraphy of the Shahadah.

A statement of faith

For Muslims, the words of the Shahadah are heard throughout the day in countless aspects of their lives. They are announced in the **adhan** (the call to prayer) from the minaret in the mosque (see page 106) and recited in each of the five daily prayers. These words are also known as the Kalimah prayer. They are the first words whispered into a newborn baby's ear and, if possible, they are the last words a dying Muslim hears on their deathbed. Muslim soldiers have these words on their lips as they go into battle.

Tasks

1. What struggles do you have to live in the right way? Do you have a battle with laziness or selfishness? Can you explain your thoughts?
2. What do you think it means to say: 'smiling in tough times is jihad'?

Key Concept

Shahadah Declaration of faith, which consists of the statement, 'There is no god except Allah, Prophet Muhammad is the Messenger of Allah'.

The Shahadah sums up the religion of Islam: the belief in the one and only Almighty God and the acceptance of Prophet Muhammad as the final messenger, a man sent by God to reveal the divine path to life (the Shari'ah).

> The words of the Shahadah ('There is no god but God and Muhammad is the prophet of God') are sometimes referred to by Muslims as the Kalimah prayer.

Key Concept

Shirk Association; regarding anything as being equal or partner to Allah.

Monotheism

The Shahadah states the existence of one God; this is called monotheism. This means that Muslims reject belief in many gods (polytheism) and they also oppose the atheist concept of a world without God. The Shahadah denies the Christian belief in the Trinity (God the Father, Son and Holy Spirit). Muslims have deep respect for Jesus (Isa), but to them he is a great prophet, not a divine being. Islam (like Judaism and Sikhism) declares that God is one.

The sin of shirk

Islam warns against the sin of **shirk**. This is when a person worships something other than God. There is one God, and there can be no pictures to represent him. Muslims must worship the true God, not an image of him created by human hands.

The prophets bring the word of God, but all Muslims understand that prophets are only human; God is divine.

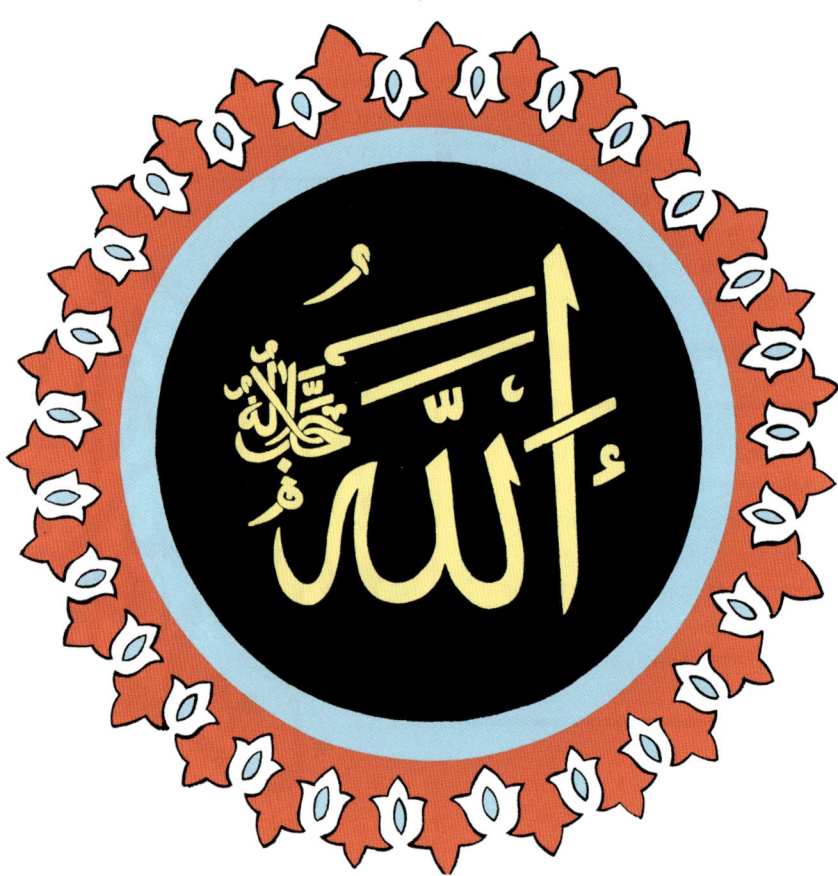

This text means Allah in Arabic. To worship anything other than Allah is to commit the sin of shirk.

▶ Prohibition of images

The Muslim teaching of Tawhid emphasises that God is one. He has no helpers, no associates and no sons. The world is here because it is his creation and he made everything in the best way possible. When people make images, it implies that they are trying to imitate God's creation and this shows disrespect towards him.

> He is the God who forms you in the wombs however He wills.
>
> (Qur'an 3.6)

> The word 'anthropomorphism' comes from the Greek words *anthropos*, meaning 'man' and *morphe* meaning 'shape'. In some religious traditions it is acceptable to picture God in human form (for example in some Christian art). Islam rejects any anthropomorphic representation of God.

Task

Choose a piece of calligraphy from the Free Islamic Calligraphy website (freeislamiccalligraphy.com) and copy it. Then, using an online version of the Qur'an, add the words of the passage in English.

Sunni Muslims are particularly strong in their belief that there can be no pictures on display in the mosque. The only art that can be used is calligraphy (artistic writing) or geometric patterns. They will not allow any pictures of the Prophet and some even avoid displaying photographs of family and friends. This is because they say that any form of representational art might lead to worshipping the picture rather than God.

On the other hand, most Muslims would say that pictures of human beings are shirk only if there is a possibility that they could be worshipped. It would, after all, be difficult to read newspapers or magazines, watch television or browse the Internet without seeing pictures of people.

All Muslims would agree, however, that depictions of the Prophet Muhammad that debase, belittle or otherwise disrespect his person and status are sinful. There have been several examples in recent years of Muslims taking offence at the publication of cartoons of Muhammad. Some of these situations, such as that involving the French magazine, Charlie Hebdo, have led to conflict and terrorist violence.

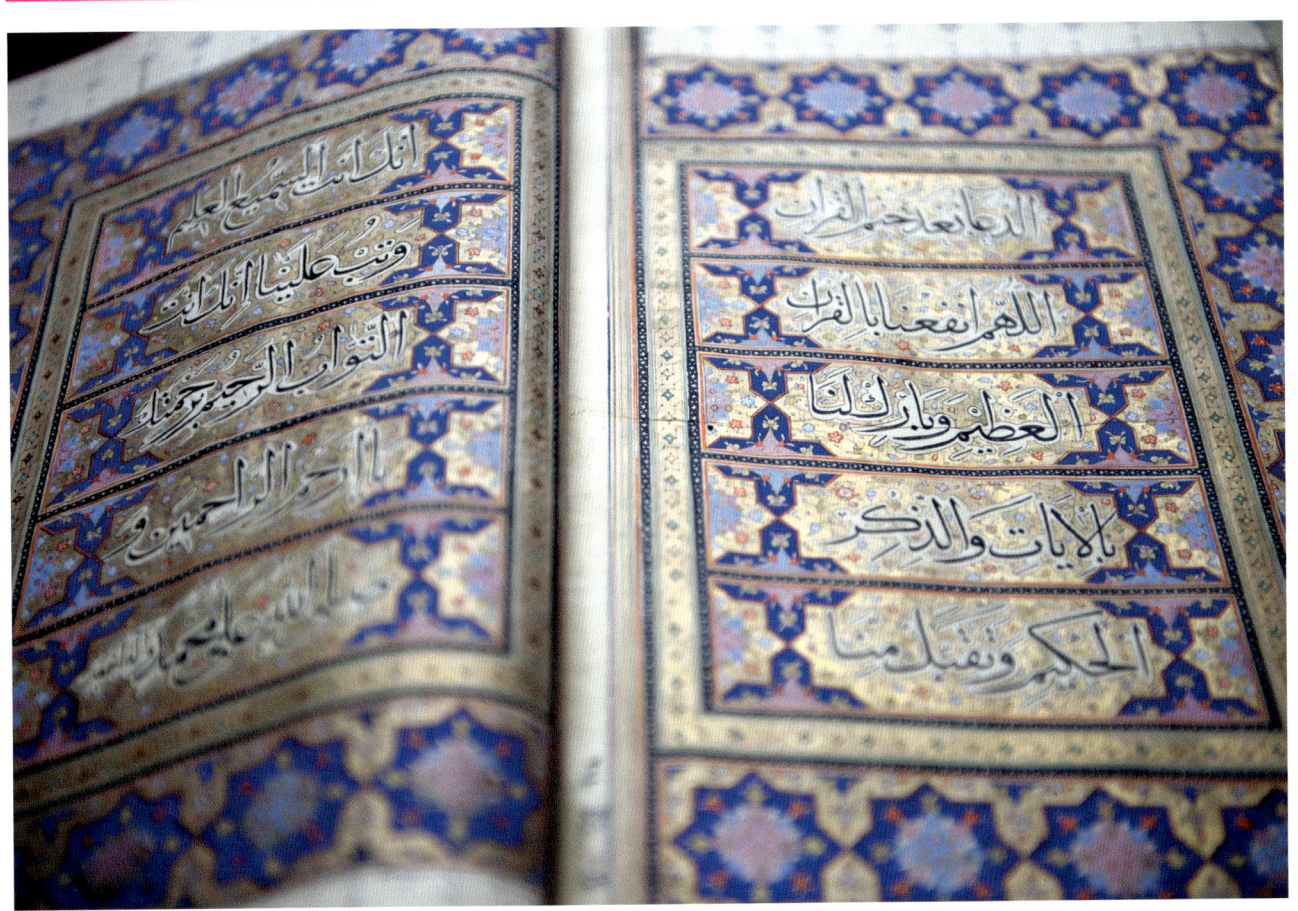

The Fatihah (the Opening) is the first chapter of the Qur'an. It is a prayer for the guidance and mercy of God. This image, drawn as a form of calligraphy, shows the way Muslims can create beautiful art without using pictures of people or animals.

The Qur'an

Sources of authority in Islam

Islam teaches that there is a divine law, sent by God, to guide human beings in the right way to live. They believe that this law is set out in the Qur'an, which is the perfect communication from God to humans. However, not every single area of life is covered by its teachings, so Muslims also look to a number of other sources of **authority** to help guide them, such as Hadith, Sunnah, Shari'ah, imams and Islamic traditions and scholars.

> **Authority** The idea that something or someone is in charge of what is right or wrong. We look to an authority to guide our own understanding and decision-making.

> **Key Concepts**
>
> **Qur'an** That which is read or recited. The divine book revealed to the Prophet Muhammad. Allah's final revelation to humankind.
>
> **Hadith** Saying; report; account. The sayings of the Prophet Muhammad, as recounted by his household, descendants and companions. These are a major source of Islamic law.

Islamic holy books: God's message

Muslims believe that God has sent messages and messengers to set out the laws and moral codes by which humanity should live. These communications are called revelations. The most significant among them is the Qur'an, God's final written word.

Islam teaches that God revealed his laws in stages, through his prophets, beginning with Adam, and so Muslims have respect for all previous scriptures from the messengers of God. However, they believe the Qur'an is the completion of all these earlier books (some of which have been lost and others corrupted). Uniquely, the Qur'an is understood to be the sacred text perfectly inspired by God and thus free from any mistakes or distortion.

> The Arabic word for book is 'kitab' (plural 'kutub'). The Qur'an is known as Umm-ul-Kitab, 'Mother of the Book' (43.4).

> **Task**
>
> Write two sentences to explain what Muslims believe is unique about the Qur'an.

> *… It is he who has brought the Qur'an down upon your heart, [O Muhammad], by permission of Allah, confirming that which was before it and as guidance and good tidings for the believers. Whoever is an enemy to Allah and His angels and His messengers and Gabriel and Michael – then indeed, Allah is an enemy to the disbelievers.*
>
> (Qur'an 2.97)

The Qur'an: God's perfect revelation

Muslims believe that the Qur'an is the direct and perfect word of God. Sunni Muslims say that it has always existed and is with God in heaven, written in Arabic on a tablet of stone. The Qur'an introduces itself as being 'the guidance for the worlds' (3.96), and Muslims believe that God has sent down this guidance in the form of a book to give a solution to any human problem.

> The Qur'an refers to Jews and Christians as the 'People of the Scripture' (29.46). It teaches that Muslims should show particular respect to them, because they too worship the one, true (Abrahamic) God.

> *… We have sent down to you the Book as clarification for all things and as guidance and mercy and good tidings for the Muslims.*
>
> (Qur'an 16.89)

Muslims respect and honour the Qur'an and use it as a guide for their lives. It teaches them how to worship, how to treat other people and how to live good lives. It contains advice on showing kindness to parents, a warning not to be wasteful, instructions on keeping promises, being honest and refraining from gossip, a prohibition on adultery and a reminder to help the poor. Some Muslims learn it by heart in Arabic, reading and reciting it daily; they take immense care in writing it out; they allow it to guide every action and thought.

The Qur'an is the perfect and direct word of God as revealed to the Prophet Muhammad.

The Qur'an is the most important source of authority in Islam. Muslims believe that the Qur'an:

- is the complete book of guidance for all human beings
- was revealed by God to the Prophet Muhammad (through the Angel Jibril) over a period of 23 years
- was written down by his followers and compiled into one book shortly after the Prophet's death in 632 CE
- must be studied and learnt in Arabic (its original language), because its words must not be altered.

Niyyah Having the right intention, having one's heart turned towards God.

Qur'an means reading or recitation. The Angel Jibril instructed Prophet Muhammad to recite or proclaim the words God was giving him. The Qur'an was revealed as a living sound and it must be spoken to reveal its beauty and truth.

Niyyah: intention

Niyyah means having the right intention to worship God. Muslims believe that it is important to have 'God consciousness' (taqwa). They may not always be in the right mood to worship God, or they may feel unworthy to meet him, but it is important to dedicate that time to being in his presence in prayer. Sometimes there may be a strong feeling that God is present and at other times he may seem distant, but God is merciful and judges the desire to communicate with him, even if someone feels they do not succeed.

Many Muslims report that the practice of reciting the Qur'an in Arabic is a deep and overwhelming experience. The words have a power and a beauty that outsiders find hard to grasp.

In fact, Islam teaches that the Qur'an is meant to be recited and heard, and when it is spoken in the presence of others it brings blessings and spiritual awareness. For many Muslims it is an

Hafiz Someone who has succeeded in memorising the whole Qur'an in Arabic.

ambition to be able to learn all 114 surahs and thus recite the whole Qur'an from heart; such a person is called a **hafiz**.

> As the students learn these surahs, they are not simply learning something by rote (off by heart), but rather interiorising the inner rhythms, sound patterns, and textual dynamics – taking it to heart in the deepest manner.
> (Michael Sells, *Approaching the Qur'an*)

Muslims believe it is important to respect the Qur'an as God's eternal message to human beings. It contains powerful accounts that are memorable for young and old alike. For example:

- The Garden of Paradise, Adam and Eve, Satan and the Tree
- The Ark of Nuh and the great flood
- The Prophet Yusuf who had an unusual dream
- The Prophet King Dawud who defeated a giant
- The honourable young girl Maryam who gave birth to a son (Isa) who performed many miracles
- The teachings and wise actions of Muhammad, often referred to as the Prophet or the Messenger.

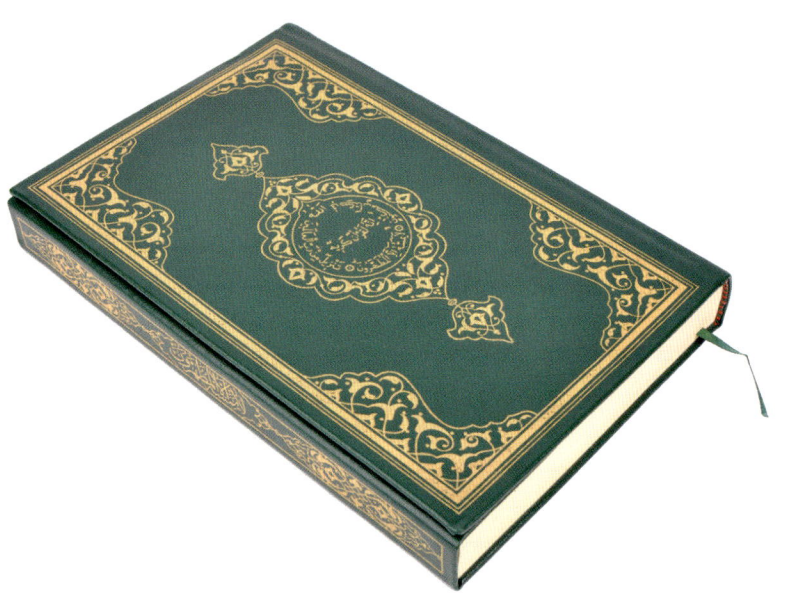

Tasks

1 Who are the 'People of the Book'?
2 Explain why the Qur'an instructs Muslims to show respect to the People of the Book.
3 Make a list of the things Muslims do which shows they treat the Qur'an with honour and respect.
4 Why do Muslims say the Qur'an should be read and studied in Arabic?
5 What is a hafiz?
6 Why do you think Muslims believe it is a special achievement to become a hafiz?

> The Qur'an is not the Qur'an unless it is heard.
> (Kristina Nelson, *The Art of Reciting the Qur'an*)

Tasks

1 Use the Search Truth website to listen to some Surahs from the Qur'an: www.searchtruth.com/quran_recitation/recite.php.
2 Look up the translations of these passages and copy out some of the verses (ayat). Try to write down what the sound of the Qur'an being read makes you feel like.

The Qur'an is arranged into chapters (surahs) and verses (ayat). It contains 114 surahs and 6,616 ayat.

The Shari'ah: the Muslim way of life

The **Shari'ah** law sets out the moral and religious rules that Muslims must follow. It puts into practice the principles set out by the Qur'an, the Sunnah and the Hadith, so by following Shari'ah law, Muslims can know that they are obeying the will of God. Shari'ah lays down laws about what is **fard** (obligatory or compulsory), **halal** (allowable) and what is **haram** (forbidden). It deals with many everyday topics, setting out rules for Muslims on personal matters like prayer, food (see page 117), clothing, crime, money, sex and relationships.

Shari'ah (straight path) A way of life for Muslims; Islam teaches that God has set out a clear path to guide how people should live. Shari'ah law is the set of moral and religious rules that puts the principles set out by the Qur'an and the Hadith into practice.

Fard (obligatory) Actions that must be carried out, such as wudu before the five daily prayers.

Haram (forbidden) Any actions or things which are forbidden within Islam, such as eating forbidden foods.

Kutub: holy books

The Qur'an names four other holy books, known in Arabic as kutub. These are from the Jewish and Christian traditions and, according to Islam, in their original form, they were true revelations from God. However, Muslims believe that because they were not properly written down or preserved, they are now said to be corrupted. So, unlike the perfect Qur'an, they cannot be trusted to be the true word of God.

- Sahifah: the Scrolls of Ibrahim, now lost
- Tawrat (Torah): the revelation given to Musa (Moses)
- Zabur (Psalms): given to Dawud (David)
- Injil (Gospel): the teaching given to Isa (Jesus)

Tasks

1. What books, other than the Qur'an, are sacred to Muslims?
2. Can you explain why these books have special status?
3. Why do they have less significance than the Qur'an?

> We believe in God, and the revelation given to us, and to Abraham, Isma'il, Isaac, Jacob . . . Moses and Jesus, and that given to all prophets from their Lord: We make no difference between one and another.
>
> (Qur'an 2.136)

Revelation A message sent by God and 'revealed' or shown to the human mind.

▶ Revelation: God reveals his truth

Islam teaches that God does not communicate directly with humans, but instead he uses special beings (prophets and angels) to carry his message to us.

Muslims believe that, because all humans have a duty to serve God, he must have shown us what his will is. As humans, we can only know what is truly right and wrong by understanding God's laws. Since God is just, it makes sense to believe that God has a duty to show us the right path to follow.

The channel of communication between God and humanity is called risalah; the prophets are our guides. They are human beings chosen to carry guidance from God to people, but their wisdom does not come from within themselves; it comes from God.

The Qur'an teaches that every generation has been given its own prophet, bringing God's message in a book. The message brought by the Prophet Muhammad is essentially the same message as had been preached by all the prophets back to Adam: the need to worship the one, true God, who will be the judge of all.

Revelation is the idea that God has made known his special truth to humans. Islam teaches that the prophets received God's divinely inspired message, instructing humans how to live. God's final and perfect message was given to the Prophet Muhammad, sent down to him over the last 23 years of his life. Each passage was memorised and recorded by his followers and then later written down to form the Qur'an, the final revelation.

> This is the Book about which there is no doubt, a guidance for those conscious of Allah.
>
> (Qur'an 2.2)

Tasks

1. What do Muslims call the people who receive God's divinely inspired messages?
2. Why is the idea of revelation important in Islam?

> Indeed, We sent the Qur'an down during the Night of Decree. And what can make you know what is the Night of Decree? The Night of Decree is better than a thousand months. The angels and the Spirit descend therein by permission of their Lord for every matter. Peace it is until the emergence of dawn.
>
> (Qur'an 97.1–5)

God reveals the Qur'an to Muhammad

God's first revelation to Muhammad occurred in the year 610 CE. Muhammad was praying in a cave near Makkah (Mecca) and he had an experience that would change his life. As he sat meditating, the Angel Jibril appeared before him and ordered him to recite the words that had miraculously appeared before him. Muslims call this event Laylat-ul-Qadr, the Night of Power, and they remember it today on the 27th day of Ramadan. It is one of the holiest days of the Muslim year.

The Qur'an itself emphasises that Jibril brought God's words to Muhammad with full authority:

> Say (O Muhammad, to mankind): Who is an enemy to Gabriel! For he it is who hath revealed (this Scripture) to thy heart by Allah's leave, confirming that which was (revealed) before it, and a guidance and glad tidings to believers; Who is an enemy to Allah, and His angels and His messengers, and Gabriel and Michael! Then, lo! Allah (Himself) is an enemy to the disbelievers.
>
> (Qur'an 2.97–98)

Pilgrims at the Cave of Hira where the Qur'an was first revealed to the Prophet Muhammad on Laylat-ul-Qadr, in 610 CE.

Task

Write a summary (2–3 short paragraphs) of the Prophet Muhammad's message to the people of Makkah.

> Say, 'I am not something original among the messengers, nor do I know what will be done with me or with you. I only follow that which is revealed to me, and I am not but a clear warner.'
>
> (Qur'an 46.9)

Revelations such as these were to continue for the next 23 years, until the Prophet Muhammad's death. He did not always see the Angel Jibril. Sometimes he heard a voice speaking to him, sometimes these revelations took place while he was in prayer and at other times when he was going about his everyday life, but they always had a dramatic effect on him.

> Not once did I receive a revelation without thinking that my soul had been torn away.
>
> (Hadith)

Prophet Muhammad brought God's message to the people of Makkah. In essence, it was:

- There is one true God, Lord of goodness and power.
- We need to show thanks to God through worship.
- There will be a judgement day where God will judge our lives.

Many in Makkah did not receive this message well. The Prophet Muhammad was ridiculed and insulted. However, some did follow him and they became known as 'Muslims'.

The Sunnah and the Hadith

Muslims believe the Qur'an is perfect and complete, but there are occasions when they need to understand things that are not covered in its pages. At these times they turn to the **Sunnah** and the Hadith, the actions and words of the Prophet Muhammad. What the Prophet Muhammad said the Qur'an meant, or what Muhammad did or said is the next best guide for a Muslim.

Sunnah The actions of Prophet Muhammad.

The Sunnah: the way of the Prophet

The Sunnah is the record of all that Prophet Muhammad did, and this helps guide Muslims today to live a life that is pleasing to God. The Prophet Muhammad is an inspiration to all Muslims, so they try to imitate the way he lived. The Sunnah:

- is the second most important source of authority for Muslims
- describes the customs, practices and traditions of the Prophet Muhammad
- teaches the perfect path or model of how Muslims should live.

Some Sunnahs provide practical examples of daily living from the life of the Prophet:

> Aisha [the wife of the Prophet] said about the Prophet: 'He used to sleep early at night, and get up in its last part to pray, and then return to his bed.'

Some give details of what the Prophet Muhammad was like:

> I'bn Jaz reports: 'I have not seen anyone who smiled more than the Messenger of Allah.'

There is even dietary advice:

> Miqdam bin Madikarib said: 'I heard the Messenger of Allah say: "A human being fills no worse vessel than his stomach. It is sufficient for a human being to eat a few mouthfuls to keep his spine straight. But if he must (fill it), then one third of food, one third for drink and one third for air."'

The Hadith: the sayings of the Prophet

Muslims love and respect the words of Prophet Muhammad because he was such an outstanding character. He had deep devotion to God, but he was also a man of enormous wisdom, kindness and compassion. The Hadith is a book that contains his sayings, as recorded by his family and companions. There are different collections of these sayings, each accepted by different Muslim groups.

> The warrior who truly fights for God's cause is he who looks after a widow or a poor person.
> (Hadith)

> If you think of God, you will find Him there before you.
> (Hadith)

> **Tasks**
>
> 1 What is the Sunnah?
> 2 What is the Hadith?
> 3 Although Muslims treat the Hadith with enormous respect, explain why you think it is not regarded as sacred in the same way as the Qur'an?

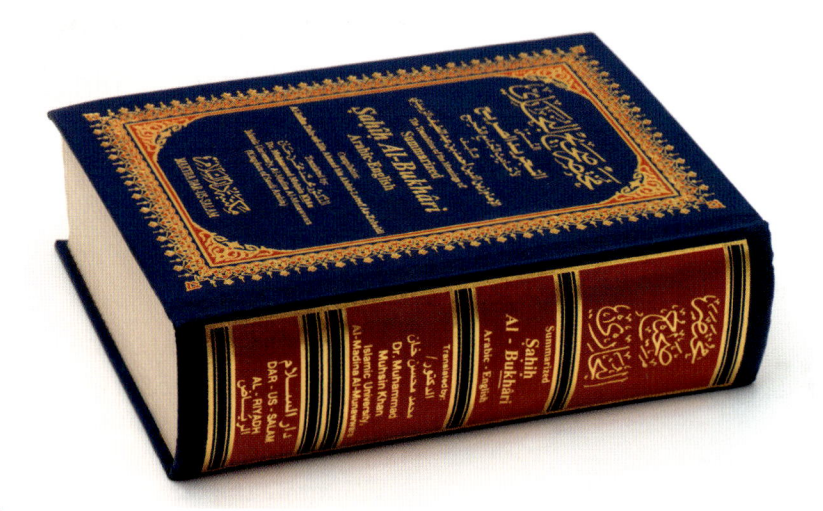

The Hadith are the sayings of the Prophet Muhammad.

In the Hadith, there is an account of Prophet Muhammad's last sermon, delivered in Makkah shortly before his death. Here he instructed his followers to be obedient to the teachings set out in the Qur'an and the Sunnah:

> I have left among you that which if you hold fast to, then you would never go astray, clear things, the book of God and the Sunnah of his prophet.

▶ How Muslims show respect for the Qur'an

Since Islam teaches that the Qur'an contains the same words from God that were revealed to Prophet Muhammad, the book is treated with great respect. It has been passed on unchanged to this day. This is why it is important that Muslims, whatever their nationality and native tongue, will recite and study the Qur'an in its original Arabic. In this way, they can be sure that the meaning of what they read has not been altered in translation.

It is usually wrapped in a cloth to protect it and placed on a higher shelf than other books to show its superiority. Muslims wash thoroughly before touching it and, when reading from it, place it on a stand rather than directly on a table that is used for everyday tasks. Muslims' respect for the Qur'an is shown in practical ways. For example, while it is being read, they must not eat or drink, speak or make any unnecessary noise. Before reading, it is important to wash carefully and make sure you are in the right frame of mind (niyyah). It is not permitted for a woman to read it if she is having a period.

> Indeed, it is a noble Qur'an in a Register well-protected; None touch it except the purified.

(Qur'an 56.77–79)

Because the Qur'an is believed to be the direct of word of God, the words themselves have great significance. Some Muslims (hafiz) try to immerse themselves in the message of God by learning it and being able to recite it from memory.

Ultimately, Muslims show respect for the Qur'an (as God's messages to humankind) by trying to live out its message in their daily lives.

> **Task**
>
> Make a bulleted list of ways in which Muslims show respect for the Qur'an.

End of Section Review

Stickability

Key concepts:
- Hadith
- Qur'an
- Shahadah
- Shirk
- Tawhid

Key teachings:
- The nature of God
- The Shahadah
- The meaning of submission
- The Qur'an and other sources of authority in Islam

Skills Link

1. What is meant by 'hadith'?
2. Explain the Muslim belief about the oneness of Allah.

Knowledge Check

1. Write a short paragraph (roughly three sentences) to explain what Muslims believe about God (Allah).
2. Why is 'submission to God' important to Muslims?
3. Where do Muslims believe the Qur'an came from?

The Big Question

'The Qur'an is the only book Muslims need.'

Your Task

Respond to the statement above, showing that you have considered more than one point of view. Give reasoned judgements on the validity and strength of these views.

Task

You need to explain in detail religious teachings about shirk (different views on the core beliefs of Islam). Use the guidance below to help you to write a developed explanation for Islam. Ensure that you use key terms fluently and frequently.

All/many/most Muslims believe that _____.

This comes from the teaching/ quote _____.

This means that/Because of this they _____.

Some/other Muslims such as _____ believe that _____.

This comes from the teaching/ quote_____.

This means that/Because of this they _____.

Finally, Muslims such as _____ believe that _____.

This means that/Because of this they_____.

Their beliefs do/do not differ because _____.

6 Islam: Practices

■ The Five Pillars of Sunni Islam

> **Ibadah**
>
> For Muslims, actions speak louder than words, and it is not enough just to have faith in God; they believe it is necessary to show religious commitment through the way they live their entire lives. Every action is a form of worship; this is called **ibadah**. People in Western countries sometimes think that religions are just sets of beliefs, or a collection of optional faith-based activities. However, Muslims have always been very clear that Islam is a complete way of life. Worship is a 24/7 reality, to be lived fully, not just as an after-thought to add on to our secular lives.

Ibadah Acts of worship; any permissible action performed with the intention of obeying God.

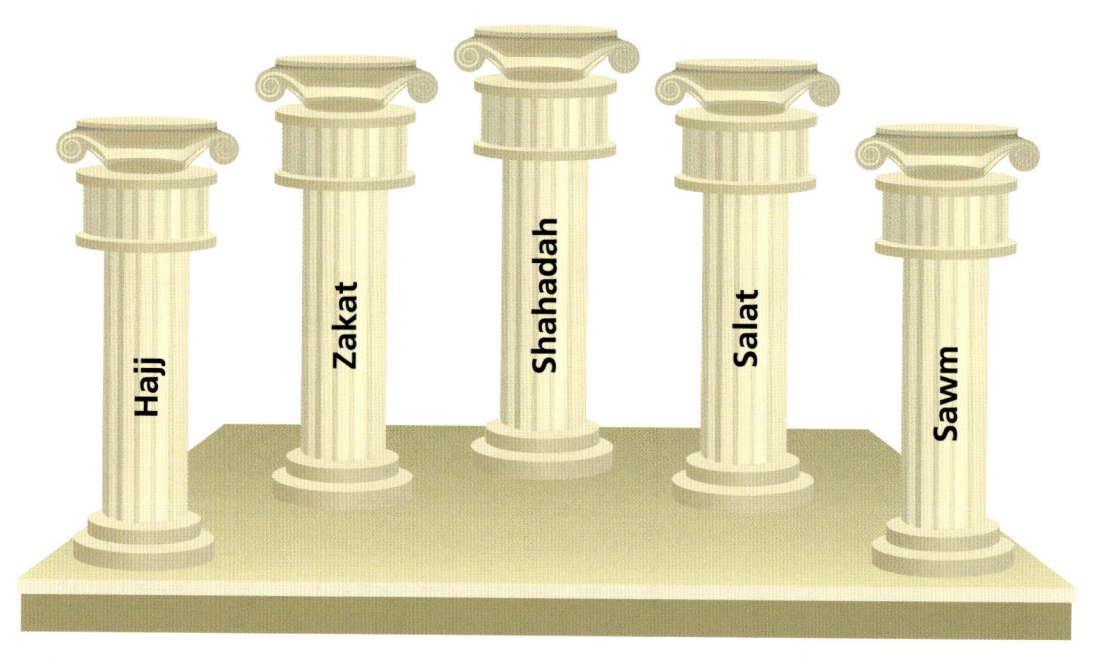

The Five Pillars

Islam teaches that all Muslims have a duty to worship God by following the Five Pillars. These actions are all ibadah, acts of worship carried out with the intention of obeying God. They are:

- Shahadah: the declaration of faith that says 'There is no god but God and Muhammad is his prophet'
- **Salat**: prayer, five times a day
- **Zakat**: charity, giving money to the poor
- **Sawm**: fasting during the month of Ramadan
- Hajj: pilgrimage to Makkah.

By following these rules, Muslims believe that they can show their obedience to the will of God. The Shari'ah (Islamic law) sets out the Five Pillars as religious duties; they are practical signs that demonstrate true submission to the divine creator. They must be carried out with niyyah, the true intention to submit to the will of God (see page 97). Muslims say that there can be no doubt that they have been instructed by God to complete the Five Pillars. The Qur'an contains many references to their importance and, in his last sermon, Prophet Muhammad makes clear mention of them:

> O People, listen to me in earnest, worship God, perform your five daily prayers, fast during the month of Ramadan, and offer Zakat. Perform Hajj if you have the means.
>
> (The Prophet Muhammad's last sermon, Hadith)

Tasks

1. Summarise the Five Pillars. Draw an image of a building with the roof supported by Five Pillars. On each of the pillars write the name of one of the five Pillars of Islam, with a brief description of each duty.
2. In pairs, test each other at matching the names of the pillars (in English and Arabic) to the descriptions.

Obligatory Acts in Islam

According to Islamic Law (Shari'ah), certain acts are fard (**obligatory**) (see page 98). This means there is a list of things that a Muslim must do, if they are to follow their religion. Examples of these compulsory practices are: the five daily prayers (Salat), paying some of their earnings to the poor (Zakat) and fasting during Ramadan (Sawm). Muslims who follow these duties will be rewarded. If they fail to carry them out, they will face punishment from God.

Obligatory acts (fard) Practices that a Muslim must follow. These are set out in the Islamic Law (Shari'ah).

▶ Prayer (Salat)

One of the Five Pillars is Salat, the practice of prayer.

For Muslims, prayer is the most important way to worship God. It is a duty for all Muslims to pray five times a day. Prophet Muhammad called prayer the 'pillar of religion' and it reminds Muslims to give thanks for God's blessings and of the importance of submitting to God's will. It is a physical, mental and spiritual activity that draws believers close to God.

Muslims should try to pray at the allocated times, set out clearly in the Islamic prayer schedule for every day of the year but, if they miss a prayer, then it is acceptable to catch up later. However, it would be seen as a sin to miss prayers regularly without a valid reason.

> If one of you sleeps and misses a prayer, or forgets it, let him offer the prayer when he remembers.
>
> (Hadith)

Tasks

1. Explain why you think Muslims believe it is so important to follow their religious duties?
2. Which of the Five Pillars would you argue to be the most important to Muslims? Explain why.

> ### Why do Muslims pray five times a day?
>
> Both the Qur'an and the Hadith contain the story of Prophet Muhammad's night journey. It tells how Muhammad was woken from his sleep and taken on a winged horse to Jerusalem and then up through seven levels of heaven, to the very presence of God. Here, God revealed to Prophet Muhammad that Muslims must pray continuously, 50 times a day. Worship must be a constant presence throughout life. However, Musa (Moses) intervened and said this was too much, and eventually it was agreed that there must be five prayer times each day.

Salat is a duty for all Muslims.

The call to prayer (adhan)

The **adhan** is the Islamic call to prayer which is heard before each of the five daily prayer times (Salat). Traditionally, a muezzin would call the adhan from the top of a **minaret**, but nowadays it is usually broadcast around the building through the mosque sound system. When a faithful Muslim hears the adhan, they will respond to the call of the **muezzin** by starting their preparations for prayer.

> **Minaret** Tall tower connected to a mosque from which the call to prayer is made.
> **Muezzin** The man who recites the call to prayer from a mosque.

> ### Key Concepts
>
> **Salat** Prescribed communication with and worship of Allah, performed under specific conditions, in the manner taught by the Prophet Muhammad, and recited in Arabic. Muslims believe that the five times of Salat are fixed by Allah.
>
> **Adhan** Call to prayer, usually performed by a muezzin.

6 Islam: Practices

[1] Allahu Akbar
God is Great
(said four times)

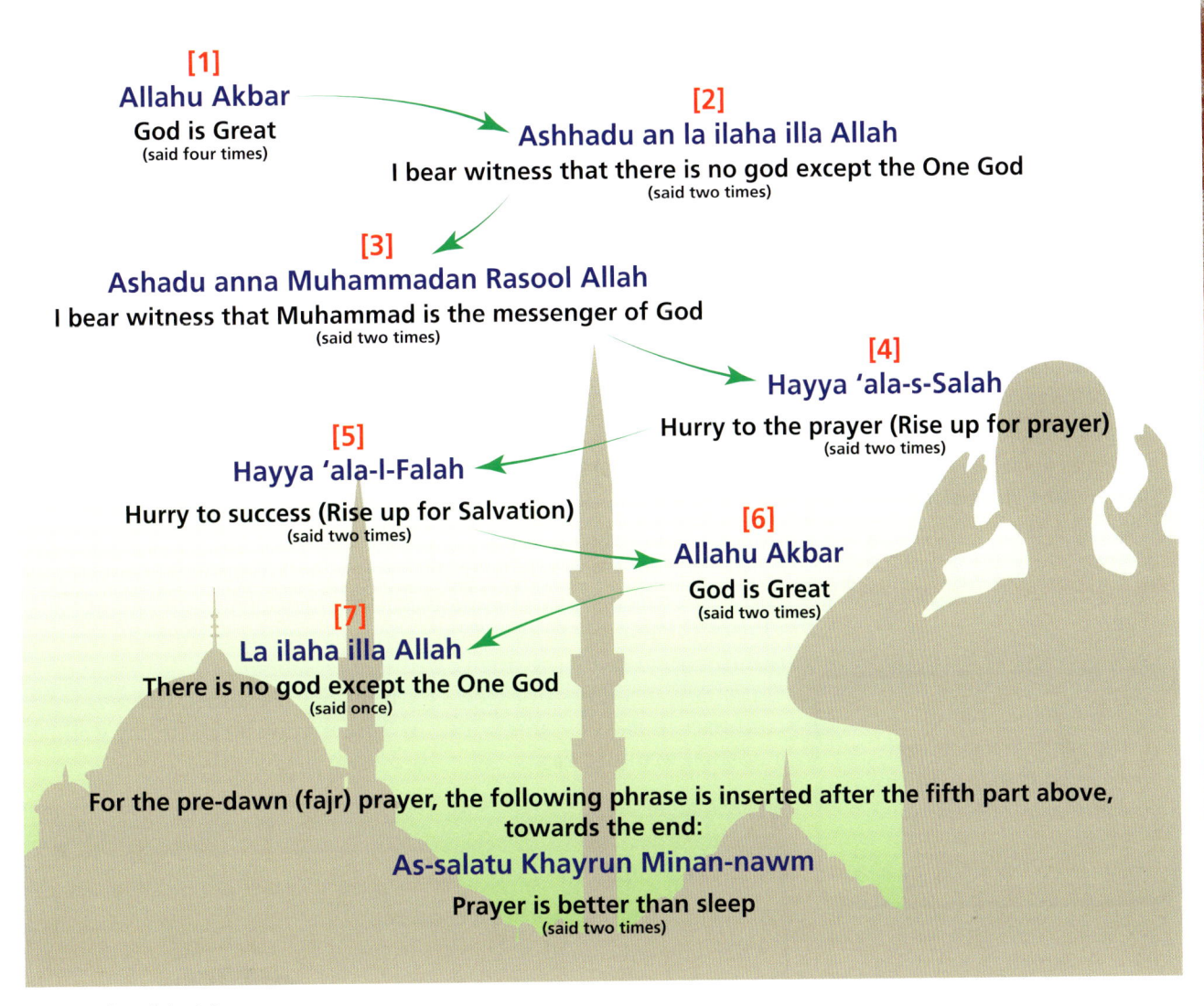

[2] Ashhadu an la ilaha illa Allah
I bear witness that there is no god except the One God
(said two times)

[3] Ashadu anna Muhammadan Rasool Allah
I bear witness that Muhammad is the messenger of God
(said two times)

[4] Hayya 'ala-s-Salah
Hurry to the prayer (Rise up for prayer)
(said two times)

[5] Hayya 'ala-l-Falah
Hurry to success (Rise up for Salvation)
(said two times)

[6] Allahu Akbar
God is Great
(said two times)

[7] La ilaha illa Allah
There is no god except the One God
(said once)

For the pre-dawn (fajr) prayer, the following phrase is inserted after the fifth part above, towards the end:

As-salatu Khayrun Minan-nawm
Prayer is better than sleep
(said two times)

The meaning of the Adhan.

Tasks

1 The website www.haqaonline.com/multimedia/audio/Azan has a number of different renditions of the adhan. Listen to the adhan being called in different ways. How do they compare? Write down your impressions of each.

2 In these video clips, what do the images suggest about the importance of the call to prayer?
- www.youtube.com/watch?v=4_LN0hznp-A
- www.youtube.com/watch?v=zBNUdeWw-wE
- www.youtube.com/watch?v=Dw3kRv6SVN0

The Five Pillars of Sunni Islam

Praying at the mosque

Many Muslims like to go to pray at the mosque, especially for Friday prayers, because praying with others builds the ummah (community of Muslims) and strengthens personal faith. Some also believe that an individual who prays at the mosque receives a greater blessing from God. Worshippers often gather informally in the prayer room before and after Salat prayers, to say their own **du'ah** (personal) prayers. When it is time for the Salat prayers, the adhan will be heard and they will line up, shoulder to shoulder, at the front of the prayer room, facing **qibla**. Women will pray in a separate area or at the back of the prayer room, behind the men.

Jummah prayers

In Islam, Friday is the day when Muslims come together at the mosque for **congregational** prayers. Muslim men are expected to gather for the Friday midday (Zuhr) prayers. Women may attend these community prayers, but traditionally they pray at home. One of the main features of the Jummah prayers is the sermon (khutbah) given by the imam. Unlike the Sabbath for Jews and Christians, Friday is not seen as a 'holy' day. In some Muslim countries, it is a day of rest, but in Western countries it may well be a normal working day.

Mosque A 'place of prostration' for Muslims; it is a communal place of worship for a Muslim community (Arabic: masjid).

Qibla The direction to face during prayer (towards Makkah).

Congregational All together, praying as a whole community (the ummah). Jummah prayers in the mosque are congregational prayers.

Salat is the pillar of the Islamic religion, and whoever abandons it, demolishes the very pillar of religion.

(Hadith)

How to pray

The Qur'an and the Sunnah give Muslims clear guidance on how and when to pray. Salat takes place five times a day:

- Fajr (just after dawn)
- Zuhr (just after midday)
- As'r (late afternoon)
- Maghrib (just after sunset)
- Isha (after dark).

■ Time given for each of the daily prayers.

Task

What are the key features of Jummah prayers?

Praying at home

When Muslims pray at home they must ensure they have a quiet, clean place to bow and prostrate. If possible they will use a room set aside for prayer where people never wear their shoes, ensuring that no dirt has been trodden into the carpet. Women and children often pray at home rather than the mosque, but there are no fixed rules about this. Praying at home allows the worshipper to feel more comfortable about the way they pray. They may feel less inhibited about performing their own du'ah (private) prayers too.

Du'ah (personal) prayer

Salat prayers are a duty for all Muslims (apart from young children), five times a day, but people who love God will often choose to find time to make their own personal connection with God. There are no set times for du'ah prayers; they are spontaneous opportunities to spend time in the presence of God. A prayer for yourself, for your family or to ask for help for someone else is a du'ah prayer. Some Muslims try to make their first thought when they wake in the morning, and their last thought before sleep at night, to be focused on God. Du'ah prayers may take many forms such as:

- thanking God for a blessing
- pleading to God for help
- asking for forgiveness
- requests for guidance and blessings.

After the Salat (obligatory) prayers, Muslims may continue to praise God through their du'ah prayers. Some Muslims use prayer beads (subhah) to help them as an aid. The Prophet Muhammad advised Muslims to recite Subhanallah ("Glory be to Allah"), Alhamdulillah ("Praise be to Allah"), and Allahuakhbar ("Allah is great"), 33 times each, after each Salat. So a subhah may consist of 33 beads or 99 (33 x 3). 99 beads also represent the names of Allah. Some sects recite Subhanallah 34 times, so they use a subhah of 100 beads.

> **Key Concept**
>
> **Du'ah** Varying forms of personal prayer.

> **Tasks**
>
> 1. What are the key features of Du'ah prayers?
> 2. What are the key differences between Salat and Du'ah prayers?
> 3. Explain which type of prayer you think is the most important for a Muslim? Why?

Prayer beads consist of 33, 99 or 100 beads.

Preparation for prayer

A Muslim can pray anywhere, so long as it is clean and there is enough space to stand, kneel and bow, facing towards the Ka'ba in Makkah. Muslims often pray at home, but they are encouraged to go to the mosque to pray whenever they can, because congregational prayers increase the togetherness they experience when they gather in one place. This emphasises the importance of the ummah, the Muslim community.

Finding a place to pray

Prayer can never be an ordinary act for Muslims, because they believe that in prayer they make direct contact with God. So, wherever a Muslim prays, it must be done with the right intention and with proper preparation.

Muslims usually pray using a prayer mat. This literally separates them from the ordinary world and symbolises the connection between the person praying and God. It also ensures that the place of prayer is clean. Cleanliness is the most important thing, so if the place of prayer is already clean, a mat is not necessary. However, many Muslims prefer not to pray directly on the ground, so might use any clean object, such as a sheet or towel, if a mat is unavailable or inconvenient.

Muslims must pray facing Makkah (this direction is called qibla). They use special compasses that show the *qibla* from any place in the world. Some prayer mats have *qibla* compass sewn into them, and *qibla* apps can be downloaded onto phones and tablets.

Niyyah (intention)

Preparation for prayer is vital because coming into the presence of God requires a deep sense of respect and reverence. Prayer begins with a declaration of intent (niyyah). It must be a deliberate act, to set aside a few minutes to focus on God and enter into a state of 'God consciousness'. This allows Muslims to concentrate on God's greatness, to thank and praise him and ask for his forgiveness.

Wudu: ablution (washing)

Before starting to pray, Muslims must practise **wudu**, washing specific parts of the body: hands, mouth, nose, face, arms, head and feet, in a particular order. This is an outward sign of the inner cleanliness needed to face God.

The aims of prayer

The aims of prayer are:

- to be a constant reminder of the presence of God
- to show submission to the will of God
- to cleanse away the corruption of the world
- to unite all Muslims
- to bring about peace in the world
- to remove sins, just as water removes dirt.

Task

Recite, [O Muhammad], what has been revealed to you of the Book and establish prayer. Indeed, prayer prohibits immorality and wrongdoing, and the remembrance of Allah is greater. And Allah knows that which you do.
(Qur'an 29.45)

So exalt [Allah] with praise of your Lord and be of those who prostrate [to Him]. And worship your Lord until there comes to you a certainty [i.e. death].
(Qur'an 15.98–99)

Use the above quotations to explain why prayer is important for Muslims.

Wudu Washing in preparation for prayer.

Task

Why do you think is it important for a Muslim to be in the right frame of mind (niyyah) as they prepare for prayer?

> And when you have completed the prayer, remember God standing, sitting, or [lying] on your sides. But when you become secure, re-establish [regular] prayer. Indeed, prayer has been decreed upon the believers a decree of specified times.
>
> (Qur'an 4.103)

The rak'ats

A **rak'at** is a sequence of movements, following a set pattern, which make up the prayer routine. The different prayers during the day require different numbers of rak'ats. Prayers follow a set pattern, but the physical movements are less important than the intention in the heart.

At the appropriate point during worship, the worshipper will:

- stand quietly, reciting prayers from the Qur'an. This acknowledges the majesty of God, shutting out all other distractions, thoughts and desires.
- bow low, with hands on knees. This shows respect and love for God.
- prostrate on the floor. This shows full submission to God.
- kneel with feet folded under body. A posture of humility.
- stand, reciting 'Peace be upon you, and God's blessing', once facing to the right, once facing to the left. This shows respect for other worshippers and for the guardian angels.

Takbeerat   Al-Qiyam   Ruku'   Qiyam

Sajjah   Tashahhud   Salam

The sequence of movements that make up a rak'at.

Tasks

1. What is the meaning of the physical activities during Salat?
2. Can you explain how these physical movements might make a difference to the way a Muslim feels?

> And when you have completed the prayer, remember God standing, sitting, or [lying] on your sides. But when you become secure, re-establish [regular] prayer. Indeed, prayer has been decreed upon the believers a decree of specified times.
>
> (Qur'an 4.103)

The Five Pillars of Sunni Islam

Obligatory acts

Shahadah: the declaration of faith

The Shahadah is the Muslim declaration of faith in Allah and the Prophet Muhammad, and it forms the central pillar of belief in Islam.

The Shahadah says:

> There is no god worthy of worship except for God (Allah), and Muhammad is the messenger of God.

These words sum up all you have to believe to be a Muslim: to accept the unity of God and the prophethood of Muhammad. By saying these words, a Muslim is showing their commitment to the whole religion of Islam.

Muslims will say and hear the words of the Shahadah repeated many times every day:

- in the prayer rituals (Salat)
- in their own private prayers (du'ah)
- announced from the minaret in the call to prayer (the adhan).

We have seen that the Shahadah is recited:

- when a baby is born. In the **aqiqah** ceremony, the father whispers the Shahadah into the ear of a new born baby, making them the first words a child hears on coming into this world.
- when a Muslim is about to die. A Muslim who knows they are about to die will try to make these the final words they utter with their dying breath.
- when a soldier is going into battle. These may be the words on their lips as a commitment to their submission to the will of God.

It is also said when someone becomes a Muslim. All they have to do is to recite the Shahadah in front of witnesses.

Conversion or reversion

There are no ceremonies or rituals to welcome new believers to Islam. All one needs to do to become a Muslim is to recite the Shahadah. Some people refer to this as conversion, to change from one religion to another. Others call it reversion, saying that, because God is our creator, we were all born as worshippers of the true God and so, when we discover faith, we return (revert) to our natural faith.

Aqiqah A Muslim ceremony welcoming the birth of a baby.

Tasks

1. List the occasions when the Shahadah may be heard.
2. Why do you think it is so important for the Shahadah to be spoken at these times?

Famous converts

Famous people who are reported to have converted (or reverted) to Islam include: Yusuf Islam (Cat Stevens), Muhammad Ali, Shaquille O'Neal, Mike Tyson, Ellen Burstyn, Janet Jackson and Malcolm X.

> Whoever says, 'There is no god but God,' enters Paradise.
>
> (Hadith)

Tasks

1. Find out about people who have converted to Islam.
2. When someone accepts the religion of Islam, is it more accurate to call this conversion or reversion? Explain your views.

▶ Zakat: giving to the poor

The third pillar of Islam is Zakat, the practice of charity, giving money to the poor. All Muslims are expected to be charitable as a regular duty, giving 2.5 per cent of their wealth every year. Although Zakat is sometimes called a tax, most Muslims do not think of it in this way, but rather as a religious obligation. All Muslims can be sure that God will reward them for their acts of giving.

The Qur'an makes a clear command: to give to those in need, to widows, orphans and travellers. It is an obligation and a form of worship, to be generous and kind for the benefit of humanity. Zakat is closely associated with prayer; what value is it to pray for others if you are not prepared to share with them?

Giving is a sign of cleansing and purity. The Qur'an teaches that money may have a corrupting influence; wealth can be an evil thing, because it may cut people off from each other and from God. Zakat is a purifying influence, giving Muslims the opportunity to share their wealth and offering them a means of purification.

According to Islam, our wealth and our property are not ours; wealth is given to us by God, for the benefit of all humans. It is our duty to share the good fortune that we have received, not to hoard it and spend it purely for selfish reasons. Islam disapproves of gambling. Money should be shared, not wasted for personal satisfaction. Gambling is seen as a great sin, because it makes people dependent on chance rather than relying on God to provide.

> O you who have believed, spend from that which We have provided for you before there comes a Day in which there is no exchange and no friendship and no intercession. And the disbelievers – they are the wrongdoers.
>
> (Qur'an 2.254)

Khalifah A representative of God; a steward.

The Qur'an teaches that humans are **khalifahs** (God's representatives on earth). This means that we are stewards or trustees of the world; we do not own it, we are looking after it in trust, for God, to hand it on to our children and to future generations. Therefore, we should not view possessions as our own; they are on loan to us from God, so we do not have the absolute right to spend our money as we choose.

The practice of giving Zakat began when Prophet Muhammad was the ruler in Madinah. Muhammad had to fight many battles against those who persecuted Muslims. After the first battles, there were many orphans and widows, and the prophet instructed people to care for all those in need.

> The one who looks after and works for a widow and for a poor person is like a warrior fighting for God's cause.
>
> (Hadith)

Shi'a Muslims point out that the Qur'an demands that Zakat be paid on profits from farming or trading in gold and silver. This means it applies to very few people. Instead, they focus on the following verse from the Qur'an:

> And know that anything you obtain of war booty – then indeed, for Allah is one fifth of it and for the Messenger and for [his] near relatives and the orphans, the needy, and the [stranded] traveller
>
> (Surah 8.41)

So Shi'a Muslims pay 20 per cent of their surplus wealth in an act called Khums. Half of Khums money goes to Shi'a lawyers and scholars (for spending on their religious education or on their daily life), and half of it goes to the poor, orphans and the homeless.

How should Zakat be spent?

The Qur'an identifies a number of people who can receive Zakat: the poor, the needy and travellers. Today there are many Muslim aid agencies that distribute Zakat to support development in community projects in areas such as water supply, sanitation, healthcare and education.

Zakat cannot be used to build mosques, for funeral expenses, or to clear the debts of the deceased.

Muslim Aid is a charity that receives and distributes Zakat.

Saddaqah: giving from the heart

It is a duty for all Muslims to pay Zakat once a year, but Islam also teaches that voluntary giving is important too. **Saddaqah** is any good deed done out of compassion or generosity. It could be a gift of time, or of money to a homeless person. It might be a gift of help for others or a donation to a charity. Muslims often give saddaqah if they want forgiveness for a sin they have committed or if they want to thank God for something.

> A Muslim who plants a tree or sows a field, from which man, birds and animals can eat, is committing an act of charity.
>
> (Hadith)

Key Concepts

Zakat Purification of wealth by payment of annual almsgiving. An obligatory act of worship.

Saddaqah Voluntary payment or good action for charitable purposes.

Tasks

1. Explain the difference between Zakat and saddaqah.
2. Do you think it is a good attitude to think of our property as belonging to God, not us? Explain your views?
3. Why do Muslims disagree with gambling?
4. Do you agree that gambling is harmful?

Sawm, fasting during Ramadan

The fourth pillar of Islam is **Sawm**, the practice of fasting during the month of **Ramadan**. For Muslims, it is the holiest month of the year, being a time dedicated to self-discipline and spiritual reflection. Ramadan holds a special place in the Muslim calendar because it is believed to be the month in which the Prophet Muhammad received the first verses of the Qur'an, revealed to him by God.

Fasting is the deliberate control of the body and Muslims are expected to refrain from eating, drinking (including water), smoking and sexual intercourse from dawn to dusk for a period of 29/30 days. They must also abstain from evil thoughts, harmful actions and unkind speech.

The beginning of Ramadan is marked by the appearance of the new (crescent) moon in the sky, signalling the start of the new month. It ends 29/30 days later with the beginning of the tenth month, Shawwal, heralding the start of celebrations for **Id-ul-Fitr**.

According to the Qur'an, the fast must begin each day at first light and continue until dusk. At dawn, eating and drinking must cease at the moment when it becomes light enough to distinguish a black thread from a white one. Food and drink may only be consumed again at the end of the day, after dark.

A special meal, known as **suhur**, is eaten before dawn, and at dusk the fast is broken by the **iftar** meal, often consisting of dates and water, before a bigger meal is shared. These meals during Ramadan are often very social events, with family, neighbours and friends gathering in homes and mosques to provide for each other. In this way, Ramadan brings a very happy, community focus to Islamic society.

Celebrating the Qur'an

During Ramadan, Muslims gather at the mosque for extra night prayers. This includes the recitation of a section of the Qur'an each day, so that, by the end of the month, the whole Qur'an has been recited. All Muslims should try to attend the mosque on the 27th day of Ramadan to celebrate Laylat-ul-Qadr, the Night of Power (see page 100). This is remembered as the date of the first revelation of the Qur'an, when the Angel Jibril first visited Prophet Muhammad.

Why do Muslims fast?

Fasting during Ramadan is obligatory in Islam. That means it is not a matter of choice, it is a duty. Muslims believe that this was not a new instruction, from God to Prophet Muhammad, to fast. Many years before, Isa (Jesus) had taught his disciples to fast. Fasting has always been understood to be a spiritual act that brings a believer closer to God.

Muslims believe that the fast is important because it:

- is commanded in the Qur'an by God
- follows the example of the Prophet Muhammad (as set down in the Sunnah)
- celebrates the fact that God has given humans the Qur'an
- brings people closer to God
- is a reminder of the mercy and blessings of God
- helps Muslims to identify with the poor

Key Concept

Sawm Fasting from just before dawn until sunset. Abstinence is required from all food and drink as well as smoking and sexual relations.

Ramadan The ninth month of the Islamic calendar and the month of fasting.

Suhur The meal eaten before dawn, before fasting begins.

Iftar The meal eaten after the sun has set, when fasting has ended.

Id-ul-Fitr Celebrations marking the end of Ramadan.

Ramadan is the ninth month of the Islamic year. Muslims follow a lunar calendar which lasts 354 days; it is 11 days shorter than the solar year. This means every year Ramadan will come around one and a half weeks earlier that it did the previous (solar) year.

Task

Draw up a timetable for a Muslim teenager for a day during the month of Ramadan, showing when they would get up, go to bed, eat, pray, go to school etc. You might need to look up prayer times for your local mosque and times of sunrise and sunset.

- promotes self-control
- helps to recharge spiritual batteries
- unites Muslim communities (ummah).

Who should fast?

God has instructed all adult Muslims to fast during Ramadan. Children, from quite a young age, may begin to fast for just a few days in the month.

The Qur'an does allow certain people to be excused from the fast, for instance, if they are ill or travelling. However, they would be expected to make up the days at a later time.

The following passage from the Qur'an makes it clear that fasting has been 'decreed' by God: it is not an option. By fasting you will 'become righteous'; fasting will help you to develop into a more spiritual person.

> O you who have believed, decreed upon you is fasting as it was decreed upon those before you that you may become righteous – [Fasting for] a limited number of days. So who ever among you is ill or on a journey [during them] – then an equal number of other days [are to be made up]. And upon those who are able [to fast, but with hardship] – a ransom [as substitute] of feeding a poor person [each day]. And whoever volunteers excess – it is better for him. But to fast is best for you, if you only knew.
>
> (Qur'an 2.183–184)

'RAMADAN FAST IN UK "SHOULD BE SHORTENED" SAY SCHOLARS.'

Breaking the fast at the end of each day of Ramadan is often a social occasion, shared with family and friends.

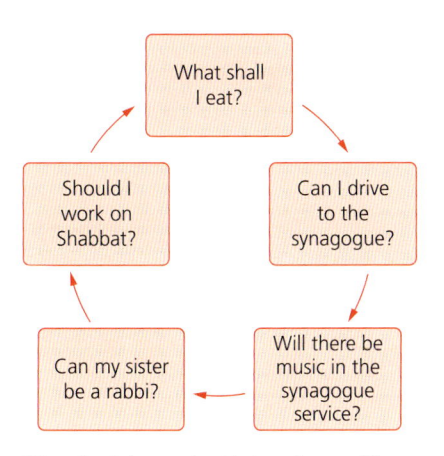

What shall I eat?
Should I work on Shabbat?
Can I drive to the synagogue?
Can my sister be a rabbi?
Will there be music in the synagogue service?

What Jewish people think on issues like these will be based on their interpretations of teachings from the Torah.

communities of Jews originally from different parts of the world. Although they have some different practices and use some different terms in worship, they have the same basic beliefs.

There are many different views among Jews concerning the degree of observance that is paid to the teachings of the Torah. Each Jew must decide if they will follow it all as originally intended or whether they believe that religion should adapt and change. The decision will make a difference to the way in which they live their lives.

Because there is a great diversity of beliefs and practices among Jews, it is difficult to specify exactly which beliefs they all have in common. In the twelfth century, **Rabbi** Moshe ben Maimon (known as Maimonides) put together 13 principal beliefs that were in the Torah. For many Orthodox Jews, these remain central beliefs. Some principles are accepted by all Jews, such as the belief in one God. For some principles, such as a belief in a Messiah, there are many different views and interpretations.

Maimonides' 13 principles of faith

1. God exists, is perfect and created everything in existence.
2. Belief in God's unity.
3. God does not have a physical body and so is not affected by the same needs as humans.
4. God is eternal.
5. Only God should be worshipped.
6. God communicates with people through prophets.
7. Moses is the most important prophet.
8. The Torah was given to Moses by God.
9. The Torah is God's law and cannot be changed.
10. God is all knowing and knows everything that is going to happen.
11. God will reward good and punish evil.
12. The belief that the Messiah will come.
13. The dead will be resurrected.

Tasks

1. Which of these statements do you think Maimonides would agree with?
   God's laws are given through human beings
   God only existed at the time of creation
   There is only one God
   God looks like a human being
   God doesn't care about human beings.
2. 'Maimonides' principles were written in the twelfth century. They aren't relevant today.'
   How might an Orthodox Jew reply?

7 Judaism: Beliefs and teachings

The concept of God

A central belief in Judaism is that there is one God who alone should be worshipped (monotheism). This belief is declared twice a day by observant Jews when they recite the Jewish prayer the **Shema** (Hebrew for 'Listen'). Taken from Deuteronomy 6.4, the important prayer begins: 'Listen, Israel, God is our Lord, God is One'.

The teaching about the oneness of God means two things:

- God is a unity
- there is only one God.

> **Key Concept**
>
> **Shema** A prayer declaring Jewish faith that is said by many Jews twice a day. The Shema states that there is only one God. It is placed in the mezuzah case and tefillin.

Judaism was one of the first religions to emphasise the unity of God. Maimonides' second principle of faith says:

> God, the Cause of all, is one. This does not mean one as in one of a pair, nor one like a species (which encompasses many individuals), nor one as in an object that is made up of many elements, nor as a single simple object that is infinitely divisible. Rather, God is a unity unlike any other possible unity.

The belief that there is only one God came about over time. In the ancient world, each state had its own god, so it was believed that there were many gods. Each state was concerned that its god was more powerful than the others. The belief that the God of Israel was the only God and was God of the world came about in the 6th century BCE.

Jews consider it difficult, if not impossible, to describe the nature of God. This is because they believe humans don't have the language to do so. Indeed, some Jews argue that God is genderless, as when we talk about male or female we are referring to physical features of the body, which is not relevant in describing God. They believe that God is indescribable in human terms and can only be described through the different characteristics that are shown throughout the Torah.

These characteristics show the different natures of God and are often used as names when describing God, such as 'creator' or 'judge'.

The Torah tells that, when God gave the ancient Jewish people the Ten Commandments (Exodus 20.1–17), he made statements about himself and how humans should think of him. He emphasises his uniqueness, his power and his authority. He says:

- He is the God of the Jewish people.
- Jews should worship no other gods and should make no images of God to worship.
- Jews should not use God's name to make blessings or curses.
- Jews should set aside a day each week for rest and to worship God.

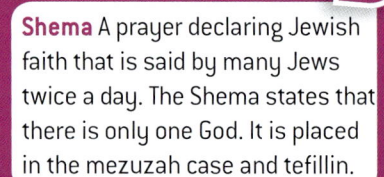

▶ God as creator

The Torah begins by showing how God created the world:

> In the beginning God created heaven and earth.
>
> (Genesis 1.1)

It continues by describing how he created human beings and gave them special and individual roles:

> God said, 'Let us make man with our image and likeness. Let him dominate the fish of the sea, the birds of the sky, the livestock animals, and all the earth – and every land animal that walks the earth.
>
> God [thus] created man with his image. In the image of God, he created him, male and female, he created them. God blessed them. God said to them, 'Be fertile and become many. Fill the land and conquer it. Dominate the fish of the sea, the birds of the sky, and every beast that walks the land.'
>
> (Genesis 1.26–28)

A depiction of the creation of the universe. The Hebrew letters spell 'YHWH', the name of God.

God is believed to be the creator, who exists always (omnipresent), is all powerful (omnipotent) and is all loving (omnibenevolent), acting like a judge in punishing and rewarding actions. For Jews, God is the creator of the universe and as such transcends above the universe. According to the Midrash (commentary on the Jewish Bible), he can do things all at once:

> God can do everything simultaneously. He kills us and makes alive at one and the same moment.
>
> (Exodus Rabbah Yitro 28:4)

Tasks

Look at the picture of creation on page 123.

1. Why isn't God shown in the picture?
2. In your own words, explain what point you think the rabbi in the adjacent box was making.
3. A famous 18th-century rabbi, Nachman of Bratislava, wrote, 'God is higher than time.' Explain in your own words what you think he meant.
In your answer you need to include the following words: creator, omnipotence and omnibenevolence.

Jewish beliefs about creation

For Jews the world is too wonderful and complex to have happened by chance. So it must have had a creator. Celebrating God as the creator is an important part of Judaism. Prayers said in Orthodox services illustrate how God created the world:

> Blessed be He who spoke, and the world existed.

Each week, Jews celebrate **Shabbat** (see page 147). This is a day, not only of rest, but also of celebration of creation. Just as God rested on the seventh day, so observant Jews do not work on Shabbat.

> A traditional story is told about a rabbi who wanted to show how the world was created. He turned a bottle of ink on its side so it poured into a poem. 'Look,' he said, 'The wind knocked over the ink and spilled out a poem onto the paper.' The people laughed at him. 'Such an act is impossible. Look at the poem. It has too much design for it to have been composed by accident.' 'Ah,' said the rabbi, 'then how could you look at the world and think it was designed by accident?'

▶ God as omnipotent, omnipresent and omnibenevolent

God's omnipotence

Jews believe that God is omnipotent. He created the universe and has absolute power and control over it. They believe that God has an ultimate purpose and plan for his universe, though we don't know what it is. So everything works together according to God's plan: the stars and planets, plants and animals, molecules and atoms all act in the way they do directed by God and with no responsibility for the outcome.

Only human beings are free to make choices. They can even choose not to believe in God and to act against God's wishes. However, as far as Judaism is concerned, this does not challenge the belief that God is omnipotent; rather, it supports it. That God can create a universe with beings in it who exercise free will, yet whose free will cannot divert his ultimate plan, is proof of his omnipotence.

> I say, 'My counsel shall stand, and all my desire I will do… I formed it, I will also do it.'

(Isaiah 46.10–11)

God's omnipresence

The Jewish belief in God's **omnipresence** is the belief that God has no physical form. For this reason, he cannot be represented in drawings or sculptures, in two or three dimensions.

This means that God can fill the universe, but not in a physical way. He is always close, to hear his people when they call him.

It also means that God is not just the God of the Jewish people; he God of all nations.

Key Concept

Omnipotence The all-powerful, almighty and unlimited nature of God.

Omnipresence The idea that God is everywhere throughout time.

> The mountain of the Lord's house shall be firmly established at the top of the mountains... and peoples shall stream upon it. And many nations shall go, and they shall say, 'Come, let us go up to the Lord's mount... and let Him teach of His ways, and we will go in his paths.'... And he shall judge between many peoples.
>
> (Micah 4.1–3)

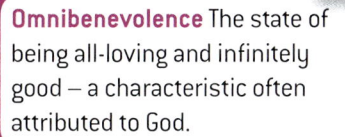

God's omnibenevolence

> **Key Concept**
>
> **Omnibenevolence** The state of being all-loving and infinitely good – a characteristic often attributed to God.

Judaism teaches that God is a God of justice. He rewards those who obey his commands and punishes those who go against them. However, Jews believe that justice cannot work without compassion, mercy and kindness. This is because God loves his people: he grieves when they disobey him and weeps when they suffer. Two of the most common names for God in the Torah – Elohim and Yahweh - are used to show the balance between his justice and his benevolence.

> The Lord is gracious and compassionate, slow to anger and of great kindness. The Lord is good to all, and his mercies are on all His works.
>
> (Psalm 145.8–9)

▶ The teachings of the Shema

The Shema is a prayer that consists of three passages from the Bible: Deuteronomy 6.4–9, Deuteronomy 11.13–21, and Numbers 15.37–41. The first section announces the oneness of God and the command to worship him. It says that these statements should be passed from generation to generation, and there should be constant reminders of them.

The other two sections repeat the necessity of being reminded of the statements.

The first section runs as follows:

| It starts with a command: 'Hear' or 'Listen' (Shema in Hebrew). This shows that God has a relationship with his people and they are able to experience him and interact with him. | The command is to a particular group of people: Israel, or the Jewish people. They are the people of God. | God has a name: his name is Yahweh. So holy is this name that no Jew will say it. It is substituted in Hebrew by the word Adonai, meaning Lord. |

> Listen, Israel, God is our Lord, God is One. Love God with all your heart, with all your soul, and with all your might. These words which I am commanding you today must remain on your heart. Teach them to your children and speak of them when you are at home, when travelling on the road, when you lie down and when you get up. Bind [these words] as a sign on your hand, and let them be an emblem in the centre of your head. [Also] write them on [parchments affixed to] the doorposts of your houses and gates.

| The second part of the first sentence contains two important beliefs about the oneness of God. First, there is only one God, Yahweh, and he is the God of the Jewish people. Second, God is a unity; he cannot be divided or adequately described as if his qualities and characteristics are separate from each other. | The second part of the passage is another command: to love God to the exclusion of all else. It gives instructions as to how Jews should express their love for God in practice (we shall examine these in the section on Jewish Practices, page 138). |

▶ God as transcendent

In Isaiah 55.8–9, differences between humans and God are described. He is transcendent – above and beyond all earthly things.

> 'For my thoughts are not your thoughts,
>   neither are your ways my ways,'
> says the Lord.
>
> 'As the heavens are higher than the earth,
>   so are my ways higher than your ways
> and my thoughts than your thoughts.'

The Jewish belief that God created the universe and everything in it suggests his transcendence. As we have seen (page 123), he predates the universe, he is able to observe the universe and he is beyond human understanding. He is omnipotent, omniscient (he knows everything) and omnipresent. He cannot be seen; he chooses how he reveals himself.

The teaching that God is unique runs throughout Jewish belief, worship and lifestyle. Nearly 2,000 years ago Rabbi Akiba said that God's uniqueness is shown by his knowing the character of every single creature and their minds. Jews sometimes talk of Shekhinah, God's unseen presence in the world (see page 128). This is an example of God's transcendence.

▶ God as eternal, merciful and a judge

Jews believe that God is eternal (always existing). God existed before the universe was created and Jews accept that he has always existed and will always exist. In the Bible, the Psalmist says:

> Before the mountains were born, and You brought forth the earth and the inhabited world, and from everlasting to everlasting, You are God.

(Psalm 90.2)

God's existence is accepted as fact and Jews feel no need to argue for or attempt to prove his existence.

In the Torah, when Moses asked God his name, God replied, 'I am what I am.' This can be translated in other ways: it can mean, 'I am what I will be' or 'I will be what I will be'. Jews often cite this as evidence that God is timeless.

Throughout history Judaism has taught that God is a judge but acts with mercy. God revealed to the prophet Moses laws and duties that are expected of all Jews. These are recorded in the Torah. The Ten Commandments or Sayings (Exodus 20.1–17) that God gave to Moses are the framework of how a just society that is close to God could be established.

> I am the Lord thy God who brought you out of the land of Egypt, the house of bondage.
>
> Thou shalt have no other gods before me
>
> Thou shalt not take the name of the lord thy God in vain
>
> Remember the Sabbath day to keep it holy
>
> Honour thy father and thy mother
>
> Thou shalt not kill
>
> Thou shalt not commit adultery
>
> Thou shalt not steal
>
> Thou shalt not bear false witness
>
> Thou shalt not covet

God gave Moses the Ten Sayings.

God judges how each Jew follows the laws. By obeying the laws, Jews are not only fulfilling what God wants but they are forming a close relationship with him. Judaism teaches that God is a God of both justice and mercy and that he will judge each person. The Book of Exodus describes how God balances justice with mercy:

> God, God … merciful and kind, slow to anger, with tremendous [resources of] love and truth. He remembers deeds of love for thousands [of generations], forgiving sin, rebellion and error. He does not clear [those who do not repent]

(Exodus 34.6–7)

God is prepared to forgive people who sin, provided they are truly sorry for what they have done.

Although God's ways may not be understandable by humans, they are considered to be just. God has no pleasure in judging humans wrongly, so any judgements he makes will be just.

The Jewish festival of Rosh Hashanah celebrates the creation of the world. At this time it is believed God will judge every person. The **Talmud** describes how God brings out scales to weigh the deeds (**mitzvot**) of each person. On one side he places the good deeds and on the other the bad deeds.

As God is believed to be a God of mercy, ten days are given after Rosh Hashanah before Yom Kippur (the Day of Atonement), during which humans can try to make up for any bad deeds and ask for forgiveness. After death it is impossible to repent, so this time allows humans to reflect on their deeds and make amends.

As eternal and omnipotent, God has a continuing presence in the world.

> **Talmud** The written version of the Jewish oral law and commentaries on it.
>
> **Mitzvah (Mitzvot, pl.)** 1. A commandment. 2. A good deed.

Task

In what ways might observant Jews believe God continues to have a presence in the world?

Sacred places

Shekhinah God's presence in the world.

Task

Do you think that people need to go to places of worship to feel God's presence?

Jews can worship anywhere although, where possible, they should worship in a community. Through worship, Jews are able to gain a sense of the **Shekhinah** a place where God's presence rests and can be felt. It is believed by many that the Shekinhah, or God's presence, would be brought into a place by doing good things there, such as praying, studying or performing mitzvot. Shekhinah is sometimes used to refer to God himself, but more usually to God's presence in the world.

If God is meant to be everywhere, what is special about the Shekhinah? Most Jews would explain that the Shekhinah is not just where God is, but where the presence can be felt – something that cannot be seen but can be experienced.

When I light the candles and bring Shabbat into my home, then I feel the presence of God.

Leonard Nimoy, who acted the part of the Vulcan Mr Spock in Star Trek, was Jewish. He wrote a book that included his interpretation of Shekhinah. He was asked to explain how the presence of Shekhinah felt.

'I think – I hope that most people at one time or another in their lives have a feeling of being in a state of grace for a moment or two, feeling that all has come together for them, that they're in a sense of harmony, a sense of inner peace, a sense of successful combining of instinct and will and the coincidence of events that makes one feel that you're in the right place at the right time and doing the right thing.'

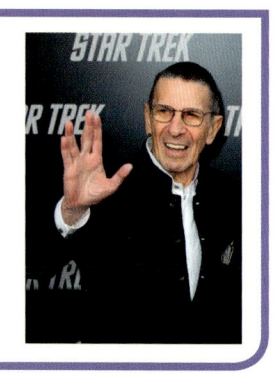

Although Jews can worship anywhere, there are two main places of worship: the synagogue and the home. Many Jews will consider that both are important for their beliefs and practices and as a support for maintaining family traditions.

The synagogue

> **Key Concept**
>
> **Synagogue** House assembly; building for Jewish public prayer, study and assembly.

There are many different types of **synagogues** throughout the world.

The Jubilee synagogue in Prague.

The former synagogue in Cardiff, Wales.

Older synagogues are often large so that they can hold a large number of worshippers. Today when synagogues are built, they are often smaller and easily accessible for older and disabled people.

The practices and design of synagogues also reflect the particular tradition they belong to, for example, Orthodox, Reform, Ashkenazi or Sephardic. Despite the many differences that might appear, there are also many similarities. Each synagogue across the world has four main functions.

- **As a beit tefilah, a house of prayer.** It is the place where Jews come together for community prayer services. Although Jews can pray anywhere, there are certain prayers that can only be said in the presence of a minyan (ten adult men, although in some traditions women are included). It is believed by many Jews that gathering for group prayers creates a more spiritual experience. It is for this reason that many observant Jews will go to the synagogue each evening.
- **As a beit midrash, a house of study.** Indeed many Ashkenazi Jews refer to their synagogue as shul, from the Yiddish word for school. For the observant Jew, the study of sacred texts is a life-long task. Thus a synagogue normally has a well-stocked library of sacred Jewish texts for members of the community to study. It is also the place where children receive their basic religious education.
- **As a place of celebration.** Although many festivals are celebrated at home, the synagogue is a place where celebrations such as a boy's coming of age (Bar Mitzvah) or weddings can be recognised communally. Many festivals are celebrated communally throughout the year in the synagogue.
- **As the central focus of Jewish life.** In Hebrew the synagogue is called beit knesset, which means 'house of assembly'. It is here that Jews will worship and celebrate or commemorate festivals throughout the Jewish year. The synagogue acts as a social hall for religious and non-religious activities. The synagogue often functions as a sort of town hall where matters of importance to the community can be discussed. Each synagogue normally has a programme of social events, which will include opportunities to learn more about religious and cultural traditions. An important role of the synagogue is its function as a social welfare agency, collecting and dispensing money and other items for the aid of the poor and needy within the community. Many are connected with Jewish Care agencies.

Tasks

1. What is a synagogue?
2. Draw a table like the one below. Under each heading, list the relevant activities that take place in the synagogue.

A place of worship	A place of study	A place for social and community events

Merseyside Jewish Community Care initiatives

- **Care and shopping services:** Providing personal support and advice and coordinating clubs and activities to meet the needs of the community. Shopping services for those unable to shop for themselves.
- **Carers services:** Giving short respite breaks for carers.
- **Financial support:** Giving financial advice and relief grants to families and individuals in financial need.
- **Hospital visiting:** Visiting and supporting patients in hospital.
- **The Gesher Group:** Providing a support group for adults with learning disabilities and mental-health or stress-related problems.
- **Supported Living Scheme:** Merseyside Jewish Community Care is operating the first Jewish Supported Living service for adults with learning disabilities in Liverpool.
- **Kosher meals and activity clubs:** Providing nearly 5,000 kosher meals each year. The cooks work to provide what may be for some recipients the only hot kosher meal they receive each week through the weekly lunch club and meals on wheels for senior citizens.
- **Yom Tovim:** Arranging celebrations for Jewish festivals. They provide traditional food at the parties and, through the meal-delivery service, every Friday, a traditional meal is delivered for Shabbat. At Rosh Hashanah, cards, apples and honey are sent to all those who use the meal service. These are particularly important for people with no family.
- **Visual Support Group (VSG):** Arranging support and organising activities such as keep fit and visits to the theatre.
- **Funerals:** In some cases the deceased may have no synagogue affiliation, relatives or friends. Under these circumstances, the synagogue organises the funeral and ensures a Jewish burial. They work closely with the Chevra Kadisha (burial society) of the synagogue.

Initiatives to increase support offered by a Jewish Care agency.

Although the synagogue is important for worship, learning and community activities, there are many challenges synagogues face in modern Britain. There has been a decline in the number of practising Jews and many synagogues have very small memberships. This is a situation also relevant to many churches, but the issue with synagogues is more difficult because Orthodox Jewish law prohibits travelling on Shabbat, so synagogues need to be situated within the Jewish neighbourhood and accessible on foot. Many Jewish communities need to make decisions regarding the upkeep and role of the synagogue.

WANTED: A RABBI
Synagogue has been without a rabbi for two years!

There are few people who are willing to take on the role of and be trained as a rabbi; sometimes small communities can only afford to pay a rabbi a low salary. Small Jewish communities find it difficult to attract rabbis; some rabbis disapprove of some of the customs that the community have adopted, such as driving to synagogues.

SECURITY ALERT AT LOCAL SYNAGOGUE

The Community Security Trust provides security and vigilance at times of worship and when the building is empty. Synagogues are often vandalised, sometimes with anti-Semitic graffiti. In some countries there have been terrorist attacks on synagogues.

DECREASING NUMBER OF WORSHIPPERS

Many synagogues were built in the 1900s and are often larger than needed today. There are changing patterns of residence as Jews move out of areas to other locations and there is an increase in the number of elderly Jews who are unable to attend places of worship.

CARDIFF SYNAGOGUE TURNED INTO OFFICES

Some synagogues have been converted into houses and even a spa. Other changes of use have included becoming museums.

Pop-Up Pair Launch New Kind Of Prayer

Orthodox Jewish couple, Naftali and Dina Brawer, have being running experimental Shabbat services in locations around London for some years. Now they are taking their 'pop-up' services to a new level: Mishkan, 'a community without borders'.

- Dina and Naftali Brawer

Mishkan is the Hebrew name for the portable sanctuary (holy place) that the Israelites carried with them in the desert before they settled in the Promised Land.

'Pop-up is a new interpretation of that,' says Mrs Brawer. 'The idea of creating a community around what people are passionate about is really important, rather than limiting yourself to the particular geography of where you happen to be or the particular denomination you're in or the group of friends you are with. What's beautiful is that it brings people together interested in the same thing, who would otherwise not meet.'

Rabbi Brawer adds: 'For many Jews, having a one-stop shop for their Judaism doesn't work. They move around, they flit about. They are more used to picking and choosing. We go out to where people are.'

While some people are drawn to 'sacred space' such as a synagogue, others find that intimidating, he observes. 'By popping up in a café or bar and studying Torah in a public space, we are able to transform secular into sacred, which is a very Jewish concept. There is a kedusha, holiness, everywhere.'

The initiative was motivated particularly by Mrs Brawer's own experiences of returning too often from a conventional synagogue service 'feeling depleted rather than uplifted. I felt I needed something different, but we realised other people were in the same situation for various reasons.'

'We see this as being part of a new way of imagining vibrant Jewish life,' Rabbi Brawer says.

(Adapted from an article in the *Jewish Chronicle*. www.thejc.com/news/uk-news/pop-up-pair-launch-new-kind-of-prayer-1.52865)

Task

'You need to go to a synagogue to feel God's presence.'

Identify three different arguments a Jew might use to disagree with the statement. In your answer use the words: omnipotent, Shabbat, Shekhinah.

▶ Differences in tradition

Judaism is an ancient religion that has developed over many millennia. As it has evolved, different communities have responded to changing times in different ways. They have also responded differently in different parts of the world. Over time, therefore, Judaism has grown and progressed through different branches or movements. Each movement has its own distinctive beliefs and ways of doing things within the broader Jewish tradition.

Orthodox Jews

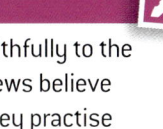

> **Key Concept**
>
> **Orthodox** A major branch within Judaism which adheres faithfully to the principles and practices of traditional Judaism. Orthodox Jews believe that the Law of the Torah is eternal and unchanging, and they practise observance of the Sabbath, religious festivals, holy days, and the dietary laws.

Orthodox Jews try to live as close to the teachings of the Torah as possible. They believe it came from God, and so it cannot be changed. God is the law-giver whose words must be obeyed rather than interpreted. Orthodox Jews will try to observe the 613 mitzvot (commandments). They believe that God gave rules about how lives should be lived and those rules are constant. Any technological or scientific advances must be considered within Jewish teachings. Society may change, but Jewish teachings don't.

It must be remembered that within the Orthodox community there are many different communities. A growing movement in Britain are the **Charedi**, sometimes known as Ultra-Orthodox, whose ideal lifestyle is dedication to the study and practice of the Torah.

Charedi Groups of Ultra-Orthodox Jews whose devotion to their religion separates them from aspects of secular culture.

Reform Jews

> **Key Concept**
>
> **Reform** A major branch of Judaism which seeks to embrace a diversity of interpretations of Jewish Law and customs, whilst preserving the beliefs, values and traditions central to the faith. Reform Jews believe that Jewish law is inspired by God and people can choose which laws to follow.

It wasn't until the **Reform** movement that large numbers of Jews departed from more traditional Orthodox teachings. Most Reform Jews believe that only the ethical laws of the Torah are binding. Additionally, they believe that other laws, like those in the Talmud, were products of their time and place, and so it is not necessary to treat them as absolute. Jews from the Reform movement consider the Torah and its teachings to be important; but they believe that religion should move with the times, and they do not take the teachings of the Torah literally. How far they interpret teachings depends upon their own reasoning and conscience.

Liberal Jews

Liberal Jews, like Reform Jews, believe that their faith should fit into modern ways of thinking, including scientific and moral thinking. So Liberal Judaism encourages people to make up their own minds about what to believe, how to interpret the Jewish scriptures, what is right and wrong, and which traditions to follow and which to reject.

The movement describes itself as 'the dynamic cutting edge of modern Judaism'.

Country of origin

Throughout history, Jews have been forced to move between countries. This is one of the reasons why there are small communities of Jews scattered throughout the world.

Secular Jews

Some Jews do not believe in God and do not see that the teachings of the Torah are sacred. They are secular Jews who are born to Jewish parents but do not observe the religious practices or teachings of Judaism. They are not a movement as such, but many secular Jews are proud to be Jewish and follow Jewish traditions.

Tasks

1 What is the Torah?
2 Consider the quotations below. Decide whether a Reform or Orthodox Jew is more likely to say one or the other. Copy and complete the table below.

Quote	Reform or Orthodox?
The Torah is important but we have to move with the times.	
The Torah came from God and must not be changed.	
God gave the rules to live by and those are eternal.	
We need to interpret the mitzvot of the Torah according to the circumstances in which we live.	

3 In your own words explain why there are different beliefs and practices among Jews.

▶ The home

Jewish identity and the home

The family home is greatly valued by many Jews who consider it to be a sanctuary. Of course, there are many differences between families, but generally the home is considered a place where the values and beliefs of Judaism are learnt and reinforced, and where a sense of Jewish identity is shaped. The home is also a place where Jewish practices are taught. In his book *Faith in the Future*, the former Chief Rabbi Jonathan Sacks shows the importance of the home for future generations:

> Its effects stay with us for a lifetime. It is where one generation passes on its values to the next and ensures the continuity of a civilisation.

> In most Jewish homes there is a pushke box in which money is collected for charity. In Judaism giving to the poor is not considered an act of charity but an act of justice or tzedakah.

Worship and prayer in the home

The home is a place of worship and prayer, both important features of daily life. As in the synagogue, observances have continued from the time of the ancient Jewish Temple. The lighting of Shabbat candles recalls the menorah (candle holder) in the Temple, and the dining table symbolises the altar (table of sacrifice). On waking up in the morning, many Orthodox Jews will thank God by saying the modeh ani while still in bed. This is a prayer that says, 'I offer thanks before you, living and eternal king, for you have mercifully restored my soul within me. Your faithfulness is great.' The Shema is a declaration of faith recited at prayer times, but also at other points during the day.

Mezuzah

Many Jewish families will have a **mezuzah** on the front door post of their house and each of the door posts inside, apart from the bathroom. The mezuzah is a parchment scroll which is placed inside a case. On the scroll is written the Shema prayer (see page 138). The parchment is prepared and written by a scribe, called a sofer, in indelible black ink with a special quill pen. It must be written on parchment made from the skin of a kosher animal, such as a cow, sheep or goat.

Usually, on the back of the parchment, the word Shaddai is written. This means 'almighty' and is one of the many names for God. The mezuzah case is affixed on the right-hand side of the door as you enter the room. It should be placed at a slight angle, with the top of the mezuzah pointing toward the inside of the room and the bottom pointing toward the outside. Often Jews will touch the case as they pass through the door and then kiss their fingers as a reminder that the family should live according to the words of the Shema. For many, the mezuzah symbolises God's protection of the house.

Siddur A book of daily prayers.

Mezuzah A small case containing the Shema inscribed on parchment. It is attached to a door frame.

The siddur

The **siddur** is a prayer book, an important part of Judaism that guides Jews through daily prayers both in the synagogue and at home. It begins with the modeh ani and contains prayers for daily services as well as those for Shabbat and other holidays. Just as the Torah is considered a gift from God, so the siddur is considered a gift to God. The siddur is considered holy and, as such, if it falls to the ground, it will be picked up as quickly as possible and kissed.

Touching the mezuzah case is a reminder to live by the words of the Shema.

Task

There is a famous saying in Judaism: 'If you are looking for God, go home.'

Explain what this saying means, and include at least three examples.

End of Section Review

Stickability

Key concepts:
- Omnipotence
- Omnibenevolence
- Reform
- Orthodox
- Shema
- Synagogue

Key teachings:
- The characteristicsz of God
- The Shema
- God's transcendence
- God as eternal
- God's mercy
- God as judge
- The synagogue
- Branches of Judaism
- The importance of the home

Skills Link

1. What is meant by 'omnipotence'?
2. Describe how the home is a place of Jewish traditions.

Knowledge Check

1. Write a short paragraph (roughly three sentences) to explain what Jews believe about the nature of God.
2. Write a long paragraph (roughly eight to ten sentences) to explain how the home shapes Jewish identity.
3. Explain the Jewish beliefs expressed in the Shema. Try to make at least three points.
4. Write a developed paragraph (approximately six to eight sentences) to explain the different functions of a synagogue.

The Big Question

'Jews need not go to the synagogue to worship.'

Your Task

Respond to the statement above, showing that you have considered more than one point of view. Give reasoned judgements on the validity and strength of these views.

Task

You need to explain in detail religious similarities and differences between the branches of Judaism. Use the guidance below to help you to write a developed explanation for Judaism. Ensure that you use key terms fluently and frequently.

All/many/most Jews believe that _____.

This comes from the teaching/Bible quote _____.

This means that/Because of this they _____.

Some/other Jews such as _____ believe that _____.

This comes from the teaching/Bible quote _____.

This means that/Because of this they _____.

Finally, Jews such as _____ believe that _____.

This means that/Because of this they _____.

Their beliefs do/do not differ because _____.

8 Judaism: Practices

■ Practices that demonstrate beliefs about God

Throughout daily life many Jews show their reverence to God through actions, worship and what they wear.

▶ The Shema

Beliefs about God are shown in the central prayer of Judaism, the **Shema**. As we have seen, this prayer is made up of three passages from the Torah and is the most important prayer in Judaism.

The Shema itself contains the command to recite it 'when you lie down and when you get up' (Deuteronomy 6.7). Therefore, Jews repeat the Shema every morning and every evening. They do this whether they are at the synagogue, at home, or any other respectful place. They may do it alone or with other Jews. It is said that the reward for observing the recitation of the Shema at the proper times is greater than the reward for studying the Torah at any time.

Morning recitation: The morning recitation should be performed as early as possible, after it has started to get light, but before the sun has risen. If this is not possible, it is advised to recite at least the first of the three sections before sunrise – and before taking a cup of tea or coffee. In any event, the morning Shema should be said within the first quarter of daylight hours.

Evening recitation: The recitation of the evening Shema should take place when three stars are visible in the sky, and before midnight.

The command to recite the Shema does not apply to women, as women may have to be available at the specified times to care for children, and Jewish tradition supports this. However, in practice, Jewish women do recite it. Children who are too young to read do not have to say it, but their parent will teach it to them from an early age.

Reciting the Shema is important because, according to Jewish teaching, it is commanded by God, and God rewards those who follow his commands. As with all traditions, it is also important simply because it is a tradition: it ensures the continuation of Jewish teachings and the Jewish community.

How do Jews pray?

Before they pray, Jews will wash and make sure they are comfortable and able to concentrate. They do not have to recite the Shema in Hebrew (the language in which it is written in the Bible), but is thought that doing so gives it a special power. They may say it while sitting or standing – or even walking. At least the first section should be said aloud. The eyes should be covered by the right hand to cut out distractions and aid concentration.

▶ Representations of God

Artwork

Because they believe they should only worship one God, Jews never have statues or representations of human beings in synagogues. They believe this is obeying the second commandment given to Moses:

> Do not represent [such] gods by any carved statue or picture of anything in the heaven above, on the earth below, or in the water below the land.

(Exodus 20.4)

This means that images of God are forbidden in case they are used for worship. So it is God alone who should be worshipped. Synagogues will often have stained glass windows, but there will be no human representation in their designs.

Written representations of God

The holiness of God extends to his name. Jews will not write the word God out of respect. Instead, they will write G-d. There is another reason, though. Many Jews believe that no books that have the actual name of God should be destroyed. It would not be considered disrespectful to write God's name on the computer, but could be considered a violation if that document was printed and then thrown away. Instead such documents would need to be stored in a genizah, which is a special storage space sometimes found in a synagogue, until they can be given a proper burial in a Jewish cemetery. Because of this, many Jews substitute 'God' with 'G-d' so that they can erase or dispose of the writing without showing disrespect to God.

▶ Items worn for worship

Kippah

> **Key Concept**
>
> **Kippah** A cap worn by Jewish boys and men (and sometimes women) during services. Some Jews wear a kippah at all times. It is a reminder of God's presence. A kippah is often also known as a yarmulke.

The kippah has become a source of identity for Jews so I wear mine with pride.

As I believe the whole of my life is worship to God I wear a kippah all the time as a symbol of my respect.

I only wear a kippah in the synagogue as I don't always feel safe to wear it in the streets where I live.

Many Jewish men choose to wear a **kippah** (plural kippot) when they are awake to show their respect to God. The exact meaning of the kippah is unknown, but for most Jews, it is a symbol of identity and a sign of respect to God.

Throughout Jewish history, the attitude towards head covering has varied. Drawings from the third century depict Jews without hats, but in the Middle Ages many Jews wore hats during prayer and study. Today there is much debate about why the kippah is worn and whether it is a duty to wear the kippah all the time or just during worship.

The shape and size of the kippah also differs depending upon the community.

The tallith

A **tallith** is a fringed shawl that can cover the shoulders of a Jewish man. It is worn during morning prayers. The tallith itself has no significance. Its importance lies in the **tzizit**, or tassels, which represent the 613 mitzvot or commands given by God to the Jewish people in the Bible.

Wearing the tzizit on the tallith reminds Jews that God is the lawgiver who gave the mitzvot that they base their lives around. In the Bible, God tells Moses that the tzizit should remind them to obey the commandments and worship God:

> '… speak to the Israelites and have them make tassels on the corners of their garments for all generations. They shall include a twist of sky-blue wool in the corner tassels. These shall be your tassels, and when you see them, you shall remember all of God's commandments so as to keep them.'

(Numbers 15.38–39)

The tzizit are found on the four corners of the tallith, which is worn during services in the synagogue. The Talmud refers to 613 mitzvot in the Torah. This number is represented by the number of knots on the fringes of the tallit. Hebrew letters also have numerical values. The values of the letters of the word 'tzizit' in Hebrew add up to 600; each tassel has eight strings and five knots, making a total of 613.

Jews wear the fringes outside their clothing to remind them of the mitzvot that God gave. However, a prayer shawl is not worn all the time, and so some observant Jews wear a tallith katan (little tallith) under a shirt throughout the day.

Traditionally only men wear the tallith for worship, but there is an increasing number of women, especially in the Reform movement, who choose to wear a tallith for worship.

A Jewish man prepared for worship. He is wearing a kippah (head covering) and a tallith (shawl), with tzitit (tassels).

Tzitzit Fringes attached to the corners of garments as a reminder of the commandments.
Shema A prayer declaring a belief in one God. It is found in the Torah
Tallith A fringed shawl worn by Jewish men when praying.

Task

'There is no need for Jews to wear special clothing.'
Discuss this statement showing that you have considered more than one point of view.

Worship in the home and synagogue

The importance of the synagogue: internal features

We have seen that statues and representations of living beings, including God, will not be found in synagogues. This is to prevent **idolatry** – the worship of images.

> Do not represent [such] gods by any carved statue or picture of anything in the heaven above, on the earth below, or in the water below the land.

(Exodus 20.4)

In the following pages, each main area of the synagogue will be explained. There are references to the specific differences between Reform and Orthodox communities. The tasks on page 143 will require you to be able to identify and explain those differences.

Aron HaKodesh

Idolatry The worship of images.

The Aron HaKodesh

> **Key Concept**
>
> **Aron HaKodesh** The holy Ark containing the Torah scrolls. It is on the wall facing Jerusalem and is the focal point of the synagogue.

The **Aron HaKodesh** (also known as the ark) is the most important place in a synagogue as it is here the Torah scrolls are kept. It is permissible to sell the seats or the reading desk of a synagogue and apply the proceeds to the purchase of an ark, because they have a lesser holiness; but it is forbidden to sell an ark, even in order to build a synagogue. In the Sephardic tradition the ark is called herkal or sanctuary.

During certain prayers the doors and curtain of the ark may be opened or closed. Some have a curtain outside the doors of the ark (Ashkenazi custom) or inside the doors of the ark (Sephardi custom).

There are several customs and traditions connected with the ark. It is opened for certain prayers and during the Ten Days of Penitence, between Rosh Hashanah and Yom Kippur. Opening the ark emphasises the importance of prayer. It is normal for everyone to stand whenever the doors of the ark are open. In Britain there are many different designs of arks, with some being made from glass and concrete.

The ner tamid.

Bimah A platform that supports the desk from which the Torah scrolls are read.

The bimah.

The Torah scroll being read with a yad (often referred to as a Torah pointer).

The Ten Sayings (Commandments) can be seen on the top of the Aron HaKodesh.

Ner tamid

> **Key Concept**
>
> **Ner tamid** 'Eternal light'; a constantly lit lamp near the ark in the synagogue that symbolises God's presence.

In front of and slightly above the Aron HaKodesh, is the **ner tamid**, often called the eternal lamp. This is kept continually burning and should never be extinguished. This lamp symbolises the menorah (seven-branched lamp) which was kept burning in the Temple. Many Jews consider it as a symbol of God's eternal presence. The ner tamid used to be an oil lamp but now most are fuelled by gas, electric lightbulbs or solar power.

The bimah

The **bimah** is a central platform in the synagogue on which stands the desk from which the Torah scrolls are read. In Orthodox synagogues, the bimah is usually in the middle so the rabbi faces the congregation. In Reform synagogues, everyone sits together and the bimah is at the front, combined with the ark, rather than in the middle.

The Torah scrolls

The Torah scrolls are the most sacred part of any synagogue. They are made from animal skins and are handwritten. Each scroll is one continuous Torah written in columns. Each end is stitched to a pole, called the 'tree of life'. The scrolls are wrapped in silk or velvet when not used and often decorated with silver. Such a handwritten scroll is called a Sefer Torah. The scrolls are carried carefully to the bimah during a service where the weekly portion of text is read.

Ten Commandments

The Torah contains 613 mitzvot (commandments). According to the Torah, God gave ten of them to Moses, inscribed on two tablets of stone. It is said that all of the other 603 mitzvot can be grouped using the ten as headings. Although they are usually called the Ten Commandments, the Bible refers to them simply as 'sayings' or 'statements'.

The Ten Commandments (or Ten Sayings) are clearly mounted in synagogues. They are often placed near to or above the ark to remind the congregation that the original tablets on which they were written were carried in an ark. More importantly, they remind worshippers of their duty to follow God's commands.

The Sayings are written in Hebrew, usually just the first two words of each of them. They are displayed on two plaques – five on each – because the Bible says that Moses received the original Sayings on two stone tablets.

Seating

Women sitting with men in a Reform synagogue.

Women sitting separate from men in an Orthodox synagogue.

The seating for women is one of the main differences between Orthodox and Reform synagogues. In Orthodox synagogues there is a separate area where women are seated. This might be an upper-floor balcony or an area separated by a wall or curtain. The Talmud says that men and women can concentrate more on their worship if they are separated. There are different practices among Orthodox synagogues. Some argue that, although men and women should be separated, they should each be close to the ark. For some synagogues it is important to have an opaque curtain separating the women's gallery so that the male worshippers cannot see the women's gallery.

In Reform synagogues there is no partition between males and females, and they may sit together throughout the worship.

Tasks

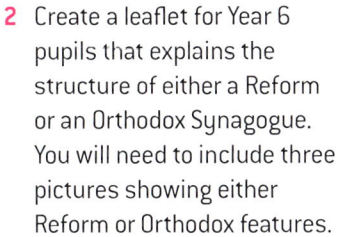

1. What is the difference between Sefer Torah and the Torah?
2. Create a leaflet for Year 6 pupils that explains the structure of either a Reform or an Orthodox Synagogue. You will need to include three pictures showing either Reform or Orthodox features.
3. Answer the following question in 30–35 words.

   Why don't synagogues have statues or pictures in them?

   In your answer you need to include the following words: Shema, idolatry, monotheism. Pages 140–141 will help you.

> Worshipping at home and worshipping in the synagogue cannot be separated. The way I celebrate Shabbat shows the link between home and synagogue.

▶ Reading of the Torah during worship

> **Jewish books**
>
> The Jewish Bible is often called TeNaKh. It is spelt this way because it contains three sections, the initial letters of which are TNK:
> - Torah: the books of the Law; the first five books of the Bible, often called the Books of Moses.
> - Nevi'im: The books of the prophets.
> - Ketuvim: The other writings.
>
> Some of the laws were not written in the Torah originally and were preserved in oral form. They were finally written down in 200CE in a book called the Mishnah. A commentary on the Mishnah, known as the Gemara, was completed in 500CE. The Mishnah and the Gemara together are known as the Talmud.

The Torah consists of the first five books of the Jewish Bible. They are sometimes called the Books of Moses. For the purposes of worship, they are divided into 54 portions. Each portion (parsha) consists of between three and five chapters. By reading one portion each week (sometimes two) at the Shabbat service, the whole of the Torah is read over the course of a year. The cycle begins and finishes at the end of Sukkot (an autumn festival).

The portions are recited in their original Hebrew and sung rather than said. This requires skill, because ancient Hebrew words contain no vowels. The reader needs to know his portion very well to be able to recite accurately and fluently.

The Torah scrolls (Sefer Torah) are kept in the ark. When the ark is opened to reveal the scrolls, the congregation stands to show their respect and chants the words Moses is reported to have said when setting out with the original ark:

'Arise, O God, and scatter your enemies!

Let your foes flee before You!'

(Numbers 10.35)

It is a great honour for a member of the congregation to be asked to take a scroll and carry it to the bimah to be read. As he carries it, fellow worshippers try to kiss it to show their love and respect for the word of God, all the while singing verses from the Bible.

When the scroll reaches the bimah, the scroll is 'undressed': the coverings and decorations in which it is kept are removed. Either before the reading (in Sephardi synagogues) or afterwards (in Ashkenazi congregations), the scroll is slightly unrolled and held up so that everyone can see the writing on it. The congregation says together: 'This is the Torah that Moses set before the people of Israel; the Torah, given by God, through Moses.' There are usually three people in the bimah: an official who calls people up to the Torah, a reader and a person to help the reader's pronunciation of the Hebrew.

As the portion is read from the scroll, the reader uses a yad to indicate his place in the text. A yad is a silver pointer, about 15–20 centimetres long, usually made in the shape of a human

> **Task**
>
> Explain what is happening in the photo using the words: parsha, tallith, yad, Sefer Torah, bimah.

hand with a pointing finger. Out of respect for the Torah, the scroll is not touched with a hand. Each portion is divided into seven sections and members of the congregation are called to the bimah to make blessings (aliyah) before and after each section.

It is customary to take the scroll up to the bimah from the right-hand side, and take it down from the left. It is also a tradition for the person who carries the scroll to take the shortest route from his seat to fetch it from the ark – to show anticipation – and to take a longer way back – to show reluctance to leave it. As it is placed back in the ark, the congregation again quotes the words of Moses recorded in the Bible:

> When [the Ark] came to rest, he said,
> 'Return, O God, [to] the myriads of Israel's thousands.'

(Numbers 10.36)

Diverse practices within Orthodox and Reform synagogues

Orthodox and Reform synagogue services

Prayers may be said anywhere in Judaism. For many Jews, however, it is important to join with others for communal prayers. In order for this to happen, a minyan (ten men) has to be present. This is to create a more spiritual experience than people can have on their own.

It is believed that communal prayers are less selfish than individual prayers. When praying with others, there is a communal responsibility, and prayers are said for the whole community. Although each synagogue usually has daily prayers, the time when the community comes together is for the Shabbat service.

Prayers are an important part of any synagogue service. For many centuries, rabbis have taught that prayer is one of the best ways of communicating a love of God. It forms the bridge between humans on earth and God. Prayer is so important that a whole section of the Talmud, called Berachot, is based on prayer.

Historically there were no special prayers, but as time progressed different types of set prayers were established.

- **Praising God** – This involves praising God for his qualities. By thinking of specific qualities of God such as justice, Jews think about the qualities they should aim for.
- **Requests of God** – These aren't just requests for what people want, but what God thinks is best for them.
- **Thanksgiving** – These show gratitude for the life God has given and the blessings granted.

Examples of these prayers can be found in the prayer book (siddur), which contains many of the prayers used in daily life and festivals. Some Jews prefer to recite their prayers in Hebrew, as they argue this is a holy language and it connects all Jews worldwide. Other Jews consider it more important to understand what is being said. Orthodox services normally include many prayers in Hebrew, while Reform services have a mixture of prayers in Hebrew and in the language of the country.

Although all prayers are important in Judaism, the Amidah and the Shema (see page 138) are considered two of the most important.

The Amidah

The Amidah is the core of every Jewish worship service, and is therefore also referred to as HaTefillah, or 'The prayer'. Amidah literally means 'standing', and people stand throughout the prayer to show they are in God's presence. The Amidah consists of 18 blessings and can be divided into three sections, each of which reflects a different type of prayer. The three types of prayer in the Amidah are praise of God, requests of God, and thanksgiving.

The Amidah is recited silently by all members of a congregation or by individuals praying alone, and then, in communal settings, repeated aloud by the prayer leader or cantor, with the congregation reciting 'Amen' to all the blessings of the Amidah.

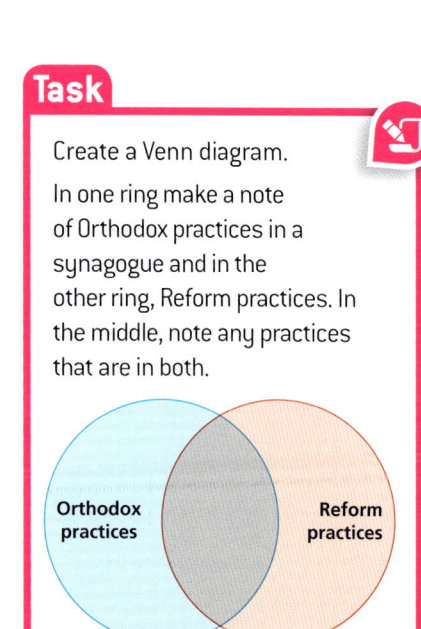

> **Task**
>
> Create a Venn diagram.
>
> In one ring make a note of Orthodox practices in a synagogue and in the other ring, Reform practices. In the middle, note any practices that are in both.

The Amidah formally concludes with the recitation of the line:

May God, who brings peace to the universe, bring peace to us and all of the people, Israel. Amen.

This is recited while taking three steps backward, bowing to both sides, and taking three steps forward again, formally retreating from God's symbolic presence.

Tasks

1. Read about the importance of the Shema on page 138 and about the Amidah above and then create and complete a table like the one below.

	Shema	Amidah
What is it?		
Why is it important?		
How is the prayer shown to be important?		

2. A famous Rabbi once said, 'Prayer is for the soul what food is for the body.' (Rabbi Halevi, 1095–1150)

   Explain in your own words what you think he meant.

Shabbat service in the synagogue

Although it is very important for Jews to have a private relationship with God, it is also important to unite the community through worship. Important ceremonies happen at festival times, but each week, the Shabbat service (the weekly festival that is celebrated from sunset on Friday to sunset on Saturday) brings the community together. Many Jews attend synagogue services on Shabbat even if they do not do so during the week. Services are held on Shabbat eve (Friday night), Shabbat morning (Saturday morning) and late Shabbat afternoon (Saturday afternoon). Fixed periods of prayer correspond with the times when sacrifices were offered in the Temple in ancient times.

The Shabbat morning service is the longest of the week and can last between two and three hours. The service includes important prayers such as the Shema, Amidah and Kaddish. At each service, selected portions of the Torah and **haftorah** are read. It is common for rabbis to deliver a weekly sermon, which draws upon the meaning of the readings from the Torah and haftorah.

After the service, a Kiddush is usually held. This is the special blessing recited over a cup of wine or Shabbat wine before Friday night dinner.

The service in a Reform synagogue is based on traditional elements, but contains more use of the language of the country in which the service is taking place and far less Hebrew. Reform Judaism has made changes to services to reflect the differences in their beliefs from those of Orthodox Judaism. Prayers and readings usually leave out beliefs about bodily resurrection, a personal Jewish Messiah, and references to angels. Reform services often play instrumental or recorded music, while Orthodox synagogues have unaccompanied singing.

Key Concept

Shabbat Day of spiritual renewal and rest. Beginning at sunset on Friday and closing at nightfall on Saturday.

Haftorah A passage from one of the books of the Nevi'im (prophets), which is read after the Torah reading.

Key Concept

Rabbi A religious teacher and leader with authority to make decisions on issues of Jewish law. A rabbi is the chief religious official of a synagogue, who often (but not always) leads worship and conducts rites and rituals.

The role of the rabbi

Each synagogue has a board of synagogue members who, with the rabbi, have charge of the synagogue. A rabbi is normally chosen by the synagogue community to teach and provide spiritual and religious guidance and offer advice. Usually, the most important quality of a rabbi is their understanding of Judaism. This is because their role is to make decisions and rulings about Jewish law issues. The rabbi often leads services, such as Shabbat services and religious festivals. Although other members of the community may lead acts of worship, rabbis normally take part in ceremonies and celebrations, such as marriages, to make sure they are legally correct.

There are differences between the Orthodox and Reform movements regarding who can be a rabbi. Reform synagogues allow both males and females to be rabbis. The Senior Rabbi for Reform Jews in Britain is Laura Janner Klausner.

In Orthodox synagogues in Britain, only men are allowed to be rabbis. In America, however, there have recently been some female rabbis ordained. The Chief Rabbi in Britain is Ephraim Mirvis. He was installed in September 2013 in a ceremony attended by HRH The Prince of Wales, the first time that a member of the royal family has attended a service for the Installation of a Chief Rabbi.

In Orthodox Judaism, only men can be rabbis.

Laura Klausner is the Senior Rabbi for Reform Jews in Britain.

Rabbi Kagedan has been ordained as the first Orthodox woman rabbi in North America. She studied at a women's seminary (religious college) in New York where, in the past, graduates have taken on the title of maharat (female spiritual leader) rather than rabbi. She said she had wanted to take the title of rabbi as she wanted to serve the community, and people would know that her role is the same as that of a male rabbi. Although many Jews have been actively supporting her, there have been many Jews unwilling to accept a female Orthodox rabbi.

Rabbi Lila Kagedan, the first female Orthodox rabbi in North America.

Tasks

1. Write a job description for a rabbi. Remember to include areas that you think would be important for the community.
2. Why do you think Rabbi Kagedan did not want to be called maharat?
3. 'Judaism is a religion of tradition. Rabbis should be male.'
   Give one reason for and one against the statement.

The importance of the home for worship in Judaism

Challenges and benefits of observing Shabbat

The importance of the home is shown in the weekly Shabbat celebrations.

The keeping of Shabbat obeys two interrelated mitzvot contained in the Torah.

> Remember the Sabbath day [the Shabbat] by keeping it holy. Six days you shall labour and do all your work, but the seventh day is a Sabbath to the Lord your God. On it you shall not do any work, neither you, nor your son or daughter, nor your male or female servant, nor your animals, nor any foreigner residing in your towns.
>
> (Exodus 20.8–10)

Remembering Shabbat means remembering the importance of it as a celebration of creation and also of the freedom of the Israelites from slavery in Egypt. Keeping Shabbat means showing it is holy through worship in the home and synagogue. For many Jews, observing Shabbat means recognising the types of activities and work that are not allowed.

Shabbat is considered by many Jews to be the most important festival. They see it as a gift from God, when weekday worries can be forgotten. Throughout history, Shabbat has been an important festival for Jews. Even in times of persecution, Jews tried to celebrate Shabbat.

There are many different opinions among Jews regarding what can and cannot be done on Shabbat. For many observant Orthodox Jews, all forms of work must be avoided unless it is a matter of life and death. Also, articles should not be carried between private and public places. In some areas, this has led to Orthodox Jews creating a special enclosure (eruv) in their neighbourhoods. Inside the **eruv**, Jewish residents or visitors are permitted to carry objects from one place to another on Shabbat.

> **Eruv** Area of a town enclosed by wire, extending the space in which objects may be carried on Shabbat.

> As Jewish men and women were being taken in crowded trucks to concentration camps…
>
> One elderly woman had a small bundle with her and with a lot of effort slowly managed to open it. She drew out two candlesticks and two hallot [ceremonial bread]. She had just prepared them for Sabbath when she was dragged from her home that morning. They were the only things she had thought worth taking with her. Soon the Sabbath candles lit up the faces of the tortured Jews and the song of Lekhah Dodi transformed the scene. Sabbath with its atmosphere of peace had descended upon them all.
>
> (Extract from *The Sabbath* by Dayan Grunfeld, 1981)

Each family celebrates Shabbat in its own way, although there are some features which are common to most Shabbat celebrations.

Shabbat starts a few minutes before sunset on Friday night. The time is different according to the location and the time of the year.

Eruv makes a difference in Manchester

Observant Jews are prohibited from pushing or carrying everyday items between sundown on Fridays and sundown on Saturdays unless they are in a special area known as an eruv. This includes pushchairs, wheelchairs, house keys or mobile phones. In some parts of Britain, like Manchester, an eruv is created using physical features, like walls and hedges, railway lines and roads, to completely enclose an area of land. To be accepted, it must satisfy strict laws, including being 'completely enclosed' by existing natural boundaries or by wires from the top of posts.

Task

Look at the differences in times for Shabbat between December and April. What differences to someone's lifestyle might this make?

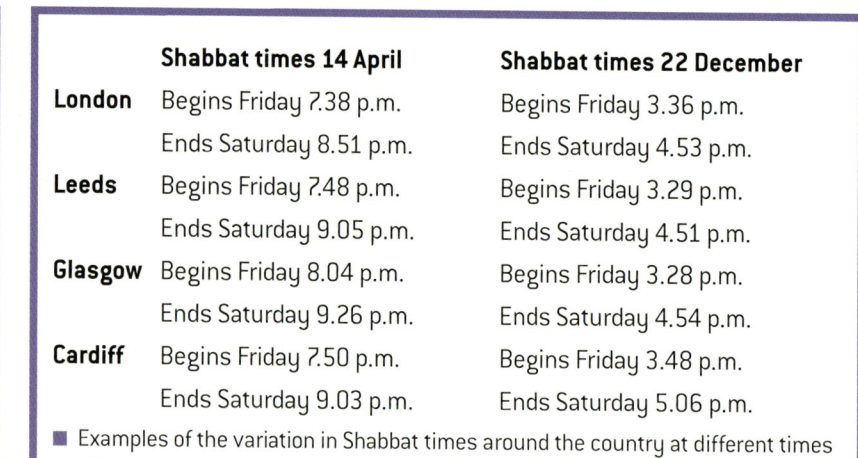

	Shabbat times 14 April	**Shabbat times 22 December**
London	Begins Friday 7.38 p.m.	Begins Friday 3.36 p.m.
	Ends Saturday 8.51 p.m.	Ends Saturday 4.53 p.m.
Leeds	Begins Friday 7.48 p.m.	Begins Friday 3.29 p.m.
	Ends Saturday 9.05 p.m.	Ends Saturday 4.51 p.m.
Glasgow	Begins Friday 8.04 p.m.	Begins Friday 3.28 p.m.
	Ends Saturday 9.26 p.m.	Ends Saturday 4.54 p.m.
Cardiff	Begins Friday 7.50 p.m.	Begins Friday 3.48 p.m.
	Ends Saturday 9.03 p.m.	Ends Saturday 5.06 p.m.

■ Examples of the variation in Shabbat times around the country at different times of year.

The woman of the family lights two candles to bring the presence of Shabbat into the home. This is a ritual that happens worldwide at the same time. In many families, the father welcomes Shabbat in the synagogue and when he returns home, the family sits down to a special meal. All the preparation will have taken place before Shabbat begins.

Meals begin with a blessing over two loaves of bread, usually braided loaves (challah). These two loaves symbolise the double portion of manna, which were eaten by the Israelites in the desert after the Exodus from Egypt. The Kiddush prayer is recited over a cup of wine at the beginning of Shabbat meals. The meal is a time of happiness and relaxation with all the family, if possible.

Candles are lit, loaves are blessed and the Kiddush prayer is said over a glass of wine at the start of the Shabbat meal.

Shabbat continues as a day of rest until sunset the next day. On the Saturday morning the family usually goes to the synagogue for the Shabbat service. For Orthodox Jews, it is important that they walk to synagogue, as driving a car would be considered as work, which is forbidden. After the synagogue service most families relax and enjoy the day. For Orthodox families, it is important that anything that could be considered work is avoided. This might include turning on electricity, cooking or driving.

> ### Shabbat unplugged
>
> Having a day off from technology is becoming more common for non-Jews as well as Jews. An increasing number of people now close down computers and phones for a day so they can focus on friends and family.
>
> For the past six years, Shlain and her family have observed Technology Shabbat, a modernised version of the Jewish day of rest. They turn off every screen in sight – phones, laptops, TVs – before dinner on Friday night and do not reconnect for 24 hours.

At sunset on Saturday, the importance of Shabbat is shown again as the family joins together to say 'goodbye' to Shabbat. This is shown through the lighting of the havdallah candle – a plaited candle. Havdallah means 'separation' and symbolises the distinction between Shabbat and the rest of the week now the day is over. A glass of wine is passed around for the family to take a sip from, and a sweet-smelling spice box is sniffed to symbolise the hope of a sweet week ahead.

Shabbat is celebrated through many rituals in both the home and the synagogue. What is most important is people's intention during Shabbat. Their behaviour shows that Shabbat is a special day and God is worshipped by people being kind to each other.

> ### The Chief Rabbi's Shabbat UK
>
> Each year there is a special Shabbat which all Jews may celebrate, regardless of their level of religious observance.
>
> The weekend's festivities usually commence on Thursday with mass 'Challah (plaited loaves) Bakes' in various locations and communal meals, and culminates in a huge concert to mark the end of Shabbat (Havdallah) and to welcome in the new week. Synagogues, Jewish schools and other Jewish organisations across the UK organise series of events to mark the weekend. Everybody can participate in Shabbat UK, from the most observant Jews to those who may have never experienced the beauty of a Shabbat.

Tasks

1. Select three different words from the word puzzle below. Explain why each is important.

> Shabbat kiddush friday
> friday relax
> siddur Saturday candles
> blessings Saturday candles Shabbat dinner
> Shabbat meal fun reflect
> service
> dinner Shabbat
> friends service
> prayer songs meal reflect

2. Look back at pages 149–151 where the different attitudes to keeping the Torah are described. Decide which of the following is most likely to be said by an Orthodox Jew, a Reform Jew or both Orthodox and Reform Jews.
   - It is not up to us to question the ways of God. The Shabbat laws are to be obeyed.
   - By keeping the Shabbat we are showing our thanks to God.
   - If we can't work, then how can rabbis lead the Shabbat services?
   - We have to act on our conscience and remember we live in modern times.
   - The duties given to us by God do not change over time. They are eternal.
   - Practising a religion is not picking the bits you want to obey and ignoring those you don't.

3. Complete the following mnemonic, adding in a relevant statement about Shabbat that begins with the first letter of each line. Three examples have been completed for you.

   Sunset on Friday starts Shabbat
   H
   All the family together at home
   B
   B
   A
   Time for rest, family and reflection

4. Make a list of what you think are the benefits of keeping Shabbat and what you think are the challenges.

▶ Observing Kashrut

Keeping Kosher

> **Key Concept**
>
> **Kashrut** The body of Jewish law dealing with what foods can and cannot be eaten and how those foods must be prepared. The word 'Kashrut' comes from the Hebrew, meaning fit, proper or correct. The word 'kosher' describes food that meets the standards of kashrut.

Kosher Fitting, proper; often used for foods that are permitted to be eaten.

Kosher means 'fitting' or 'proper' according to Jewish law. Although it can be used to describe certain actions, it is more often used to describe foods that can and cannot be eaten by observant Jews. The opposite of kosher is **treifa**, which is used to describe actions and foods that are forbidden. The Jewish food laws about what is kosher and what is treifa are called **kashrut**.

The laws concerning kosher food are found in the Torah. There are many references not only to what can and cannot be eaten, but also to the way foods should be prepared. According to Genesis 1.29, the first humans were vegetarians. It was only after the flood that God allowed Noah and his family to eat meat.

Leviticus 11.1–24 refers to many issues of keeping kosher that influence the lifestyle of many Jews today. In this passage God gives Moses instructions regarding what the Israelites can and cannot eat. Forbidden are:

- many types of birds
- shellfish
- fish without fins and scales
- animals that don't chew the cud and have hooves completely parted.

Animals that are permitted to be eaten are considered kosher only if they are killed in a certain way. Causing pain to any living creature is strictly forbidden in Jewish law, and so a method is used called **shechitah**, which is supposed to cause less pain to animals. The animal's throat is cut with a razor-sharp knife, causing immediate loss of consciousness and death. The slaughter of animals for meat is carried out by a person called a **shochet**. The role of the shochet is very important, and a shochet must live a good moral life. He must be Jewish, as the method of killing of the animal is a form of dedication to God. The Torah commands Jews not to eat the blood of animals and birds, so after being slaughtered, the meat is laid out to let the blood drain away before rinsing.

Fruit and vegetables are kosher and may be eaten however they are prepared.

Although the Torah is quite clear about permitted and forbidden foods, and about how to prepare them, it does not give any reasons for the laws. For Jews, it is enough to know that kashrut is commanded by God for them to obey it.

> **Words associated with kashrut:**
> **Kosher** Fitting; foods that observant Jews may eat.
> **Treifa** Forbidden.
> **Parev** Permitted to be eaten with meat or milk.
> **Shechitah** Ritual slaughter.
> **Shochet** A Jew trained in ritual slaughter.

▶ Separation of milk and meat in a kosher kitchen

Keeping a kosher diet doesn't just mean selecting the right animals to be eaten and preparing them in a fit way. There are certain combinations that are forbidden. Exodus 23.19 states:

> Bring your first fruits to the Temple of God your Lord. Do not cook meat in milk, [even] that of its mother.

For Jews who keep kosher homes, this means that meat and dairy products must be kept separately, and they should not be eaten in the same meal. Any kitchen utensil that is used in the preparation or consumption of meat cannot be used for dairy products, and vice versa. Although meat and milk dishes should be kept separately, there are foods that can be eaten in any meal. These are called **parev** and include vegetables, eggs and plants.

There are many different decisions that families have to make regarding how far to keep kosher. Both religious and practical considerations can impact upon their practice.

Tasks

1. What does 'kosher' mean?
2. Kieran has been asked to consider the following statement: 'Keeping kosher is not important anymore.' From Sara and Tanya's discussion on page 154, identify six different points he could make in his answer.

Sara is from an observant Orthodox Jewish family. She has invited Tanya, her non-Jewish friend, to a kosher restaurant.

Sara: Here's the menu – don't look so worried.

Tanya: But how will I know what to eat. I know there are many things you can't eat and I don't want to offend you.

Sara: This is a kosher restaurant. Did you see the certificate on the shop window that shows that it has been inspected and all the preparations of the food are fit and proper.

Tanya: What do you mean 'fit and proper'? Do you mean they are clean?

Sara: Well yes. But it's more than that. This is a 'meaty' restaurant so there will be no dishes here with milk and all the meat will have been killed according to the rules we must follow.

Tanya: Is that why I don't see cheeseburger on the menu?

Sara: Exactly. At home we have a set of plates for our meaty dishes and a set for our milky dishes. They are all kept in separate areas of the kitchen.

Tanya: But that must be really expensive.

Sara: It is. To buy kosher food can be really expensive. Especially where there are no Jewish shops. I know some people who have had to give up keeping kosher because they can't afford it.

Tanya: What happens to them?

Sara: What do you mean? Do you think they would be struck down by thunder and lightning! Well each individual has to make their choice and then live by it. I consider it a blessing to keep a kosher lifestyle. It helps my relationship with God. He gave us the duties we should follow and I feel I owe it to him.

Tanya: But those rules come from ages ago. They can't be relevant to today.

Sara: That's what some of my Jewish friends say as they are eating their bacon sandwich! It has to be an individual choice as our relationship with God is individual. For me I keep kosher and hope I always will. It binds us together as a family. I also think that God made those rules for all time and I shouldn't change them just because it is difficult or inconvenient.

Tanya: But how do you know what to eat? Here it's easy as all the menu is kosher but what about if you are somewhere else?

Sara: It's natural to me now. It's just like people who have gluten free diets know what they can and can't eat. I look at the food labels and there will be signs that tell me if it is kosher or treifah. Also technology helps. My friend has a device, which lets them know what they can eat. It's really useful when she is travelling.

Tanya: All this talk of food is making me hungry – let's order.

End of Section Review

Stickability

Key concepts:
- Ner tamid
- Rabbi
- Kashrut

Key teachings:
- The concept of God
- Worship in the home
- Worship in the synagogue
- Observing Shabbat
- Observing kashrut

Skills Link

1. Explain why it is important for Jews to maintain a kosher kitchen.
2. 'Maintaining Shabbat is too time consuming.'
   Discuss this statement showing that you have considered more than one point of view. (You must refer to religion and belief in your answer.)

Knowledge Check

1. What does the term 'kashrut' mean?
2. Write a short paragraph (roughly three sentences) to explain what is meant by 'synagogue'.
3. Draw a Venn diagram. In the middle, write three beliefs that Orthodox and Reform Jews share. In the outer rings, write two beliefs on which they have different views.
4. Explain what Jews believe about keeping Shabbat. Remember there are different views.

The Big Question

'What you eat doesn't matter to God.'

Your Task

How do you think someone who is Jewish might respond to this statement?

Write a minimum of two developed paragraphs.

You must include two references to sacred texts and references to Orthodox, Reform, Kashrut.

Task

You need to explain in detail religious teachings about the synagogue. Use the guidance below to help you to write a developed explanation for Judaism. Ensure that you use key terms fluently and frequently.

All/many/most Jews believe that _____.

This comes from the teaching/Torah quote _____.

This means that/Because of this they _____.

Some/other Jews such as _____ believe that _____.

This comes from the teaching/Torah quote _____.

This means that/Because of this they _____.

Finally, Jews such as _____ believe that _____.

This means that/Because of this they _____.

Their beliefs do/do not differ because _____.

9 Issues of life and death

Key Concepts

Abortion When a pregnancy is ended by the deliberate removal of the foetus from the womb so that it does not result in the birth of a child.

Afterlife Life after death; the belief that existence continues after physical death.

Environmental responsibility The duty upon human beings to respect, care for and preserve the natural environment. Crucial to environmental responsibility is the idea of sustainability.

Euthanasia From Greek, *eu* 'good' + *thanatos* 'death'. Sometimes referred to as mercy killing. The act of killing a person, either directly or indirectly, because a decision has been reached that death would be the best option.

Evolution The process by which different living creatures are believed to have developed from earlier, less complex forms, during the history of the earth.

Quality of life The extent to which life is meaningful and pleasurable.

Sanctity of life The belief that life is precious or sacred because humans are made 'in God's image'. For many religious believers, only human life holds this special status.

Soul The spiritual aspect of a being; that which connects someone to God. The soul is often regarded as non-physical and as living on after physical death, in an afterlife.

Core Questions

- Could life have developed by itself?
- Are there different ways of understanding religious scriptures?
- Do humans have an immortal soul?
- Are the lives of people more valuable than those of animals?
- What is environmental stewardship?
- Does the unborn baby have a right to life?
- Should we be able ask someone to help us die?

The world

The origin of the world: religious and scientific perspectives

Religion: creation stories

Many of the world's religions have beliefs about how the world came into being. The monotheistic traditions of Judaism, Christianity and Islam believe that there is one, all-powerful creator God who is the source of all life. Their creation stories, found in their holy books, tell of a creation event at the beginning of time, when life sprang into existence from nothing at the command of God. These three religions all share common roots, so there are elements of the Genesis creation stories in the Bible, which also appear in the Qur'an.

Hinduism and Buddhism do not teach the existence of a single monotheistic creator god. In general, the Eastern religions see the origin of the universe in a more mysterious and mythological way. Their belief in a cyclical world-view tends to suggest that the world may have been formed, destroyed and reformed countless times.

The ways in which religious people understand their creation stories today vary enormously

- **Literal interpretation** Some religious believers are literalists. They believe that their holy text should be understood word for word. Creationists are literalists: for them the creation of the world happened exactly as it is described in sacred texts.
- **Liberal interpretation** Other religious people take a liberal view. They believe that people should be free to understand the holy books in any way they choose. They say that the stories they contain should be understood more as metaphors or symbolic stories. They are true because the stories carry real meaning, but they don't refer to actual historical events.

Interpretation The way people make sense of a piece of writing. Different believers interpret passages from the holy books in different ways.
Literal Understanding something exactly as it is written.
Liberal Free-thinking.

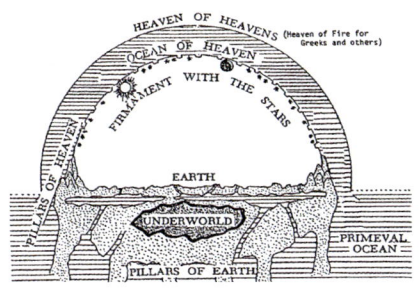

An ancient Hebrew view of the world: an attempt to picture the flat earth and dome-like heavens above, as described by the Genesis creation stories.

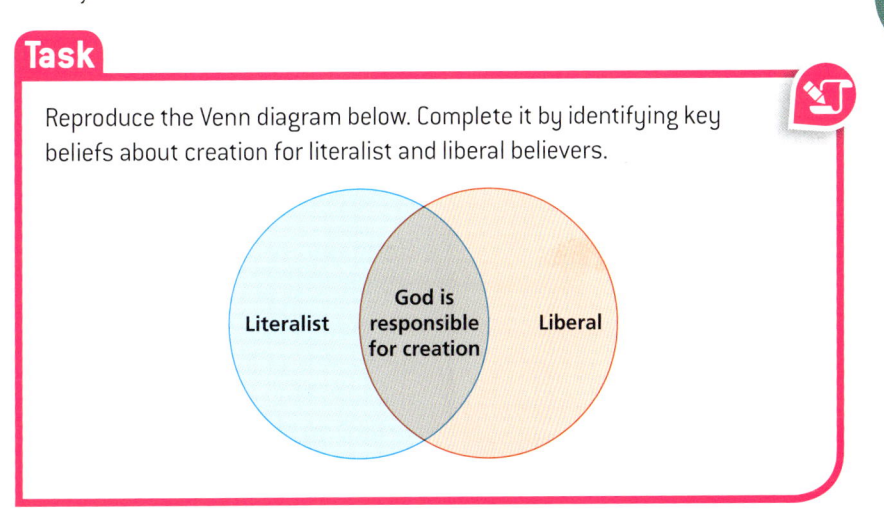

Task

Reproduce the Venn diagram below. Complete it by identifying key beliefs about creation for literalist and liberal believers.

Literalist | God is responsible for creation | Liberal

> **Tasks**
>
> 1 What is a creationist?
> 2 How do creationist ideas about the natural world differ from non-religious ones?
> 3 Read the following statement from Pope Francis.
>
> > When we read about Creation in Genesis, we run the risk of imagining God as a magician, with a magic wand able to do everything. But that is not so. God created human beings and let them develop according to the internal laws that He gave to each one so they would reach their fulfilment.
>
> Explain whether or not you think Pope Francis is a creationist. Use quotes from his statement to support your point.

> **Stephen Hawking**
>
> One of the physicists to have made the biggest contributions to the field of cosmology for over half a century is Stephen Hawking. In the late 1960s, his ground-breaking research showed that, at the birth of the universe, the cosmos must have emerged from a singularity. His studies demonstrated that the universe may look as if it is static, but it is actually expanding at an astonishing rate, and that this expansion can be traced back to an initial event: the Big Bang.

Science: the Big Bang theory and evolution

Since the sixteenth century there has been a massive shift in the way people in the West understand the natural world. Until the rise of scientific thinking, there was an acceptance within Christian society that the Bible was the absolute, unchanging word of God. The traditional Christian view was that the earth had been created by God, as described in the Book of Genesis.

In the seventeenth century, Archbishop Ussher in Ireland pronounced that the world had been created in 4004 BCE. However, as more evidence built up in the fields of geology and biology, it became clear that the earth is far older than had previously been understood. Charles Darwin was the first person to show convincingly that life had arisen through the slow, natural process of **evolution**, and therefore the earth must be many millions of years old.

In the twentieth century scientists began to look beyond the earth to space for an explanation of how the world was created, but it was not until 1965 that the Big Bang theory became the accepted explanation for the origin of the universe.

The Big Bang theory

The scientific study of the origins of the universe is called cosmology. Throughout history, some thinkers have argued about whether the universe had an origin, or whether it has always existed; whether it is expanding, or whether it is static (at rest). In 1965, cosmologists published evidence to show that the universe did, in fact, have a beginning. This theory, that time and space began around 15 billion years ago, became known as the Big Bang theory.

According to the Big Bang theory, the universe began from a 'singularity', an infinitely tiny point. This singularity was infinitely hot and infinitely dense and, as it expanded, sub-atomic particles and then atoms began to appear. This led to the formation of stars and planets, which make up the universe as we know it today. Most physicists believe that the universe will continue expanding for billions of years to come, becoming bigger and colder.

Today most scientists accept this as an accurate explanation for our world. The evidence for the Big Bang theory comes from the discovery of background radiation, which is thought to be left over from the initial expansion at the start of the universe. This can be detected with powerful telescopes.

Religious reactions to the Big Bang theory

Buddhists, Hindus and Sikhs tend to be quite accepting of the Big Bang theory. They believe that the world has been formed, destroyed and re-formed countless times, and so this fits well with the idea that the universe is in a state of development.

Liberal Christians, Jews and Muslims find no problem in accepting the Big Bang theory. They have no reason to question the evidence on which it is based and accept that this is a way that God may have chosen to allow the universe to create intelligent life.

Religious creationists are very critical of these ideas. For them they contradict the truth that God has formed all life through his own power.

Even if scientists are correct in saying that the universe began with a Big Bang, have they really solved the question 'where does the universe come from'? We are still left with the question of what caused the Big Bang. Some Christians have argued that it was God.

Tasks

1. a. In one sentence, describe the Big Bang theory.
   b. Outline the process of the Big Bang using a flow chart.

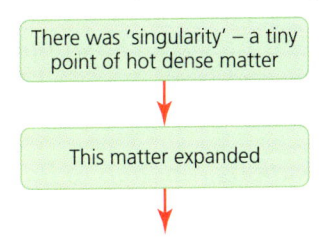

   > There was 'singularity' – a tiny point of hot dense matter
   >
   > ↓
   >
   > This matter expanded
   >
   > ↓

2. What are the problems with the Big Bang theory? Refer to two different problems in your answer.
3. Copy and complete the table below by placing the following words in the correct column:

   chance, design, faith, evidence, change, accident, purpose, plan, origin, probability, value, life, beliefs, reasoning, hope, trust, facts, proof

Scientific concepts	Religious concepts

Key Concept

Evolution The process by which different living creatures are believed to have developed from earlier, less complex forms during the history of the earth.

Natural selection The idea that the species that flourish are those which are best suited to their environment.

The theory of evolution

In 1859, Charles Darwin published *On the Origin of Species*. This controversial book set out his theory of evolution by **natural selection**, explaining how living creatures have developed through a process of gradual change over millions of years. His ideas were backed by the detailed evidence gathered through over 30 years of scientific research.

[Evolution is] the single best idea anyone has ever had.

(Daniel C Dennett)

Blind evolution

On the Galapagos Islands, off the coast of South America, Darwin had observed birds (finches) on the different islands. He noticed that different types of finches lived on different islands. Some had fat beaks – they tended to be found on islands where seeds were the main food-source. On other islands, where fleshy cactus fruits were abundant, the finches had thin, pointed beaks.

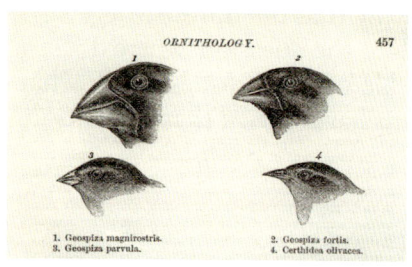

Darwin observed differences in the beaks of finches. He assumed that all finches had a common ancestor. This led him to the theory of evolution by natural selection.

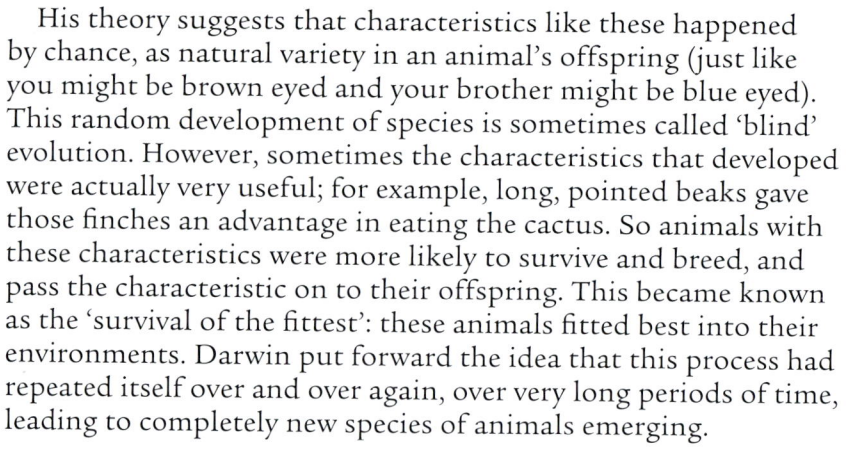

His theory suggests that characteristics like these happened by chance, as natural variety in an animal's offspring (just like you might be brown eyed and your brother might be blue eyed). This random development of species is sometimes called 'blind' evolution. However, sometimes the characteristics that developed were actually very useful; for example, long, pointed beaks gave those finches an advantage in eating the cactus. So animals with these characteristics were more likely to survive and breed, and pass the characteristic on to their offspring. This became known as the 'survival of the fittest': these animals fitted best into their environments. Darwin put forward the idea that this process had repeated itself over and over again, over very long periods of time, leading to completely new species of animals emerging.

Religious reaction to Darwin

Today, there are many religious believers who welcome Darwin's theories. Liberal Christians accept the idea that science can teach us things that the writers of the Bible had no understanding of. Most Jewish people have no problem in accepting the theory of evolution.

However, some Evangelical Christians and many mainstream Muslims see Darwinian evolution as an attack on their beliefs. These are some of the objections that some religious people have to the theory of evolution:

- Evolution implies that life has developed by chance, whereas religious scriptures (for example, the Bible, the Torah and the Qur'an) teach that God is the creator.
- Undermining the Bible, the Torah or the Qur'an risks undermining the morals we share as human beings, leading to crime and disorder.
- Religious scriptures teach that humans alone have a God-given soul, but if we have evolved from animals, there is no special place for the human soul.
- Evolution challenges the teachings of the Bible, because Genesis says that each species was made 'according to its kind' (species don't change, they are fixed for all time).

This 'Jesus fish' is a Christian symbol, which was used by the early Church.

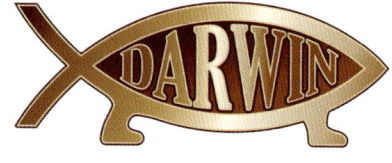

This is a 'Darwin fish'. Do you think it is a symbol used by Christians who believe in evolution, or a symbol used to mock Christian beliefs about creation? Can you explain your answer?

Tasks

1. Explain what evolution is. Ensure that you use the following terms in your answer: theory, natural selection, survival of the fittest, Charles Darwin.
2. Summarise the main problems some religious believers have with the theory of evolution.
3. Look at the quotation from Charles Darwin. Do you think he is an atheist or a theist? Explain your opinion.

   It seems to me absurd to doubt that a man may be an ardent Theist and an evolutionist… I have never been an atheist in the sense of denying the existence of a God.

   (Charles Darwin, 1879)

Was the world designed?

The design argument

Many religious believers say that the fact that the world is so beautiful and well-ordered gives us strong evidence for the existence of a creator God. They argue that the complexity and interconnectedness of nature could not have come about by itself. There must be a divine mind behind creation.

> **William Paley**
>
> In 1802, the theologian William Paley put forward his famous watch analogy. If you were to find a watch by accident, you would think that it must have been designed by a watch-maker. In the same way, when looking at the world with its complex patterns and structures, you would come to the conclusion that there must be a cosmic world-maker, a designer God.

Intelligent design

Intelligent design is a popular belief in the USA today among Christians. The theory states that there are some organisms alive today that cannot have come about through the process of slow, random evolution.

Intelligent design The idea that certain features of life are best explained by an intelligent cause, rather than an undirected process, such as natural selection.

The illusion of design

The biologist Richard Dawkins claims that the theory of evolution is the best explanation of how life has come about. He argues that the world might appear to have been designed, but that raises the question: who designed the designer? Dawkins believes that natural selection gives the solution to the question, 'Where do we come from?' As an atheist, he argues that evolution needs no help from God.

The illusion of design in the living world is explained with far greater economy ... by Darwinian natural selection.

(Richard Dawkins)

Richard Dawkins argues that evolution is the best explanation of how life has developed on Earth.

> **Tasks**
>
> 1 Summarise what is meant by 'intelligent design'.
> 2 Outline the main argument (The Watch) offered by William Paley.
> 3 Give two examples that suggest that the world appears to be designed. Include things that show order in the world, such as the seasons.
> 4 Richard Dawkins says that the appearance of design is an illusion. What does he mean by this?
> 5 Do you agree with William Paley or Richard Dawkins? Explain the reason for your opinion.

Tasks

1. What is the key difference between science and religion when thinking about creation?
2. Is it possible for Christians to believe in both the biblical creation story and the theory of evolution?
3. a) Analyse the results from 'Evolution without God? What do people think?'
   b) Explain what the results tell us about modern ideas of creation. Why might some people find these results surprising?

Evolution without God? What do people think?

In a survey of 2,060 adults in Great Britain (carried out by Comres in 2008), people were told:

'Atheistic evolution is the idea that evolution makes belief in God unnecessary and absurd.'

Then they were asked:

'In your opinion, is atheistic evolution …?'

The results are shown in the table.

	%
Definitely true	13
Probably true	21
Probably untrue	27
Definitely untrue	30
Don't know	9

Conclusion: 34 per cent of British people accept the idea of atheistic evolution.

▶ Religious teachings about the creation of the world

Christian attitudes to the creation of the world

There are two stories that describe God's creation of the world, both found in the Book of Genesis. (For more detail see pages 7–12.)

Genesis 1.1–2.3

The first creation story describes how God created the universe over six days: from the creation of earth and sky, through the making of the sun, stars, plants, animals and then finally human beings. Humans are the peak of God's creation, made in his image, giving them a unique status as God's stewards of the earth. On the seventh day God rested.

> And God said: 'Let there be light', and there was light.
>
> (Genesis 1.3)

> Then God said, 'Let us make mankind in our image, in our likeness…'
>
> (Genesis 1.26)

Genesis 2.4–2.25

The second creation story teaches that God made the man, Adam, first, before the animals, and placed him in the Garden of Eden to live in paradise. Adam was formed from the dust of the ground and the breath of God (symbolising the human soul), making him the son of the earth, but also a child of God. To give Adam a partner and a companion, God created Eve out of one of Adam's ribs.

Christian sacred writings and science

For Christians, the Bible has a unique status as the inspired 'Word of God'; it is unlike any other piece of writing. However, the way in which Christians interpret the Bible varies considerably.

Evangelical Christians

Many Evangelical Christians are **creationists**. They say that scientific theories of evolution and the Big Bang must be false because they contradict the literal understanding of the creation stories. However, there are different ways of understanding creationism:

- **Young – earth creationism** is the view that the world was created by God, in six actual days, and this happened less than 10,000 years ago.
- **Old – earth creationism** agrees that God must have created the world, but it accepts the idea that creation took place millions of years ago. The six days of creation refer to long eras of time, rather than 24-hour periods.

9 Issues of life and death

162

Liberal Christians

Liberal Christians say that it makes more sense to understand the Bible accounts as myths (stories which contain religious wisdom) written thousands of years ago by people living in a pre-scientific age; they should not to be understood as historical events. The very fact that the two creation narratives in Genesis seem to contradict each other is evidence that these are stories, not factual accounts. (Genesis 1 says humans were created on the last day of creation; Genesis 2 says that humans were created first, before the animals.)

Liberal Christians accept that scientific thinking gives us an accurate picture of reality. Liberal Christians tend to agree with evolution, but believe that God planned that life should develop in this way. However, they may disagree on the way God was actually involved in bringing life into being:

- **Theistic guided evolution** The belief that life came about through evolution, but this process was guided by the direct intervention of God.
- **Natural evolution** Many Christians accept the evidence put forward by science, which says that evolution is the natural process through which life has emerged. However, they would say that God set down these laws of nature before the universe existed.

> **Creationism** The belief that all life was made by God, exactly as it is.

Buddhist attitudes to the creation of the world

Buddhism does not teach about a creator god. In fact, Buddhism does not concern itself with how the world was created at all. The Buddha said that the question of how to overcome suffering in the world is far more urgent.

Generally, Buddhists would say that questions about the origin of the universe are scientific, and they would be content to accept the scientific explanation of the Big Bang. In the same way, Buddhists are likely to accept evolutionary theory. However, they would not accept that these things develop randomly. Addressing evolution, the Dalai Lama, spiritual leader of Tibetan Buddhists, has said,

> From the Buddhist's perspective, the idea of these mutations being random events is deeply unsatisfying for a theory that purports to explain the origin of life.
>
> (Dalai Lama, *The Universe in a Single Atom: The Convergence of Science And Spirituality*)

Change (mutation) is a core principle of Buddhism; everything constantly changes, but change does not come about by accident. Buddhism teaches that everything in the cosmos is interrelated; everything depends on everything else for its existence. This is called 'Dependent Origination' (pratityasamutpada). The existence of all things is caused by the existence of other things: their 'origination' is 'dependent' on others. Things develop and change as the conditions around them develop and change. The Buddha said:

> When there is this, that comes to be;
> with the arising of this, that arises.
> When there is not this, that does not come to be;
> with the ending of this, that ends.
>
> (Samyutta Sutta 12.61)

For example, an oak tree grows from an acorn; it depends on the acorn for its existence. But it depends on other things, too: soil conditions, climate, rain, temperature, sunshine and so on. As these conditions change, the tree changes.

The principle of Dependent Origination is not meant to explain how the universe or life came about. But it does suggest that there is no first cause: nothing arises out of nothing, and nothing was created. It means that God did not create the universe and did not create life.

Buddhism teaches that events arise when the right conditions are present, they persist, and then they cease. This happens in regular ways and the laws of physics, chemistry, biology and zoology for instance, are acceptable to Buddhists. However Buddhism adds in an extra level of conditionality for humans: the law of karma, which shows how our motivations and actions can keep us in a cycle of painful birth and death (samsara) or gradually release us to the liberation of Nirvana.

When speaking of how Buddhists view creation, the Dalai Lama said:

> This is significant because it precludes two possibilities. One is the possibility that things can arise from nowhere, with no causes and conditions, and the second is that things can arise on account of a transcendent designer or creator. Both these possibilities are negated.
>
> (Quoted in *The New Mandala – Eastern Wisdom for Western Living*, John Lundin)

Muslim attitudes to the creation of the world

The Qur'an teaches that God is the creator and sustainer of all life but, unlike the Bible, there is no single creation story. Passages about the creation are scattered throughout the Qur'an. Muslims believe that God created the heavens and the earth from formless matter over six long periods of time. He created humans out of clay, moulding Adam and breathing life and power into him. He took Adam to paradise and made a wife for him.

> Indeed, your Lord is God who created the heavens and earth in six days and then established Himself above the Throne. He covers the night with the day, [another night] chasing it rapidly; and [He created] the sun, the moon, and the stars, subjected by His command. Unquestionably, His is the creation and the command; blessed is God, Lord of the worlds.
>
> (Qur'an 7.54)

Islamic sacred writings and science

Islam teaches that the Qur'an is a sacred text and that the words it contains are the actual word of God. Most Muslims believe that the Qur'an must be understood literally, not metaphorically. Because of this, many Muslims are creationists: they say it was God who made the earth; it could not possibly have come about by itself. Islam tends to teach old-earth creationism, the idea that God created the world over six long periods of time.

Some Muslims will criticise the theory of evolution. The Qur'an makes specific reference to Adam's creation by God, so many Muslims, even if they accept most aspects of evolution, refuse to accept the idea of human evolution.

Although, like the Bible, the Qur'an refers to creation taking six 'days', the Arabic word used in the Qur'an is understood to mean six long periods of time, rather than exactly 24 hours.

> Is not He who created the heavens and the earth able to create the likes of them? Yes, [it is so]; and He is the Knowing Creator.
>
> (Qur'an 36.81)

However, there are also many Muslims who have no difficulty accepting scientific explanations of the world, while also believing in the Qur'an. They have no major disagreement with science and they accept evolution, because they say that scientific ideas cannot disprove the existence of God. An important part of being a Muslim is to strive for better understanding of the world, so greater scientific knowledge gives a deeper awareness of the way God has created the world.

> Have those who disbelieved not considered that the heavens and the earth were a joined entity, and We separated them and made from water every living thing? Then will they not believe?
>
> (Qur'an 21.30)

> The book of God and the book of Nature can be aligned.
>
> (Dr Hasan)

Jewish attitudes to the creation of the world

Jews believe that there is one God who is the source and purpose of all life. The Book of Genesis, which is the first book in the Torah, tells two stories about the origins of the world.

The first creation story says:

> In the beginning of God's creating the heavens and the earth when the earth was astonishingly empty … God said: 'Let there be light'.
>
> (Genesis 1.1–3)

This account goes on to describe the six 'days' of creation. On the sixth day, God created human beings: 'So God created Man in his image…'

The second creation story (Genesis 2.4–25) gives a different account of God's creation, with Adam and Eve being created and placed in the Garden of Eden.

Many Jews believe that the Torah is the 'Word of God', but if this is the case, then how can both these stories be true?

Orthodox Jews take a literalist view: they believe that these stories are true accounts of the origin of the world. They say that they were revealed to Moses by God, and they argue that the different accounts only appear to contradict each other because we have not understood them properly.

Reform Jews would take a more liberal view and question whether Moses was the actual author of

Genesis. They might argue that there are different stories because they were written by different authors and only put together in the Torah at a later date.

Jewish sacred writings and science

Some Orthodox Jews would understand the Genesis creation passages to be historical fact, so they would have difficulties accepting modern scientific ideas. The creation stories picture God creating all species of animals just as they are today, fixed forever. This leads them to reject ideas of evolution, where species emerge and change over millions of years.

Other, more progressive Jews have no problem in accepting scientific theories like the Big Bang and evolution. However, they would not accept the conclusion that humanists come to, namely that therefore there is no need for God. They still have faith in God as a sustainer and provider, but they argue that God kick-started the universe through the Big Bang and has guided the creation of life through evolution.

Humanist attitudes to the creation of the world

Humanists believe that we can understand the world through science and that religious explanations of the world are unreliable. They say that there are no good reasons for believing in the existence of God, and there is plenty of evidence to suggest that the world formed by itself, through slow, gradual processes over billions of years. Evolution can help us to understand the way species are related to each other today, rather than relying on the religious belief that the creation of life is a 'mystery'.

Tasks

1. What are the key differences between the creation stories in Christian, Jewish and Muslim traditions, compared with Buddhism?
2. How do Creationist Christians view creation stories?
3. How do Liberal Christians view creation stories?
4. Using the table below, create a glossary of key terms linked with creation.

Term	Definition	Summarised
Monotheism		One God
Religious belief	Accepting that there is a spiritual purpose in life.	

5. Explain why ideas about creation have changed over time.

Stewardship and the relationship between humans and the natural world

What is stewardship?

Stewardship means caring for the planet and managing its resources. Stewards are like trustees or caretakers; they are responsible for looking after someone's property while that person is away. Many believers say that God has given humans the special duty to care for the world in his place, since they are his precious possession.

Earth provides enough to satisfy every man's need, but not every man's greed.

(Mahatma Gandhi)

Stewardship implies that human beings have a duty to ensure that the demands placed on natural resources can be met without reducing capacity to allow all people and other species of animals, as well as plant life, to live well, now and in the future. This is known as **environmental sustainability**.

This, in turn, means that we should think of ourselves as **global citizens**. We should view the whole world as our home, not just the town where we live or our country of birth. We have a responsibility to care for the Amazonian rainforests and for global climate change as much as for pollution in our own local communities.

> **Key Concept**
>
> **Environmental responsibility**
> The duty upon human beings to respect, care for and preserve the natural environment. Crucial to environmental responsibility is the idea of sustainability.

Environmental sustainability Ensuring that the demands placed on natural resources can be met without reducing capacity.

Global citizenship The idea that we should see ourselves as part of a world community.

Stewardship means caring for the planet.

Christian Aid and Global Citizenship

In 2015, countries that make up the United Nations agreed to 17 goals to end poverty, protect the planet and ensure prosperity for all as part of a new sustainable development agenda. Each goal has specific targets to be achieved by 2030. Of course, governments must play their parts in meeting the targets but, says the United Nations, each citizen has a part to play in acting as global citizens to create a sustainable future for all on the planet.

Christian Aid is a Christian organisation that works throughout the world to create the conditions in which everyone can live with dignity, free from poverty. Part of their work involves working for environmental sustainability so that people can live in prosperity.

Christian Aid, therefore, has developed a programme to help deliver the Sustainable Development Goals. The charity sees education as the key to achieving the goals and has produced curriculum materials for use in schools to get the message across. Dr Tanya Wisely of Christian Aid says:

> Education is key to delivering the Global Goals, and the ideas of fairness and equality behind much of the Global Goals are key to a good education. It's a virtuous circle.

Religious teachings about stewardship

Christian attitudes to stewardship

Christians believe that life is a gift from God and that God has given humans the role of stewards in the world. Genesis 1.26 teaches that God made men and women in his own image, meaning that humans have a soul, which is unique among all creatures. Genesis 2.7 says that God formed Adam from the dust and breathed his divine life into him.

Both these passages imply that humans were created with a special status above the rest of nature. However, this leads to a disagreement among Christians about how we should treat the environment.

> *You have made them (humans) a little lower than the angels and crowned them with glory and honour. You made them rulers over the works of your hands; you put everything under their feet.*
>
> (Psalm 8.5–6)

> *God blessed them and said to them, 'Be fruitful and increase in number; fill the earth and subdue it. Rule over the fish in the sea and the birds in the sky and over every living creature that moves on the ground.'*
>
> (Genesis 1.28)

Dominion: to rule over nature

Evangelical Christians tend to take the Bible literally so, when it says in Genesis 1.28 that God created humans to 'rule over' nature, they believe that this gives us the right to use the world's natural resources for our own benefit. In other words, they believe humans have 'dominion' over nature.

Stewardship: to live in harmony with nature

More Liberal Christians, however, argue that humans should be stewards of the earth, rather than exploiters. Genesis 2.15 speaks of God placing Adam in the Garden of Eden to 'cultivate and care for it'.

They say that humans have a responsibility towards the environment, looking after the planet's precious resources. God has entrusted us to live as stewards and we should be responsible global citizens, using the earth's resources in a sustainable manner.

Some 'Green Christians' are environmental activists who promote awareness and action at church, community and national levels.

Buddhist attitudes to stewardship

Pratityasamutpada (Dependent Origination)

The Buddhist principle of pratityasamutpada (Dependent Origination) says that everything is interrelated, dependent on everything else for its existence. Nothing comes into existence independently, nothing continues to exist unconnected to anything else.

In considering the relationship between human beings and their environment, Dependent Origination suggests that as we affect our environment, so our environment affects us. The idea of karma says that human action has proportionate consequences. So actions that harm the environment come to affect humanity negatively. On the other hand, when humans take responsible care for the natural world, they create the conditions for the earth to support and sustain their existence.

For example, human activity has involved the use of so-called 'greenhouse gases' that cause global warming. The effect of this is climate change: melting ice sheets, rising sea levels, increase in rain and snowfall and so on. If it continues, fresh water will be harder to obtain, places where crops thrive will become rarer, animal habitats will move and diseases will spread.

Conversely, when humans take steps to reduce their negative influence on the environment by, for example, recycling, then landfill is reduced, energy consumption is lowered, and pollution decreases. These things lessen the effects of global warming and enable the earth to produce food, water, medicines and so on, in a sustainable way.

Causing harm

The principle of Right Action, the fourth component of the Noble Eightfold Path, is essentially guidance to avoid any actions that harm one's surroundings, including, of course, the natural environment. The second of the Five Precepts also warns against taking what is not freely given, and there is a sense in which human beings have taken from the environment in ways that are not sustainable.

The Vietnamese Zen Buddhist, Thich Nhat Hanh, says:

> We should not harm ourselves; we should not harm nature. Harming nature is harming ourselves, and vice versa.
>
> (*The Individual, Society and Nature*, from *The Path of Compassion: Writings on Socially Engaged Buddhism*)

The status of human beings

While Buddhism teaches that humans should care for the environment, it is not simply to make human life comfortable; it is out of respect for all living beings, in recognition of our interrelationship.

So Buddhism cannot agree with those religions that say that human beings have a special status on earth, which includes dominion or stewardship on behalf of God. The status of human beings is not higher than that of other living beings, but the abilities humans have to develop wisdom, compassion and loving-kindness give them a special responsibility to extend them to all living beings.

Some Buddhist organisations have set up retreat centres to provide models of sustainable living, based on Buddhist principles. For example, the Lam Rim Centre in Raglan, Monmouthshire, was established in 1978 to offer a peaceful setting for people to experience the application of Buddhist values. Their intention is:

> To cultivate awareness within ourselves and others to highlight the current urgency of climate change and to establish a means of preventing this from continuing.

Their aspiration is to reverse climate change, starting with individuals and small groups:

> We will initiate simple, practical, achievable, and realistic steps from a grass-roots level so that we can develop a personal and collective ability to respond to the current climate crisis we all face.

Muslim attitudes to stewardship

Stewardship

Islam teaches that animals must be respected, but, unlike human beings, they are not sacred. Muslims, like Christians, believe that God is the all-powerful creator of all life, and that humans have been created with particular responsibilities. We are his trustees (**khalifahs**), appointed to care for the world and rule it as God would wish. It is not ours to waste or spoil; it must be safeguarded for future generations.

Khalifah The Arabic word for 'steward'.
Fitrah Natural order, balance.

Environmental responsibility

Islam teaches that there is a pattern and balance in the universe, known as **fitrah**.

The survival and continuation of the planet relies on this balance being maintained. It is the role of humans, as khalifahs, to work to maintain this fitrah (balance) by being aware of the need to use the earth's resources fairly.

Many Muslims say that this means that they should act as global citizens, living sustainable lifestyles. Others argue that the reason Muslims should treat the earth with care is because they will be judged by God on the way they have looked after the natural world.

> The earth is green and beautiful. God has appointed you his stewards over it.
>
> (Hadith)

The Prophet Muhammad said animals must be treated with care, and he told a story about how, on a very hot day, a prostitute took water from a well to give to a dog. He pronounced that, for this act of kindness, all her sins would be forgiven by God.

> And it is He who has made you successors upon the earth and has raised some of you above others in degrees [of rank] that He may try you through what He has given you.
>
> (Qur'an 6.165)

Yet the Qur'an makes it clear that the world belongs to its creator:

> Indeed, your Lord is Allah, who created the heavens and earth in six days and then established Himself above the Throne. He covers the night with the day, [another night] chasing it rapidly; and [He created] the sun, the moon, and the stars, subjected by His command. Unquestionably, His is the creation and the command; blessed is Allah, Lord of the worlds.
>
> (Qur'an 7.54)

9 Issues of life and death

> So direct your face toward the religion, inclining to truth. [Adhere to] the fitrah of God upon which He has created [all] people. No change should there be in the creation of God. That is the correct religion, but most of the people do not know.
>
> (Qur'an 30.30)

Jewish attitudes to stewardship

Jewish leaders today teach that human beings must behave as responsible global citizens, acting as the stewards of God's creation. There are a number of teachings about how to care for the earth, some originating in the Tenakh, others from the Talmud or from Jewish traditions.

Stewardship and dominion

Genesis 1 explains that God gave humans control over nature:

> Rule over the fish of the sea, the birds of the air and everything living that moves on the earth.
>
> (Genesis 1.28)

> It is our Jewish responsibility to put the defence of the whole of nature at the very centre of our concern.
>
> (Rabbi Arthur Hertzberg)

Humans must treat the environment with respect because the earth is God's possession, and we are the temporary caretakers. Stewardship is both a gift and a duty.

Environmental sustainability

The annual festival of Tu B'Shevat (New Year for Trees) is a powerful reminder that humans must learn to live environmentally sustainable lives. Tu B'Shevat comes at the beginning of spring, and Jewish people in Israel and around the world mark the event by planting trees wherever they can. They also celebrate the day by eating fruit, especially from varieties that are mentioned in the Torah: grapes, figs, pomegranates, olives and dates.

There is a story in the Talmud that is often told at Tu B'Shevat that serves as a reminder to Jewish people about the need to safeguard the environment for future generations. It tells of a character called Honi the circle-drawer, who lived in the first century BCE. On one occasion, Honi was travelling along a road when he met a man planting a carob tree. He asked the man how long it takes for a carob tree to bear fruit. The man replied, 'Seventy years'. Honi asked the man if he was certain that he would still be alive in 70 years' time, and the man replied, 'I found already grown carob trees in the world; as my forefathers planted those for me, so I too plant these for my children.'

Animal rights

The Jewish scriptures do not have very much to say about the rights of animals, but they make it very clear that animals are an important part of God's creation. Today most Jewish people are happy to eat certain types of meat, provided it is killed according to kosher food laws. It must be carried out by a certified person, and the animal's throat must be cut with a swift action, using a special knife with a sharp blade. Others are vegetarians, believing that this is the way God created us to be, living in harmony with animals as Adam and Eve did in the Garden of Eden.

One of the great Jewish thinkers is Maimonides who lived in the twelfth century. He taught that animals must be respected for themselves; they were not created by God just for the benefit of humans. The Torah teaches that, although humans have been given dominion over animals, this does not give us the right to exploit and harm them. The tenth of Maimoides' 13 Principles concerns God's omnipotence and his omniscience: even though human beings have dominion over the world, God has the ultimate power.

Care for the environment

The Torah does not say much about how to treat the environment, but there is a passage in Deuteronomy that says:

> When you lay siege to a city . . . do not destroy its trees by putting an axe to them.
>
> (Deuteronomy 20.19)

This teaching is known as **bal tashchit**. Jewish people see it as an instruction to use the earth's resources wisely and not to waste or exploit them for short-term gain.

In Jewish tradition there is a strong emphasis on the importance of caring for others. The phrase **tikkun olam** is an instruction to 'repair the world'. It encourages Jewish people to work to conserve the earth's resources through sensible use and recycling. In Judaism it is a mitzvah (duty) for individuals to be generous, making **gemilut hasadim** (acts of loving kindness) towards others. Caring for the environment might mean going out of your way not to be wasteful or being prepared to pay more for ethical products.

So important is caring for the environment, it ranks above other religious duties:

Rabbi Yochanan Ben Zakkai said… If you have a sapling in your hand, and someone says to you that the Messiah has come, stay and complete the planting, and then go out to greet the Messiah.

(Avot de Rabbi Natan, 31(B))

Tend well to the earth, for there will be no one to make it right after you.

(Talmud)

> **Bal tashchit** Referred to in the Torah; literally, it means 'do not destroy'.
>
> **Tikkun olam** Literally means 'repair the world'. Jewish people believe it is important to work to make the world a better place for everyone.
>
> **Gemilut hasadim** Literally means making 'acts of loving kindness'. It emphasises the need to be charitable, caring for others and for the world.

Humanist attitudes to stewardship

Humanists try to base their thinking on reasoning and evidence, rejecting ideas that rely on belief in a supernatural being (God). Most humanists agree with the ideas of stewardship; they say that we have a responsibility to work for a more sustainable world, causing as little harm to the environment as possible. However, they believe this because they say it makes sense, not because God has placed us here for that purpose.

Social and community responsibility: Humanists for a better world

Humanists for a Better World (H4BW) is an interest group, linked with the British Humanist Association, which grew out of the Stop Climate Chaos coalition. The basic principles of H4BW are to protect human rights, where they are under threat from poverty, hunger and exploitation; and to act against climate change and in favour of environmental sustainability. Their aim is simple: 'Putting humanist values into action – because the whole world is in our hands.' They actively lobby for environmental causes and have been vocal on issues such as fracking, global warming and issues linked with animal welfare.

> The humanist perspective places a strong emphasis on personal responsibility for our actions and the importance of social co-operation, and we very much hope that Humanists for a Better World can build upon this tradition.
>
> (Andrew Copson, Chief Executive of the British Humanist Association)

Humanists UK

Tasks

1. Explain the key difference between 'inheriting' the earth and 'borrowing' it.
2. Look at the saying below. How might it affect the way people treat the earth?

   We didn't inherit the land from our fathers, we are borrowing it from our children.
3. What is environmental sustainability? Support your answer by giving three different examples.

▶ End of Section Review

Stickability

Key concepts:
- Environmental responsibility
- Evolution

Key teachings:
- The origin of the universe
- Stewardship and environmental responsibility
- Dominion
- Sustainability
- Global citizenship
- Social and community responsibility

Skills Link

1. What is meant by environmental responsibility?
2. Explain why there may be differences in belief within a religion about creation.

Knowledge Check

1. What does the word 'stewardship' mean?
2. In your own words, explain the difference between evolution and creation.
3. Explain ideas about creationism in two different religions or religious traditions.
4. Explain what Richard Dawkins means by the 'illusion of design'.

The Big Question

'Life must have come about by itself.'

Your Task

Respond to the statement above, showing that you have considered more than one point of view. Give reasoned judgements on the validity and strength of these views.

Task

For both of the religions you are studying, explain in detail religious teachings about stewardship.

Use the guidance below to help you to write a developed explanation for Christianity and a second one for your other chosen religion. Ensure you use key terms fluently and frequently.

All/many/most Christians believe that _____ .

This comes from the teaching/Bible quote _____ .

This means that/Because of this they _____ .

Some/other Christians such as _____ believe that _____ .

This comes from the teaching/Bible quote _____ .

This means that/Because of this they _____ .

Finally, Christians such as _____ believe that _____ .

This means that/Because of this they _____ .

Their beliefs do/do not differ because _____ .

The origin and value of human life

What is sanctity of life?

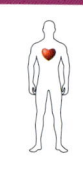

> **Key Concept**
>
> **Sanctity of life** The belief that life is precious or sacred, because humans are made 'in God's image'. For many religious believers, only human life holds this special status.

Most people, whether they hold a religious belief or not, would accept that human life is special and worthy of being preserved. For most religious believers, life is special because it comes ultimately from God. For those without a religious faith, life is no less precious, but its importance does not hail from God. Life is priceless because it is the only life we have.

This belief has a huge impact on various issues of **medical ethics**, especially those which relate to life-creating or life-ending procedures.

What makes us human?

Ingredients for human beings:

Seven bars of soap

Lime – to whitewash a chicken coop

Phosphorous – for 2,200 match heads

Magnesium – a small dose

Iron – for a medium-sized nail

Potassium – enough explode a small toy cannon

Sugar – to fill a sugar sifter

Water – five buckets

Sulphur – a pinch

The nine images above show the physical elements that make up human beings. What do you think is missing?

Religious teachings about the sanctity of life

Christian attitudes to the sanctity of life

Christians believe that life is created by God, protected by God and valued by God. God is interested and involved in each human's life. God has created each individual person and made them unique in their own right, just as he made Adam and Eve. Genesis 1.27 states that God created humankind in his own image. For literalist Christians this means that every human being who has ever walked the earth bears God's image. It is for this reason that all Christians, irrespective of denomination, believe that life is sacred and is a gift from God.

Because of the belief in the sanctity of life, many Christians also accept that only God should take life away. Quaker Christians oppose the death penalty and fighting in wars because of the belief that each person contains a reflection of the image of God, which makes every human sacred. This is clearly shown in the Bible:

> Don't you know that you yourselves are God's temple and that God's Spirit dwells in your midst?
>
> (1 Corinthians 3.16)

Similarly, only God should choose when life begins. Catholics hold strictly to this belief and as such disagree in practice with artificial methods of contraception and in vitro fertilisation (when an embryo is created outside of the human body in a laboratory using sperm and an egg).

Jesus also showed through his teachings and practice that all life should be valued. The way in which he tended to a leper, visited the sick and spoke to a Samaritan woman demonstrated that all lives are worthy of respect and compassion because all life comes from God and is therefore sacred.

The story of the creation in Genesis says that God created human beings and was pleased with what he created:

> God saw all that he had made, and it was very good. And there was evening, and there was morning – the sixth day.
>
> (Genesis 1.31)

Moreover, the Bible says that God creates every person individually and has plans for each of them:

> Before I formed you in the womb I knew you, before you were born I set you apart; I appointed you as a prophet to the nations.
>
> (Jeremiah 1.5)

Buddhist attitudes to the sanctity of life

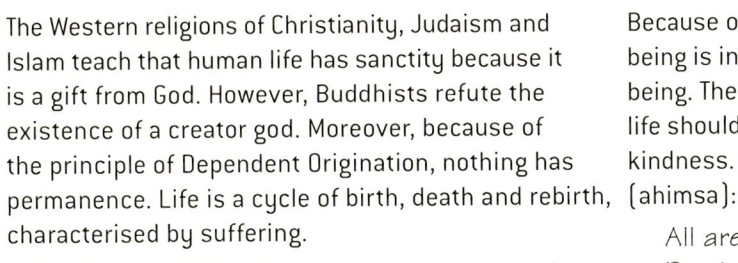

The Western religions of Christianity, Judaism and Islam teach that human life has sanctity because it is a gift from God. However, Buddhists refute the existence of a creator god. Moreover, because of the principle of Dependent Origination, nothing has permanence. Life is a cycle of birth, death and rebirth, characterised by suffering.

This is not to say, however, that life has no meaning. For Buddhists, part of the significance of human life lies in their belief that only humans can reveal the buddha-nature (Mahayana) or attain arahanthood (Theravada). Not having life denies the opportunity for humans to experience the bliss of nirvana. Buddhism teaches that it is very rare to be born as a human being and incredibly fortunate. So, although life is not sacred, in the sense that it is not holy or divine, it is infinitely precious.

Because of Dependent Origination, the life of each being is inextricably bound up with that of every other being. Therefore, Buddhism teaches that all forms of life should be treated with compassion and loving-kindness. It teaches harmlessness and non-violence (ahimsa):

> All are afraid of danger, all fear death. Putting oneself in another's place, one should not hurt or kill others.
>
> All are afraid of danger, all hold their lives dear. Putting oneself in another's place, one should not beat or kill others.
>
> (Dhammapada 129–130)

In fact, ahimsa is the first of the Five Precepts, part of the Noble Eightfold Path, and is therefore an important feature of the Middle Way: the practice that leads to nirvana.

Muslim attitudes to the sanctity of life

Muslims believe that all life is created by God and only he has the right to take it away. This teaching applies to all creations of God, and murder is explicitly forbidden in the Qur'an:

> And do not kill the soul which God has forbidden [to be killed] except by [legal] right.
>
> (Qur'an 6.151)

Every soul has been created by God. God has a plan for each life, written before each person is 'planted as a seed in your mothers' womb'.

No one has the right to take their own or anyone else's life. This is discussed in the Qur'an:

> We decreed upon the children of Israel that whoever kills a soul unless for a soul or for corruption [done] in the land – it is as if he had slain mankind entirely. And Our messengers had certainly come to them with clear proofs. Then indeed many of them, [even] after that throughout the land, were transgressors.
>
> (Qur'an 5.32)

This essentially means that the killing of just one soul carries the sin of killing all of humanity. Those who commit such crimes will face a severe punishment by God on the Day of Judgement.

The Qur'an makes it clear that the life of each human being is sacred and provided for by God. Therefore, no-one should take the life of another, even when they believe they are doing the right thing:

> Say, 'Come, I will recite what your Lord has prohibited to you. [He commands] that you not associate anything with Him, and to parents, good treatment, and do not kill your children out of poverty; We will provide for you and them. And do not approach immoralities – what is apparent of them and what is concealed. And do not kill the soul which God has forbidden [to be killed] except by [legal] right. This has He instructed you that you may use reason.'
>
> (Qur'an 6.151)

Jewish attitudes to the sanctity of life

The Torah teaches that humans are created in God's image. Their lives are a gift from God and are therefore sacred. This means that the life of each person is infinitely precious and cannot be thrown away. Therefore, murder is forbidden for all people. The Talmud explains that Adam was created to teach us the significance, importance and sanctity of each individual:

> Anyone who destroys a human life is considered as if he had destroyed an entire world, and anyone who preserves a human life is considered to have preserved an entire world.
>
> (Sanhedrin 37a)

Pikuach nefesh is the principle in Jewish law that the preservation of human life overrides virtually any other religious consideration. This means that if a person's life is in danger, other mitzvot (duties) from the Torah become irrelevant. Human life is so precious that most other laws should be put aside to enable it to be protected and preserved, for example, the laws of Shabbat or other Jewish holidays are to be suspended for the purposes of pikuach nefesh.

The Talmud discusses a number of cases as examples in which mitzvot can be disregarded for the sake of saving a human life (Yoma 84b 8–9).

Humanist attitudes to the sanctity of life

Because humanism is an atheistic tradition, humanists do not believe that the value of life comes from God. Humanists do not believe that people have souls, or that there is an **afterlfe** in heaven, hell or purgatory, or that there is a God who judges where people go in an afterlife. They believe that we only have this life and that it ends forever when we die. Life therefore has special importance because it is our only life.

As humanists believe that one of the central purposes of life is to make ourselves and others around us as happy as possible, life is imbued with importance because it is our opportunity to benefit others through compassion and kindness. As such, life is not seen as sacred but is worthy of the highest respect.

9 Issues of life and death

174

Peter Singer: speciesism

Moral philosopher Peter Singer popularised the word 'speciesism', which he defines as 'a prejudice or bias in favour of the interests of members of one's own species and against those of members of other species.' He argues that it is wrong to give human beings greater rights than other animals, in the same way as it wrong to give greater rights to one group of humans than another. Singer's opposition to speciesism means that he believes that humans and other animals should be treated with equal consideration. He is therefore against the use of animals for experimentation and promotes veganism.

▶ The quality of life

Key Concept

Quality of life The extent to which life is meaningful and pleasurable.

Many people believe that the quality of their life is more important than whether it is special or sacred. If life is relatively free from pain and anxiety, and if we live with freedom and dignity, then we have what is considered a good **quality of life**. If the degree of pain and suffering that we endure exceeds the pleasure that we gain from other areas of our life, then we would be considered to have a poor quality of life.

How do we measure quality?

Assessing the extent to which a life has quality is a difficult philosophical problem. One person can no more appreciate how another experiences and tolerates pain than they can guess how much pleasure they might get from eating a bar of chocolate. As such, measuring the quality of a person's life is incredibly difficult.

Quality of life indicators are used by governments across the world. They look broadly at material living conditions, health and education provision, leisure and social interactions, as well as economic factors and the extent to which human rights are granted. Doctors and clinicians also have tools to measure the quality of life of their patients, looking at levels of pain, the extent of disability, the ability to feed and toilet oneself, among other indicators. Most doctors, however, understand that there are real limits to how accurate these measurements can be. They similarly appreciate that there are genuine ethical problems with trying to evaluate quality of life.

If a person's life has insufficient quality, some would argue that they should have the right to die if they wish. Some would also say that attempts to treat a person's illness should be weighed against the extent to which they are going to live a life free from pain and suffering afterwards.

Tasks

1. In your own words, explain what is meant by sanctity of life. Aim to include the following terms: sacred, priceless, value, God.
2. In a short paragraph, explain the differences between quality and sanctity of life.
3. In a mind map, identify six different ways in which quality of life can be measured (for example, material living conditions).
4. What is the difference between a religious believer's ideas on why life is special and those of an atheist, for example, a humanist?
5. Explain the teachings about why life is sacred from one religious tradition.

▶ When does life begin?

Although it seems obvious to state that life begins at birth and ends at death, there are real questions as to when a 'person' is first created. When does a person actually become a person?

Some would argue that a person 'begins' when they are first aware of their own existence; others when independent life is possible. Some would claim that from the point a foetus can feel pain, they are a person in their own right. Many religious believers would assert that from the moment of conception, a life and therefore a person has been created. There are no definitive or clear answers to this question, and any answers offered are affected by what we think being a 'person' is all about.

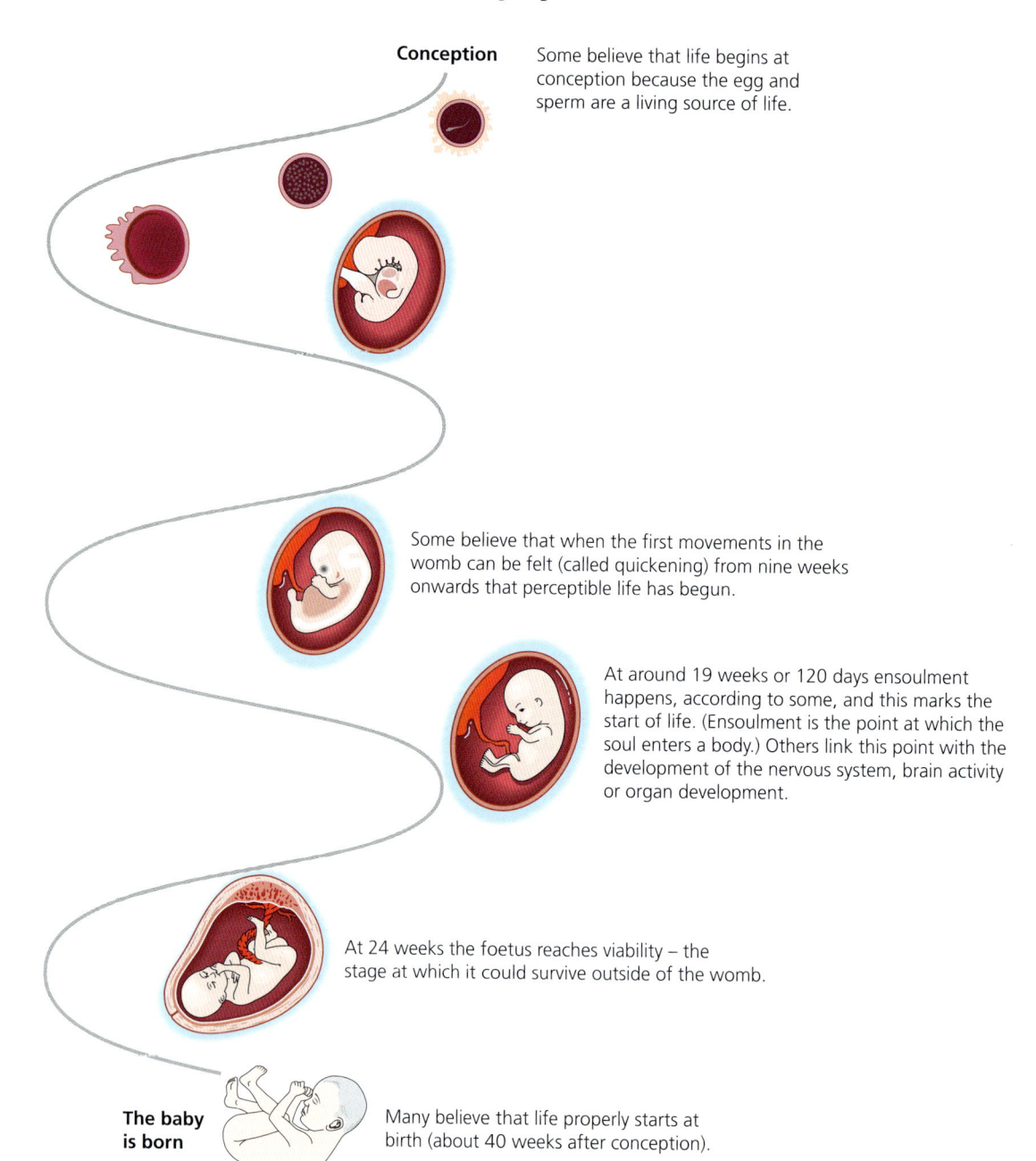

Conception — Some believe that life begins at conception because the egg and sperm are a living source of life.

Some believe that when the first movements in the womb can be felt (called quickening) from nine weeks onwards that perceptible life has begun.

At around 19 weeks or 120 days ensoulment happens, according to some, and this marks the start of life. (Ensoulment is the point at which the soul enters a body.) Others link this point with the development of the nervous system, brain activity or organ development.

At 24 weeks the foetus reaches viability – the stage at which it could survive outside of the womb.

The baby is born — Many believe that life properly starts at birth (about 40 weeks after conception).

Key Concept

Abortion When a pregnancy is ended by the deliberate removal of the foetus from the womb so that it does not result in the birth of a child.

Tasks

1. Construct a timeline of the different stages of pregnancy. Identify each key development point (for example, when the foetus can survive on its own) and the points at which different people believe that the foetus is a person (for example, at 120 days when ensoulment happens).
2. Briefly explain when you believe life begins and mark it on your timeline. Give a clear reason or justification for your belief.
3. Define what is meant by 'pro-life' and 'pro-choice'.
4. What are the legal restrictions to abortion in twenty – first-century Britain?
5. Draw a table with two columns – one for each of the religions that you are choosing to study. For each, summarise the religious attitudes to abortion as bullet points. Remember to mention where there are differences of belief within each religion.

Task

'It takes two to create a human life, but only one to end it.'

What is your opinion on the fact that fathers have no legal rights when it comes to the abortion decision?

The great abortion debate

The ethics of **abortion** have been widely debated, and it was first legalised in Britain in 1967. Those against abortion claim that it is simply immoral to kill unborn babies, irrespective of the circumstances of the mother. Others argue that a foetus is not a baby. They would say further that it is the quality of life that matters, and that sometimes in modern society procedures like abortion are necessary. If a baby is going to be born severely disabled or with a terminal or life-limiting condition, if the mother is going to suffer mentally or physically as the result of the pregnancy, or even if the pregnancy was the result of rape, some people feel that it is kinder to permit an abortion so that quality of life is maintained. For reasons such as these, abortion has become a massively controversial issue. Beliefs about abortion are generally divided into two categories, pro-life and pro-choice:

- **'Pro-life'** is a term used to describe the view that abortion is always wrong and that every human being has a right to life (even tiny embryos).
- **'Pro-choice'** is a term used to describe the belief that every woman should be able to choose what happens to her body. That right includes choosing whether or not to continue with a pregnancy and have a baby. This does not mean that a pro-choice advocate is necessarily in favour of abortion absolutely – there may well be some situations in which they would morally disagree with abortion. Rather, it means that they support a woman's right to choose for herself.

The rights of the unborn child

Many people (religious and not religious) who oppose abortion, argue that the unborn (potential) child has rights – most specifically a right to life. The law, however, is unclear about the rights of the unborn child, and, in practice, their rights are not distinguishable from those of the mother. In December 2014, as part of a court case not related to abortion, the UK Court of Appeal ruled that an unborn child 'was not a person'.

Abortion: facts and figures

Abortion is legal in Britain before 24 weeks of pregnancy. Two doctors must consent to the procedure by deciding whether there will be a risk to the mother's physical or mental health if the pregnancy were to continue that would be greater than the risk to her health if the pregnancy were not to continue. In very rare cases, such as severe foetal abnormality or grave risk to the life of the mother, an abortion can be performed after 24 weeks.

It is estimated that one in three women will, at some point in her life, have an abortion. At the moment, the father of the foetus has no legal right to participate in the decision process – even if the couple are married.

Religious teachings about abortion

Christian attitudes to abortion

There is no single view on abortion in Christianity. Views differ according to the different priority given to concerns over the sanctity of life and the teaching of Jesus to act with compassion.

The Roman Catholic Church

Catholics and Orthodox denominations agree that abortion should be forbidden in all circumstances as life is sacred and God given. From the moment of conception, a new and unique life begins. This is not a potential life, but rather a human being with potential. Abortion is therefore murder and against the Ten Commandments. Catholics believe that the foetus has a right to live and develop and that terminating this life is a great moral evil. The Catholic Church condemned abortion as early as the second century CE. The Didache, written in the second century, states:

> You shall not kill the embryo by abortion and shall not cause the newborn to perish.

The Anglican Communion

The Anglican Churches do not share a single view about abortion, but there is similarity among them.

The Church of England, for example, states:

> The Church of England combines strong opposition to abortion with a recognition that there can be – strictly limited – conditions under which it may be morally preferable to any available alternative.

The General Synod, the Church's governing body, clarifies this position. It holds that all life is precious as it is made by God. Abortion should not be allowed for social reasons; however, if the mother's life is in danger, abortion may be permitted but not encouraged.

Similarly, for 'quality of life' reasons and out of compassion, abortion is permitted if the female has been raped. Taking all of this into consideration, the Synod also believes that the law in Britain has been interpreted too liberally and that this has resulted in the performance of an excessive number of abortions.

The Church in Wales has published no official position in relation to abortion. It is likely to share the view of the Church of England.

The Episcopal Church in America supports the right of a woman to have an abortion, but only in extreme situations. The newly formed Anglican Church in North America, however, is strictly pro-life.

Methodist Churches

The Methodist Churches of Great Britain take a generally anti-abortion view, but would permit abortions in extreme circumstances. They advocate providing social support for mothers so that there is no need for abortion.

Buddhist attitudes to abortion

As far as Buddhists are concerned, life is an endless cycle of birth, existence, decay, death and rebirth, and there is no point at which the embryo or foetus is not a living being. It follows that Buddhists consider abortion to be the deliberate taking of a human life. The first of the Five Precepts guides against taking life. The principle of ahimsa, endorsed by Buddhism, is often translated as 'non-violence', but it really means 'no harm'. Abortion would seem to go against this principle.

However, the Precepts are guidelines for moral action and not hard and fast rules. Issues such as abortion are rarely clear-cut, and their complexity must be considered in making ethical decisions. If a woman is pregnant and is thinking about the possibility of having the pregnancy ended, all the factors of her unique circumstances must be considered. A Buddhist would want to make a decision that is 'skilful'. A skilful action is one that is based on awareness, kindness and taking responsibility for your own actions.

It may be that pregnancy is the result of rape and continuing with it would cause great mental and emotional suffering to the mother. It may be that the pregnancy is endangering the mother's life. In these cases, suffering is inevitable, whatever decision is made about abortion. Buddhists would feel compassion (karuna) for the mother in circumstances such as these and respect her decision.

> 'Of course, abortion, from a Buddhist viewpoint, is an act of killing and is negative, generally speaking. But it depends on the circumstances... I think abortion should be approved or disapproved according to each circumstance.'
>
> (Dalai Lama, interview in *The New York Times*, 28.11.1993)

Muslim attitudes to abortion

The Qur'an does not explicitly refer to abortion but offers guidance on related matters. Muslims believe that God creates life and only he can end it (sanctity of life). Abortion for purely economic reasons is forbidden in the Qur'an:

> Do not kill your children out of poverty; We will provide for you and them.
>
> (Qur'an 6.151)

While many Muslims believe that abortion is wrong and haram (forbidden), some also accept that there are situations in which an abortion can be permitted. Many will allow abortion if the mother's life is in danger or if the child is likely to be seriously deformed or diseased. However, such decisions should not be entered into lightly. The taking of the life of a child is a sin and, on the Day of Judgement, a child will have the right to ask why it was killed.

There exists real debate about the acceptability of abortion and the conditions under which it should be permitted. Some schools of Muslim law say abortion is permitted in the first 16 weeks of pregnancy, while others only permit it in the first seven weeks. These different interpretations exist because each sets a different 'point' at which the embryo or foetus becomes a person. Even those scholars who permit early abortion in certain cases still regard abortion as wrong, but do not regard it as a punishable wrong. They would argue that the more advanced the pregnancy, the greater the wrong.

The Hadith says that ensoulment takes place (the foetus gets its soul) 120 days after conception. Muslim scholars have traditionally held that, until that time, the mother's rights are greater than those of the foetus. Islam allows abortion to save the life of the mother because it sees this as the 'lesser of two evils' and there is a general principle in Shari'ah (Muslim law) of choosing the lesser of two evils.

Nevertheless, the Qur'an makes it clear that, ultimately, life comes from God and he is in control of it:

> Allah is the one who created you, then provided for you, then will cause you to die, and then will give you life. Are there any of your associates who does anything of that? Exalted is He and high above what they associate with Him.
>
> (Qur'an 30.40)

Jewish attitudes to abortion

Judaism as a whole does not forbid abortion, but it does not permit abortion on demand; abortion is only permitted for serious reasons. Every case is expected to be considered on its own merits, and the decision should be taken only after consultation with a rabbi. The unborn foetus is not considered a 'person' in Jewish law until it has been born, and the principle of pikuach nefesh (see page 174) allows for the life of the mother to be saved. There are, however, differing beliefs among Jews as to when and whether abortion is permissible.

Abortion is largely opposed by Orthodox Jews. This is because they believe that life is God's greatest gift and it should be preserved at all costs. God is the creator and he alone can take life. Destroying a life is therefore a heinous crime.

Reform and liberal Jews believe that abortion may be permitted in some circumstances, such as if the mother's life is at risk. In such circumstances (where allowing the pregnancy to continue would kill the mother), Judaism insists that the foetus must be aborted, since the mother's life is more important than that of the foetus.

Some Jews accept abortion in cases of rape or incest, or if the health of the mother is generally poor.

However, abortion may take place only when the foetus is in its mother's womb. Once it is born, it becomes a person in its own right, including the right to life. Birth means that more than 50 per cent of the baby has left its mother's body. The Mishnah says:

> 1. If a woman is having trouble giving birth, they cut up the child in her womb and bring it forth limb by limb, because her life comes before the life of [the child].
>
> 2. But if the greater part has come out, one may not touch it, for one may not set aside one person's life for that of another.
>
> (Mishnah Oholot 7.6)

Humanist attitudes to abortion

In considering abortion, a humanist would consider the evidence, the probable consequences, and the rights and wishes of everyone involved. They would do this with the aim of trying to find the kindest course of action or the one that would do the least harm.

It is difficult to say what makes an action right or wrong. There are two views about this:

- **Moral relativism**, which says that the rightness or wrongness of an action depends on its social, cultural or personal context.
- **Moral absolutism**, which says that there are universal moral principles that exist regardless of context.

Humanists reject absolutism as being 'doctrinal'. They would say that no individual or institution is in a position to decide which moral principles should apply to everyone.

On the other hand, they are reluctant to call themselves relativists. They prefer to think of themselves as 'situationists', believing that moral decisions should be made on a case-by-case basis.

Because of this **situation ethics** approach, there is not one single humanist view on abortion, but humanists tend to take on a liberal, pro-choice stance. Humanists value happiness and personal choice, and many actively campaigned to legalise abortion in the 1960s. As humanists do not believe that life is sacred, the debate hinges on when one thinks human life begins, and a foetus does not become a person with its own feelings and rights, until well after conception. As humanists take happiness and suffering as foremost moral considerations, quality of life will often outweigh the preservation of life

> **Situation ethics** Judging the rightness or wrongness of an act on a case-by-case basis.

at all costs. They believe that abortion is often a morally acceptable choice to make. It is, however, a personal choice that should be made in an informed fashion which considers both the long- and short-term effects.

▶ Euthanasia

Key Concept

Euthanasia From Greek, *eu* 'good' + *thanatos* 'death'. Sometimes referred to as mercy killing. The act of killing a person, either directly or indirectly, because a decision has been reached that death would be the best option.

Why might people want to end their own life?

People suffering from incurable, chronic, degenerative diseases (illnesses that steadily grow worse over time, for which there are no known cures) like motor neurone disease, might choose to end their own lives before their illness reaches its final stages, and they are unable to communicate with others. Some people, for example, those suffering from terminal cancer, may choose to end their lives before the most painful and life-limiting phase of their illness sets in. For others, living with constant and unmanageable pain (maybe linked to an injury, disability or side-effect from previous illnesses) is reason enough to consider seeking euthanasia.

Also known as mercy killing or assisted suicide, **euthanasia** comes from the Greek words for 'good death'. It is usually when a peaceful and pain-free end is brought to a person's life.

There are technically four different types of euthanasia.

- **Voluntary euthanasia** (or assisted suicide, as it is known in law) is the ending of the life of a person who explicitly asks for help to die. Often this would be due to a life-limiting or terminal illness.
- **Active euthanasia** is when a person takes a specific course of action to end their own life, for example, by taking an overdose.
- **Passive euthanasia** is the removal of life-sustaining treatment, for example, a feeding tube or respirator. Often this would be because it is believed that the patient would have wished for a 'dignified death' or if there is no hope of recovery.
- **Involuntary euthanasia** refers to death being forced upon a person, for example, during ethnic cleansing or the death penalty.

The issue of euthanasia calls into question many different religious, philosophical and ethical issues, in particular as to whether we have the right to end our own lives.

The 'right to die' debate – For

Free will

Daniel James was paralysed in a rugby accident at the age of 22. He was in constant pain, had no movement in any limbs and felt his body was a prison. He decided to go to the Dignitas clinic in Switzerland to end his life. He was assisted by his parents. Despite being investigated, they were not charged for helping him. The Crown Prosecution Service has now said that families who help relatives die in this way are unlikely to be prosecuted.

Campaigners supporting the 'right to die'

Many people with chronic degenerative diseases want to control when and how they die. For them it is not just a matter of free will, but rather a matter of maintaining human dignity. For example, Dr Anne Turner, who suffered from a fatal degenerative nerve disease, decided to end her own life before she reached a point when she could not walk, feed, dress or speak for herself.

Those who believe that people should be free to decide their own future think it is ethically wrong to keep someone with no hope of recovery on expensive life-support treatment.

Baby RB

In November 2009, the father of a severely disabled baby boy, known as Baby RB, went to court to fight the hospital's decision to turn off his son's life-support machine. At 13 months old, Baby RB was incapable of moving his limbs, breathing or swallowing on his own. He had a severe and incurable neuromuscular disorder and had been on a respirator since an hour after his birth. His mother supported the hospital's decision, as she felt that her son had no quality of life.

The father eventually agreed with the hospital's doctors, and both parents were present when Baby RB's life support was turned off.

Stephen Hawking

In 2013, Stephen Hawking offered his public support to the argument for assisted dying, saying, 'We don't let animals suffer, so why humans?' He said that he would consider euthanasia if he reached a point where he felt he had nothing left to offer or was a burden to others.

Stephen Hawking is a supporter of assisted dying

LOST
General human dignity
If found
Please call
077 3858 1664

The 'right to die' debate – Against

Harold Shipman

Harold Shipman (1946–2004) was a British doctor and one of the most prolific serial killers in recorded history. On 31 January 2000, a jury found Shipman guilty of 15 murders. He was sentenced to life imprisonment and the judge recommended that he never be released.

After his trial, the Shipman Inquiry began. Lasting almost two years, it was an investigation into all deaths certified by Shipman. About 80 per cent of his victims were women. His youngest victim was a 41-year-old man. They died as the result of being given lethal injections of morphine. Much of Britain's legal structure concerning health care and medicine was reviewed and modified as a direct and indirect result of Shipman's crimes. Shipman is the only British doctor to have been found guilty of murdering his patients.

Legalising doctor-assisted euthanasia would make it easier for people like Shipman to commit horrific crimes.

■ Harold Shipman was convicted of murder in 2000

If euthanasia is legalised, the stimulus or drive to research into terminal illnesses lessens.

It's murder

All life is special and worthy of protection.

The slippery-slope argument

The slippery-slope argument claims that the acceptance of certain practices, such as physician-assisted suicide or voluntary euthanasia, will invariably lead to the acceptance or application of practices that are currently deemed unacceptable, such as involuntary euthanasia. In order to prevent these undesirable practices from occurring, we need to resist taking the first step.

Legalising euthanasia could lead to those in the latter stages of life feeling that they are a burden or, even worse, feeling obliged to consider ending their life.

Hospices provide a real alternative to those feeling unable to deal with the symptoms of terminal illnesses.

▶ Hospices

In 1967, St Christopher's Hospice was opened in Sydenham, London. It was the first hospice in Britain and was opened by Dame Cicely Saunders. Her aim was to provide physical, spiritual, emotional and psychological support to those in the final period of their illnesses/lives. She wanted to offer care that considered all elements of a patient's needs rather than simply treating the physical symptoms of a patient. The Hospice Movement, as it has since become known, was born.

Although hospices are not specifically religious places, Dame Cicely Saunders did acknowledge that her Christian beliefs were the main motivation for her work. In addition, many hospices are supported or sponsored by religious institutions. They fulfil the Christian desire to relieve the suffering of both patients and family in the final moments of life, as well as enabling believers to preserve the sanctity of life rather than resorting to euthanasia.

Many people believe that hospices provide a real alternative to euthanasia. They allow people to die with their dignity intact in a loving, caring environment, surrounded by family if desired. Patients need not feel a burden and can still benefit from a quality of life, as pain relief is palliative and focused on managing symptoms while maintaining consciousness.

> We should concern ourselves with the quality of life as well as its length.
>
> (Dame Cicely Saunders)

Dignified dying, dignified living

There are currently over 260 inpatient hospices in Britain.

Some are dedicated entirely to the care of children and infants, and offer invaluable support to both patient and family – providing respite care and end-of-life palliative treatment. Others focus purely on adult end-of-life care, with some specialising in specific diseases such as cancer.

The myth that people only go into hospices to die is slowly being dispelled, as more and more patients are admitted for short periods of time (between 12 and 14 days is the average stay) to help manage pain and relieve other symptoms of their illness.

Upwards of 4 per cent of deaths occur in a hospice setting, with many more patients and their families benefiting from time spent in a hospice before their death.

A Katharine House hospice for adults with life-limiting conditions.

The origin and value of human life

Religious teachings about euthanasia

Christian attitudes to euthanasia

Most Christians agree that euthanasia is not acceptable because:

- All life is sacred (sanctity of life) and taking any life is wrong.
- Those who assist are involved in murder, which is against the Ten Commandments.
- Life is a gift from God and therefore is precious.
- Suffering can have a purpose and should be endured, as God will not give us more suffering than we are truly able to cope with.
- Hospices offer an alternative where care and support can be given to the patient. This allows patients to die with dignity while their pain is managed.

Some liberal Christians believe that it is acceptable to turn off life-support if there is medical evidence that a person is brain-dead. This is because they believe that the person has already died and that the machine is just performing bodily functions. They would also consider withholding treatment that prolongs a painful illness as they follow Jesus' teaching of acting in the most loving and compassionate way towards another person.

The Catholic Church is absolutely opposed to euthanasia. In spite of arguments that prolonging a life of pain and suffering may not be the most compassionate course of action, the Church says that there are no circumstances that justify the killing of a human being; palliative care is a viable alternative. In 2006, the Catholic Archbishop of Cardiff said:

> There's a fierce ethical battle here with how we deal with the terminally ill, with the very vulnerable, with the very sick. We're saying, you don't kill people off. What they need is to be loved and cared for.

While the Church in Wales broadly agrees that a life given by God cannot be ended by human intervention, its policy on euthanasia is neutral. It recommends further study and prayer before it takes a firm position.

Buddhist attitudes to euthanasia

Buddhism teaches that living beings go through an endless cycle of birth, existence, decay, death and rebirth (samsara). It teaches that there is no such thing as a 'soul', an unchanging essence of an individual. What goes through the cycle of samsara is karma. Karma continually changes as new causes are made and old ones come into effect. Therefore, the karmic state of one's life at the moment of death is the same karmic state that is reborn.

Therefore, according to Buddhism, there is no point in committing euthanasia or assisting suicide: it will not relieve suffering (dukkha) in the world of samsara. In fact, Buddhist monks can be ejected from the monastic Sangha if they encourage others to commit suicide. The only circumstance in which euthanasia may relieve suffering is in the case of an enlightened being who is about to be released from samsara. Indeed, Buddhist scriptures recount cases of the Buddha approving the suicide of monks in the state of nirvana who wish to be released from the sufferings of life.

Furthermore, the Buddha himself, as an enlightened being, hastened his own death by eating food he knew to be lethal, while forbidding others to eat it.

So some Buddhists would say that euthanasia, in some very specific cases, may be acceptable in order to relieve suffering. It may be considered to be an act of compassion (karuna). The Dalai Lama has compared euthanasia with abortion, saying that, with both issues, cases must be considered individually:

> ... the Buddhist way is to judge the right and wrong or the pros and cons... (There) are, I think from the Buddhist viewpoint, exceptional cases, so it's best to be judged on a case-by-case basis.
>
> (Dalai Lama, quoted in *World Tibet Network News*, 18.09.1996)

On the other hand, it should be remembered that the deliberate taking of a human life goes against the first of the Five Precepts and against the principle of ahimsa (not to harm). Buddhists consider human life to be exceptionally precious. For this reason, the Dalai Lama says about euthanasia, 'I think it's better to avoid it.'

Muslim attitudes to euthanasia

Islam is clear that life is made by God (sanctity of life) and only God can decide when a person dies. Everything that happens does so because God wants it to happen. Even suffering has a purpose.

It is important to show compassion to those who are in pain or are suffering. When this happens, there should be no need for euthanasia. No matter what state the body is in, the soul is still perfect and that is what matters to God.

Muslim lawyers have recently agreed that it is acceptable for a person who is in a coma, being kept alive by machines and who has no hope of recovery, to have the machines turned off. This is because their life has already ended and the machine is of no real use as treatment.

Jewish attitudes to euthanasia

Jews are largely opposed to euthanasia. Active euthanasia is seen as murder. All life is precious and a gift from God – it is not ours to throw away. Only the Creator can decide when life should end. Every moment of human life is considered equal in value to many years of life. 'The value of human life is infinite and beyond measure, so that any part of life - even if only an hour or a second – is of precisely the same worth as seventy years of it, just as any fraction of infinity, being indivisible, remains infinite.'

Lord Jakobovits, former UK Chief Rabbi

The Talmud says, 'And let not your evil nature assure you that the grave will be your refuge.' (Ethics of the Fathers 4.22). In other words, both the living and the dead are accountable to God. Euthanasia cannot be seen as an escape from God's judgement.

Medicine that relieves pain can be administered, even if it hastens death as a side effect. Crucially, the purpose or intention here cannot be to kill, but to relieve pain. Similarly, Jews can pray to end a person's pain and suffering, but it is wrong to shorten a person's life (even if it would naturally end very soon).

Some Jews believe that a life-support machine can be turned off if the patient has no chance of recovery. There is also a belief that doctors should not make a person suffer more by artificially extending their life.

Humanist attitudes to euthanasia

Humanists have supported attempts to legalise assisted dying, assisted suicide and voluntary euthanasia across the UK. They believe that assistance should not be limited to terminally ill people alone and want to see reform of the law that considers the needs of other people who are 'permanently and incurably suffering', for example, people who are paralysed.

Humanists uphold the right to life but don't believe that life should be prolonged in the face of pointless suffering. Being able to die, with dignity, in a manner of one's own choosing, must be understood to be a fundamental human right.

Dignity in Dying

The Dignity in Dying movement lobbies for choice, access and control in issues of death and dying.

- They want people to be able to have the right to choose where they die, who is present and what treatment options are available.
- They want people to have access to expert information on end-of-life options and good quality end-of-life care.
- They also call for control over how people die, what symptoms they are left to manage, pain relief and planning their own death.
- They work with a sister group – Compassion in Dying – to provide advice and support to any who are contemplating end-of-life issues and assisted dying.

As a group, they believe the right law for the UK is one that allows dying people, with six months or fewer to live, the option to control their death. They do not support a wider law or one that encompasses all life-limiting conditions. Dignity in Dying would like the UK to adopt a model used successfully in some states in the USA. There, in states like Oregon and California, a terminally ill patient can submit their request for assisted dying to a panel of doctors and a high court judge. Once approved, and after a 'cool-off' period for reflection, the patient receives a lethal dose of drugs which they take at home. Critically, this means that the patient can plan their own death, and die in their own home.

Organ donation in Wales

Wales is unique among the nations of the United Kingdom to have an 'opt-out' system of consent to organ donation. This means that, after a person's death, their organs may be given to someone who needs a transplant, unless they have specified in advance that they do not want this to happen.

What is unique about the Welsh system is that it is assumed that a person consents to organ donation, unless they indicate that they do not ('opt out'). This is called 'deemed (or presumed) consent'.

So each adult in Wales can choose between four options:

- Opt in to donation by registering while still alive. This means that there is no doubt about the decision.
- Opt out of donation by registering not to donate.
- Do nothing, in which case deemed consent is presumed.
- Appoint a relative or friend to decide about donation after death.

In general, most religions in Wales support the idea of organ donation, or, at least, are not wholly against it. They tend to teach that it is an individual choice.

Christianity is in favour of organ donation:

- Christians consider organ donation an act of love and a way of following Jesus' example.
- Christians believe in eternal life, and preparing for death should not be feared.
- Christians believe that nothing that happens to our body, before or after death, can impact on our relationship with God.

The Christian Churches in Wales fully support the 'opt-out' system.

- In 2011, Barry Morgan, Archbishop of Wales, declared that organ donation is an act of agape: 'Giving organs is the most generous act of self-giving imaginable'.
- In 2015, the bishops of the Church in Wales issued a statement: 'As Bishops we are wholeheartedly in favour of organ donation. It is love in action and a wonderful example of what it can mean to love our neighbours, especially those in need. Such generosity is a response to God's generosity towards us.'
- In 2000, Pope John Paul II said: 'There is a need to instil in people's hearts, especially in the hearts of the young, a genuine and deep appreciation of the need for brotherly love, a love that can find expression in the decision to become an organ donor.'
- The Methodist Church says: 'The Methodist Church has consistently supported organ donation and transplantation in appropriate circumstances, as a means through which healing and health may be made possible.'

▶ # End of Section Review

Skills Link

Describe religious teachings about the value of human life.

Stickability

Key concepts:
- Abortion
- Euthanasia
- Sanctity of life
- Quality of life

Key teachings:
- The sanctity of life
- Abortion
- Euthanasia

Knowledge Check

1. What is a hospice? How does it differ from a hospital?
2. Create a Venn diagram to compare sanctity and quality of life.
3. Give three different reasons why Christians would disagree with euthanasia. After you have given each reason, extend your explanation with a connective, such as, 'This means that ... ', or 'This is because ... ', or 'This comes from the teaching ... '.

The Big Question

'Everyone should have the right to choose how and when to die.'

Your Task

Respond to the statement above, showing that you have considered more than one point of view. Give reasoned judgements on the validity and strength of these views.

Task

For both of the religions you are studying, explain in detail religious teachings about euthanasia. Use the guidance below to help you to write a developed explanation for Christianity. Ensure that you use key terms fluently and frequently.

All/many/most Christians believe that _____ .

This comes from the teaching/Bible quote _____ .

This means that/Because of this they _____ .

Some/other Christians such as _____ believe that _____ .

This comes from the teaching/Bible quote _____ .

This means that/Because of this they _____

Finally, Christians such as _____ believe that _____ .

This means that/Because of this they _____ .

Beliefs do/do not differ because _____ .

Beliefs about death and the afterlife

The soul

> **Key Concept**
>
> **Soul** The spiritual aspect of a being; that which connects someone to God. The soul is often regarded as non-physical and as living on after physical death, in an afterlife.

Belief in the existence of a **soul** is a central feature of many religious and philosophical traditions. According to Christianity, Islam and Judaism, only human beings have immortal souls, other species do not. Buddhists do not believe that human beings possess a soul that gives them identity. They believe that all living beings are connected, and none has a fixed, unique identity. Humanists, too, refute the existence of a soul.

There are two distinct views about the soul and its relationship with our physical body:

- **Dualism** is the belief that we are made of two separate parts: a physical body and a spiritual soul. Dualists believe that our soul (or spirit) lives in our physical body. This soul is the true, inner part of us, and it will live on after our material body dies.
- **Materialism** is the view that nothing else exists apart from matter. All we have, as human beings, is a physical body; there is no soul or spirit.

Religious teachings about the soul

Christian attitudes to the soul

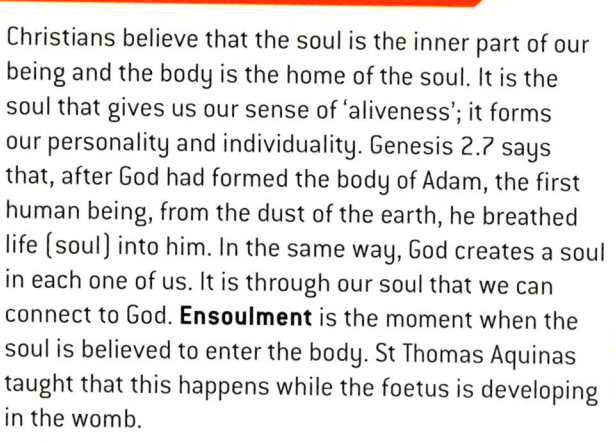

Christians believe that the soul is the inner part of our being and the body is the home of the soul. It is the soul that gives us our sense of 'aliveness'; it forms our personality and individuality. Genesis 2.7 says that, after God had formed the body of Adam, the first human being, from the dust of the earth, he breathed life (soul) into him. In the same way, God creates a soul in each one of us. It is through our soul that we can connect to God. **Ensoulment** is the moment when the soul is believed to enter the body. St Thomas Aquinas taught that this happens while the foetus is developing in the womb.

Some Christians are dualists. They believe that we are made from two distinctive parts: body and soul. They say that the soul is the true, inner part of us; it is eternal and will continue to live on, even after the death of our material body. It is our soul that will rise to everlasting life in heaven.

Other Christians are non-dualists. They say that the body and soul are one and they cannot be separated. They agree that we have a soul, but believe it is an integral part of us, which is indistinguishable from the body. After death the soul is temporarily apart from the body, but body and soul will be reunited on Judgement Day. At the resurrection on that day, we will rise bodily from the dead, just as Jesus rose from the dead and ascended into heaven as a physical being.

> **Ensoulment** The moment when the human soul is said to enter the baby's body (usually thought to happen in the womb, at an early point in the pregnancy).

> The philosopher Gilbert Ryle used the phrase the 'ghost in the machine'. This refers to the idea that humans may think they have a soul, but in reality there is nothing there.

Buddhist attitudes to the soul

Buddhists believe in samsara: life is an endless cycle of birth, existence, death and rebirth. Existing in the world and being dead are as much a part of life as being awake and being asleep are part of one's day-to-day existence.

Buddhists do not believe that human beings have souls (anatta); rather it is karma that moves from lifetime to lifetime. So it is not the case that a soul is reborn into a new body: there is no soul and nothing can arise spontaneously (see Dependent Origination, page 163). The 'new body' that is born is simply the effect of karma: its colour, size, sex, personality – all karma. These things that come together to make a person are called skandhas (sometimes called kandhas). They give the impression that they form a person; they appear to make you you.

Yet Buddhism teaches that everything is conditioned by everything else. Nothing is permanent, nothing lasts, everything changes, everything is interrelated. So there is no permanent you.

As you get older, your body changes: it grows taller, fatter; hair and nails grow longer; your mind changes: ideas and views mature; likes and dislikes come and go. Nothing remains the same. Body cells, like everything else, decay and die, to be replaced by new ones. Where do the new ones come from? They do not spontaneously arise. They are the result of what you eat – hamburgers, chicken nuggets, brussels sprouts: this is Dependent Origination. There is no you.

Clinging to the idea of me is an illusion. It brings about dukkha and keeps samsara moving around.

So death is a stage in the cycle of samsara. And there is no afterlife: there is just life.

Muslim attitudes to the soul

Islam teaches that, as humans, we have both physical and non-physical aspects. The soul is an invisible part of an individual's existence that is 'pure' at birth. According to the Qur'an, God made Adam from the 'earth', so we have a physical body. We are also blessed with a soul (ruh); this is the non-physical part of our being that makes us a real person.

The Qur'an teaches that humans are created when God 'breathes' a soul into them. In the Hadith there is a passage that says that this ensoulment happens in the womb at 120 days after conception.

Islam teaches that, when a child is born, its soul is imprinted with a belief in God. This natural belief in God is called fitrah. For Muslims, the idea of fitrah describes our human nature: we are born in a state of purity, with an inbuilt, natural instinct to submit to God and live by his laws. So, according to Islam, this means that the true nature of our soul is for us to grow up as a Muslim and submit our lives to God.

> Every newborn child is born in a state of 'fitrah' (purity).
>
> (M Hanif)

Fitrah The natural instinct all humans have, from birth, to know and worship God.

Jewish attitudes to the soul

In the Jewish tradition, the soul is a divine energy in each person, a fragment of God within each human being. Body and soul are different aspects of a person, but they cannot be separated. For Jews, the breath is often a symbol of the soul (or spirit) within.

In Judaism, the soul is the 'I' that inhabits our body. A being without a soul would be like a candle without a flame or a food without any flavour. The soul gives the body life, personality, emotions and identity.

The soul is the spark of godliness in each one of us. It is the expression of God's desire for each of us to be an individual, unique being. It is more than the engine of life, because it is the *why* of our existence: the soul embodies the meaning and purpose of our lives.

Humanist attitudes to the soul

Humanists are materialists, so they dismiss any suggestion that we have a soul. They believe in a scientific description of human life and they reject beliefs about our spiritual existence. We are physical beings who will decompose when we die. No eternal, supernatural part of us will live on.

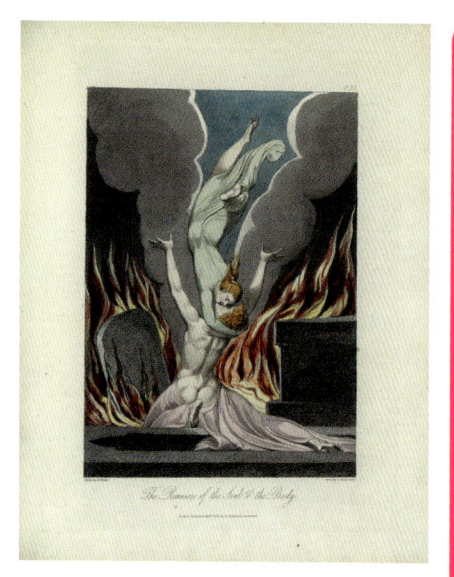

'The Reunion of the Soul and the Body' by William Blake.

Tasks

1. Create a mind map for the concept of 'soul'. Include religious and non-religious ideas and beliefs.
2. **a)** Explain what is meant by 'dualism'.
   b) How is dualism different to materialism?
3. Reproduce the Venn diagram below and use it to write down the key ideas about the soul in Islam, Christianity and Judaism.

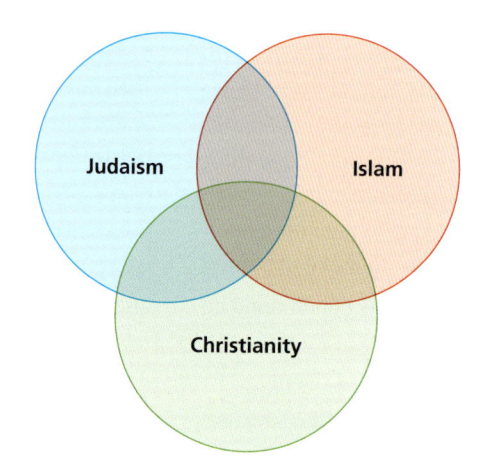

[Venn diagram with three overlapping circles labelled Judaism, Islam, and Christianity]

4. Where would you put Buddhism on your Venn diagram?

What happens when we die?

Key Concept

Afterlife Life after death; the belief that existence continues after physical death.

There are three main types of belief about what happens after death:

- **Atheists and humanists** believe that nothing survives death. They are certain that humans do not have a soul; we are just physical, material beings, so when we die that is the end. Nothing exists beyond the grave – the chemicals of our bodies are recycled into the environment.
- **Hindus, Buddhists and Sikhs** share a belief that life is a cycle of birth, death and rebirth (samsara), with the form of our next life being determined by our karma (good or bad actions). The aim of every living being is to escape from the cycle of samsara by gaining enlightenment. However, most of us will be reborn again and again countless times on the way. Buddhists believe in rebirth; after death the karmic energy of our previous life will take on a new physical form.
- **Jews, Christians and Muslims** believe that, as humans, we only live one earthly existence, followed by eternal life in the world to come. Many traditional believers hold that after death we will rise from the dead to be judged by God, with those whom God deems worthy (the good or righteous) being raised to eternal life. There is less agreement amongst Jewish, Christian and Muslim believers about the existence of hell.

The story of Jesus and the empty tomb gives Christians the confidence to believe that, after death, God will raise the dead to eternal life.

▶ Concepts of heaven and hell: Are they real places?

A simple view of heaven pictures it located in the clouds, where angels drift around and God sits on a golden throne. According to this view, it is a 'place' where the souls of people go to be rewarded for living a good life. However, we know enough about the universe today to be certain that heaven is not a place just above the earth. For this reason, many religious people say that the concept of heaven is better understood as a metaphor representing the peace and harmony to be found when we are in a relationship with God.

Is hell really a fiery place of everlasting torment, deep beneath the earth? Could the concept of hell be a description of a state of mind when someone is full of hatred, anger and resentment, rejecting all kindness and love, and cut off from God/goodness?

Tasks

1. Reproduce the table below. Complete it by outlining the belief about the afterlife for each group of religious traditions; then summarise each in three words.

Tradition	Belief	Summarised in three words
Atheists and humanists		Nothing survives death
Hindus, Sikhs and Buddhists		
Jews, Christians and Muslims		

2. Read this quotation from John's Gospel and study the comments about it.

> At the time of Jesus many Jewish people believed that God would raise people from the dead on the Day of Judgement.

> Jesus is teaching that anyone who believes in him will live again after death. But in what form? Will people live as eternal spirits, or will they have a resurrected 'body' like Jesus?

> Martha answered, 'I know he [Lazarus] will rise again in the resurrection at the last day.' Jesus said to her, 'I am the resurrection and the life. The one who believes in me will live, even though they die; and whoever lives by believing in me will never die. Do you believe this?' 'Yes, Lord,' she replied, 'I believe that you are the Messiah, the Son of God, who is to come into the world.'
> John 11:24–27

> By claiming to be the 'resurrection' and the 'life' Jesus is saying that he is the source of both: there can be no life after death without him.

> Most Christians hold the view that only those that 'believe in' Jesus will be given the gift of eternal life.

> The 'Messiah' is the special, chosen one who the Jews believed God would send to save the world.

3. Explain what Christians can learn about life after death from this quote.

Religious teachings about judgement, heaven and hell

Christian attitudes to judgement, heaven and hell

Christians believe in resurrection and eternal life; death is not the end, but a gateway to a perfect existence. Some Christians say that heaven is our true home, and our lives here on earth are the testing ground for life in eternity.

Judgement

Christians believe that, just as Jesus rose again after death, so will we. The Bible teaches that God is the Divine Judge and, on Judgement Day, he will decide who will be rewarded with eternal life in paradise and who will be punished. Those who believe in Jesus and have lived a good life will be taken to heaven. Those who have rejected God's love and caused harm to others will be sent to hell.

Resurrection

Some Christians are dualists. They believe that at the moment of death our soul separates and leaves the body. The body will decay while the immortal soul is united with God in heaven.

Other Christians (for example, Catholics) say that, after death, we will experience a 'bodily resurrection', like Jesus, who came back to life in physical form. In his Letter to the Corinthians, St Paul says that, after our deaths, we will be raised as spiritual bodies, not just disembodied souls.

> So will it be with the resurrection of the dead. The body that is sown is perishable, it is raised imperishable; it is sown in dishonour, it is raised in glory; it is sown in weakness, it is raised in power; it is sown a natural body, it is raised a spiritual body. If there is a natural body, there is also a spiritual body.
>
> (1 Corinthians 15.42–44)

What does St Paul mean when he talks about a 'spiritual body'? Probably the closest we can get to understanding this idea is to picture an angel. Angels are thought to be physical, but they are also spiritual and immortal. They can be seen, but they are not of this world. Is St Paul saying that we will exist for eternity like angels?

Read the Parable of the Sheep and the Goats (Matthew 25.31–46). Explain what this story teaches Christians about how Jesus' followers should live their lives.

Heaven and hell

Christians believe that to be in heaven is to be in God's presence, existing in a state of pure beauty and kindness. To be in hell is to be in constant torment, cut off from all that is good and loving.

Many Evangelical Christians refer to heaven and hell as if they are real places where humans will spend eternity. Liberal Christians say these ideas are symbolic. They remind us that there are consequences to our thoughts and actions.

One question which troubles many Christians is: How can a loving God condemn people to hell? Some reply that it is not God, but us, as individuals, who send ourselves to hell.

Buddhist attitudes to judgement, heaven and hell

Buddhism teaches that death is not the end of life. Buddhism also teaches that there is no creator god who controls the universe and holds individuals accountable for their moral actions.

Instead, Buddhism says that death is part of life. If there are such things as heaven and hell, they exist in our lives. Samsara, conditioned (dependent) existence in the world of suffering, consists of the movement of karma from lifetime to lifetime. Karma is itself conditioned, in the sense that actions are influenced by emotions and circumstances; sometimes they generate positive effects, sometimes negative. These effects in turn create the conditions for new actions to be taken.

These conditions are mental states. A person's mental or emotional state is dependent on their karma. In turn, it will influence that person's thoughts and actions; in other words, it will condition more karma.

For example, a person may, through carelessness, lose their money. This is their karma – to experience the effects of their carelessness. The effect of that karma is to experience an emotional state: misery. The person's misery now determines what sort of karma they go on to create – they may steal, for example, to regain some cash.

The emotional states are known as the Six Realms of Existence. Together they describe almost every human emotion: misery, arrogance, greed, anger, serenity, happiness, and everything in between.

It may appear that the Six Realms are judgements on the actions a person has made; it is better to be happy ➡

than miserable. But all of these states are temporary, impermanent, and so forms of dukkha. There is no judgement. Although misery is called the Realm of Hell, and happiness is called the Realm of Heaven, they are not punishments and rewards. They are just life states that everyone finds themselves in from time to time. Buddhism says you cannot prevent your karma from taking effect; but you can take action to improve your karma.

In the end, the aim of Buddhism is not to experience the Realm of Heaven as much as possible, but to escape from the Six Realms in samsara altogether: nirvana.

Triratna is a form of Buddhism that started in the West. Its founder, Sangharakshita (born Dennis Lingwood) admits that it is hard for Westerners to accept the idea of rebirth. On the other hand, he says that a problem with accepting the idea of rebirth is that it is too easy to focus on the future rather than living here and now. Some Triratna followers therefore concentrate on 'moment-to-moment' rebirth. This emphasises that karma is the cause of whatever happens in life at every moment. And, as each moment leads on to another moment, karma continues like a thread being woven through cloth. Karmic continuity means that, at every moment of life, a person has freedom to respond to whatever it is that their karma produces. While acknowledging that 'traditional' forms of Buddhism do teach rebirth in samsara, Sangharakshita encourages Triratna Buddhists to keep an open mind about rebirth.

Muslim attitudes to judgement, heaven and hell

For Muslims, this world is not all that there is. Our human existence will continue after death; our earthly life is just a preparation for the eternal life to come (**akhirah**).

Muslims believe that at the end of the world there will be a Day of Judgement. Only God knows when the Day of Judgement will come. Muslims believe that, for those who die before that day, the archangel of death, Azrail, will come to take their souls to await the day. They will be kept in a state of **barzakh** (waiting) until the archangel Israfil blows his trumpet to announce the resurrection of all from the dead.

Islam teaches that, on the Day of Judgement, the dead will be raised from their graves and all people will stand before God to be sentenced according to the way they have lived their lives. A book, which represents everything an individual has done, is presented to each of them. The Qur'an explains: 'And everything they did is in written records' (Qur'an 54.52).

If the person's good deeds outweigh the bad, then they will receive the book in their right hand and pass into heaven. If it is placed into their left hand, they will be among the damned. Each person is responsible for their own destiny:

> And the evil consequences of what they did will appear to them, and they will be enveloped by what they used to ridicule.
>
> (Qur'an 46.33)

The coming of the Mahdi

Muslims believe that the Mahdi (the 'guided one') will come on the Day of Judgement. He is the long-awaited saviour who will come to rescue the world. Sunnis believe that he will appear in the End Times, with Isa (Jesus). Shi'as too are awaiting the Mahdi, but they believe his identity will be revealed as the Hidden (or 12th) Imam (see page 87).

Heaven and hell

Most Muslims understand accounts of the afterlife in a very literal way. In the Qur'an, heaven (Janna) and hell (Jahannan) are described in very physical terms. Heaven is a garden of contentment, full of flowers, fruits and fountains. Hell is a state of torment and terror, where the damned are separated from God; they face boiling water, scorching fire and black smoke. There are some Muslims who interpret these descriptions symbolically.

The Qur'an explains that God will be merciful to those who believe in him and save them from the fires of hell:

> The righteous people are those who pray: 'Our Lord! We sincerely believe in You: please forgive our sins and save us from the agony of the Hellfire.'
>
> (Qur'an 3.16)

Akhirah The Islamic term for the afterlife. There are many references to it, and warnings about it, in the Qur'an.

Barzakh A place of waiting, after death, before Judgement Day comes.

Jewish attitudes to judgement, heaven and hell

Judaism teaches that the body and the soul are one; they are inseparable. The soul has no existence without the body. When Adam was created, it says that God 'breathed into his nostrils the soul of life' (Genesis 2.7). Jews see this soul as the 'aliveness' of a person. It is a metaphor for what makes us living beings; it is not a separate thing that has a life of its own without the body.

Early Judaism

The Jewish scriptures say almost nothing about the afterlife; there is no reference to figures like Adam, Abraham, Moses and David living on after death. It was accepted that when they died, although they would live on in the memories of generations to come, their bodies and souls passed away forever. If there was any understanding of an afterlife, it was that the dead were transported to **Sheol**, a shadowy, dreary underworld existence, but this was not a common idea.

> **Sheol** A place of darkness where the dead, both good and evil, are sent.

Present-day Judaism

More recently, Jewish thinking has come to accept the idea of an afterlife (**Olam Ha-Ba**). Today, Judaism tends to teach that at death there will be a temporary separation of body and soul, but they will be reunited on the Day of Judgement.

Many Orthodox Jews nowadays believe in some form of resurrection, believing that people will be raised to eternal life in a bodily resurrection at the end of time. Righteous people will be rewarded with eternal life in paradise, while the wicked will be sent to a place of punishment. Many Jewish people believe that this judgement and resurrection will take place after the coming of the **Messiah (Mashiach)**.

> **Olam Ha-Ba** The afterlife. It means 'the world to come'.
>
> **Messiah (Mashiach)** The one who will be anointed as king to rule in the world to come.

Humanist attitudes to judgement, heaven and hell

One of the questions that has concerned humans since the dawn of time is what happens after death. The humanist answer is: nothing; we live only once, and there is no second chance. There is no soul or immortal consciousness, no cosmic judge, divine paradise or fiery hell. Because of this, we should make the most of our existence while we can, living moral lives, not because God will judge us, but because it shows compassion for others and respect for ourselves.

Most humanists are materialists; they believe that we are nothing more than matter. There is no spiritual or supernatural aspect to life.

Task

For both of the religions you are studying, explain in detail religious teachings about the afterlife. Use the guidance below to help you to write a developed explanation for Christianity. Ensure that you use key terms fluently and frequently.

All/many/most Christians believe that _____ .

This comes from the teaching/Bible quote _____ .

This means that/Because of this they _____ .

Some/other Christians such as _____ believe that _____ .

This comes from the teaching/Bible quote _____ .

This means that/Because of this they _____ .

Finally, Christians such as _____ believe that _____ .

This means that/Because of this they _____ .

Their beliefs do/do not differ because _____ .

9 Issues of life and death

194

How do funeral rites reflect people's beliefs about the afterlife?

When someone dies, it is common to mark their death and celebrate their life in some sort of ceremony. Different religions have their own specific rituals and practices. This section gives details of religious and non-religious funeral **rites**, explaining how these ceremonies reflect beliefs about the afterlife.

Rite A ritual or solemn ceremony.

Christian funeral rites and their meaning

When a Catholic is close to death, if it is possible, a priest is called to say the last rites. Prayers are said for the dying person, and they can ask God for forgiveness of their sins. The last rites is a Catholic practice, which might also involve the priest giving Holy Communion.

Meaning This helps to ease the dying person into the afterlife, enabling them to die at peace, having asked for God's forgiveness.

In the Catholic Church and the Church in Wales, the funeral itself is usually held in a church. The coffin is carried to the front of the church, and a service is held in honour of the dead person: flowers are displayed, prayers said and candles may be lit. The minister reads the words of Jesus:

> I am the resurrection and the life.
>
> (John 11.25)

Meaning The candles represent Jesus as the 'light of the world', because he guides a path into heaven. The passage 'I am the resurrection' reminds the congregation that those who believe in Jesus will be resurrected, to spend eternity with God.

Psalm 23, 'The Lord is my shepherd', is often read at funerals. It says that even when I am 'in the valley of the shadow of death', God is still by my side. Catholics may hold a mass (communion service) with bread and wine at a funeral.

Meaning We are not forgotten by God; he will comfort those who mourn and accompany those who have died.

After this, the person is buried, with the words 'ashes to ashes, dust to dust'. Today, many Christians prefer to be cremated, but traditionally the dead had to be buried.

Meaning Christianity used to teach that the bones of the dead must be left intact, so that on the Day of Judgement they could reform, rising to bodily resurrection with God in heaven. Some Christians today believe that only the soul goes to heaven, so it is acceptable to cremate the body.

Although the Catholic Church teaches the resurrection of the body, it recognises that many people opt for cremation. It therefore permits cremation, even though it calls it a 'brutal destruction' of the body and makes it clear that burial is preferable.

Buddhist funeral rites and their meaning

For Buddhists, death does not mark the end of life; it is just a stage of life between existence and rebirth. However, it is a stage when the deceased has no influence over their karma: they cannot make causes that will benefit them in the future.

Therefore, funerals are important opportunities for the living to help the dead and have a positive influence on the circumstances of their rebirth. This is known as 'transferring merit'. 'Merit' is good or fortunate karma and Buddhists believe they are able to donate their merit to the deceased in order to facilitate a favourable rebirth. The transfer is made through positive thought, but must be motivated by generosity and a whole-hearted wish for the deceased to receive benefit.

In Theravadin funeral rites, monks will chant each day for seven days for the deceased to receive merit. Over this time, a young male relative may become a monk, as it is believed that monks have greater power than lay people to exert spiritual influence. Water is poured from a jug to a small dish. The deceased is washed and relatives sprinkle scented water onto his or her right hand, again as a symbol of the transfer of merit.

Meaning These actions symbolise the transfer of merit from the living to the deceased.

Afterwards, white thread is used to bind the dead person's hands and feet. The thread is unwound outside the coffin and held by the monks. The coffin is carried to the local temple for cremation. The funeral procession is led by close relatives holding a picture of the deceased. They are followed by monks, who hold the white thread that is connected to the deceased in the coffin carried on a cart behind them.

Meaning Linking the deceased person to monks via the thread enables him or her to maintain contact with the monks' merit-giving energy.

At the temple, relatives place a monk's robes on the coffin. The monks take them from there, as if they are a gift from the deceased.

Meaning The deceased can acquire more merit in this way.

There are many different Mahayana funeral traditions from many countries. Usually, as in Theravadin rites, chanting takes place over seven days, then every seven days for seven weeks.

Meaning These 49 days are thought to be especially significant for the deceased, for this is the period during which the deceased person's karma is being channelled into rebirth.

Tibetan death rites reflect the mystical beliefs that Tibetan Buddhists hold about death. Stages between lifetimes are called 'bardos'. They are described in a book called *Bardo Thodol*, the Tibetan Book of the Dead. It is read to a person as they lie dying.

Meaning This reminds the dying person what to expect as they move from death to rebirth.

After death, the body may be cremated, or in Tibet it may be offered in a sky burial. In a sky burial, the body is taken to a site in the mountains where it is hacked into pieces that are fed to vultures.

Meaning Sky burial shows, in a dramatic way, the impermanence of life and the interrelation (Dependent Origination) of all things.

In Wales, Buddhism is still a young religion so there are no Buddhist funeral directors. If a Buddhist dies, the funeral arrangements are usually made by the Buddhist organisation to which the deceased belonged, along with his or her relatives.

The service is likely to take place in a crematorium, though prayers and chanting may take place at a Buddhist centre or a fellow-Buddhist's home beforehand. It is likely that most of the mourners at a Welsh Buddhist's funeral will not be Buddhists, so the service will be simple, involving readings from Buddhist texts and positive wishes, so it is accessible to all.

Muslim funeral rites and their meaning

When a Muslim is close to death, they try to repeat the final words of Prophet Muhammad: 'God, help me through the hardship and agony of death'. Those around the person will respond: 'To God we belong and to God we return'.

The **Kalimah** (often referred to as the **shahadah**) is whispered into their ears, just as these words were whispered into their ears as a new-born baby.

Meaning: This emphasises the belief that, at death, we are returning to our creator (God).

If possible, funerals take place within 24 hours of death. The dead person's body is washed: this is called ghusl. The body is then wrapped in a white shroud. In Britain it will be put into a coffin, but in some Islamic countries Muslims prefer to be buried without one.

Meaning: The simple white shroud represents purity and equality: all are equal before God in death.

Muslims do not approve of cremation. Bodies are buried facing Makkah.

Meaning: Muslims believe that the body must remain intact, facing the Holy City. This will allow the person to be resurrected on the Day of Judgement.

At the graveside they recite the first chapter (Surah) of the Qur'an (the al-Fatihah):

In the name of God, Most Gracious, Most Merciful. Praise be to God, the Cherisher and Sustainer of the worlds …

During prayers, takbir (Allahu Akbar) is recited, four times by Sunni Muslims and five times by Shi'a.

When the body has been lowered into the grave, the following words are spoken:

From the earth We created you. And into it We shall cause you to return and from it We shall bring you forth once more.

(Qur'an 20.55)

In addition, Shi'a Muslims recite Talqin: instructions to the deceased. This is a statement of reassurance spoken directly to the deceased, confirming that they are a Muslim and reminding them of what will happen to them.

Meaning: These prayers emphasise the greatness of God and the belief that he will bring people back to life.

Muslims do not usually have gravestones, but the site of the grave is often raised in a mound, above the level of the ground and identified with a simple marker.

Meaning: Everyone is equal in death.

> **Kalimah (shahadah)** The statement: 'There is no god but God, and Muhammad is his prophet'.

9 Issues of life and death

196

Jewish funeral rites and their meaning

As they are dying, Jews try to say the Shema prayer: 'Listen, Israel, God is our Lord, God is One.'

Meaning: This shows their deeply held belief in one God.

When someone dies, arrangements must be made for burial as soon as possible, preferably within 24 hours of death. The body will be washed and dressed in a simple white shroud (tachrichim). Men may also be wrapped in their prayer shawl (tallith), which is sometimes cut. The body will then be placed in a simple coffin.

Meaning: Being washed and dressed in a simple white shroud and placed in a simple coffin is to show that the rich and poor are alike in death.

Before the burial takes place the mourners make a tear in their clothes. This is called a keriah.

Meaning: The prayer shawl fringes are cut off to show that now they are dead they are now free of any religious laws. Tearing their clothes represents the grief felt by close family and friends.

Orthodox Judaism does not permit cremation, but some progressive Jews allow it. After the burial a blessing is said: 'May God comfort you among all the mourners of Zion and Jerusalem.'

For the next seven days the family observes shiva, when they stay at home and a candle is kept burning. Kaddish is said three times a day. All the mirrors in the house are covered, people sit on low stools and do not shave or cut their hair.

Mourning continues for 30 days after the burial and mourners do not go out for pleasure. This is called 'Sheloshim'.

The dead person is remembered each year, on the anniversary of their death, by the lighting of a candle and reciting the Kaddish.

Meaning: These rituals and prayers are to show respect to God and to the dead person and to help to keep them in the memories of their loved ones.

Merthyr Tydfil Jewish Cemetery.

Non-religious funeral services

Many people today are uncomfortable with religious ceremonies and, as a result, non-religious funeral services are becoming increasingly popular. Many people want a more informal, personal ceremony, where they can choose the songs and readings and where there is no mention of God.

A humanist funeral will be led by a humanist celebrant. At a humanist funeral, those present will remember the life of the person who has died, reflecting on their contribution to the world and to others. The ceremony may include:

- music
- a non-religious reflection on death
- readings of poetry
- reminiscences about the person
- a eulogy (a description of why they were special)
- lighting candles
- moments of quiet reflection.

Meaning: The service will try to show respect for the dead person without suggesting that they are going to a better place. They will be remembered for their special, unique qualities, the life they led and the achievements they made.

> …a funeral that focuses on the person who had died and the life they led – not on the idea of an afterlife – and provides a dignified and sincere way of saying goodbye.
>
> (Wales Humanists)

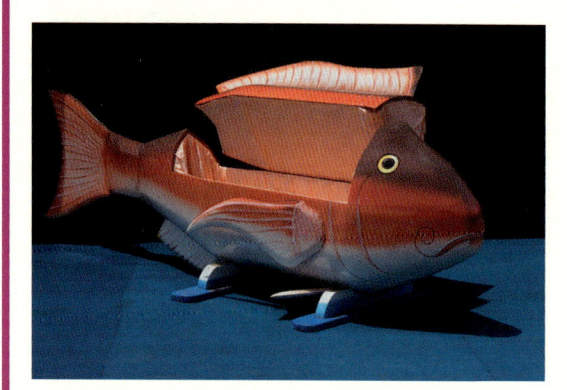

Unusual coffins, designed to show something special about the life of the person who has died, are now available.

Green burials are becoming more common in the UK. A growing number of people are choosing to have woodland burials.

Tasks

1. Copy and complete the table below, identifying the key rites during a Christian funeral and their symbolism or meaning.

Funeral Rite	Symbolism/Meaning

2. Explain the key benefits of a funeral for both the living and dead. Where possible provide specific examples from the religious traditions you are studying.

9 Issues of life and death

▶ **End of Section Review**

Stickability

Key concepts:
- Afterlife
- Soul

Key teachings:
- The afterlife
- Judgement

Key practices:
- Religious and non-religious attitudes towards funerals

Knowledge Check

1. Write a short paragraph (roughly three sentences) to explain what is meant by the soul.
2. Why might there be differences of belief about the afterlife within one religion?
3. Explain how a funeral reflects religious beliefs about the afterlife.

Skills Link

"The belief in the afterlife is the most important one."
Discuss this statement showing that you have considered more than one point of view. (In your answer, you must refer to religious and non-religious beliefs)

The Big Question

'Death is the end.'

Your Task

Respond to the statement above, showing that you have considered more than one point of view. Give reasoned judgements on the validity and strength of these views.

Task

For both of the religions that you are studying, you need to explain in detail religious teachings about **judgement**. Use the guidance below to help you to write a **developed explanation** for Christianity and a second one for your other chosen religion. Ensure that you use key terms fluently and frequently.

All/many/most Christians believe that _____ .

This comes from the teaching/Bible quote _____ .

This means that/Because of this they _____ .

Some/other Christians such as _____ believe that _____ .

This comes from the teaching/Bible quote _____ .

This means that/Because of this they _____ .

Finally, Christians such as _____ believe that _____ .

This means that/Because of this they _____ .

Their beliefs do/do not differ because _____ .

10 Issues of good and evil

Key Concepts

Good That which is considered morally right, or beneficial and to our advantage.

Evil That which is considered extremely immoral, wicked and wrong.

Forgiveness To grant pardon for a wrongdoing; to give up resentment and the desire to seek revenge against a wrongdoer.

Free will The ability to make choices (particularly moral choices) voluntarily and independently. The belief that nothing is pre-determined.

Justice Fairness; where everyone has equal provisions and equality of opportunity and receives what they are due.

Morality Principles and standards determining which actions are right or wrong.

Pacifism: The belief that war and violence are unjustifiable.

Conscience: A person's moral sense of right and wrong. Religious people may believe that the conscience is their inner guidance from God.

Suffering Pain or distress caused by injury, illness or loss. Suffering can be physical, emotional/psychological or spiritual. spiritual.

Core Questions

What makes an act wrong?

Why do people suffer?

What causes crime?

What are the aims of punishment?

How are criminals treated in the twenty-first century?

Is it ever right to execute someone?

Is it really possible to forgive?

200

Crime and punishment

How do people make moral decisions?

Making moral decisions is not a straightforward, risk-free process. We all have a **conscience**, which helps us to assess the right choice to make when reviewing a situation. Some believe that our conscience develops as we grow older, and that it grows through the process of making right decisions. It also grows through the guilt felt when making the wrong decisions. Some people also believe that our conscience gives us advance warning of whether the decision we are about to make is right or wrong. We then choose, it is our **free will** that enables us to make decisions and choices that are genuinely our own.

However, there are a number of factors that influence our moral decision making. Here are some of them.

- Our past experiences allow us to learn the rightness and wrongness of our actions, partially through the responses of others to our behaviour and choices. The human brain has evolved to learn from previous experiences and use these reflections to help us to make decisions in the future.
- The law offers us strict guidance for our behaviour. Laws are made by our elected representatives in government and by judges, and exist to help maintain order, peace and harmony. Breaking these laws is met with punishments such as fines, community service and prison.
- Many people, especially religious believes, consult either religious leaders or community elders for advice and guidance before making difficult moral decisions. It is widely accepted that these leaders have the wisdom, experience and knowledge to offer counselling. They have usually received special training to understand and interpret holy scriptures and teachings, and many are seen to be God's representatives on earth.
- Religious believers also look to their religion's teachings before making moral decisions. These are found in the sacred texts of each tradition: the Bible; the Tipitaka or the sutras; the Qur'an and Hadith; and the Torah. In the modern world, there are many moral decisions for which ancient sacred texts are unable to provide specific guidance. In situations like these, believers look to religious leaders to interpret and attempt to apply the teachings of their religion. They also look towards the example of prophets such as Muhammad or other notable individuals from within the religious tradition, such as Martin Luther King or Archbishop Desmond Tutu.

Other forms of belief that sit outside strict moral codes and religious beliefs can also guide decision-making. For example, many people take what is known as a situation ethics approach to making decisions.

Key Concepts

Morality Principles and standards determining which actions are right or wrong.

Conscience A person's moral sense of right and wrong. Religious people may believe that the conscience is their inner guidance from God.

Every single instance of moral decision-making is viewed as totally unique because the circumstances of each case are always different, and choices are made with the guiding principle that the well-being of people is the most important thing.

Another example of a system of moral guidance that does not rely on a moral code is utilitarianism. In utilitarian decision-making, choices are made based on the principle of creating the greatest happiness for the greatest number of people.

Finally, some people look to reason and logic to guide their moral decision-making. This is when decisions are made according to strict principles. In practice, it means looking at the moral problem away from emotions and ideas from religion, law or accepted codes of moral behaviour, and making a decision rationally, according to a set of agreed principles.

Types of morality

There are two common forms of **morality**.

- **Absolute morality** is when a person has a principle such as 'it is wrong to kill' and never alters it. They apply this principle or moral standard to all situations, no matter what the context or circumstance. This person might believe that all killing, including in war, is wrong. Within both the Islamic and Christian traditions there are examples of groups who traditionally adopt a moral absolutist approach, to certain issues, for example the Catholic view on abortion and Quaker views about war. Islamic Shari'ah law is grounded in moral absolutism.
- **Relative morality** is when a person holds a moral principle but is prepared to adapt or adjust it in certain situations. This person might believe that, if it reduces suffering in the future, killing in war might be necessary. Buddhists and many Protestant Christian denominations, like the Church in Wales, would be considered moral relativists.

Tasks

1. In your own words, explain what moral decision-making is and summarise five ways of making moral decisions.
2. Explain the difference between absolute and relative morality. For each, give an example of a viewpoint that would be held (for example, abortion is always wrong) and a religious group that would follow that stance.
3. Choose three different factors that help us to make moral decisions. For each, explain their importance and how they work.
4. Read and reproduce the quote below from William Penn. Is he a moral absolutist or relativist? Explain how you can tell.

   Right is right, even if everyone is against it, and wrong is wrong, even if everyone is for it.

   (William Penn, a seventeenth-century Quaker and founder of Pennsylvania, USA)

Crime

What is crime?

Crime can be defined as any offence that is punishable by law. The government makes laws that govern our behaviour, the police prevent and detect crime, and the principal job of the criminal justice system (including courts and judges) is to enforce these laws and punish crime. Throughout the course of history, what constitutes a crime, ideas about the causes of crime, and how criminals should be punished have changed.

Crime versus sin

Although there are many sins that can be punished by law, a great many sins are not considered crimes in modern society. For example, while it goes against the Ten Commandments to commit adultery (to have an affair) and to work on the Sabbath, neither is a crime according to the law.

The consequences of committing a sin are critically different in different religious traditions:

- For Christians, sinful behaviour can lead to personal suffering, offending God, excommunication (being cut off from the Church), or even exclusion from heaven.
- Jews believe that, while to sin is part of human life, those who sin will suffer in this life in order to atone for their behaviour.
- The idea of sin does not exist in Hinduism and Buddhism. Actions that are intended to cause harm are likely to have negative effects for the person who performs the action, either in this lifetime or a future rebirth.
- Through **Shari'ah law**, Muslims who openly go against accepted religious codes can receive specified punishments that are fixed by God. Those people who have rejected God, or whose bad deeds outweigh their good ones, will be sent to hell after the Day of Judgement.

Shari'ah law Muslim law based upon the Qur'an. Most Muslim countries incorporate aspects of Shari'ah into their national legal frameworks.

Examples of Sins

The seven deadly sins originate in Christian tradition. They are believed to be the source of all other forms of immoral behaviour.

- Pride
- Greed
- Lust
- Envy
- Gluttony
- Wrath
- Sloth

Crime statistics

In Britain, over 30,000 crimes are believed to be committed each day. These range from crimes against property and people, to Internet crime and fraud. Many of these crimes are not reported to the police, which means it is very difficult to know the true extent of criminal behaviour in Britain. Recent crime statistics show that people are at more risk of falling victim to cybercrime than ever before.

Despite the fact that statistically the most danger is posed by anti-social behaviour, society has become most concerned with extremism, terrorism and sexual offences.

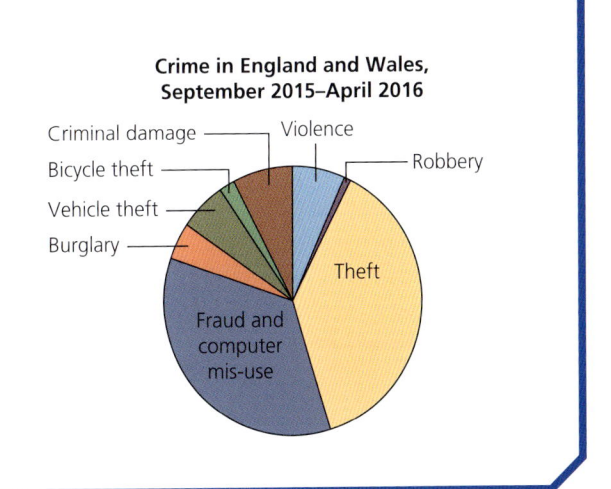

Crime in England and Wales, September 2015–April 2016

- Criminal damage
- Bicycle theft
- Vehicle theft
- Burglary
- Violence
- Robbery
- Theft
- Fraud and computer mis-use

Causes of crime

The causes of crime are complex. Most people today accept that poverty, parental neglect, low self-esteem and alcohol and drug abuse are all connected in explaining why people commit crimes. Some people are simply at greater risk of becoming offenders because of the circumstances into which they are born.

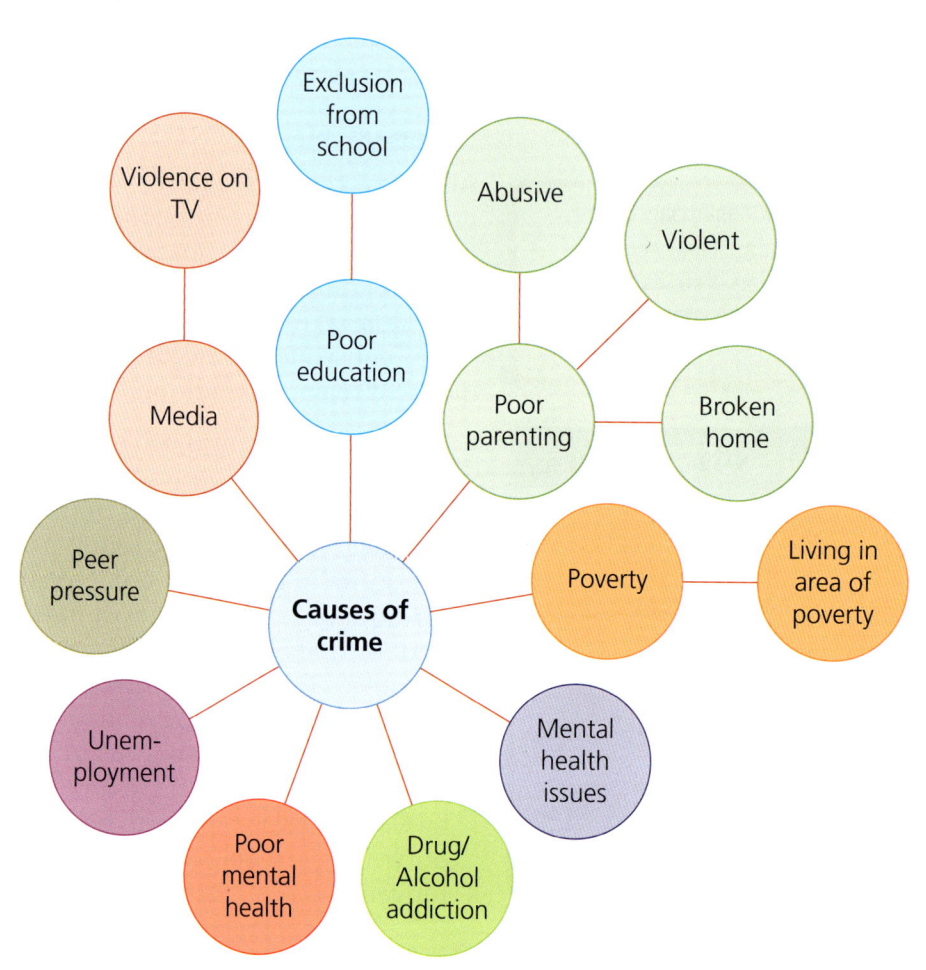

Causes of crime:
- Exclusion from school
- Violence on TV
- Abusive
- Violent
- Poor education
- Media
- Poor parenting
- Broken home
- Peer pressure
- Poverty
- Living in area of poverty
- Unemployment
- Mental health issues
- Poor mental health
- Drug/Alcohol addiction

In society, it is important that people are brought up with a good understanding of the concepts of good and bad and the difference between the two. Members of any society have a duty to follow the laws of the country. When citizens choose not to be law-abiding, chaos ensues. Because of this, parents and schools have a moral responsibility to teach the difference between right and wrong so that young people will be respectful of others and, critically, not commit crime. All major religions agree on the importance of law in society and the role it plays in maintaining order and protecting citizens.

Tasks

1. Define what 'crime' is.
2. Explain the difference between crime and sin. Give two examples for each.
3. Write a short paragraph to identify the main causes of crime. Give clear examples of three.

Aims of punishment

Punishment A penalty given to someone for a crime or wrong they have done.

When detected and prosecuted, criminal behaviour results in **punishment**. There are a number of different punishment options available to judges (such as community service, fines and prison terms). Often, a judge will consider several different purposes when sentencing a person for committing a crime.

Protection
Punishment often aims to protect more people from becoming victims of crime. As a prison sentence removes a criminal from society, innocent people are prevented from suffering from wrongdoing as the criminal has no option to commit further crime. Terrorists, murderers, rapists and drug dealers are given prison sentences as they pose a danger to the rest of society.

Retribution
In simple terms, this means revenge. 'Getting even' with a person who has committed a crime means that the criminal suffers just as they have made others suffer. For some victims of crime, this is the only way that they feel that justice can been done.

Reparation
Reparation simply means repairing the damage done through crime. Restorative justice programmes, such as community service clean-up schemes for vandals, allow offenders to attempt to make up for the crime they have committed.

Aims of punishment

Deterrence
For many people, one of the main aims of punishment is to deter or put people off committing crime altogether. Historically in England this was the main purpose of the death penalty, and is still seen to be the aim of capital punishment in some states in the USA where executions take place for murder. For a deterrent to work, the criminals who are caught need to be made an example of in order to warn others in society not to commit crime.

Vindication
Through effective punishment the government and the law can prove that it deserves respect and should be followed. Punishment exists to prove the authority of the law, and to remind people that without law and order there is chaos. This aim of punishment allows people to have confidence in the law and respect for the role it plays in creating order.

Reformation
Punishment can only go so far if it does not address the causes of crime and the reasons why some people become criminals. Because of this, one of the main aims of modern punishment is to reform or rehabilitate offenders so that they can understand why they committed offences and attempt to 'fix' these problems. Reform can take the shape of therapy, counselling, education or training.

Task

Draw a table like the one below. Copy the six aims of punishment from the diagram above into the first column. Explain what each aim means in the second column and then summarise each, in no more than four words, in the final column.

Aim	Explanation	Summary (four words)
Retribution		Getting your own back

205

Crime and punishment

Key Concept

Justice Fairness; where everyone has equal provisions and equality of opportunity and receives what they are due.

Punishment and justice

What is justice?

Strictly speaking, **justice** simply translates as fairness. When talking about crime and punishment, most people take justice to mean that a criminal is caught, fairly tried in court, and given a punishment that both fits the crime and allows the victim to overcome their resentment.

Both religions and governments focus upon maintaining justice as a key feature of a moral society.

The relationship between justice and punishment

Many people would agree that justice cannot be achieved without some form of punishment. For justice to truly be achieved, however, the punishment must address the cause of the crime and reflect the severity of the crime. It would be totally inappropriate to give a murderer a community service order, but similarly it would be ineffective to give a drug addict a life sentence in a high-security prison.

> It is better to risk saving a guilty person than to condemn an innocent one.
> (Voltaire, 18th-century writer and philosopher)

Are prisons schools for crime?

The prison system in Britain is at breaking point. Numbers in prison have never been so high, and yet neither have rates of reoffending on release. Something, it seems, is not working properly. There are many benefits to prisons. They protect society from violent and dangerous criminals, and remove those who have done wrong from their families, friends and communities (retribution). Criminals are given the opportunity to reflect on their actions and potentially reform. Furthermore, prison can be seen as a deterrent.

On the other hand, many prisoners reoffend on release, the rates being higher for those who have received short sentences of less than a year. Prison has a poor record for reducing reoffending – 47 per cent of adults are reconvicted within one year of release. For those serving sentences of fewer than 12 months, this increases to 60 per cent. Over two-thirds (68 per cent) of under-18-year-olds are reconvicted within a year of release. There are several reasons for this. It can be incredibly difficult to get a job with a criminal record, which can add to the bitterness and resentment felt at having served a prison sentence. On top of this, prisons are often referred to as 'schools of crime' – and it is well known that many prisoners educate each other in criminal methods.

(Statistics from PrisonReformTrust.org. Bromley Briefings, Summer 2016)

Tasks

1. What is 'justice'?
2. Explain why it is important to think about justice when punishing someone for a crime.
3. For the religions that you are studying, explain their attitude to punishment and justice. Make sure you outline both beliefs (teachings and ideas) and practice (actions or behaviour).
4. Look the quotation from Voltaire above. What view on punishment do you think he holds?

Religious teachings about punishment and justice

Christian attitudes to punishment and justice

Christianity is a religion of forgiveness and, as such, Christians do not support the idea of retribution as a purpose of punishment. Christians do, however, believe in justice, which means that forgiveness and punishment should go together. Christians should try to follow the example of Jesus, who forgave those who betrayed him. Because of this, many support punishment practices that lead to forgiveness, for example, **restorative justice** programmes in prisons.

Similarly, Jesus taught compassion and not revenge and, because of this, many Christians have been actively involved in prison reform to ensure that people are treated humanely in prison. They also believe that it is important to recognise and address the causes of criminal behaviour, such as poverty, unemployment and poor social conditions, as a means of restoring social justice and preventing crime. Most Christians also firmly believe that punishment should enable a person to reform – to change their ways on release from prison and add value to the community. Some Christians have become prison chaplains (see page 210) so that they can help prisoners to reform effectively.

> But let justice roll on like a river, righteousness like a never-failing stream.
>
> (Amos 5.24)

Restorative justice A system of justice that enables criminals to make amends for their behaviour by meeting with their victim and apologising.

Buddhist attitudes to punishment and justice

When Buddhists think about justice, they think about justice for all. In a situation where a crime has been committed against an individual, of course they would be concerned that justice is carried out on behalf of the victim. But they would also want to ensure that the criminal is treated fairly.

Criminal behaviour itself is conditioned; it is motivated by the Three Poisons: greed, anger and ignorance. It is also conditioned by a person's circumstances and background, and these conditions are products of karma. For example, a person's karma may cause them to be born into a dysfunctional family. Their circumstances might 'condition' them into becoming angry and violent. Their violent actions will harm others and they will face the consequences of that, perhaps by being imprisoned.

Buddhists see karma as natural justice: those who harm others will reap the effects. Sometimes, simply living with the knowledge of one's actions is a punishment.

Of course, this does not mean that criminal behaviour can be excused on the grounds that it is conditioned by karma. Buddhists believe that people can overcome their karma through the discipline of the Noble Eightfold Path. People choose to behave badly and they should face the consequences of their actions. So punishment imposed on people for their criminal behaviour is karmic justice.

However, Buddhists also see that it is difficult to escape from the negative karmic cycle of criminality. They would support programmes whose aims are to help reform criminals and to give them opportunities to create better karma and lead more positive lives. The Angulimala organisation is an example of this (see page 215).

Buddhists would also support initiatives to reduce poverty and social inequality so that people are less likely to be motivated to commit crimes.

Islamic attitudes to punishment and justice

Islam teaches that every person's life is predestined: nothing happens that Allah does not will to happen and he knows in advance what each person will do. This means that God knows a criminal's activities before they are committed. This does not mean, however, that criminals are not responsible for their actions. Although actions are predetermined and although God knows what each person will do, the individual does not know in advance.

He or she still has free will and so makes freely chosen decisions. Therefore, criminals are still responsible for their crimes, even though they are doing the will of Allah.

Although forgiveness is very important in Islam, so is the need to protect society (called the ummah) and keep law and order. Punishment is therefore seen as central to justice and essential in keeping people from straying from what is good and just. 'Shari'ah' translates as 'straight path' and Shari'ah law outlines both the rules to live by and the punishments if these laws are broken.

Shari'ah law is laid down in the Qur'an, the word of God. Muslims are therefore bound by Shari'ah law.

Many Shari'ah law punishments are designed to deter as well as protect society from further wrongdoing, for example, cutting off a hand for theft, or a receiving a beating in full view of the local community. Although Muslims are bound by Shari'ah law, no country has completely incorporated Shari'ah into its nation's legal system. Some Muslim countries have mixed systems and this is the usual model. Shari'ah has no legal status in the UK and Muslims must obey British law. There are, however, Shari'ah Courts in the UK for Muslims who want to use them, though judgments made by the courts are not legally binding and must be lawful – so, for example, amputation and beatings are not allowed. For Muslims, punishment has nothing to do with removing sin, as only God can forgive – it is a way of keeping law and order. Muslims do hope, however, that offenders will repent, reform and seek forgiveness both from God and their victims.

> Indeed, God orders justice and good conduct and giving [help] to relatives and forbids immorality and bad conduct and oppression. He admonishes you that perhaps you will be reminded.
>
> (Qur'an 16.90)

Shari'ah law in Wales

Shari'ah law has no legal authority in Wales and there is no Shari'ah court in Wales. There is, however, a Shari'ah Council, which advises Muslims on how to apply Shari'ah to commonplace situations and problems such as marriage and divorce, inheritance and personal disputes. The Council is a source of reference for Welsh lawyers who want to understand Islamic perspectives on cases relating to Muslim families.

Saleem Kidwai, Secretary of the Muslim Council of Wales, says:

> A Shari'ah Council doesn't have the same power as a Supreme or High Court. It simply gives advice, and it is up to the individual whether to follow that advice or not. A Shari'ah Council has no legal authority. You cannot force religion on anybody.

In fact, he does not believe it is appropriate for England and Wales to adopt Shari'ah law, in spite of their growing Muslim populations:

> Whenever Shari'ah law is mentioned, people talk about floggings, hands being cut off and executions.
>
> It upsets us. These are deterrents which are only used in extreme circumstances abroad – and we are not asking for that to be brought here.

Jewish attitudes to punishment and justice

In Judaism, there is a firm principle that people have been given free will and must therefore take responsibility for their actions. Jews believe that punishment should deter, protect society, provide retribution and promote justice. Just as God created a just world, Jews believe that they must practise justice themselves. Judges must be appointed to rule over the actions of others. They should be fair and incorruptible.

The Torah also contains many laws giving instructions on how crime should be punished. There are many different views on the issue of punishment in Judaism. Members of the Reform Jewish community are often active in protesting for the fair treatment of prisoners in jail. Like other religions, Jews are taught that they should be forgiving; however, within Judaism, only the victim is able to forgive, as no one can be forgiven on behalf of others. Offenders should repent and ask God's forgiveness by avoiding repeat offending, giving money to charity and fasting, especially on the Day of Atonement.

▶ The treatment of criminals in the prison system

How are criminals treated in modern prisons?

How should prisons treat criminals?

Since prisons were first built, there has been concern about how the prisoners within them are treated. There are many different opinions about what prison should achieve, and because of this there are a great many opinions about the kind of treatment prisoners should receive. Some feel that prison should be a place of isolation and punishment and that prisoners should have few if any privileges, such as access to television or computers. Many others, however, see prisons as a place of rehabilitation and reform. Because of this, they believe that the treatment that prisoners receive should enable them to address the root cause of their criminality and equip them for life as responsible citizens.

The treatment of prisoners is carefully monitored. Prisoners are entitled to humane treatment that shows respect for their human rights. No matter what the arguments about prison regimes, the fact remains that many prisoners continue to complain about overcrowding, poor treatment and a lack of access to important services. Many argue that the impact of poor prison conditions can be seen in rising rates of assault, self-harm and suicide among inmates.

Prison reformers

Britain has a proud history of prison **reformers**, many of whom were inspired by their religious beliefs to lobby for change.

John Howard was a committed Calvinist (Protestant Christian) and inspected prisons in the late eighteenth century. He found them to be diseased, dirty and corrupt, and gave evidence to Parliament with recommendations that conditions and practices be improved. He called for basic but essential provisions, such as clean running water, separate cells for men and women, access to doctors and greater numbers of prison officers to support and ensure the safety of inmates. This was at a time when the majority of prisons were privately run for profit.

Elizabeth Fry was a nineteenth-century **Quaker** prison reformer, who dedicated her life to improving the state of British prisons after visiting Newgate Prison in London in 1813. She was a passionate advocate of education in prisons and looked towards reforming prisoners as opposed to simply isolating them from society. She is most famous for teaching female prisoners to read and write and holding Bible readings for inmates.

By the 1870s, ideas about prison and prisons themselves had changed dramatically. Purpose-built institutions (like Pentonville Prison in London) were to be found across the country, and a lively debate about how to treat prisoners once in jail had been born. Finally, real thought was being given to how we should approach the reform of individuals once in prison.

Reformer Someone who lobbies or pressurises for change.

Quaker Member of the Society of Friends, a Christian denomination whose central belief is that every human being contains a reflection of the image of God.

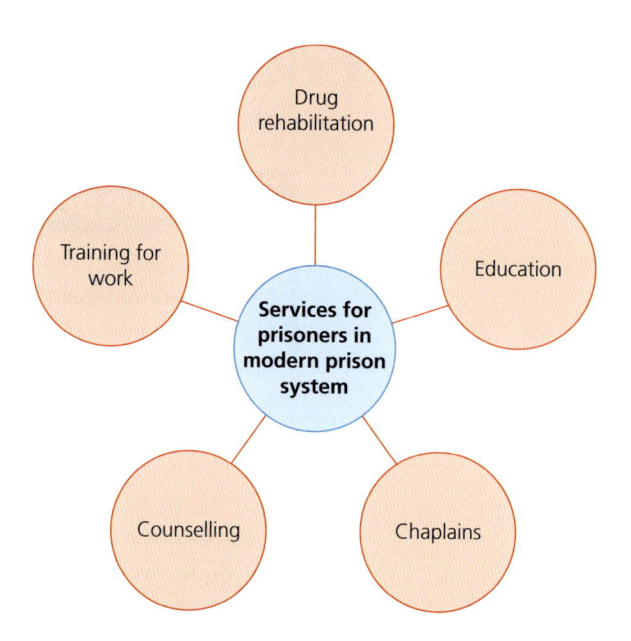

Services for prisoners in modern prison system:
- Drug rehabilitation
- Education
- Chaplains
- Counselling
- Training for work

Prison reform in the twenty-first century

The current prison population of England and Wales is 85,442, compared to 44,246 in 1993. Reoffending rates are high. According to the National Audit Office, reoffending costs us the equivalent of staging another Olympic Games every year. In light of these figures, many again are calling for a reform of prisons and prison regimes.

According to Government statistics, only 53 per cent of the prison population have any qualifications, compared to 85 per cent of the working-age population. The key focus of current discussions about prison reform is, therefore, education. The government recently announced plans to overhaul the prison system in Britain, calling for prisoners to be viewed and treated as 'potential assets, not liabilities'.

Tasks

1. In your own words, explain what the term 'reformer' means.
2. What was wrong with the early prisons in Britain?
3. In a mind map, identify the four main suggestions that John Howard made to improve prisons in the eighteenth century. For each, suggest how it would improve prisons.
4. Explain the current concerns with prisons in twenty-first century Britain. What does the government think is the most important way to reform prisons? Why?

Care for prisoners – chaplains

What is a chaplain?

For many of us, our only experience of chaplains is through movies or television. Here they are often portrayed as people on the sidelines, without a uniform or an easily defined role, who give out quick slices of advice. Traditionally, a chaplain is a minister, such as a priest, pastor, rabbi, imam or community leader of a religious tradition. They are attached to non-religious institutions such as hospitals, prisons, schools or universities. Their job is to provide pastoral care for patients, pupils, or in this case, prisoners.

What is their role?

Prison chaplains have a demanding and essential job, providing counselling to inmates, supporting them through their rehabilitation and seeing to their spiritual (and often religious) needs. Prisoners have to deal with a complex mixture of emotions and needs during their sentence and they often need someone who is not a prison officer or warden to offer support. Fear, loneliness, guilt, concerns about family or children on the outside – all of these become the concern of the prison chaplain. In addition to this, chaplains often help prisoners re-enter the community, working with **parole officers** and other volunteers. Families of inmates also have access to prison chaplains. Family members can be the victims of the inmates' crimes and require the care of the chaplain just as much as the inmate.

Parole officer A person who supports a prisoner on their release from prison and their return to the community.

> You are there primarily for the inmates. Most offenders are also victims. That doesn't mean that we feel sorry for them; but we do offer them enough compassion.
> (Kate Johnson, Quaker and prison chaplain)

Prison chaplains help prisoners deal with both their emotional and practical needs.

Chaplains do not have to be religious and it is documented that 32 per cent of the prison population have no religious faith. Since 2011, the British Humanist Society has been running a project with Humanist Pastoral Support Volunteers at Winchester Prison. This involves meeting inmates with 'nil' religion on admission, holding discussion groups and providing counselling, such as bereavement support, for inmates. This is especially important as often prisoners are unable to attend funerals of loved ones or benefit from the type of community support offered to those who have suffered the loss of family or friends.

Task

What is a prison chaplain and what is their role?

The death penalty

The death penalty has been a feature of punishment practices for thousands of years. It has been used by societies across the world to deter crime and to punish the very worst criminal behaviours. Also referred to as capital punishment or execution, the death penalty is still legal in over 80 different countries (although 50 of these countries have not used execution as a punishment in the last ten years). The majority of the countries that retain the death penalty are African or Asia-Pacific nations like China, Afghanistan and Iran. A notable exception to this is the United States of America. Of the 50 states in America, 31 allow execution in both law and practice for the crimes of murder and treason. Death row, the name given to the area where death penalty convicts reside in prison, has now become a popular feature of film, TV programmes and documentaries.

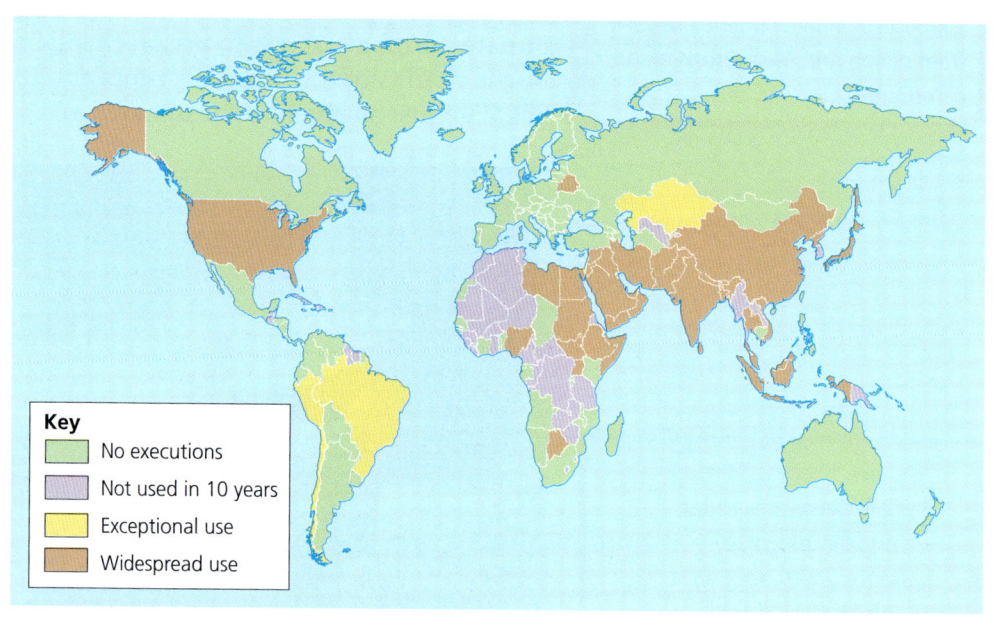

Worldwide use of the death penalty, 2016.

Methods of execution have changed over the past century as governments look for cheaper but more humane ways to end the lives of convicts. In America, executions take the form of lethal injection, electric chair, gas chamber, firing squad or hanging (although in practice lethal injection is most widely used). Other less humane methods still in use include decapitation (North Korea and Saudi Arabia), being shot under anaesthetic (Taiwan) and stoning (Sudan).

Tasks

1. Copy and complete the table below. Add five statements that support the death penalty and five that oppose it.

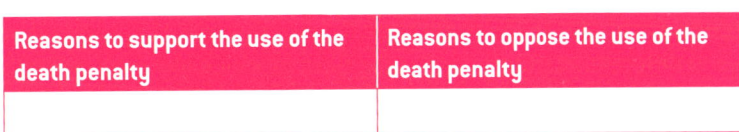

Reasons to support the use of the death penalty	Reasons to oppose the use of the death penalty

2. Write down what you believe the death penalty is designed to achieve.

The death penalty in Britain

The UK parliament abolished the death penalty in 1969. Although public opinion has at times been in favour of reinstating execution for the worst criminals, all attempts to bring it back have failed. Some of the last people to be executed, including Derek Bentley, who was convicted of being involved in the killing of a policeman, have since received pardons after their death. Essentially this means that they should not have been convicted in the first place.

Last discussed in parliament in 1998 during the passage of the Human Rights Act, the death penalty has always been hotly debated. The British Social Attitudes survey has recorded popular attitudes to the death penalty since 1983. Since then, the number of those in favour of execution has fallen from 75 per cent to 48 per cent in 2015. The UK is now among the 82 per cent of global nations that do not use the death penalty.

- The death penalty is just state-sanctioned murder.
- There is evidence that innocent people have been executed.
- The death penalty does not deter murderers.
- Only God has the right to end a life.
- Two wrongs do not make a right.
- The state should be a moral force for good.
- Forgiveness is important.
- The death penalty disproportionately affects members of racial, ethnic and religious minorities, as well as those living in poverty.
- Life terms in prison are very expensive – £40,000 per year.
- Some people – such as the criminally insane – cannot be reformed.
- It is the only way that victims can experience closure.
- There has to be an ultimate punishment for the very worst crimes.
- In Britain, life sentences amount to 15 years.
- Execution is the only way to truly protect society from very dangerous murderers and terrorists.

There are a number of key arguments and beliefs linked with the death penalty.

▶ Religious teachings about the death penalty

Christian attitudes to the death penalty

Christian attitudes to the death penalty vary. This is due to different interpretations of the Bible (specifically the Old Testament) and the extent to which teachings about the sanctity of life and Jesus' examples of compassion and forgiveness overrule early biblical teachings about justice.

Liberal Christians

Most Christians believe that only God has the right to take a life. Execution goes against the sanctity of life, as all life is precious and only God should end it. Christians believe that God commanded, 'Thou shalt not kill' (Exodus 20.13) and that this is a clear instruction. Christians should also follow the teachings of Jesus to be compassionate and forgiving. Jesus was openly forgiving to an adulterous woman (John 8) and also pleaded with God for his executioners to be forgiven when he was on the cross:

> Father, forgive them, for they know not what they do.
>
> (Luke 23.33–34)

Many Christians favour reform over execution and because of this, many have been involved in prison reform and continue to work in prisons as chaplains. Jesus also taught us to 'turn the other cheek' (Matthew 5.38–39), to love our enemies and to forgive (Matthew 5.43–47). Execution makes all of these impossible. The Golden Rule to 'do to others as you want them to do to you' also compels us to treat others as we would wish to be treated.

Quakers

Quakers have campaigned against the death penalty since 1818. For Quakers, all human life should be respected, as every person is a reflection of God and contains something of God. Quakers firmly believe that punishments should be used to reform. Some of the first prison reformers were Quakers, who worked to maintain the dignity and humanity of prisoners.

> Do not repay anyone evil for evil. Be careful to do what is right in the eyes of everyone. If it is possible, as far as it depends on you, live at peace with everyone.
>
> (Romans 12.17–18)

Conservative Christians

Some very traditional or literalist Christians advocate the death penalty, seeing it as following the Old Testament law of 'an eye for an eye'. In the Old Testament it states:

> Whoever sheds the blood of man, by man shall his blood be shed.
>
> (Genesis 9.6)

In total, the Old Testament specifies 36 capital offences, including crimes such as idolatry, magic and blasphemy, as well as murder. Some Christians would therefore argue that the death penalty was not only approved, but created by God. Some Christians also argue that capital punishment upholds the commandment, 'Thou shalt not kill' by showing the seriousness of the crime of murder.

Catholics

Catholic Christians are also divided. Traditionally the Catholic Church has allowed (but not encouraged) capital punishment. In 1997, the Vatican issued a statement saying that execution was acceptable where the identity of the criminal was absolutely confirmed and where execution was the only means to protect society from the aggressor. It did, however, state that non-lethal means of punishment were:

> ... more in keeping with the concrete conditions of the common good and ... the dignity of the human person.
>
> (Pope John Paul II – The *Gospel of Life*)

Buddhist attitudes to the death penalty

The principle of ahimsa (non-violence, harmlessness) is of prime importance in Buddhism. It is at the heart of the first of the Five Precepts, not to take life.

Karuna (compassion) means putting oneself in another's place, trying to imagine their feelings and exercising metta (loving-kindness). The Buddha said:

> All tremble at violence; all fear death.
> Putting oneself in the place of another,
> one should not kill nor cause another to kill.
>
> (Dhammapada 129)

10 Issues of good and evil

214

Capital punishment therefore seems to go against Buddhist principles. Since Buddhism teaches that all beings have the capacity to become enlightened or reach nirvana, the death penalty denies a criminal the opportunity to work at self-improvement and to make amends for their actions. The Dalai Lama has said:

> The death penalty fulfils a preventive function, but it is also very clearly a form of revenge. It is an especially severe form of punishment because it is so final. The human life is ended and the executed person is deprived of the opportunity to change, to restore the harm done or compensate for it.
>
> (Dalai Lama, Message Supporting the Moratorium on the Death Penalty, 09.04.1999)

No doubt the Dalai Lama was thinking of the story of Milarepa, a Buddhist teacher from medieval Tibet. Milarepa practised black magic as a young man and killed a large number of people, including members of his own family. Later, he was remorseful and practised hard to became a Buddhist lama (teacher). All the energy that had been used destructively was channelled into doing good – but only after a great deal of effort to break his selfish and destructive impulses.

Milarepa was able to work through the effects of his negative karma to become enlightened and a great Buddhist sage. Had his life been taken for his destructive acts, he would not have been able to lead others to enlightenment.

Similarly, the Theravada scriptures tell the story of Angulimala. Angulimala became a ruthless killer, collecting fingers from his victims and wearing them on a necklace. One of his intended victims was the Buddha, but the Buddha was able to stop Angulimala's murderous rampage. Angulimala repented of his horrific deeds and practised the Dharma. He still had to experience the karmic effects of his actions and was attacked and beaten many times. However, he was able to attain arahanthood (see page 173).

Buddhists believe that even the most violent and depraved of criminals can change and should be given every opportunity to.

The Angulimala organisation offers chaplaincy services to prisoners in England, Wales and Scotland. They aim to offer Buddhist teaching to prisoners and help them with their Buddhist practice. They liaise with prison and probationary services to ensure that prisoners in their care have opportunities to work through their karma and lead constructive lives.

Muslim attitudes to the death penalty

Islam as a whole accepts capital punishment. Muslims believe that capital punishment is a severe sentence, but one that can be issued for the most severe crimes. While criminals will be punished by God on the Day of Judgement, Muslims also believe that they should be punished on earth.

Forgiveness is important (and is preferred if possible), but so is the need to protect the ummah (Muslim community). Islam sees punishment as being central to justice. This means that all punishment is part of justice and stops people from straying down the wrong path.

The Qur'an 17.33 forbids the taking of life except in extreme situations:

> Nor take life – which God has made sacred, except for just cause.

Most Muslims agree that this 'just cause', for which the death penalty is permitted, includes the crimes of murder and 'spreading mischief in the land', which means attacking authority or destabilising the state.

Most Muslim countries (for example, Saudi Arabia and Iran) retain the death penalty. Methods of execution in Islamic countries vary but include beheading, firing squad, hanging and stoning. In some countries, public executions are carried out to provide a deterrent. Islamic countries that practise very strict Shari'ah law are associated with the use of capital punishment as punishment for the largest variety of crimes, (including some acts that are not considered to be crimes in the West), for example, for adultery, homosexuality, terrorism and treason.

There is a small but growing number of Muslims who disagree with the death penalty and call for it to be abolished. They argue that Shari'ah law is often used by repressive governments to attack women and the poor. In addition, there are examples of these countries executing the accused while denying them access to a lawyer or a proper trial. These acts are totally against the concept of Islamic justice.

Jewish attitudes to the death penalty

There are many different Jewish views on the death penalty.

The Torah stipulates several offences for which capital punishment could be used and is clear in its guidance concerning the justice of using the death penalty:

> One who takes a human life must be put to death. If one kills an animal, he must pay for it, [the value of] a life for a life. If one maims his neighbour, he must be penalised accordingly. Thus, full compensation must be paid for a fracture or the loss of an eye or a tooth. If one inflicts injury on another person, he must [pay as if the same injury were] inflicted on him.
>
> (Leviticus 24.17–20)

According to the **Mishnah**, the death penalty could only be inflicted, after trial, by a **Sanhedrin** composed of 23 judges, and there were four types of death penalty: stoning, burning, slaying (by the sword) and strangling. Heavy restrictions and conditions are placed on the use of execution, for example, the requirement for two witnesses to the crime itself and for both of those witnesses to have issued warning prior to the crime being committed.

> **Mishnah** The Oral Torah.
> **Sanhedrin** A council or assembly of men appointed in every city in the land of Israel.

Orthodox Judaism

As the death penalty is allowed in the Torah, some Orthodox Jews believe that it should be allowed for certain crimes today. However, many rabbis and Jewish academics view this guidance with suspicion, as it means that, in practice, it is virtually impossible to issue a death sentence. What it shows is that the death penalty is permitted, but should only be used with the greatest of caution.

Israel allows the death penalty for acts of genocide, treason and murder – although, in practice, it is rarely used. In fact, when Israel was made the Jewish State, there was wide debate about whether or not to abolish the death penalty entirely. The last person to be executed in Israel was Nazi war criminal, Adolf Eichmann, in 1962. Now the death penalty exists purely as a deterrent and not as retribution.

Reform Judaism

Since 1959, the Union for Reform Judaism (URJ) has formally opposed the death penalty. They say that 'both in concept and in practice, Jewish tradition found capital punishment repugnant' and there is no persuasive evidence 'that capital punishment serves as a deterrent to crime'. The death penalty also goes against the commandment not to kill (Exodus 20.13).

47% of all criminals leaving prison reoffend within the year

▶ Arguing for the death penalty

For those arguing from outside a strict religious belief, views about the death penalty are affected by a number of factors. Some people argue that there needs to be an ultimate punishment to act as a deterrent and feel that, for the greater good of society, the death penalty is necessary. Some religious believers agree with these arguments and believe that religious teachings on justice allow for the use of the death penalty.

Arguments for Britain using the death penalty

Over the last few years, there have been plenty of examples of the system of justice and punishment in the UK failing to work and many more examples of dangerous criminals some think need to be permanently removed from society. Here are some examples of those cases, and of the victims who paid the price:

- Jonathan Vass, 30, from Blackpool, murdered his ex-girlfriend Jane Clough, 26, after he had been released on bail for raping her. He was jailed for 30 years.
- Mark Bridger, from Powys, was found guilty of the murder of 5-year-old April Jones in 2013. He had previous convictions, including firearms offences, battery and assault, over a period of 30 years. He was given a life sentence for April's murder, and is unlikely ever to be released from prison.
- David Cook, from Caerphilly, was convicted of the murder of Beryl Maynard in 1988. He was jailed and released in 2009, having escaped from an open prison in 2008. In 2012, he was convicted of the murder of his next-door-neighbour.

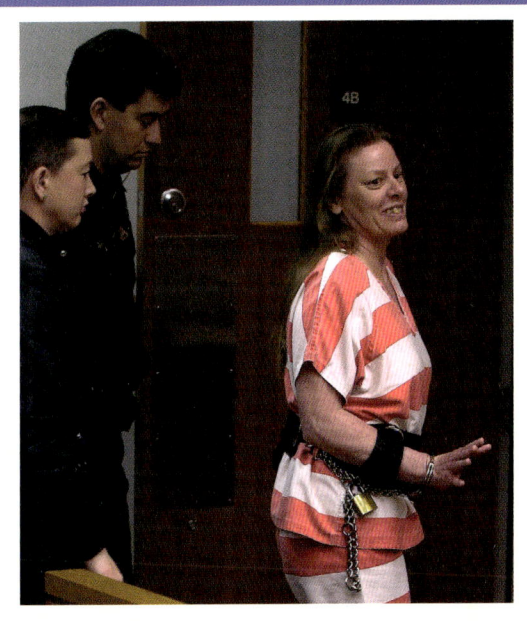

■ 'You have to kill me. I am evil. If you don't I'll just kill again.' Aileen Wuornos, convicted serial killer, Florida. Executed 2002.

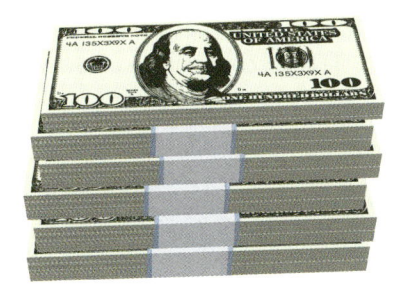

■ Average cost of keeping a person in jail for a year in the US: $58,351.

■ Average cost of a lethal injection in the US: $1,300.

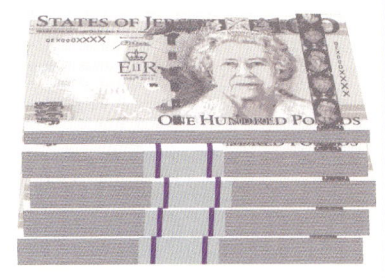

■ Cost of keeping a person in a category A prison for a year in the UK: £41,200.

Arguing against the death penalty

Some people see execution of any form as morally wrong and might argue that there is little evidence that the death penalty works as a deterrent. Religious people might agree with these views; many believe that life is sacred and shouldn't be ended by human beings.

'You can't have a penalty that isn't reversible – that you can't take back later and say, "I'm sorry, we got it wrong"... It is given out by human beings, and human beings make mistakes.' Ray Krone, former death-row inmate who was wrongly convicted of murder.

Amnesty International

Amnesty International opposes the death penalty absolutely – for all crimes without exception. They believe that:

- The death penalty violates basic human rights in every case.
- Evidence shows that it doesn't deter crime. It is often used within skewed or unfair and corrupt justice systems.
- It discriminates. Statistics show that the death penalty is used disproportionately against the poor, members of minority racial, ethnic and religious communities. It also discriminates based on the race of the victim: in the USA you are several times more likely to receive the death penalty if the victim was white than if the victim was African-American.
- It can be used as a political tool. In the USA, many state governors have fast-tracked the executions of inmates during re-election time to prove that they are 'tough on crime'. Similarly, many politicians use the issue of the death penalty to prove that they prioritise protection and justice.

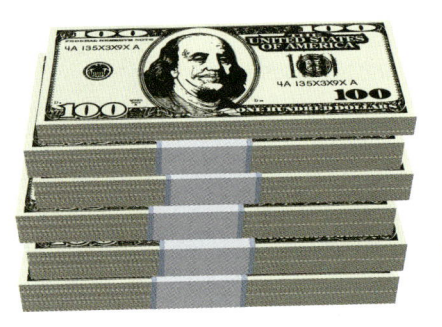

Average cost of a prisoner being sentenced to the death penalty in the US: $3 million.

Average cost of a prisoner being sentenced to life imprisonment in the US: $1.1 million.

My objection to the death penalty is based on the idea that this is a democracy, and in a democracy the government is me, and if the government kills somebody, then I'm killing somebody.

(Steve Earle, musician)

I do not think that God approves the death penalty for any crime, rape and murder included. Capital punishment is against the better judgment of modern criminology, and, above all, against the highest expression of love in the nature of God.

(Martin Luther King, Jr)

Task

'All murderers should be executed.'

Look at the previous pages and respond to the statement above, referring to both sides of the argument.

Aim for at least one paragraph for each side of the debate and give a reasoned judgement on the validity and strength of that argument. Conclude your answer with a justification of your own viewpoint.

▶ **End of Section Review**

Stickability

Key concepts:
- Morality
- Conscience
- Free will
- Justice

Key teachings:
- Crime and punishment
- The death penalty

Knowledge Check

1. List at least four aims of punishment. For each, write one sentence to explain it.
2. Explain the differences between absolute and relative morality.
3. Draw a table with two columns. Add five reasons for agreeing and five reasons for disagreeing with the death penalty.
4. Create a Venn diagram to summarise the main beliefs of your two chosen religions about punishment. Ensure that where they overlap, you identify similarities.
5. Write a short paragraph (three or four sentences) on the role of a prison chaplain.

Skills Link

What is meant by 'conscience'?

The Big Question

'The aim of punishment should be to reform.'

Your Task

Respond to the statement above, showing that you have considered more than one point of view. Give reasoned judgements on the validity and strength of these views.

Task

For both of the religions you are studying, explain in detail religious teachings about the death penalty. Use the guidance below to help you to write a developed explanation for Christianity and a second one for your other chosen religion. Ensure that you use key terms fluently and frequently.

All/many/most Christians believe that _____ .

This comes from the teaching/Bible quote _____ .

This means that/Because of this they _____ .

Some/other Christians such as _____ believe that _____.

This comes from the teaching/Bible quote _____ .

This means that/Because of this they _____ .

Finally, Christians such as _____ believe that _____.

This means that/Because of this they _____ .

Their beliefs do/do not differ because _____ .

■ **Forgiveness**

▶ # Peace and conflict

Conflict is disagreement between two or more parties, particularly if the parties hold negative or hurtful feelings for each other. When conflict happens on a national or international scale, it is called war.

Most religions teach that, ideally, people should live alongside each other in mutual tolerance and respect. In reality, however, most accept that war is sometimes inevitable.

Some people (religious or otherwise) are **pacifists**. They believe that there can never be justification for war or violence.

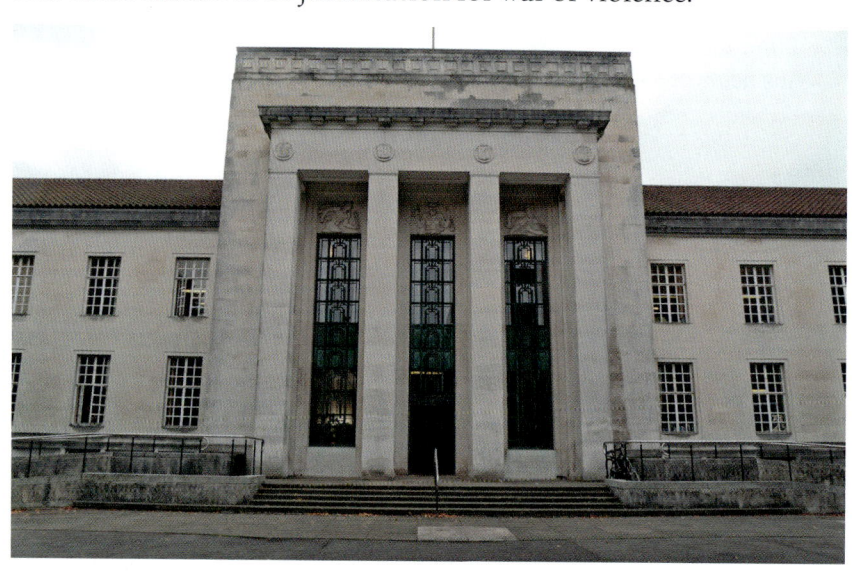

> **Key Concept**
>
> **Pacifism** The belief that war and violence are unjustifiable.

The Temple of Peace and Health in Cardiff

Christian attitudes to peace and conflict

The Bible contains many references opposed to violent conflict, and many that promote peace. One of the Ten Commandments is an instruction not to kill. In his Sermon on the Mount, Jesus goes further, saying that even anger and hatred are destructive:

> I tell you that anyone who is angry with a brother or sister will be subject to judgment.
>
> (Matthew 5.22)

He urges his audience not just to avoid conflict, but to take steps to stop it:

> Blessed are the peacemakers, for they will be called children of God.
>
> (Matthew 5.9)

In light of this, many Christians believe that war can never be justified and are pacifists. An example of a pacifist Christian group is the Religious Society of Friends, sometimes known as Quakers.

Welsh Society of Friends/Quakers

Quakers share a conviction that all people are created by God as equals and they should demonstrate their equality by showing respect for each other. They believe that each person has something of God in them and that their actions should be motivated by the love that God has given them.

Therefore, Quakers are opposed to violence and war. Many work for peace, attempting to bring together communities in areas of conflict. Quakers refuse military service in times of war. A person who does this is called a conscientious objector.

The Welsh Society of Friends is called Quakers in Wales. They say:

> Quakers recognise the equal worth and unique nature of every person. This means working to change the systems that cause injustice and hinder true community. It also

means working with people who are suffering from injustice, such as prisoners and asylum seekers.

Just War theory

However, many Christians recognise that, although war is terrible, it is sometimes less terrible than not fighting. In the 13th century, Thomas Aquinas, a Christian thinker, developed conditions that, if they were to be fulfilled, would justify war. A war that meets these conditions is called a Just War.

The conditions are:
1 The war must be for a just (fair/good) cause.
2 A war must be declared or agreed by a lawful authority: a government or the United Nations.
3 A war must be fought to bring about good or get rid of evil.
4 War must be a last resort.
5 There must be a reasonable chance of success.
6 Only necessary force must be used.
7 Only legitimate targets must be attacked.

Most Christian denominations agree with the Just War theory.

Buddhist attitudes to peace and conflict

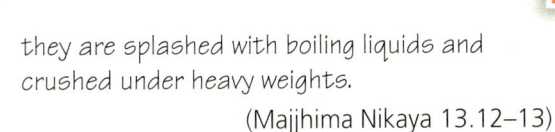

Conflict is caused by want and attachment and these, in turn, are grounded in the Three Poisons of greed, anger/hatred and ignorance. The desire for land, resources, control or revenge can often lead to war. The karma it creates is a collective karma: it applies to a whole nation. Countries that go to war against others will themselves suffer losses.

> Men take up swords and shields, buckle on bows and quivers, and charge into battle… where they are wounded by arrows and spears, and their heads are cut off by swords… and they are splashed with boiling liquids and crushed under heavy weights.
>
> (Majjhima Nikaya 13.12–13)

Buddhism teaches ahimsa, which suggests that nations should not fight wars. However, in reality, situations that require moral decisions are rarely simple, and such decisions should be considered in full recognition of all the facts of a situation. In one Buddhist teaching (Samyutta Nikaya 4.20), the Buddha asks whether it is possible to rule a country without having recourse to fighting wars to resolve conflict. It is a question he does not answer.

Muslim attitudes to peace and conflict

The Arabic word jihad means 'struggle'. Islam teaches that it is important to fight against negative forces to achieve something good.

The most important kind of jihad for Muslims is the internal struggle against temptations to avoid doing what is right. This is called the Greater Jihad (see page 92). By engaging in the Greater Jihad, a Muslims can develop their commitment to Islam and fully submit to God.

Lesser Jihad and Just War

Islam teaches that sometimes it is necessary to engage in a physical jihad to defend Islam, if its beliefs, principles, values or practices are being disrespected or attacked. This is known as the Lesser Jihad. Sometimes, the Lesser Jihad may involve armed conflict. However, in order for a war to be jihad, it must fulfil a number of conditions. If it does, it may be called a Just War. These conditions are as follows:

1 It must be fought for a Just Cause: Islam is being attacked or people are suffering.
2 It must be a last resort: all possible non-violent means of resolving the situation have been tried.
3 It must be authorised by a Muslim authority – that is by a religious leader or council of leaders.
4 It must cause minimal suffering.
5 It must not target innocent civilians, especially the elderly, women and children.
6 It must end when the enemy surrenders; prisoners of war must be returned.

The word Islam derives from the word salaam, which means 'peace'. However, this does not mean that Islam is a pacifist religion. Muslims who support the idea of the Lesser Jihad justify it on the following grounds:

- The Qur'an teaches that Muslims may fight to defend themselves, provided the war is just:

  Fight in the way of Allah those who fight you but do not transgress. Indeed, Allah does not like transgressors.

  (Surah 2.190)

- The Prophet Muhammad himself fought in battle.
- The Prophet Muhammad said that fighting to defend Islam is acceptable:

  The person who struggles so that Allah's word is supreme is the one serving Allah's cause.

  (Hadith)

Pacifism

On the other hand, there have been and are Muslim pacifists. One example is Abdul Ghaffar Khan (1890–1988). He was an activist who opposed British rule in India, but was committed to non-violence. He said:

'I am going to give you such a weapon that the police and the army will not be able to stand against it. It is the weapon of the Prophet, but you are not aware of it. That weapon is patience and righteousness. No power on earth can stand against it.'

In the same way, some individual Muslims have refused to fight in wars, citing Islamic teachings on peace as reasons. In the 1960s, African-American boxer Muhammad Ali refused to fight in the Vietnam War. He applied to be a conscientious objector, but his application was refused. This decision was reversed, however, by an appeal to the United States Supreme Court:

[Ali's] beliefs are founded on tenets of the Muslim religion as he understands them.

Jewish attitudes to peace and conflict

The Jewish Bible provides many examples of the ancient Israelites engaging in armed conflict. In some cases, it is explicit that God supports them in battle:

When you go to war against your enemies and see horses and chariots and an army greater than yours, do not be afraid of them, because the Lord your God, who brought you up out of Egypt, will be with you.

(Deuteronomy 20.1)

Just War

So Judaism is not a pacifist religion. Judaism identifies three kinds of war that are justified.

- Obligatory wars. These are wars that God has commanded. Two are recorded in the Jewish Bible.
- Defensive wars. These are fought either in self-defence or to prevent being attacked.
- Optional wars. These are Just Wars that fulfil certain conditions:
  1. It must be a last resort: peaceful means of settling the dispute must be exhausted.
  2. Every attempt must be made to limit killing to combatants and avoid civilians.

In addition, the enemy should be treated humanely:

If your enemy is hungry, give him food to eat; if he is thirsty, give him water to drink.

(Proverbs 25.21)

Although Judaism accepts that war may be unavoidable in certain circumstances, the ideal is always to strive for peace, both at a personal level and at an international level:

In God's eyes the man stands high who makes peace between men... But he stands highest who establishes peace among the nations.

(Talmud)

Pacifism

There are a significant number of Jews who believe that the teachings of Judaism inspire non-violence. The Jewish Peace Fellowship is an organisation that supports conscientious objectors. Two of its aims are:

- to work to abolish war and to create a community of concern transcending national boundaries and selfish interests
- to refrain from participation in war or military service.

Forgiveness

Religions teach that, when working for peace and harmony, when trying to rebuild relationships after a wrongdoing, or when differences of opinion and hostility arise, **forgiveness** is essential. Forgiveness enables wrongs to be acknowledged and relationships to be rebuilt.

Can true forgiveness exist?

True forgiveness is not about forgetting about wrongs done to us – in fact, it often involves exactly the opposite. To forgive properly, we have to remember the wrongs done, analyse them, understand them, accept them and then continue to live our lives.

All religions have clear teachings about the importance of forgiveness. They do not suggest that forgiving is easy or that it comes without further conflict, but they are clear that forgiving enables believers to reach a deeper spiritual understanding about themselves.

Forgiving cannot be taught. We learn to forgive through our own human experience; through reading religious teachings, through being forgiven by others and through learning about others who have forgiven, in spite of the great wrongs done to them.

> **Key Concept**
>
> **Forgiveness** To grant pardon for a wrongdoing; to give up resentment and the desire to seek revenge against a wrongdoer.

Following the destruction of Coventry Cathedral during German bombing in 1940, a commitment was made not to seek revenge, but to work for forgiveness and reconciliation with those responsible. The altar, which stands in the remains of the destroyed cathedral, features a cross made out of charred wood from the ruins and has the words 'Father forgive' inscribed on the wall behind it. The cathedral now houses the Centre for Reconciliation which has provided support to thousands of Christians addressing issues of conflict and forgiveness.

Religious teachings about forgiveness

Christian attitudes to forgiveness

Forgiveness is a prominent theme in the Bible and in Christianity as a whole. Christianity is known as a religion of forgiveness, love and compassion, and these themes are evident in religious teachings and the example of Jesus and other leaders within the faith, such as Martin Luther King.

Jesus' teachings

The Bible clearly instructs Christians to forgive:

> Do not judge, and you will not be judged. Do not condemn, and you will not be condemned. Forgive, and you will be forgiven.
>
> (Luke 6.37)

The importance of forgiveness is emphasised in the Lord's Prayer. Christians ask God to 'forgive our sins, as we forgive those who have sinned against us.' This means that Christians can expect to receive forgiveness from God only if they are forgiving towards others.

Jesus teaches further about the importance of forgiveness in his Sermon on the Mount, in the **Beatitudes**:

> Blessed are the merciful, for they will be shown mercy.
>
> (Matthew 5.7)

Beatitudes The blessings listed by Jesus in the Sermon on the Mount.

His words from the cross demonstrate how central forgiveness is to the Christian tradition:

> Father, forgive them, for they know not what they do.
>
> (Luke 23.35)

Jesus' actions

The actions of Jesus offer further examples for Christians to follow, and they are expected to do so. He visited the tax collector, Zacchaeus, despite his cheating and selfishness and, in doing so, enabled Zacchaeus to make amends and reform (Luke 19.2–10). He similarly forgave an adulterous woman (John 8.1–11), imploring her to 'go and sin no more'.

Bible stories

Bible stories clearly demonstrate the importance of forgiveness. The story in the Bible of the prodigal son teaches explicitly about forgiveness and repentance. Sometimes known as the Parable of the Forgiving Father, it tells the tale of a son who demands his inheritance from his father, abandons the family home to seek his fortune elsewhere, and returns years later, poor and hungry. The father forgives his son and welcomes him back, despite his wrongdoing (Luke 15.11–24).

The Parable of the Unmerciful Servant (Matthew 18.21–22) reinforces the teachings that we must forgive others in order to be forgiven ourselves, and that forgiveness is something which should have no limits. In this parable, the servant refuses to forgive a friend for borrowing a small sum of money when he had received a very large sum of money from his master. This teaches Christians to forgive a limitless number of times because they will be forgiven by God for all of their many sins.

> For if you forgive other people when they sin against you, your heavenly Father will also forgive you. But if you do not forgive others their sins, your Father will not forgive your sins.
>
> (Matthew 6.14–15)

How to get forgiveness

For Catholics, forgiveness is supported through confession and religious acts of atonement, for example, saying specific prayers. The Catholic Church teaches that Jesus instituted the sacrament of penance, and they believe that God's forgiveness is granted through the priest's pardon after confession. Many other Christians, including Evangelical Christians, however, believe that forgiveness of sins is granted by God and is reliant upon faith. Here, confession is not accepted as a route to forgiveness.

Buddhist attitudes to forgiveness

> 'He insulted me, he beat me, robbed me!'
> Think this way and hatred never ends.
> 'He insulted me, he beat me, robbed me!'
> Give this up and in you hatred ends.
> Not by hate is hate defeated; hate is
> Quenched by love. This is eternal law.
>
> (Dhammapada 3–5)

Buddhism teaches that holding grudges perpetuates hatred and suffering. In a situation where one person has hurt another, the hurt the victim feels can never be healed as long as he or she continues to hate. Their hatred contaminates them.

With reference to holding on to hatred and anger, the fifth-century Buddhist commentator, Buddhaghosa, said:

> By doing this you are like a man who wants to hit another and picks up a burning coal or excrement in his hand; he first burns himself or makes himself stink.
>
> (Buddhaghosa, Visuddhimagga 9.23)

Buddhism says that only love (metta) has the power to overcome hate. The application of love in a situation of mutual hate is expressed though forgiveness. Forgiveness takes account of the offenders' ability to reform and allows them to change.

For Buddhists, the application of loving-kindness (metta) and compassion (karuna) removes suffering and brings about happiness.

Conflict is caused by desire and attachment. It is natural to want to respond when others hurt us and it is difficult to let go of this desire. But Buddhism says that, if we hurt someone who hurts us, we simply join their negative karma, creating a vicious cycle that only forgiveness can break.

Muslim attitudes to forgiveness

The Qur'an states that those who forgive others will be rewarded by God and that forgiveness is the path to peace. Islam accepts that human beings are not perfect and that everybody makes mistakes in life and unknowingly sins.

According to Islam, there are two kinds of forgiveness: God's forgiveness and human forgiveness. Human beings are in need of both, as they make mistakes in their actions towards each other and their actions towards God. According to the Qur'an, there is no limit to God's forgiveness, and God is prepared to ignore many human failings in those who believe in him:

> Whatever affliction befalls you, it is because of what your hands have earned; and yet, He overlooks many of the wrongs you do.
>
> (Qur'an 42.30)

The words 'God is Oft-forgiving, Most Merciful' are repeated many times throughout the Qur'an. In Islam, individuals who commit a sin ask for forgiveness directly from God; there is no intermediary. They believe that God will forgive all those who are truly repentant. In the Qur'an it says:

> God loves those who turn unto Him in repentance and He loves those who keep themselves pure.
>
> (Qur'an 2.222)

Muslims are to follow the example of the Prophet Muhammad, who helped an old woman who became sick, even though she had regularly brushed dirt in his direction.

Even in punishment, forgiveness is important and valuable.

> (O you who have believed, indeed, among your spouses and your children are enemies to you, so beware of them. But...) if you pardon and overlook and forgive — then indeed, God is Forgiving and Merciful.
>
> (Qur'an 64.14)

Jewish attitudes to forgiveness

Jews believe that it is a mitzvah, a divine command or duty, to forgive. The Torah explicitly forbids Jews from taking revenge or bearing grudges. It also commands:

> Do not hate your brother in your heart.
>
> (Leviticus 19.17)

In Judaism, it is firmly believed that humans are responsible for their actions. If someone does wrong, they have the responsibility to recognise it, regret it, decide never to do it again, admit it to the one who was mistreated and ask for forgiveness. Once the person who has caused harm has sincerely apologised, then the wronged person is religiously bound to forgive. Only the victim, however, can forgive. Even without an apology, forgiveness is considered a worthy and virtuous act (Deuteronomy 6.9).

Repentance is important. Teshuva (literally 'returning') is a way of atoning. This requires cessation of the harmful act, regret over the action, confession and then repentance. Yom Kippur is the Day of Atonement, when Jews particularly strive to perform teshuva. It is one day that is set aside to atone for the sins of the previous year. Jews fast, attend synagogue, and abstain from work, sex, bathing and the wearing of cosmetics for 25 hours. Much of this time is spent in prayer and reflection in order to seek forgiveness for sin.

The Talmud teaches that holding on to resentment is itself painful, that a person who fails to forgive hurts themselves:

> Who takes vengeance or bears a grudge acts like one who, having cut one hand while handling a knife, avenges himself by stabbing the other hand.
>
> (Jerusalem Talmud, Nedarim 9.4)

Humans should follow the example of God, whose love cannot allow him not to forgive:

> Who is a God like You, Who forgives iniquity and passes over the transgression of the remnant of His heritage? He does not maintain His anger forever, for He desires loving-kindness.
>
> (Micah 7.18)

10 Issues of good and evil

▶ Examples of forgiveness arising from personal beliefs

- Mahatma Gandhi – Hindu leader of the Independence Movement in British-run India, 1869–1948.

The weak can never forgive. Forgiveness is the attribute of the strong.

- Dominique Walker – sister of Anthony Walker, murdered in a racially motivated attack in Merseyside in 2005.

"Seventy times seven we must forgive, that's what we were taught, that's what the Bible said, that's what we have to do. It's an everyday thing. It is hard, it is so hard, but you get through it. It eases the bitterness and the anger if you can wake up in the morning and think, 'Forgive, forgive, forgive'."

Victims' relatives and members of the Emanuel African Methodist Episcopal Church, speaking after the South Carolina Church shooting, where nine people were killed in a racially motivated shooting by Dylann Roof:

I thank you on the behalf of my family for not allowing hate to win. For me, I'm a work in progress, and I acknowledge that I'm very angry. But…

We have no room for hate. We have to forgive. I pray God on his soul. And I also thank God I won't be around when his judgment day comes.

- Nelson Mandela, South African anti-apartheid protestor and the first black President of South Africa, 1918–2013.

Resentment is like drinking poison and then hoping it will kill your enemies.

As I walked out the door toward the gate that would lead to my freedom, I knew if I didn't leave my bitterness and hatred behind, I'd still be in prison.

To be wronged is nothing, unless you continue to remember it.

- Confucius, ancient Chinese philosopher, 551–479 BCE.

"For me forgiveness is about finding an inner peace and accepting the cards you've been handed in life. It's not that the pain has gone or that things are back to how they were before. Forgiveness is accepting that we are all human beings and that we are not separate even from those who have hurt us."

- Elizabeth Turner – wife of Simon Turner who was killed in the 9/11 attack in 2001 while she was at home in London.

Task

Select three of the forgiveness profiles. For each individual you choose, provide an excerpt or quote on forgiveness that aligns with their view and explain what it means.

Person / Individual	Excerpt on forgiveness	Meaning

▶ **End of Section Review**

Skills Link

1 "It is important to always forgive others."
   Discuss this statement showing that you have considered more than one point of view. (You must refer to religion and belief in your answer)

Stickability

Key concepts:
- Pacifism
- Forgiveness

Knowledge Check

1 In your own words, explain what forgiveness is and why it can be difficult to achieve.
2 What is important about the altar at Coventry Cathedral? What does it symbolise?
3 For each of the religions you are studying, create a detailed mind map describing the teachings about peace and conflict. Ensure that you refer to the example of religious leaders, stories from sacred texts, and at least one quotation for each religion. Your mind maps should have at least four arms each.
4 Explain the Just War theory from the point of view of Christianity and one other religion.

The Big Question

'True forgiveness is impossible.'

Your Task

Respond to the statement above, showing that you have considered more than one point of view. Give reasoned judgements on the validity and strength of these views.

Task

For both of the religions that you are studying, you need to explain in detail religious teachings about pacifism. Use the guidance below to help you to write a developed explanation for Christianity and a second one for your other chosen religion. Ensure that you use key terms fluently and frequently.

All/many/most Christians believe that _____ .

This comes from the teaching/Bible quote _____ .

This means that/Because of this they _____ .

Some/other Christians such as _____ believe that _____ .

This comes from the teaching/Bible quote _____ .

This means that/Because of this they _____ .

Finally, Christians such as _____ believe that _____ .

This means that/Because of this they _____ .

Their beliefs do/do not differ because _____ .

Good, evil and suffering

'Good' means different things to different people. It is a common word, and we all have an idea of what it means. However, it is very difficult to put that meaning into words.

What is 'good'?

One of the reasons why it is difficult to define good is the fact that people have very different ideas about what makes something good: one person's good could quite easily be another person's evil. Similarly, it is a flexible concept – we can have some elements of good and some of evil, and can even work to develop good within ourselves.

The nature of good

Some might say that good is just the absence of evil or 'badness'. Others would argue that it is something that is approved of or desired. Either way, most people would agree that good is something that is morally right.

Good qualities tend to be linked to empathy. Caring, selfless, charitable, kind and giving people are generally seen to be good. Those people who sacrifice themselves for others, who are compassionate, and who treat all people equally as human beings are also considered good. If we think of the people throughout history who we consider worthy of respect, from Mahatma Gandhi and Martin Luther King to Mother Teresa, they all possessed these qualities of compassion for others and selflessness.

However, not all agree that these were good people. So the question is whether a person can be good or whether it is just their actions that are good. Many believe that good is not an intrinsic thing – it is not something which you just possess as a natural part of you. Good actions come from conscience, and we are able to make good actions as a result of our **free will**. As such, good can come from environmental factors such as childhood or from social factors such as family and friends. A person who, of their own free will, continually makes good choices driven by the qualities of empathy would therefore be a good person.

> **Key Concepts**
>
> **Good** That which is considered morally right, or beneficial and to our advantage.
>
> **Free will** The ability to make choices (particularly moral choices) voluntarily and independently. The belief that nothing is pre-determined.

> **Goodness and British values**
>
> In modern Britain, good behaviour is often judged in terms of the moral values that are seen to be underpinning British society: tolerance, respect, democracy, the defence of individual liberty, mutual respect for different religions, faiths and beliefs and those with no faith at all. As such, any act that goes against these values is generally accepted to be wrong.

10 Issues of good and evil

Religious teachings about good

Christian attitudes to good

In Genesis, it says that God made the earth 'and it was good'. The world that God has created is basically good. God has, however, given people free will – the ability to choose between right and wrong for themselves. The story of humanity's battle with good and evil is told in the story of Adam and Eve in the Garden of Eden (Genesis 3). Adam and Eve chose to disobey God by eating fruit from the Tree of the Knowledge of Good and Evil. This is called the Fall, and explains how free will can be used to stray from what is good.

God has shown people how they should live a good life through both rules of behaviour found in the Bible, for example, the Ten Commandments (a list of religious and moral rules that were given by God to Moses on Mount Sinai), and through religious teachings. Jesus' life and example also show Christians the way to lead a moral, good and righteous life. It is up to individuals to decide whether or not to follow God's instructions.

Christianity is a religion that places good qualities at its core – tolerance, compassion and love. Jesus demonstrated all of these qualities through his life, and it is considered a Christian duty to treat others with kindness, humanity and genuine acceptance.

Buddhist attitudes to good

Buddhism teaches that morality is relative. So the stages of the Noble Eightfold Path that make up sila (Right Speech, Right Action and Right Livelihood) are not rules; they are pointers to the sort of life that enables people to be healthy, happy individuals.

A wise person, guided by these pointers, will know what to do in each particular situation, but this takes skill rather than simple obedience to rules. It means tailoring actions to particular circumstances. For Buddhists, this skill comes from practising the Noble Eightfold Path, applying the wisdom, loving-kindness (metta) and compassion (karuna) that come from it. Buddhists try to develop pure minds to act wisely. This wisdom is called upaya kausala (skilful means).

Buddhists therefore speak of actions as skilful or unskilful rather than as good or bad. A skilful action is one that minimises harm (ahimsa) and maximises happiness.

The intention behind an action is most important. Actions that are motivated by greed, hatred or ignorance are likely to be harmful; whereas those that are inspired by non-attachment, benevolence and understanding are likely to maximise happiness. Consequently, actions that have positive intentions lead to fortunate karma, and actions with negative intentions bring unfortunate karma. So a person who acts with pure intentions gains positive karma, even if their actions (unintentionally) cause harm.

The Buddha said:

> Intention, I tell you, is karma. Intending, one does karma by way of body, speech, and mind.
> (Anguttara Nikaya 6.63)

Elsewhere, he describes the relationships between different intentions and their effects:

> There are four kinds of action (karma) proclaimed by me after realising them for myself with direct knowledge. What are the four? There is dark action with dark result; there is bright action with bright result; there is dark-and-bright action with dark-and-bright result; and there is action that is neither dark nor bright with neither-dark-nor-bright result.
> (Majjhima Nikaya 57)

Muslim attitudes to good

Everyone is born with a natural instinct to understand the difference between right and wrong (fitrah). All humans have free will and they must choose between right and wrong. Some say this means choosing between the path of God and the temptations of **Shaytan** (the devil).

Doing good and having the right belief go hand in hand in Islam. The Qur'an speaks of true Muslims very often as 'those who believe and do good deeds'. Doing the will of God is indistinguishable from doing good.

The Qur'an and the Prophet Muhammad outline the qualities required for goodness, including truthfulness, patience, humility and kindness to others. Muslims are expected to follow this example to guide their actions and choices in everyday life, for example, by doing **sadaqah**.

God will judge each person individually, according to their faith and their good actions. God will show mercy and fairness in his judgement. According to Islamic teachings, those who believe in God and perform good deeds will be eternally rewarded in heaven.

> **Shaytan** Satan or the devil.
> **Sadaqah** Voluntary charity given out of kindness. The Prophet Muhammad said that every act done to please God or make life more pleasant was sadaqah.

Jewish attitudes to good

Judaism teaches that God is good and will always protect and care for people. The goodness of God is shown in the creation of the world, by the giving of the Ten Commandments and on the occasions when God saved the Israelites.

Jews believe that when God created humans, he gave them free will so that they could choose whether or not to worship him. If free will is to mean anything, then humans have to live in a world that allows them to make moral choices between good and evil. The Torah provides guidance in how to live a life of good actions, and the Ten Commandments are the ultimate guidance for how to live a good life.

Judaism recognises that people are born with the inclination to do good but also with the impulse to do wrong. Empathy, compassion and giving are encouraged as good impulses, for example, through the practice of pushke in the home. For more on Judaism and free will, see page 208.

Tasks

1. What is 'good'? Give some examples of good qualities.
2. Copy and complete the table below. For each of the religions you are studying, explain three different teachings about 'good'. Then summarise each one in no more than four words.

Religion	Teaching on 'good'	Summary (four words)

10 Issues of good and evil

What is 'evil'?

People talk about **evil** in different ways: evil people, evil deeds and evil as a force that somehow makes people do wrong.

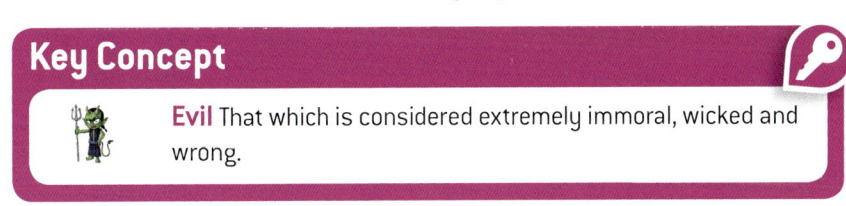

> **Key Concept**
>
> **Evil** That which is considered extremely immoral, wicked and wrong.

The question of evil is an example of an ultimate question (a question about the fundamental principles in life). There are many different answers to why evil exists in the world, and none of them is necessarily wrong. It is up to each individual to decide which is right based upon their religious beliefs, their own experiences, their own reasoning and upbringing.

There are two different types of evil in the world: moral and natural. Both lead to suffering, but each has different causes or sources.

Moral evil

Moral evil is the result of human actions and is caused by humans acting in a way that is considered morally wrong.

Natural evil

Events that have nothing to do with humans and which are to do with the way the world is, for example, natural disasters such as volcanic eruptions, floods or earthquakes, are examples of natural evil. These events cannot be stopped or affected by human action. Natural evil can also include disease and illness.

Even Britain, with its temperate climate, has had to face its own natural disasters over the years.

Human evil and natural evil can often work together, with human evil making natural evil even worse (for example, by looting after an earthquake or creating the environmental conditions for a landslide to occur).

These are all examples of moral evils.

Weather events, like hurricanes, that cause suffering are a natural evil.

> **Tasks**
>
> 1 In a short paragraph (roughly three sentences) explain what is meant by 'evil'.
> 2 Copy and complete the table below. Describe five different types of moral evil and five different types of natural evil.
>
> | Moral evil | Natural evil |
> |---|---|
> | | |
> | | |
> | | |
> | | |
> | | |

▶ Religious teachings about evil

Christian attitudes to evil

Christians have different viewpoints about the causes of evil and suffering and the origin or source of evil in the world. Many argue that God created people with free will and, because people are not programmed like computers, they can choose whether to do good or evil. When they choose evil, suffering happens.

Soul-making

Some Christians believe that God allows evil to exist because suffering through evil is necessary for individuals to develop or complete their moral souls. This concept is known as 'soul-making'. We need to learn what morality is about and we need to develop the proper virtues. We are not born knowing instinctively what morality and goodness are. Our suffering and the suffering of others are essential for us to learn lessons about morality and virtue. Without the opportunities offered by suffering and evil, people would not have the chance to develop or demonstrate moral virtues, like compassion or courage.

St Irenaeus

St Irenaeus (130–202 CE) was a father of the early Christian Church. He believed that humankind was not created as perfect, but that humans require growth in order to become spiritually perfect and moral. He argued that God does not necessarily intend evil to provide the only opportunity for this kind of spiritual growth, as a person could grow to spiritual perfection simply by obeying God's laws. Irenaeus also believed that God does not intervene in human affairs to prevent evil because that would mean interfering with free will.

St Augustine

St Augustine was an early Christian thinker. He believed that things were created good, but free will enabled things to grow away from good and become evil. Human beings use their free will to choose to do evil. Natural evils become evil only when they come into contact with people: diseases and volcanoes are not in themselves evil, but become evil when humans put themselves in harm's way.

Later in life, Augustine came to believe that we cannot understand the mind of God and that what may appear, on the face of it, to be evil may not be at all: human beings cannot judge God.

John Hick

John Hick (1922–2012) agrees with Irenaeus' theory (known as the Irenaean Theodicy). He believes that God created humans with the potential for spiritual growth. Hick argues that the process of soul-making is a response to evil in the world. If murder, cancer and natural evils did not exist, we would not have the means to develop and perfect ourselves spiritually. There is some suffering in the world that we can never understand or rationalise, which simply proves to us that we can never truly understand God's reason or plan.

Hick also believes that humans are born with an immense distance between themselves and God. On the one hand, this is good: it means that God is not so close that free will is restricted. At the same time, We are born not knowing of God's existence and it is not something that it is easy to gain knowledge of. Therefore, the process of soul-making also involves the struggle to find religious faith.

Original sin

Catholics believe that evil comes from human beings. Adam and Eve introduced sin to the world (known as original sin) when, in the Garden of Eden, they chose to disobey God and eat from the Tree of the Knowledge of Good and Evil. This act brought sin to humanity. Since then, people have been born with the ability to commit acts of evil. Within the Catholic tradition, every baby is born with **original sin**.

> **Original sin** The first sin ever committed – when Adam and Eve ate the forbidden fruit in the Garden of Eden. The action that brought sin and evil into the world.

Life as a test

Many Christians also believe that life is a test. Part of this test is whether or not an individual will tolerate suffering and keep their faith. The way people react to suffering and evil determines whether they go to heaven or hell in the afterlife. The story of Job in the Bible gives Christians an example of how suffering can come to anyone, even the most holy and good-living, and that we will be judged on how we behaved throughout our suffering. Job suffers greatly and is taken from great success to tragedy. His friends try to convince him that he is suffering due to his own past sins. Job questions God on this but is given no direct answers. He somehow maintains his faith in God and is rewarded when his suffering is brought to an end.

Evil and suffering as beyond human understanding

The story of Job also reveals to Christians that we should not question why we suffer, but simply accept that we do. Many say that 'God works in mysterious ways' and he has reasons for letting evil and suffering happen, but humans will never be able to understand the mind of God. Many religious believers accept that God has chosen suffering for us and that he has a purpose. They believe that God is compassionate and understanding and will never give us more suffering than we are truly able to cope with.

Suffering helps humans understand Jesus

Christians point to the example of Jesus as a way of explaining suffering and its purpose. Jesus chose to endure suffering and pain in order to achieve greater good. His death and Resurrection were to bring an end to death and suffering forever, with the promise of everlasting life and a new heaven and earth. For many Christians, suffering is both a way to bring them closer to an understanding of Jesus and his suffering, and a way to bring about a greater good.

Other explanations for evil and suffering

Some Christians argue that evil is simply the absence of good. Others argue that evil comes from Satan. Satan creates evil in the form of temptation, pain and suffering.

Many Christians simply argue that evil exists because good exists. The world is not perfect – evil in the world is not malevolent, it is just a natural happening.

Buddhist attitudes to evil

'Evil' is a word that Buddhists are unlikely to use. They do not believe that evil exists in the world in the same way that other abstract ideas, like loving-kindness or compassion, exist. If evil exists, it is absolute – something either is or is not evil – and Buddhists do not believe in absolute morality.

So they would never describe an individual as evil, or even an action as evil. First, Buddhists do not believe in an independent 'self': there is no such thing as an individual: we are all conditioned, interdependent and impermanent. Second, actions are just actions, karma. 'Evil' is a moral judgement; actions are just what you do. Actions, as we have seen, are skilful or unskilful according to whether they are intended to relieve suffering (dukkha) or cause it. It is the intention of an action that is karma. When people refer to the effects of an action as karma ('that was really bad karma') they are misusing the word. The effects of actions are what happens to you. They are not rewards or punishments; whether they are good or bad depends on how skilfully you deal with them.

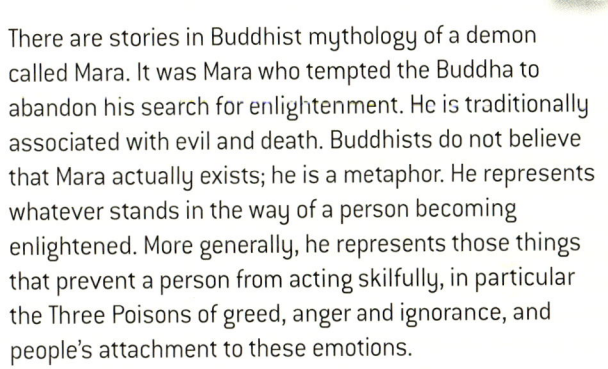

There are stories in Buddhist mythology of a demon called Mara. It was Mara who tempted the Buddha to abandon his search for enlightenment. He is traditionally associated with evil and death. Buddhists do not believe that Mara actually exists; he is a metaphor. He represents whatever stands in the way of a person becoming enlightened. More generally, he represents those things that prevent a person from acting skilfully, in particular the Three Poisons of greed, anger and ignorance, and people's attachment to these emotions.

Mara is not evil; Mara does not exist outside ourselves. Mara is whatever motivates unskilful behaviour. We are responsible for ensuring that our actions are skilful and do no harm. The Buddha said:

> By oneself, indeed, is evil done; by oneself is one defiled. By oneself is evil left undone; by oneself, indeed, is one purified. Purity and impurity depend on oneself. No one purifies another.
>
> (Dhammapada 12.165)

Killing

Gasan, a Zen Buddhist master, instructed his adherents one day:

> Those who speak against killing and who desire to spare the lives of all conscious beings are right. It is good to protect even animals and insects. But what about those persons who kill time, what about those who are destroying wealth, and those who destroy political economy? We should not overlook them. Furthermore, what of the one who preaches without enlightenment? He is killing Buddhism.

Of course killing conscious beings is wrong. But this story urges us not to be too narrow in our definition of what is wrong. It is really about what is unskilful. Is it possible to kill abstract ideas, like time and wealth? If doing so causes suffering, then yes. So if these things are unskilful, then their opposites must be skilful. We should try to develop kindness, determination and integrity.

The moon cannot be stolen

Ryokan, a Zen Buddhist master, lived the simplest kind of life in a little hut at the foot of a mountain. One evening a thief visited the hut only to discover there was nothing in it to steal.

Ryokan returned and caught him. 'You may have come a long way to visit me,' he told the prowler, 'and you should not return empty-handed. Please take my clothes as a gift.'

The thief was bewildered. He took the clothes and slunk away. Ryokan sat naked, watching the moon. 'Poor fellow,' he mused, 'I wish I could give him this beautiful moon.'

This story shows that it is greed and the attachment to things that cause unskilful action. By giving the thief his clothes, Ryokan demonstrates that he is not attached to material possessions; but the thief who takes the clothes still is. Ryokan wishes the thief could understand that non-attachment brings greater happiness: the ability to see beauty and experience peace.

Muslim attitudes to evil

In Islam it is believed that everything happens because it is the will and the plan of God. This is known as al-Qadr (pre-destination) and means that suffering and hardship are part of God's greater plan for humanity. Even though people may be unable to appreciate the value or purpose of suffering, they must accept that suffering exists and that they will never be able to truly understand God's will and purpose.

Muslims believe that all life is a test:

> We will certainly test you with something of fear and hunger, and loss of wealth and lives and fruits (earnings); but give glad tidings to the persevering and patient.
>
> (Qur'an 2.155)

Humans are given life as a gift by God and, throughout their lives, their good and evil acts are noted down by two angels. Muslims will have to answer to these at Judgement Day, and these will determine whether they will enter paradise or be sent to hell – a blazing fire that never ends.

Good can come from suffering and evil. It is a greater good when people resist temptation and follow the right path and the example set by the Prophet Muhammad. God is also known as Ar-Rahman (The Merciful), Ar-Rahim (The Compassionate) and Al-Karim (The Generous). Because of this, those who resist Shaytan and follow the straight path will be rewarded in the afterlife.

Many Muslims believe that evil comes from Shaytan. The Qur'an explains how he refused God's command to bow down before Adam:

> And when We said to the angels: 'Prostrate before Adam!' They all prostrated, but Iblis [Shaytan] did not; he refused, and grew arrogant, and displayed himself as an unbeliever.
>
> (Qur'an 2.34)

As a result of his pride and disobedience, God banished him from heaven. He now exists to tempt people to turn from God and to do wrong.

Jewish attitudes to evil

On the one hand, evil exists due to the presence of free will – in Genesis it is explained that God gave humanity free will and therefore the ability to choose between good and evil. However, evil also comes from God, as he can use it as a way to cause suffering and discipline, punish or test.

The story of Job in the Jewish Bible demonstrates that even the most righteous people can experience suffering through evil. God sends suffering in order to test Job's faith, but Job does not know why he is made to suffer. In the end, he learns not to question what God does, but to accept things as they are.

The Talmud says:

> A person is obligated to bless upon the bad just as he blesses upon the good. As it says, 'And you shall love the Lord your God, with all your heart and all your soul and with all that you have.'
>
> (Berakhot 9.5)

This teaches Jews to welcome both good and evil in their lives in a similar way, as both are sent by God and have purpose.

Jews also believe that the punishment for being tempted by evil is death and destruction, whereas the reward for resisting temptation is protection and prosperity (Deuteronomy 30.15–19).

In the same way, the Talmud makes clear that idol worshiping is outright evil because it is the same as denying God. This is explained in Avodah Zarah 3b, in which the rules regarding idol worship and interacting with those that practise it are discussed.

Task

For both of the religions you are studying, explain in detail religious teachings about evil. Use the guidance below to help you to write a developed explanation for Christianity and a second one for your other chosen religion. Ensure that you use key terms fluently and frequently.

All/many/most Christians believe that _____ .

This comes from the teaching/Bible quote _____ .

This means that/Because of this they _____ .

Some/other Christians such as _____ believe that _____.

This comes from the teaching/Bible quote _____.

This means that/Because of this they _____ .

Finally, Christians such as _____ believe that _____.

This means that/Because of this they _____ .

Their beliefs do/do not differ because _____ .

Suffering

We simply need to turn on the news or glance at the front cover of a newspaper to see examples of **suffering** in the world. Suffering, it seems, is an inevitable part of living. Why people suffer is one of the greatest of all ultimate questions (questions about the fundamental principles in life). There are many different beliefs linked with the causes of suffering, some of which we have already looked at in the previous section on evil.

> ### Key Concept
>
> **Suffering** Pain or distress caused by injury, illness or loss. Suffering can be physical, emotional/psychological or spiritual.

Types of suffering

Natural suffering is caused by events beyond human control – by natural disasters such as earthquakes, tsunamis and floods, as well as disease.

Human suffering is caused by the actions of human beings – murder, rape, terrorism and so on.

> *Try to exclude the possibility of suffering which the order of nature and existence involve, and you find you have excluded life itself.*
>
> (C. S. Lewis, the Christian author of *The Lion, The Witch and The Wardrobe*, whose wife died of cancer two years after they married.)

Religious teachings about suffering

Christian attitudes to suffering

Christians might view suffering in the following ways:
- In the Christian tradition, suffering is seen to be a test.
- Suffering is a punishment for sin and for Catholics is the result of original sin.
- Suffering is also part of God's plan – we might not understand it but should know God will never make us suffer beyond our ability to cope.
- Suffering enables us to appreciate what is good in the world and allows us to grow closer to Jesus, who also suffered.
- Stories from the Bible, such as that of Job in the Old Testament, teach Christians that anyone can suffer and that persevering with suffering can strengthen faith in God.

Tasks

1. Explain the causes of suffering in the world. Aim to include the following terms: natural, human, evil.
2. Copy and complete the mind map below, outlining the key beliefs on suffering for Christianity.

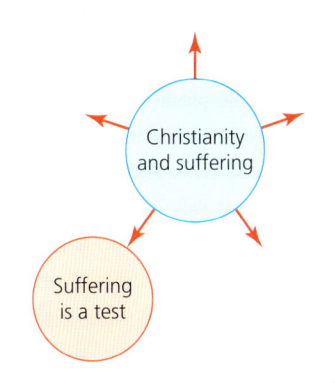

- Christianity and suffering
  - Suffering is a test

Buddhist attitudes to suffering

The analysis of suffering – what it is, what causes it, and how it can be overcome – is what Buddhism is all about.

When Buddhists talk about suffering, they use the word dukkha. Dukkha refers to the inescapable fact that things do not go the way we want them to in life. The fact that we want things to be or go a certain way is the reason why we experience dukkha – frustration and dissatisfaction. It is our wanting that causes dissatisfaction. Wanting things to be a certain way causes us to act to make that happen. Our actions are our karma: they cause things to happen to us, to which we respond by making further actions, and so on. This is the cycle of samsara: the endless round of birth, living, death and rebirth.

If we could overcome our tendency to want, we could overcome dukkha and, ultimately, escape from samsara. This is what the Four Noble Truths are about. The Noble Eightfold Path provides a way to overcome wanting and, as a result, dukkha. Extinguishing desire leads to the freedom and happiness of nirvana, offering release from the drudgery of samsara.

The word samsara literally means 'wandering'. Life, then is an aimless, unsatisfying drifting from moment to moment, lifetime to lifetime, driven by the habit we have of acting based on our desires and in spite of the fact that nothing remains the same. Contentment, on the other hand, lies in accepting things as they are and following the Middle Way between the extremes of luxury and hardship.

Muslim attitudes to suffering

Muslims might view suffering in the following ways:
- Islam teaches that everything that happens is part of the will and plan of God (al-Qadr).
- Life is a test and therefore so is suffering.
- Suffering enables Muslims to prove their faith by resisting temptation. Those who resist Shaytan and follow the straight path will be rewarded in the afterlife.
- Good can come from suffering, both because it leads to personal spiritual development and because it allows us the opportunity to support others.
- Muslims should follow the example of the Prophet Muhammad.

Jewish attitudes to suffering

Jews believe that suffering ultimately results from free will. It can also come from God as a means to discipline, punish for wrongdoing, test, or force someone to return to God. The story of Job shows that we may not be able to understand why suffering happens. Throughout history, many Jews have been persecuted for their beliefs and suffered greatly.

The Holocaust

The word 'Holocaust' means a burnt offering. The Holocaust is often referred to as the Shoah – literally 'the catastrophe'.

Between 1933 and 1945, Jews in Nazi-occupied Europe suffered prolonged **persecution**. During this period, Hitler and the Nazi regime he led carried out a programme of systematic discrimination against Jews. At first, through the Nuremberg Laws, Jews were banned from parks, theatres and universities. They were forbidden from holding positions in public office and forced out of employment. Eventually, the rights to own property and businesses were removed and Jews were rounded up and placed in ghettos. Across occupied Europe, atrocities took place, and whole communities were wiped out by military and paramilitary units tasked with rounding up and executing Jews. This programme concluded with the 'final solution' – the extermination of Jews in purpose-built concentration and death camps.

This genocide resulted in the murder of over six million Jews, two-thirds of the Jewish population of Europe. Hundreds of thousands of Jews were left displaced and homeless, as refugees in their own homeland, with no family or livelihood to return to.

> **Persecution** Persistently cruel treatment, often due to religion or belief.

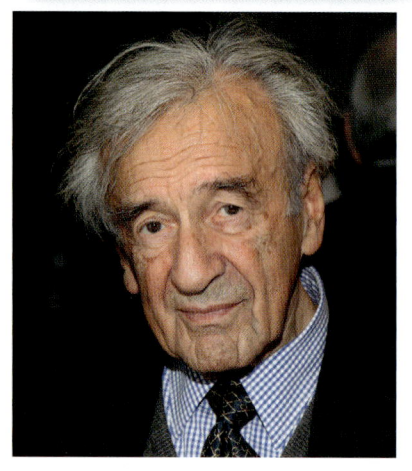

'After the Holocaust, I did not lose faith in God; I lost faith in mankind.' Elie Wiesel, who survived a concentration camp.

The entrance to the Auschwitz concentration camp in Poland. The sign reads, "Arbeit macht frei", which means "Work makes you free". It was designed to give the inmates false hope.

240

Eva Clarke: a Holocaust survivor in Wales

Eva Clarke was born Eva Bergman in Mauthausen concentration camp, Austria, on 29th April 1945. She and her mother were the only survivors of their family, 15 members of whom were killed in Auschwitz-Birkenau: three of Eva's grandparents, her father, uncles, aunts and her seven-year-old cousin, Peter.

Her parents were married in 1940 in Prague. In December 1941, they were sent to Terezín (Theresienstadt) concentration camp. They were to remain there for three years, which was very unusual: they were young, strong and well able to work.

When Eva's father was sent to Auschwitz in 1944, her mother, who was then pregnant, volunteered to follow him there. Unfortunately, he was shot dead before they could reunite.

Eva's mother was sent to work near Dresden in Germany before being sent on to the Mauthausen camp in Austria. There she gave birth to Eva. Days later, the camp was liberated by American soldiers.

When Eva's mother remarried in 1948, the family moved to Cardiff.

Holocaust Memorial Day

The Holocaust was genocide: the attempt to wipe out an entire ethnic group. It and other genocides are remembered each year on 27th January, the day when the concentration camps at Auschwitz in Poland were liberated.

Each year, the anniversary is marked by events across Wales. In 2017, a national service of commemoration was held at Cardiff City Hall. It was attended by 500 politicians, representatives of organisations, members of the Jewish community and many other faiths, as well as members of the public.

Swansea commemorated the occasion with poetry, music and memorials, with participation from a large number of young people. Neath Port Talbot hosts an annual memorial to the Holocaust, involving local schools in dance, song and poetry performances. The Borough Council says: 'Holocaust Memorial Day is a time when we seek to learn the lessons of the past and to recognise that genocide does not just take place on its own, it's a steady process which can begin if discrimination, racism and hatred are not checked and prevented.'

Exhibitions on the Holocaust and the Jewish faith were held at various locations across Wales, and many schools participated in assemblies and lessons.

Where is God? Diverse Jewish responses to the Holocaust

For some Jews, their experiences during the Holocaust – especially in the camps – were so hideous and impossible to understand that they ceased to believe in God. Many questioned how a loving, just and righteous God could allow such senseless tragedy. A great many Holocaust survivors could not reconcile their terrific suffering and personal loss with the God that they had believed in before the War. They felt abandoned by the God who, they had believed, was their protector and provider.

For some, continuing to practise their religion became their ultimate act of defiance. Some risked their lives to be able to continue to mark holy days and fulfil the ritual of prayer while in the concentration camps and ghettos. Believing in God became the key to their ability to survive.

> Is he able, but not willing? Then he is malevolent.
>
> Is he both able and willing? Then whence cometh evil?
>
> Is he neither able nor willing? Then why call him God?
>
> (Epicurus, ancient Greek philosopher)

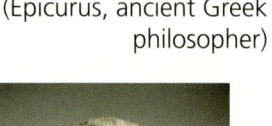

■ Is God willing to prevent evil, but not able? Then he is not omnipotent.

▶ Suffering, good and evil – a perfect link?

It is clear that suffering and evil are inextricably linked.

Evil – whether natural or moral – causes human suffering. Ironically, good and suffering are also closely linked. Good, especially the human qualities associated with good, such as compassion and empathy, have the power to alleviate the suffering caused by evil.

All religious people, and many without a religious faith, believe that it is important to try to help those around them who are suffering. This becomes a motivator for how they behave and how they treat and 'serve' others.

Ways of alleviating suffering:
- Prayer
- Fund-raising
- Counselling
- Rehabilitation programmes
- Disaster relief
- Building works
- Medical care
- Training sessions/Education

▶ The problem of evil and suffering

For religious believers, the presence of evil and suffering in the world creates a number of problems. God is believed to be omnibenevolent (all loving), omnipotent (all powerful) and omniscient (all knowing). Because of this, evil should not really exist. But it does. There are, therefore, a number of possibilities:

- ▶ God is not powerful enough to stop evil.
- ▶ God does not know that evil is happening.
- ▶ God does not love us enough to want to stop the evil.

None of these is a very satisfactory conclusion. As a result, religions have a number of teachings that help to explain how it is possible for there to be both evil in the world and a benevolent, all knowing and all-powerful God.

10 Issues of good and evil

242

▶ Are we free to choose?

Religious believers would argue that there is genuine purpose to life, and many would say that God has a plan for everyone.

Fate		Free will		Predestination
A power or force that determines the future. The idea that the outcome is predetermined or unchangeable – inevitable and irresistible.	vs	The belief that humans have free choices in life. The belief that humans were created with the ability to obey God or not according to their own choice.	vs	The belief that all events have been willed by God. The idea that God has already chosen who will receive salvation and enter heaven.

▶ Religious teachings about the problem of evil and suffering

Christian attitudes to the problem of evil and suffering

Christians believe that free will is given by God to human beings. Humans therefore have the ability to choose to do good and the ability to choose to do evil. Catholics believe that, as a result of original sin, humans find it easier to choose to do wrong, but with the help of God can choose to do good. Those who do sin can attempt to atone and gain forgiveness through prayer and, for Catholics, confession and penance.

Fate is not a Christian idea and the vast majority of Christians do not believe that their life is totally planned out for them. Some Protestant denominations (for example, Lutheran and Calvinist Christians) believe in predestination – that God has already chosen who is to reach salvation. Predestination, here, is subtly different from fate, as it particularly focuses on the notion of salvation after life on earth and not on the decisions that we make during earthly life.

Buddhist attitudes to the problem of evil and suffering

The problem of evil and suffering does not exist for Buddhism in the same way as it does for other religions. Since Buddhists do not believe in an omniscient, omnibenevolent and omnipotent god, the question of how God can allow evil and suffering is not relevant.

Nevertheless, the issue of suffering itself is fundamental to the Buddha's teachings. He ignores questions that other religions consider important, such as those that relate to the origins of the universe or the nature of life after death, and offers no explanations about them. Instead, he says:

> And what… have I explained? I have explained suffering; I have explained the origin of suffering; I have explained the overcoming of suffering; and I have explained the path that leads to the overcoming of suffering. And why… have I explained this? Because… this brings benefit, has to do with the basics of religion, and leads to… supreme wisdom and nirvana.
>
> (Majjhima Nikaya 63)

For Buddhism, the important question is not where do evil and suffering come from. It is not important, for example, to ask whether the evil is moral or natural; suffering is suffering. The important question is, how can we overcome it?

Muslim attitudes to the problem of evil and suffering

> Say, 'Never will we be struck except by what God has decreed for us; He is our protector.' And upon God let the believers rely.
>
> (Qur'an 9.51)

Teachings on free will and predestination in Islam are not straightforward. For Muslims, free will must exist as, without it, humans are simply puppets – unable to take real responsibility for themselves or offer genuine faith and submission to God. On the other hand, predestination must exist as, without it, God is not ultimately powerful and omniscient:

> God has power over all things.
>
> (Qur'an 3.159)

Islam teaches that every person is free to choose whether or not to follow God. If they choose not to, suffering occurs.

> Whatever of good befalleth thee it is from God, and whatever of ill befalleth thee it is from thyself.
>
> (Qur'an 4.79)

Al-Qadr is the will of God and translates literally as 'fate' or 'pre-ordainment'. It is one of Islam's six articles of faith or beliefs. In the Qur'an, al-Qadr is also referred to as God's 'decree'. Some Muslims believe God wrote down all that has happened and will happen (on the 'Preserved Tablet'). God has measured out the span of every person's life, their lot of good or bad fortune and the fruits of their efforts. But God does not need to force anyone to do good or evil.

Although many Muslims believe in predestination, they also believe that we have free will. It is granted by God so that people are not puppets. The idea of iktisab means that, while God knows the final outcome, a person must 'acquire' or 'merit' responsibility for their own actions. These Muslims believe there is no fate in Islam as this infers surrendering yourself helplessly. Instead there is the idea of working to understand and cooperate with God and bringing oneself to a unity with his will.

Sunni and Shi'a beliefs

Sunni Muslims believe in the concept of the 'Preserved Tablet' and that God has written down all that has happened and will happen. An individual has power to choose, but, since God created time and space, he knows what will happen.

Shi'a Muslims reject the idea of predestination. They firmly believe in the concept of bada, which states that God has not set a definite course for human history. Instead, God may alter the course of human history as he sees fit. Shi'a Muslims believe that God has definite power over the whole of the universe, however, whenever he wills, he can replace a given destiny with another one (effectively changing the course of destiny). Some of these changes of destiny are brought about by human beings, who can, through their free will, their decisions and their way of life, lay the foundations for change.

Jewish attitudes to the problem of evil and suffering

Many Jews believe that what happens in life is ultimately decided by God. In the Talmud, there is a description of an unborn child being shown the fate that awaits it. This means that predestination exists but, critically, so does free will. Jews believe that everyone is responsible for their own actions, but that God chooses the final outcome. There is an emphasis in the Talmud on everyone learning the law so that they can properly understand the difference between good and bad behaviour. Whether a person is good or bad is, therefore, a part of their free will.

End of Section Review

Stickability

Key concepts:
- Evil
- Free will
- Good
- Morality
- Suffering

Key teachings about:
- The origin of evil
- Free will and the problem of evil and suffering

Knowledge check

1. Write a paragraph outlining how Christians explain the presence of suffering in the world.
2. What is the difference between free will and fate?
3. Explain one of the problems with believing in fate and predestination.
4. Why does the issue of evil and suffering cause a challenge for believing in God?

Skills Link

1. From two different religions, explain views about 'free will'.
2. "The existence of suffering proves there is no God."
   Discuss this statement, showing that you have considered more than one point of view. (You must refer to religion and belief in your answer.)

The Big Question

You can't believe in God while there is evil in the world.

Your Task

Respond to the statement above, showing that you have considered more than one point of view. Give reasoned judgements on the validity and strength of these views.

Task

For both of the religions you are studying, explain in detail religious teachings about **suffering**. Use the guidance below to help you to write a **developed explanation** for Christianity and a second one for your other chosen religion. Ensure that you use key terms fluently and frequently.

All/many/most Christians believe that _____ .

This comes from the teaching/Bible quote _____ .

This means that/Because of this they _____ .

Some/other Christians such as _____ believe that _____.

This comes from the teaching/Bible quote _____ .

This means that/Because of this they _____ .

Finally, Christians such as _____ believe that _____.

This means that/Because of this they _____ .

Their beliefs do/do not differ because _____ .

Exam focus

Part A. Core beliefs, teachings and practices

(a) questions – AO1

These are always the first part of a question. They ask you to explain what the key concept means. Your explanation can include an example. There are 12 key concepts you need to know for Christianity and 12 for your second religion. The definition of each term is given in the textbook. Remember there are only two marks for these questions so it is important you are able to give an accurate definition.

Points are awarded for this question as follows:

- 1 mark is given for each relevant point made
- 2 marks for either two separate points or one point which is developed/explained/elaborated

Helen was asked:

(a) What do Christians mean by 'resurrection'?

Her response:

'Rising from the dead'

only got one mark. Why do you think that was? Rewrite her answer to gain two marks.

Now write a two mark answer for the (a) question for your second world religion:

- **Buddhism:** (a) What do Buddhists mean by 'samatha'?
- **Islam:** (a) What do Muslims mean by 'hadith'?
- **Judaism:** (a) What do Jews mean by 'omnipotence'?

(b) questions

In these questions you will be expected to describe a particular religious teaching, belief, idea, practice, place, event or view. There is a maximum of five marks for this type of question. To gain full marks you should be able to show your knowledge using appropriate religious terms and any relevant sources of wisdom or sacred texts.

Look at the following question:

(b) Describe the role of the church in its local community.

John has decided that there are a number of different points he could include in his answer. Select three and add any further details that could be included:

- *Worship*
- *Helps charities*
- *Celebrates important events in people's lives*
- *Helping charities*
- *Social events*
- *Activities for children and families*

Now write an answer for the (b) question for your second world religion:

- **Buddhism:** (b) Describe the ways in which Buddhists celebrate Kathina.
- **Islam:** (b) Describe how Muslims pray at home.
- **Judaism:** (b) Describe how the home is a place of Jewish traditions.

(c) questions – AO1

In these questions you will be expected to explain a key teaching, belief, idea, practice, place, event or view in the religions you have studied. There is a maximum of eight marks for this type of question. To gain full marks you should be able to show your knowledge using appropriate religious terms and any relevant sources of wisdom or sacred texts.

To gain higher marks religious language must be used in your answers. This includes the use of key concepts where relevant, as well as any particular language specific to the religions you are writing about. Look at the paragraph below. Below are some statements that might be used in response to the question, identify religious language you could include in the areas underlined.

(c) Explain Christian beliefs about the Holy Spirit.

Christians believe that God is made up of three parts, and the Holy Spirit is one of the parts.

Jesus told his followers that he would send the Holy Spirit to them once he had risen from the dead.

At the start of the Bible it says that the Holy Spirit was involved in Creation.

Now write an answer for the (c) question for your second world religion:

- **Buddhism: (c) Explain what Buddhists do when following the Eightfold Path**
- **Islam: (c) Explain the Muslim belief about the oneness of Allah.**
- **Judaism: (c) Explain why it is important for Jews to maintain a kosher kitchen.**

(d) questions – AO2

These are very important questions as they are worth 15 marks. The question requires you to:

- Read and understand the statement.
- Discuss the statement showing you have considered more than one point of view. (You must refer to religion and belief in your answer.
- Responses must analyse, evaluate, offer different and/or alternative views and reach well supported judgements.

In (d) questions different points of view are needed. These do not have to be contrasting views (though of course, they can be) but must be different.

You are expected to apply your knowledge and understanding from the whole of your study to the question. Take for example the following question:

(d) "God must be sorry he ever created humans."

Discuss this statement showing that you have considered more than one point of view. (You must refer to religion and belief in your answer.)

Marks for accurate spelling, punctuation and the use of grammar are allocated to this question [15+6]

Look on the following page at the following four areas. For each consider how this might be used in your answer.

- God's goodness and omnibenevolence
- The Fall and the existence of evil and suffering
- The work Christians do for social justice
- Jesus' life and death

Now write an answer for the (d) question for your second world religion:

- **Buddhism: (d) "The most important part of the Buddha's life was his experience as an ascetic."** *Discuss this statement showing that you have considered more than one point of view. (You must refer to religion and belief in your answer).*
- **Islam: (d) 'Muslims should only pray when they want to pray.'** *Discuss this statement showing that you have considered more than one point of view. (You must refer to religion and belief in your answer.)*
- **Judaism: (d) 'Maintaining Shabbat is too time-consuming.'** *Discuss this statement showing that you have considered more than one point of view. (You must refer to religion and belief in your answer.)*

Part B: Philosophical responses to religious themes: Questions 3 and 4

(a) questions – AO1

Just like for Part A, the (a) question will ask you for a definition of a key concept. There are 8 key concepts for each theme.

(a) What is meant by 'environmental responsibility'?

Taking care of the planet...

Tim has answered an (a) type question for 'Life and death'. If points are given as follows:

- 1 mark is given for each relevant point made
- 2 marks for either two separate points or one point which is developed/explained/elaborated

How many marks would you give Tim? Why?

Now try and write a 2 mark answer for this question from Question 4, Good and Evil:

(a) What is meant by 'conscience'?

(b) questions – AO1

In these questions you will be expected to describe a particular religious teaching, belief, idea, practice, place, event or view. There is a maximum of five marks for this type of question. To gain full marks you should be able to show your knowledge using appropriate religious terms and any relevant sources of wisdom and/or sacred texts.

(b) Describe religious teachings about the value of human life

Mark looked at this question from Question 3 on Life and Death and noted:

- *How many marks?*

Five marks are awarded so that means he has five minutes to answer the question.

- What is the question asking him to do?

He needs to show his knowledge about one religion's teaching on the value of human life. The question is not asking him about his views, he needs to focus his whole answer on religious teachings.

Have a go at the question above and also the one below from Question 4 on Good and Evil:

(b) Describe religious teachings about Free Will.

(c) questions – AO1

In the Part B (Religion and Philosophical Themes), you will be required to consider **two religious** perspectives for the (c) questions. The two perspectives must come from Christianity and the other religion you are studying in Part A. Non-religious views are NOT appropriate here.

In all (b), (c) and (d) questions references to relevant sources of wisdom or sacred texts should be included as evidence. They are important to support the point you have made. You will need to practise how you use sacred texts and other sources of wisdom and authority.

Some candidates lose marks because they have a scattergun approach. They include a reference but without any further details.

(c) Explain from Christianity and Buddhism, how religious believers respond to suffering.

Christians believe that the reasons for suffering are beyond human understanding, for example the story of Job.

Buddhists think suffering is part of life because of the Buddha.

Other candidates describe the whole of a story from a sacred text but with no reference to how it relates to the question. There are many different ways that sacred texts can be used as evidence, for example:

- Analysing the importance of a text for action or belief today:

  (c) Explain from Christianity and Buddhism, how religious believers respond to suffering.

  Stories from the Bible, such as that of Job in the Old Testament, teach Christians that anyone can suffer and that persevering with suffering can strengthen faith in God.

  In his teaching on the Four Noble Truths, the Buddha explains that dukkha is inevitable but that people can overcome some of it by avoiding craving.

- Briefly describing the text reference in relation to belief or practice today:

  The suffering of Jesus when he died in agony on the cross, means that Christians believe that when they suffer they grow closer to Jesus.

  The Noble Eightfold Path gives Buddhists a way of living that can overcome some forms of suffering.

- Making direct reference to a textual quote to support an answer:

  (c) Explain from Christianity and Judaism, why there may be differences in belief within a religion about creation.

  Orthodox Jews take a more literal view of the creation stories because they think that the Torah is the word of God, whereas more

Liberal Jews think that parts of the Torah, including the stories in the Book of Genesis, can be interpreted in light of modern day science, rather than accepted as fact.

Liberal Christians believe that the Biblical Creation stories are not scientific fact because the two accounts, Genesis 1 and Genesis 2, seem to contradict each other. Some Christians, such as many Evangelical Christians, however, think that the accounts in Genesis as literally true because they believe that the Bible is from God.

(d) questions – AO2

For (d) type questions in Question 3 on life and death unit responses must include references to non-religious beliefs. Look at the question below:

> (d) 'The belief in the afterlife is the most important one.' *Discuss this statement showing that you have considered more than one point of view. (In your answer, you must refer to religious and non-religious beliefs)*

Sammy has considered a number of points he can make. He wants to include two from different religions but also needs to identify religious teachings or a sacred text for each. He also needs to include a non-religious teaching.

Look back through the chapter; which religious views would you use and what evidence would you give to support them? Which non-religious teachings would you use?

For (d) questions on Question 4 notice that the rubric changes so that you are not required to refer to non-religious beliefs (though you may include non-religious beliefs in any (d) question where the question lends itself to such a response):

> (d) 'It is important to always forgive others.' *Discuss this statement showing that you have considered more than one point of view. (You must refer to religion and belief in your answer)*

Acknowledgements

The Publishers would like to thank the following for permission to reproduce copyright material:

Text permissions
'Skills link' questions throughout come from the WJEC sample assessment materials that can be found on their website: http://www.wjec.co.uk/qualifications/religious-studies/r-religious-studies-gcse-2017/; **p.132** © The Jewish Chronicle, 2016.

Translations of sacred texts
Quotations from the Bible: THE HOLY BIBLE, NEW INTERNATIONAL VERSION ®, NIV ® Copyright © 1973, 1978, 1984, 2011 by Biblica, Inc. ® Used by permission. All rights reserved worldwide.
Quotations from the Qur'an: Sahih International translation, www.quran.com.
Quotations from the Torah: The Living Torah by Rabbi Aryeh Kaplan.
Quotations from the Ketuvim: Judaica Press, translated and compiled by Rabbi A.J. Rosenberg.

Photo credits

p.2 © Michele Falzone/Alamy Stock Photo; **p.3** © Godong/Alamy Stock Photo; **p.4** © Blake, William/HENRY W. AND ALBERT A. BERG COLLECTION/New York public library digital collections; **p.5** *t* © Prisma Archivo/Alamy Stock Photo; **p.5** *b* © CHARLES LOMODONG/AFP/Getty Images; **p.9** © Jager/123RF; **p.10** © Granger Historical Picture Archive/Alamy Stock Photo; **p.13** © Historical Picture Archive/Corbis Historical/Getty Images; **p.16** © Allan Swart/123RF; **p.17** © Godong/Alamy Stock Photo; **p.18** © Godong/Alamy Stock Photo; **p.19** © Sergey Karpov/123RF; **p.20** © Steve Clarke; **p.22** © Ian Dagnall/Alamy Stock Photo; **p.24** © PanjarongU/iStock/Thinkstock; **p.37** © Mark Bond/Fotolia; **p.38** © John Henshall/Alamy Stock Photo; **p.39** © Paula Solloway/Alamy Stock Photo; **p.40** © Zvonimir Atletic/123RF; **p.41** © Brian Jackson /123RF; **p.44** © Adrian Sherratt/Alamy Stock Photo; **p.46** © By permission of the World Council of Churches; **p.51** *l* © Yuri/Thinkstock/iStockphoto/Getty Images; **p.51** *c* © B.S.P.I./Corbis Documentary/Getty Images; **p.51** *r* © Eddie Gerald/Alamy Stock Photo; **p.52** *tl* © Ingram Publishing Limited/Ingram Image Library 500-People; **p.52** *tc* © Guerilla/MBI/Alamy Stock Photo; **p.52** *tr* © Imagestate Media (John Foxx)/Vol 22 People & Emotions; **p.52** *bl* © Boonchob chuaynum/Shutterstock.com; **p.52** *br* © tore2527/Fotolia; **p.55** © lomography4/Fotolia; **p.57** © Sajee Rod/Shutterstock.com; **p.59** © traveler1116/Getty images; **p.60** © eroticshutter/Fotolia.com; **p.61** © Saiko3p/Shutterstock.com; **p.62** © Casper1774 Studio/Shutterstock.com; **p.70** © Mirrorpix; **p.73** © tony french/Alamy Stock Photo; **p.75** © Mar Photographics/Alamy Stock Photo; **p.78** © Tong_stocker/Shutterstock.com; **p.79** © Gavriel Jecan/DanitaDelimont/Alamy Stock Photo; **p.80** © seqoya/Fotolia; **p.82** © Granger, NYC/TopFoto; **p.86** © Trinity Mirror/Mirrorpix/Alamy Stock Photo; **p.90** © TopFoto; **p.91** © Godong/Alamy Stock Photo; **p.93** © Antony McAulay/123RF; **p.95** © Gezik/Shutterstock.com; **p.97** © Omar Mashaka /123RF; **p.98** © Gyula Gyukli /123RF; **p.100** © Ashraf Amra/APA Images/ZUMA Wire/Alamy Stock Photo; **p.102** © Art Directors & TRIP/Alamy Stock Photo; **p.106** © Ferli Achirulli /123RF; **p.109** © getideaka/Shutterstock.com; **p.114** © Muslim Aid, UK (www.muslimaid.org); **p.116** © Ria Novosti/TopFoto; **p.120** © Eddie Gerald/Alamy Stock Photo; **p.123** © Art Collection 2/Alamy Stock Photo; **p.128** *tl* © DEA/A. VERGANI/De Agostini/Getty images; **p.128** *tc* © Andrew Aitchison /Pictures Ltd./Corbis Historical/Getty Images; **p.128** *tr* © Jeff Morgan 08/Alamy Stock Photo; **p.128** *b* © Allstar Picture Library/Alamy Stock Photo; **p.129** *t* © Gonewiththewind /123RF; **p.129** *b* © gbimages/Alamy Stock Photo; **p.136** © Anyka/123RF; **p.140** © Dov makabaw Israel/Alamy Stock Photo; **p.141** © DAN PORGES/TopFoto; **p.142** *t* © Dov makabaw sundry/Alamy Stock Photo; **p.142** *tc* © Keith Levit/Alamy Stock Photo; **p.142** *tb* © Aastock/Shutterstock.com; **p.142** *b* © Shay Fogelman/Alamy Stock Photo; **p.143** *t* © DANIEL MIHAILESCU/Staff/AFP/Getty Images; **p.143** *b* © Robert Mulder/ Corbis Documentary/Getty Images; **p.145** © Howard Barlow/Alamy Stock Photo; **p.148** *tl* © Peter Marshall/Alamy Stock Photo; **p.148** *bl* © Blake Ezra Photography/Shutterstock/Rex Features; **p.148** *r* © Jta.org; **p.150** © Lisa Young/123RF; **p.151** © Office of the Chief Rabbi; **p.157** © Nicholas F. Gier, God, Reason, and the Evangelicals (Lanham, MD: University Press of America, 1987); **p.160** *t* © Classic Image/Alamy Stock Photo; **p.161** © Jeff Morgan 09/Alamy Stock Photo; **p.166** © Pakhnyushchyy/123RF; **p.170** © British Humanist Association; **p.172** *tl* © Lindsay Stone/123RF; **p.172** *tc* © Fedor Kondratenko/123RF; **p.172** *tr* © Farzana Sadat/123RF; **p.172** *cl* © Russ Lappa/Science Photo Library; **p.172** *cc* © Andrzej Tokarski/123RF; **p.172** *cr* © Astrid & Hanns-Frieder Michler/Science Photo Library; **p.172** *bl* © TAKASHI HONMA/123RF; **p.172** *bc* © Morozova Tatiana/123RF; **p.172** *br* © Winai Tepsuttinun/123RF; **p.181** *t* © Janine Wiedel Photolibrary/Alamy Stock Photo; **p.181** *b* © Geoffrey Robinson/Alamy Stock Photo; **p.182** *t* © EC/allactiondigital.com/Eamonn and James Clarke/PA Images; **p.182** *cl* © Lightpoet /123RF; **p.182** *cr* © Pauliene Wessel/123RF; **p.182** *b* © Alexander Raths/123RF; **p.183** © John Keates/Alamy Stock Photo; **p.190** © The Reunion of the Soul and the Body, illustration from 'The Grave' by Robert Blair, engraved by Louis Schiavonetti (hand-coloured etching) (see also 1785949-51), Blake, William (1757-1827) (after)/Private Collection/Photo © Christie's Images/Bridgeman Images; **p.197** © Joyce Mollet LRPS/Fotolibra; **p.198** *l* © Robert Estall photo agency/Alamy Stock Photo; **p.198** *r* © Apex News and Pictures Agency/Alamy Stock Photo; **p.211** © John Ewing/Portland Press Herald/Getty Images; **p.217** © Doug Engle/AP/Shutterstock/Rex Features; **p.218** © Danny Johnston/AP/Shutterstock/REX; **p.220** © Maurice Savage/Alamy Stock Photo; **p.223** © Travel Ink/ Gallo Images/Getty Images; **p.227** *tl* © Ullsteinbild/TopFoto; **p.227** *tr* © Trinity Mirror/Mirrorpix/Alamy Stock Photo; **p.227** *b* © IMAGNO/Votava/TopFoto; **p.228** *t* © Philipus/123RF; **p.228** *b* © Brian Moody/The Forgiveness project; **p.233** © Tomas Griger /123RF; **p.240** *t* © Taylor Hill/Getty Images; **p.240** *b* © Alessandro0770/123RF; **p.242** © Alinari/TopFoto.

Index

A
abortion 156, 177–80
adhan 84, 106
afterlife 156, 189–98
agape 1, 30–2, 45, 186
Allah 84, 85, 87–92
anapanasati 76
Anglican Church 33, 34, 36–7
Aron HaKodesh 119
Ascension 25–6
atheists 94, 161, 174, 190
atonement 1, 21–2, 225
    see also Day of Atonement

B
baptism 16
Baptist Church 34
Bible
    Corinthians 14, 173, 192
    Deuteronomy 125, 222
    Exodus 14
    Genesis 7–9, 162, 167, 173, 214
    Gospels 21–30
    Jeremiah 173
    Job 4, 16
    John 14, 22, 25, 30
    Luke 6, 23–4, 30, 32, 214, 224
    Matthew 21, 23, 29, 32, 220, 224
    Numbers 125, 145
    Proverbs 15, 222
    Psalms 5, 126
    Romans 214
    see also Torah; Qur'an
Big Bang Theory 9, 158–9
    see also creation
blasphemy 24
British values 230
buddha 50, 52–3
Buddha, The 53–72
Buddhism
    challenges of 72–3
    creation 163
    Dharma 50, 60, 62–72
    dukkha (suffering) 63–4, 239
    enlightenment 51, 53, 58–62, 66–7, 79
    festivals and retreats 79–82
    Five Precepts 69
    Five Remembrances 64
    Four Noble Truths 50, 63–6
    Four Sights 56, 62
    karma 64, 67–8, 73, 81, 163
    key concepts 50
    Mahayana 51, 53
    meditation 75–8
    Middle Way 66–7
    nirodha 66
    nirvana 66
    Noble Eightfold Path 67–72
    practices 75–82
    prajna (wisdom) 67–8
    samadhi (meditation) 70–1
    tanha (craving) 65–6
    teachings 52–72
    Theravada 51, 53
    Yanas 51

C
Calvinist Methodist Church 34
Catholic Church 33, 36, 39
Christianity
    atonement 1, 21–2, 225
    attributes of God 2–6, 16–19
    baptism 16
    beliefs 2–16
    Church 33–48
    denominations 33–4
    features of 35–6
    role of 35, 43–7
    worship practices 38
    creation 2, 7–12, 15, 162–3
    forgiveness 31, 207, 220–1
    God's role 2–6
    Gospels 21–30
    Great Schism 33
    heaven 29, 192
    Holy Spirit 18
    humanity 12–13
    image of God 12
    Jesus 18, 20–6
    birth, death and Resurrection 23–6
    teachings of 29–32
    key concepts 1
    Kingdom of God 29
    Liberal 163
    love (agape) 1, 30–2, 45, 186
    morality 14, 28–9
    practices 28–48
    prayer and worship 38, 41–2
    reconciliation 46
    Reformation 33
    sacraments 39–40
    theistic evolution 12
    Trinity 16–19
Christians, persecution of 48
Church of England 33
conscience 200, 201
craving 65
creation 2, 157–65
    Big Bang Theory 9, 158–9
    Buddhist view 163
    Christian view 2, 7–12, 15, 162–3
    Genesis 2, 7–12, 15, 123, 162
    Jewish view 164–5
    Muslim view 164
    post-scientific view 9
    scientific explanations 158–9
    theistic evolution 12
    theory of evolution 159–60

creationism 9
creativity 15
crime 203–18
	prison systems 209–18
	punishment 204–8
Crucifixion 24–5

D
Day of Atonement 127, 208, 226
day-old creationism 9
death penalty 212–18
denomination 33
Dharma 50, 60, 62–72
divine command theory 1, 18
dominion 7
du'ah 84
dukkha 63–4, 239

E
Eastern Orthodox Church 33, 39
ecumenical 46
enlightenment 51, 53, 58–62, 66–7, 79
environmental responsibility 156, 166–70
Eucharist 40
euthanasia 156, 180–5
evil 200, 233–7, 242–4
evolution 156, 159–62

F
Fall, The 11, 15
fasting 84, 115–17
fate 243
Five Precepts 69
food banks 43–4
forgiveness 31, 200, 220–8
Four Noble Truths 50, 63–6
free will 14, 200, 201, 243
funeral rites 195–8

G
God
	Allah 84, 85, 87, 88, 89–92
	Christianity 2–6, 12, 16–19, 29
	Judaism 122–7
	omnibenevolence 1, 4–5, 119, 125
	omnipotence 1, 4, 119, 124
	omnipresence 6, 124
	omniscience 1, 5–6
	problem of evil and suffering 5, 242–4
	Trinity 1, 16–19
Good Samaritan parable 30
goodness 200, 230–2, 242
gossip 68–9
grace 16

H
hadith 84
halal 84
heaven 29, 191–4
hell 191–4
Holocaust 240–1
Holy Communion 37, 39–40, 195
Holy Spirit 1, 16, 18
homelessness 44
humanists 180, 190, 194
humanity, nature of 12–13

I
Islam
	Allah 85, 88, 89–92
	beliefs 85–102
	in Britain 86
	diet 117
	fasting 84, 115–17
	Jihad 92
	key concepts 84
	practices 104–17
	prayer 105–12
	prohibition of images 94–5
	Prophet Muhammad 85, 87, 95, 99–100
	Qur'an 84, 85, 87, 88, 96–102
	Ramadan 115–17
	revelation 99
	Shadadah 84, 93–4
	Shi'a 86, 87
	sin of shirk 84, 94
	six articles of faith 88
	Sufis 86
	Sunnis 86, 87–8, 95
	zakat 84, 113–14
Islamic State 48

J
Jesus 4, 18, 20–2
	birth, death and Resurrection 23–6
	as Messiah 1, 20–1, 24–5
	teachings of 29–32
Jihad 92
Judaism
	beliefs and teachings 122–7
	Book of Exodus 127
	diet 152–4
	diversity within 120, 133–4
	Holocaust 240–1
	and the home 135, 149
	kashrut 119, 152–4
	key concepts 119
	kippah 119, 139–40
	Liberal 134
	nature of God 122–7
	Orthodox 119, 133, 143, 146
	practices 138–54
	prayer and worship 119, 122, 125, 135–6, 138, 141–52
	rabbi 119, 148
	Reform 119, 133, 143, 146
	representations of God 139
	sacred places 128–32
	Shabbat 119, 124, 147, 149–51
	Shema 119, 122, 125, 138
	sin 127
	Synagogue 119, 129–32, 141–8
	tallith 140
	Ten Commandments 142
	Torah 121–3, 142, 144–5
justice 200, 206–8

K
karma 64, 67–8, 73, 81, 163
kashrut 119, 152–4
killing 28, 69, 236

see also life: sanctity of
kippah 119, 139–40
kosher 152–4

L
life
  quality of 156, 175–86
  sanctity of 156, 172–5
Lord's Prayer 42

M
meditation 70–1, 75–8
memorialism 40
Messiah
  Islam 86
  Jesus as 1, 20–1, 24–5
  Judaism 121, 147, 170, 194
metta bhavana 50, 76–77
Middle Way 66–7
mindfulness 71
moral relativism 18
morality 28–9, 200, 202
  Buddhism 68
  Christian approach 14, 28–32
  conscience 201
  Golden Rule 29
  moral relativism 18
  situation ethics 18

N
natural selection 159
ner tamid 119, 142
nirvana 66
Noble Eightfold Path 50, 67–72
nonconformist Churches 34, 37

O
old-earth creationism 9
omnibenevolence 1, 4–5, 119, 125
omnipotence 1, 4, 119, 124
omnipresence 6, 124
omniscience 1, 5–6
organ donation 186
Original Sin 11, 16

P
pacifism 200, 220
parinirvana 50, 61–2
peace and conflict 220–2
prajna 67–8
prayer
  Christianity 38, 41–2
  Islam 105–12
  Judaism 119, 122, 125, 138
predestination 243
Presbyterian Church 34
prison 209–18
prodigal son parable 17
Prophet Muhammad 85, 87, 95, 99–100
Protestant Church 33

Q
Quakers 220
Qur'an 84, 85, 87, 88, 96–102

R
rabbi 119, 148
Ramadan 115–17
reconciliation 46
redemption 16
Reformation 33
Resurrection 1, 13, 25
Rich Man and Lazarus parable 32

S
sacraments 39–40
saddaqah 84
salat 84, 106
salvation 16
Salvation Army 44
samatha 50, 75–6
samsara 61
sangha 50
sawm 84, 115–17
Shabbat 119, 124, 147, 149–51
Shahadah 84, 93–4
Shekhinah 128
Shema 119, 122, 125, 138
Shi'a Muslims 86, 87
shirk 84, 94
sin 127
  Christianity 11
  and crime 203
  Original Sin 11, 16
social justice 45
soul 13, 156, 176, 188–9
stewardship 7, 166–70
stupa 61
suffering 63–4, 200, 235, 238–44
Sufis 86
Sunni Muslims 86, 87–8, 95
Synagogue 119, 129–32, 141–8

T
tanha (craving) 50, 65–6
tawhid 84
Tearfund 45
Ten Commandments 142
theistic evolution 12
Theravada 51
Torah 121–3, 142, 144–5
transcendence 2, 126
transubstantiation 40
Trinity 1, 16–19

V
verbal communication, Buddhism 68–9
vipassana 50, 78

W
war 220–2
wesak 50
wisdom 15, 54, 59, 67–8, 75, 78

Y
young-earth creationism 9

Z
zakat 84, 113–14